D1563232

THE CITY
IN
LATE IMPERIAL
RUSSIA

THE CITY
IN
LATE IMPERIAL
RUSSIA

EDITED BY

Michael F. Hamm

INDIANA UNIVERSITY PRESS

BLOOMINGTON

This book was brought to publication with the assistance of a grant from the Andrew W. Mellon Foundation to the Russian and East European Institute, Indiana University, and the Center for Russian and East European Studies, University of Michigan.

Manufactured in the United States of America

Library of Congress Cataloging in Publication Data
Main entry under title:

The City in late imperial Russia.

(Indiana-Michigan series in Russian and East
European studies)
Papers from a meeting of the American Association
for the Advancement of Slavic Studies, held in
Kansas City, Mo., Oct. 1983.
Bibliography: p.
Includes index.
1. Cities and towns—Soviet Union—History—Addresses,
essays, lectures. 2. Soviet Union—Economic conditions—
1861–1917—Addresses, essays, lectures. 3. Urbaniza-
tion—Soviet Union—History—Addresses, essays, lectures.
I. Hamm, Michael F. II. American Association for the
Advancement of Slavic Studies. III. Series.
HT145.S58C57   1986   307.7'64'0947   84-43082
ISBN 0-253-31370-8
1   2   3   4   5   90   89   88   87   86

For JoAnn, Sarah, Jill

CONTENTS

        Illustrations between pp. 151 and 176.

ACKNOWLEDGMENTS

Collaborative scholarship on the urban history of late Imperial Russia became possible in recent years as a small group of Western scholars began to explore in detail the nature and consequences of growth and change in the Empire's burgeoning cities. I established initial guidelines for this collection in 1982 and first met with six of the essayists at the Washington meeting of the American Association for the Advancement of Slavic Studies in October of that year. The first written drafts were exchanged the following fall, and at the Kansas City meeting of the AAASS in October 1983 I chaired a roundtable discussion of several of the themes from the collection. All of the contributors to this volume participated in this final exchange of ideas except for James Bater and Joseph Bradley, both of whom were doing additional research in the Soviet Union at that time.

Thus, *The City in Late Imperial Russia* is the product of a collaborative effort that evolved over several years. Special thanks go to Dan Brower for his thematic suggestions. John Hollingsworth of the Indiana University Department of Geography drew the city maps, and the administration of Centre College, which was very supportive of this project, helped underwrite the cost of the cartography. All of the contributors to this volume were prompt in meeting deadlines and cooperative in responding to my many requests. My wife, JoAnn Hamm, and my colleague at Centre College, David Newhall, made many helpful suggestions which are greatly appreciated.

MICHAEL F. HAMM

THE CITY
IN
LATE IMPERIAL
RUSSIA

Western Russia in 1900

I.

Introduction

MICHAEL F. HAMM

The City in Late Imperial Russia examines patterns of growth and change in eight of the Empire's largest cities from the 1860s to the First World War. In the convulsive decade of activity that followed Russia's defeat in the Crimean War, Emperor Alexander II emancipated 24,000,000 serfs, created a judicial system, revamped the military and the universities, and founded institutions of self-government for city and countryside alike. If nothing else, the Great Reforms opened an era of new opportunities for personal and geographical mobility. The explosive growth of Russia's cities that followed did not stop until the chaos of the Revolutions of 1917 and ensuing Civil War brought economic collapse and forced thousands back to the countryside in search of food.

Prior to the 1860s Russia's cities were relatively untouched by the profound changes commonly called the Industrial Revolution. In 1863 the Siemens-Martin open-hearth method of producing high-quality steel, perfected in France, made possible great advances in the metallurgical and machine-building industries. In Russia the transportation inadequacies manifested in the Crimean War brought about a new commitment to railway construction, and some 46,000 miles of track were laid between 1859 and 1914. This network of rails made large cities accessible to migrants from distant villages and greatly expanded markets for many urban manufacturers. Railway industries came to dominate the industrial economies of some cities (Khar'kov's locomotive works comes to mind), and railyards.

and related industries contributed significantly to the growth of each city in this collection.

Other industries brought together large concentrations of workers: textiles accelerated the growth of Moscow and the cities and towns of the Central Industrial Region; sugar refining and food processing contributed greatly to the growth of Kiev; and oil transformed the character of Baku. Their need for equipment and capital fostered the growth of machine-building and banking respectively, while their need for skilled workers and managers paved the way for the establishment of schools and technical institutes. Toward the end of the nineteenth century Russia's first electrical power plants added a new dimension to productive capabilities, and a bit later motorized transport further enhanced the industrial growth of cities such as Riga, where in 1914 the Provodnik Corporation employed 14,000 workers and ranked second in the world in the production of automobile tires. "The complex machine ceased to be an innovation and became ubiquitous," Sam Bass Warner has noted in his assessment of rapid urbanization in nineteenth-century America. In America, in Europe, and in Russia, where Western capital and technology blended with the creative potential of thousands who had come to the cities in search of economic opportunity, "the repeated economic successes of technological innovations led to the institutionalization of invention itself."[1]

In the mid–nineteenth century, about 9 million subjects (10 percent of the total population) lived in Russia's cities, and only St. Petersburg, Moscow, Warsaw, and Odessa had 100,000 or more inhabitants. By 1913 25 million Russian subjects (18 percent of the total population) lived in cities, and nearly three dozen cities had reached the 100,000 mark in population. From the 1860s to the First World War, St. Petersburg, Moscow, and Warsaw roughly quadrupled; Riga and Odessa quintupled; and Kiev grew tenfold.

Examined from a global perspective, even at mid-century St. Petersburg and Moscow ranked among the largest cities in the world. In Europe and America St. Petersburg was surpassed only by London (3,227,000), Paris (1,696,000), New York (696,115), and Berlin (548,000), while Moscow was outranked, additionally, only by Vienna, Liverpool, Glasgow, and Naples. Warsaw compared in size with America's second greatest city, Baltimore (169,054), Odessa with Philadelphia, New Orleans, Venice, and Baghdad.[2]

By the turn of the twentieth century, about a dozen cities in the world had a million or more inhabitants, and St. Petersburg and Moscow ranked among them. In 1910 Russia's historic capitals and Warsaw ranked among the ten largest cities in Europe. Odessa compared in size with the greatest Arab city, Cairo, and with Bangkok and Peking, Kiev with Boston and Baltimore (America's fifth and sixth largest cities) and with Amsterdam, Copenhagen, Milan, and Rome. At 300,000, Tiflis

TABLE 1.1

Population of
Imperial Russia's Largest Cities, 1856 and 1910

1856		1910	
St. Petersburg	490,808	St. Petersburg	1,566,000
Moscow	368,765	Moscow	1,481,240
Warsaw	156,072	Warsaw	781,179
Odessa	101,320	Odessa	620,143
Riga	70,463	Kiev	527,287
Kishinev	63,469	Lodz	415,604
Kiev	62,497	Riga	370,000
Saratov	61,610	Tiflis	303,150
Kazan	56,257	Khar'kov	244,526
Tula	50,641	Baku	232,200
Berdichev	50,281	Saratov	217,418
Vil'na	45,881	Ekaterinoslav	211,905
Nikolaev	44,280	Tashskent	200,191
Kursk	40,771	Vil'na	192,746
Kronshtadt	39,905	Kazan	184,465

SOURCE: Thomas Stanley Fedor, *Patterns of Urban Growth in the Russian Empire during the Nineteenth Century* (Chicago: University of Chicago Department of Geography Research Paper No. 163, 1975), 183–215.

was similar in size to Genoa, Detroit, Washington, and New Orleans. Baku and Khar'kov ranked with Minneapolis, Prague, Delhi, and Baghdad. Smaller Vil'na and Tashkent equaled Zurich in size, while Kazan and Samara had as many people as Athens or Venice, Damascus or Algiers.[3]

In the cities of Russia, as elsewhere, growth begat growth. By 1908 Moscow and St. Petersburg had 260,000 industrial workers between them in enterprises that were large enough to warrant inspection by state officials. Giant factories, each with a thousand or more workers, employed 93,000 of these laborers. Textile mills and machinery operations had particularly large workforces, and Lodz, a textile town in Russian Poland, had the Empire's third largest industrial proletariat at this time (77,000 workers), while Riga, with its machine works, ranked fourth with 53,000 mill, rail, and shipyard workers.[4] Warsaw had three giant machinery plants (which employed 31,000 workers among them by 1913), but could not really be classified as a factory town. Great factories employed relatively few of its workers and were rarer still in such rapidly growing cities as Kiev, Odessa, and Tiflis. In fact in nearly all of Russia's burgeoning cities, for every migrant who found a factory job, many more found work in countless workshops, in construction, and in the hauling, vending, and service trades. Industrialization created a great array of opportunities across the economic spectrum, for the small entrepreneur—the peasant-carpenter who hired his own crew and became a contractor, for instance—and for the artisan and the day-worker. "More brains were needed than ever before," Joseph Bradley observes in his essay on Moscow, but "at the same time more brawn was needed to build, move, haul, and clean." Social and intellectual oppor-tunity, enhanced by schools, informal educational organizations such as literacy societies, and a great variety of urban associations, also expanded rapidly, and stood in marked contrast to the timeless routines of village life. A Baltic tune popular around 1900 captures the image of the turn-of-the-century Russian city as a mecca offering all kinds of opportunities:

> Brothers, we will go to Riga
> In Riga life is good;
> In Riga golden dogs bark,
> And silver cocks crow.[5]

Each of the cities in this collection was relatively untouched by industrialization in the mid–nineteenth century, and each was pro-foundly changed by the Industrial Revolution in the decades thereafter. In age and heritage, however, these cities differed greatly. St. Petersburg, created at the beginning of the eighteenth century, and Odessa, founded at the end of that century, stood as monuments to Imperial Russian expansion, symbols of the permanence of the Russian presence on the Baltic and Black Seas. Moscow, on the other hand, was founded in 1147 and had long been the "heart" and the "hub" of the expanding Empire. "All roads led to Moscow," and most led as well to Kiev, the organizing center of ancient Rus' and "the Jerusalem of the Russian lands." A center of learning since the eleventh century, Kiev was for centuries a conduit of Western ideas into Russia and an important cultural center for Russians, Ukrainians, and Poles alike. German merchants estab-lished a community at Riga in 1158, and in 1282 the city became a member of the Hanseatic League. Long an important intermediary in Russia's trade with Western Europe, this center of Baltic German in-fluence became the crucible of Latvian national awareness in the period under review. Warsaw, founded about 1300, became the capital of Po-land in 1596 and remained thereafter the most important city of that divided country. Warsaw also housed Europe's largest and most diverse Jewish community, and, like Riga, participated in the Western intellec-tual revolution of the seventeenth and eighteenth centuries. Tiflis and Baku were part of the ancient trading networks of the Middle East and also came to nurture the national aspirations of several peoples. The capital of Georgia since the early middle ages, Tiflis was important to the growth of Armenian culture as well. Baku, which lay astride the

Christian and Muslim worlds, was drawn toward Persian influence by the spread of Shi'ite Islam, but also had a powerful Armenian community and ultimately became the cultural and political center for the Azerbaijani Turks.

Besides developing as centers of industrial and commercial might, the cities in this collection shared other common characteristics. Each was an administrative center that helped hold together the distant and disparate regions of the vast Russian Empire. The last of the Great Reforms, the Municipal Statute of 1870, provided for a council (*gorodskaia duma*) and an executive board (*uprava*) in each city except Warsaw. The Statute allowed males twenty-five years of age to vote if they paid any kind of tax or fee to the city, but established three voting curias to ensure that a minority of relatively affluent taxpayers controlled city affairs. During the decades under review, these new municipal governments were charged with protecting public health, providing utilities, extending services—in short with implementing developmental advances which became increasingly costly but critical as urban populations swelled.

The principle of self-government suffered a setback with the counterreform of 1892, which allowed state officials to nullify a municipal action if they found it to be "inexpedient." (The 1870 Statute had permitted state officials to veto city enactments only on the basis of illegality.) Although the counterreform abolished the curial system of voting, it further narrowed the franchise so that only the most affluent owners of income-producing property could vote. Thus in Saratov, where about 14,000 of the 225,000 residents owned real estate in 1913, only 2,415 could vote. In Moscow 9,431 could vote, in Riga 5,169, in Kiev 3,757.[6]

Interest among Western scholars in Russia's cities dates mainly from the late 1960s and early 1970s when efforts to build the Great Society and eradicate poverty, blight, and racial injustice in America's cities generated a wave of interest in urban history. James Bater's *St. Petersburg: Industrialization and Change*, the first major biography of a Russian city, and my own collection, *The City in Russian History*, both appeared in 1976. Mindful that the Russian Revolution remains the only example of a successful social revolution in which urban workers played a major role,[7] various scholars have subsequently examined the nature of the urban workforce and workplace and provoked debate about the ways in which the urban environment shaped attitudes and political behavior in the late Imperial period. Joseph Bradley has added a colorful study of Moscow (*Muzhik and Muscovite: Urbanization in Late Imperial Russia*), but the provincial cities still await their biographers. To date there are only a handful of articles in English on a few of these cities, and there is nothing at all on Warsaw, Kiev, Baku, or Tiflis. *The*

City in Late Imperial Russia thus adds significantly to our knowledge of prerevolutionary Russian society.

No single model of urbanization has been used in this collection. Instead I asked each contributor to provide a brief sketch of his or her city prior to the nineteenth century, and then to pursue a series of questions: Why did the city grow so rapidly beginning in the 1860s? What kinds of changes occurred in its economic fabric, in its class, occupational, or ethnic composition? In what ways was the physical environment of the city transformed and how were living conditions affected by rapid growth? What can be said about the efforts of the new institutions of self-government to cope with the profound challenges brought about by huge increases in population? What relationships can be suggested between the rapidly changing urban environment and the evolution of new forms of conflict and community in late Imperial Russia?

The City in Late Imperial Russia is thus a collaborative effort which assumes, in Theodore Hershberg's words, that there are "interrelationships among environment, behavior, and group experience—the three basic components in the larger urban system."[8] In advocating the study of "urban as process" instead of "urban as site," Hershberg argues that changing urban environments were more than passive backdrops to events; they helped shape trends and events. In this volume several contributors suggest relationships between the city and ethnicity or ethnoreligious conflict, for example. "Baku's particular characteristics fanned the flames of unrest," Audrey Altstadt-Mirhadi observes, while in Tiflis and other towns, Ronald Suny writes, "the peoples of Caucasia underwent a process of national formation, of growing awareness of their connections with their ethnic brothers, and their separation from those who could not understand their languages and customs."

Much about the urban environment remains unclear. The essayists record complaints about growing problems with crime, for example, but could not find enough data over a period of years to determine precisely new trends in urban criminal behavior. And inevitably, though the essayists pursue common themes, the results differ in emphasis and detail. Ethnic conflict, so important in the provincial cities, was not an important feature of St. Petersburg or Moscow during these decades. Likewise, the details of the upheavals of 1905 in the capitals are given relatively little attention here, for they have been recorded elsewhere.

Collectively the essays suggest a variety of factors that helped shape new attitudes, associations, and conflicts (for example, the press, literacy societies and public assistance programs, schools and universities, and political and economic competition). They document developmental advances and introduce some of the dynamic personalities who came to dominate city politics—among them George Armitstead, Riga's Oxford-educated mayor from 1901 to 1912 and the symbol of that city's administrative vigor; Isai Pitoev, whose whims had a "magic effect" on plans for the future of Tiflis; and Ivan D'iakov, Kiev's conscientious mayor, who refused to leave or interrupt a city council meeting even after receiving reports that his house was on fire. They reveal something of the other side of the urban setting as well: beggars and street people such as Moscow's matchmaking, fortune-telling cape women; "the dirty, unshaven, tattered, hideous crowd moving back and forth" in a city flea market; Warsaw's "Bloody Wola," known "for its cutthroats, audacious murders, bold robberies, and daily crimes"; and "desperate outskirts," similarly disadvantaged and forgotten peripheral neighborhoods in the other cities as well.

Contrasts were plentiful. Planned, magnificent St. Petersburg was also the unhealthiest of Europe's capitals. Moscow simultaneously conveyed the impression of a bustling modern metropolis and a backward "overgrown village." Odessa, with its multiplicity of foreign tongues and its 20,000 homeless dockworkers, had "a rough and at the same time cultivated face."

Continuities were equally apparent. Armenian merchants clung to their traditional dominance in Tiflis and Baku. Religious pilgrims continued to pour into Kiev. Street vendors, trade-row hawkers, and surly droshky drivers coexisted with new modes of manufacturing, commerce, and transport, and abounded everywhere.

The City in Late Imperial Russia highlights the distinctive features of eight very different cities while surveying their common characteristics. It provides information and insights that will enable readers to draw their own conclusions about the nature of the Russian urban environment and the ways in which it contributed to the tensions of late Imperial society and to growing demands for change. Bibliographical notes, intended for the specialist, discuss important source materials and follow each essay; for the general reader a list of pertinent English-language books and articles is included at the end of the volume. As a teacher for fifteen years, I appreciate scholarly works that are written in a style that makes them interesting to undergraduates and others who simply enjoy reading about history. These essays, I believe, accomplish that goal, for they capture elements of the color, rhythm, and drama that make the study of Russia's great cities an exciting endeavor.

NOTES

1. Sam Bass Warner, Jr., *The Urban Wilderness* (New York: Harper and Row, 1972), pp. 85–86.

2. The populations of Europe's largest cities from 1800 may be found in B. R. Mitchell, *European Historical Statistics, 1750–1970* (New York: Columbia

University Press, 1975), pp. 76–78. For America's cities in 1850 and 1900, see *The World Almanac and Book of Facts, 1984* (New York: Newspaper Enterprise Assn., 1983), p. 202. Statistics for other areas are scarce. B. R. Mitchell, *International Historical Statistics. Africa and Asia* (New York: New York University Press, 1982), lists a few cities for 1850–60 (Alexandria, 60,000; Baghdad, 105,000; Cairo, 267,000; Izmir, 160,000; Tabriz, 100,000). India's larger cities are listed first in the column for 1870 (Madras, 406,000; Delhi, 154,000). Tokyo is first mentioned in 1880 (824,000), while population data for China's cities are generally unavailable prior to the twentieth century. The population of Istanbul is first mentioned for 1890 (874,000). See pp. 66–71.

3. London, New York, Paris, Tokyo, Berlin, Vienna, Chicago, Osaka, Calcutta, Istanbul, and possibly Buenos Aires joined Moscow and St. Petersburg as cities with a million or more inhabitants in 1900. See *European Historical Statistics*, pp. 76–78, *The World Almanac and Book of Facts, 1984*, p. 202, and *International Historical Statistics*, pp. 66–71, for comparative data. Apparently no Chinese city had a million inhabitants at this time. Shanghai and Peking had about 600,000, and a comparable figure is given for Canton. See Edward J. M. Rhoads, "Merchant Associations in Canton, 1895–1911," in Mark Elvin and G. William Skinner, eds., *The Chinese City between Two Worlds* (Stanford: Stanford University Press, 1974), p. 97. For Latin America see *The World Almanac and Encyclopedia 1907* (New York, 1906), p. 394. Buenos Aires had slightly more than one million residents by 1905. In 1900–1904 Mexico City had 344,000, Santiago 334,000, and Rio de Janeiro 750,000. Figures for several Russian cities differ widely from source to source and changed sharply in accordance with the time of the year the census was taken.

4. Figures for Russia's industrial proletariat broken down by size of employing enterprise may be found in I. F. Ugarov, "Chislennost' i otraslevoi sostav proletariata Rossii v 1900 i 1908 gg.," in *Voprosy istochnikovedeniia istorii pervoi russkoi revoliutsii* (Moscow, 1977), p. 198. The towns with the largest number of industrial workers subject to factory inspection in 1908, in order, were Moscow, St. Petersburg, Lodz, Riga, Warsaw, Ivanovo-Voznesensk, Orekhovo-Zuevo, Odessa, Tver, and Iaroslavl. Many enterprises, particularly in the textile and food-processing industries, were located in the countryside. Orekhovo-Zuevo was a textile mill settlement just east of Moscow which did not have city status in 1908.

5. Translated from Latvian by Stephen D. Corrsin, "The Changing Composition of the City of Riga, 1867–1913," *Journal of Baltic Studies* 13 (1982):29.

6. For Saratov see *Saratovskii listok* (Saratov), March 13, 1913. For data on municipal elections for nineteen cities from 1900 to 1914, see Michael F. Hamm, "Khar'kov's Progressive Duma, 1910–1914: A Study in Russian Municipal Reform," *Slavic Review* 40 (1981):34–35.

7. Victoria E. Bonnell, *Roots of Rebellion: Workers' Politics and Organizations in St. Petersburg and Moscow, 1900–1914* (Berkeley: University of California Press, 1983), p. 5.

8. Theodore Hershberg, "The New Urban History. Toward an Interdisciplinary History of the City," *Journal of Urban History* 5 (1978):33.

2.

Moscow

From Big Village to Metropolis

JOSEPH BRADLEY

If ever a city expressed the character and peculiarities of its inhabitants, that city is Moscow, the "heart of Russia" in which the Russian "wide nature" (*shirokaia dusha*) is abundantly obvious. The character, life and tendencies of the people are seen in much greater purity here than in St. Petersburg and are much less influenced by Western Europe, though even Moscow is rapidly becoming modernized of late years.[1]

The European or American tourist arriving in Moscow in 1913 might have had this passage from Baedeker's *Russia* on his or her mind while descending from the train onto a crowded platform. Trite references to Russian character and to the differences between Moscow and St. Petersburg aside, the Baedeker guidebook suggested that there was a relationship between the "life and tendencies" of the people and the city in which they lived. In addition Baedeker stated that the city was rapidly becoming a modern metropolis, even in the eyes of Europeans, while at the same time it had not lost its old character and ways. Moscow conveyed the impression of a scruffy, backward, semi-Asiatic "big village" on the one hand and of a bustling, modern European city on the other.

Russians themselves were no less aware of the images of tradition and modernity and the rapid changes taking place in Moscow. The authors of a 1903 guidebook crowed:

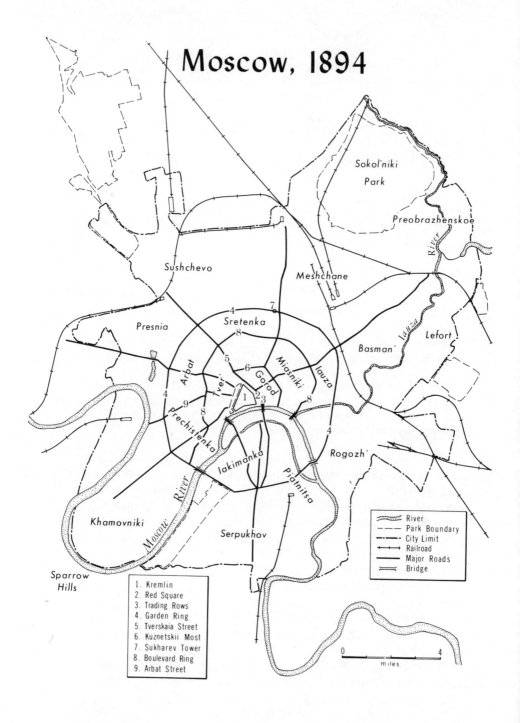

Moscow, 1894

Sokol'niki Park

Preobrazhenskoe

Sushchevo

Meshchane

Lefort

Presnia

Sretenka

Basman'

Iauza

Arbat

Miasniki

Iauza

Tver'

Gorod

Prechistenka

Iakimanka

Rogozh'

Piatnitsa

Khamovniki

Serpukhov

Moscow River

Sparrow Hills

	River
	Park Boundary
	City Limit
	Railroad
	Major Roads
	Bridge

1. Kremlin
2. Red Square
3. Trading Rows
4. Garden Ring
5. Tverskaia Street
6. Kuznetskii Most
7. Sukharev Tower
8. Boulevard Ring
9. Arbat Street

0   4
miles

> Moscow has been transformed completely from a big village . . . to a
> huge, crowded commercial and industrial city . . . adorned with
> museums, galleries, clinics, hospitals, charitable and educational
> institutions.[2]

Not only had Moscow been "transformed," but in the view of these
authors its notable features were no longer the "heavenly cathedrals,
royal palaces, aristocratic mansions and innumerable shops and stores"
that had impressed the author of an 1868 guidebook, but rather the
physical artifacts of modernity—"museums, galleries, clinics, hospitals, charitable and educational institutions." A "civic" Moscow had
been added to the earlier ecclesiastical, commercial, and "private"
Moscow. A survey of Moscow's growth, economy, social structure, city
government and cultural life will explain the images of tradition and
modernity and show the evolution of civic consciousness in Moscow.

SETTLEMENT AND GROWTH

Founded in 1147 by the Suzdal' prince Iurii Dolgorukii, Moscow
was initially no more than one of several outposts defending the western borders of the Suzdal' "lands." Yet the Kremlin, on a high bank at
the confluence of the Moscow and Neglinnaia rivers, occupied a
strategic location for the commerce and defense of northeastern Rus'.
The Moscow princes were conveniently situated to control the trade
routes from Central Europe and the Baltic to Asia via the Volga River
and to collect duties from the surrounding peasants.[3] A steadily increasing population of wholesalers, craftsmen, princes, boyars, ecclesiastical
and monastic officials, and their servitors provided the economic and
social base for a strong and vital city. As a result, in a period of two
centuries Moscow developed from a frontier post to a major administrative center, a hub of commerce and transport, and a center of production. The city was to retain this significance; one of the recurring images
of late nineteenth-century Moscow is of its importance as a hub. As the
saying went, "All roads lead to Moscow."

The city grew in concentric rings around its citadel and adjacent
trading quarters called the Walled Town. Starting at the walls of the
Kremlin itself in Red Square and extending into the Walled Town ran
rows of shops and stalls, later called the Trading Rows (*Torgovye riady*)
and now called the State Shopping Mall (GUM). The scruffiest of the
stalls, ironically, were located in Red Square itself—ironically because
the present-day authorities have imparted to the area outside the Kremlin walls a shrinelike atmosphere that it never had under the tsars.
Behind the Trading Rows was a lowland (*podol*) along the Moscow
River; this area was also known as the zariad'e and is now the site of the

Rossiia hotel.[4] Along the walls at the opposite end of the Walled Town stretched Moscow's largest open-air market:

> Every day from morning till night a most colorful and dirty crowd pushes and shoves. . . . The very essence of the flea market [literally "shoving market" (*tolkuchii rynok*)] lies in this dirty, unshaven, tattered, hideous crowd moving back and forth. Any poor man who can't spend more than a ruble for a jacket or half a ruble for a pair of pants, or who needs an old cap for a few kopeks, can go to the flea market and immediately find everything. Because of this, rubbish worn only by lower orders of Muscovites, and rags and garbage that make you sick to look at, are bought and sold here.[5]

By the end of the eighteenth century, the area of urban settlement extended in a radius of two to three miles from the Kremlin to the Garden Ring (*Sadovoe kol'tso*). A ward named Gorod (literally "the City") and known for its warehouses, shops, stores, and the stock exchange, contained the Walled Town. The other central wards were Tver', Miasniki (literally "the butchers"), Iauza, Sretenka, Arbat, and Prechistenka ("the cleanest"). This area was Moscow's nerve center, containing its government offices and institutions, stores, and best residences.

By the second half of the nineteenth century a central business district consisting of "the City," Tver', and Miasniki wards could be distinguished from the more residential wards of Arbat, Prechistenka, Sretenka, and Iauza. Within the central business district itself, "the City" and Miasniki were becoming the centers of Moscow's wholesale and financial life, while the fashionable stores along Tverskaia and Kuznetskii Most made the Tver' ward the city's retailing center. The proximity within the central business district of fashionable stores and open-air markets with their colorful assemblage of hawkers, itinerant repairmen, wandering holy men, beggars, and peasants from far-off villages contributed to the dual image—sophisticated metropolis and big village—that Moscow conveyed. Nevertheless, despite the persistence of open-air markets and peddlers, the central business district was becoming less and less "villagelike" and more and more metropolitan. In the eyes of one Russian the change was reflected in changing retailing practices:

> The old simple sign, usually black with gold letters that merely gave information rather than trying to attract attention, is being replaced by clamorous and colorful advertisements. Pressing against store windows, hanging above the sidewalks, on the empty walls of tall buildings and on roofs, these new kinds of signs gave the street a noisy and talkative appearance. Bright colors that strike the eye and involuntarily attract attention, ingenious figures and amusing inscriptions are visible everywhere.[6]

Beyond the Garden Ring lay the city's outskirts, "the other side of the tracks," as the words "za sadovoe" expressed it. As early as the seventeenth century, settlements of potters, gold- and silversmiths, tailors, armorers, and postmen began to cluster along the major trading arteries and water basins and around the best-defended points outside the fortifications. Though separated from each other by vast expanses of truck gardens and meadows, these "settlement-villages" easily made commercial contact with the "market town" of the Walled Town.[7] By the end of the nineteenth century the area of continuous urban settlement was slightly larger than that of Berlin and almost equal to that of Paris. In 1900 the outer districts contained the city's largest factories and mills, all nine of its railroad stations, as well as its freight, lumber, and stockyards, two-thirds of its inhabitants, and more than 90 percent of its factory workers.[8] Like the central business and residential districts, the outer wards were simultaneously villagelike and metropolitan in appearance. Dark, unpaved streets along which limped the barefoot and the beggars flowed into bustling railroad station squares; vast tracts of undeveloped land surrounded gigantic mills; shanties devoid of running water or sewer connections shivered in the shadow of modern factory dormitories; and sleazy taverns, inns, and tea houses were down the road from fashionable suburban restaurants and cottages. On the whole, however, while the central districts suggested a wealthy and bustling European metropolis, the sprawling outskirts suggested poverty, backwardness, and dreariness.

By the beginning of the twentieth century, its one million inhabitants made Moscow the tenth most populous of the world's cities and, among these ten, the fastest growing. In the half century preceding the outbreak of World War I, its size increased fourfold. During the period 1900–1914, Moscow's growth rate was almost 4 percent per annum, on a par with that of New York.[9] Like New York, Moscow was a city of immigrants: almost three-fourths of the city's population had been born elsewhere. Moscow's diversified economy beckoned immigrants, overwhelmingly ethnic Russians, from Moscow province and the neighboring provinces of Iaroslavl', Vladimir, Riazan', Tula, Kaluga, Smolensk, and Tver'.[10]

The immigrant population looms much larger when we realize that the census measured a mobile population frozen at only one brief moment; in any given year, let alone during the period between censuses, the number of persons in the city was much larger. The two census years 1882 and 1902 show a remarkable consistency in the number—slightly more than 100,000—of arrivals during the preceding year.[11] Considering that an undetermined number of additional immigrants entered the city but did not remain through the entire year, or were highly transient in their living habits upon arrival and therefore not counted, 100,000 to 150,000 immigrants may have come to Moscow every year during the last two decades of the nineteenth century. To put it differently, during this twenty-year period, two to three million immigrants, more than the entire population of Riazan' Province in 1897, at one time or another came to the city. Many of Moscow's newcomers remained transient residents: the median length of city residence for immigrants was approximately seven years, and the continued torrent of new arrivals from the countryside caused a slight decrease in this figure at the turn of the century.[12]

Who were these immigrants? More than two-thirds were peasants, prompting the compilers of the 1902 city census to note laconically: "The influx of immigrants is turning Moscow more and more into a peasant city."[13] The statisticians might have observed as well that Moscow was becoming a younger city: the median age of immigrants dropped from twenty-five in 1882 to twenty-two twenty years later.[14] Though the census showed a preponderance of men, more and more women were immigrating: the city had only 700 women per 1,000 men in 1871 but 839 women per 1,000 men forty years later.[15] While many peasants lived and worked in Moscow, most retained some form of tie with their native village. Such ties and the bonds shared by fellow villagers (a phenomenon known as zemliachestvo) were evidenced not only in transience of city residence, but also in marriage patterns, hiring practices, and political action.[16]

Along with the press of numbers and the transience of the immigrant population, one of the severest hardships the laboring population faced was the appalling living conditions. By the end of the nineteenth century housing had become a major issue for the city administration. Congested living conditions and the seeming breakdown in family life suggested to the municipal authorities a breakdown in traditional morals.

During the building boom at the end of the century wood continued to be the primary construction material in the metropolitan area: the proportion of wooden buildings actually increased because of the nearly exclusive use of wood in the city's rapidly growing suburbs. The continued use of wood for construction immediately suggests a predominance of one- and two-story buildings. In 1882 fewer than five percent of the city's residential buildings had more than two floors above ground. Thirty years later this proportion had increased almost threefold, and the 1915 guidebook breathlessly observed that four- and five-story buildings were growing "like mushrooms and radically altering the physiognomy of the city."[17] The fact remains, however, that on the eve of World War I seven out of every eight residential buildings were only one or two stories high.[18]

Although because of the high proportion of one and two-story structures the density of population per unit of land was relatively low in Moscow, subdivision of living space resulted in a high density per housing unit: 8.5 persons in 1912. This was far higher than Berlin (3.9 persons per housing unit), Vienna (4.2) or London (4.5).[19] And it was not much of an improvement over the 1882 density figure of 8.9; the degree of congestion had remained essentially the same for three decades, despite a 43 percent increase in the number of occupied housing units during the decade 1902–1912 alone. With nearly as many residents per housing unit as the city proper, the suburbs, sprawling and villagelike in outward appearance, were almost as densely inhabited.[20]

The housing market in turn affected other aspects of the urban environment for the laboring population, most notably family life. Little more than one-third of the city's inhabitants lived with relatives. Among men, only slightly more than one-quarter lived with members of their own family, the lowest proportion recorded in any Russian city.[21] The families of the remainder were elsewhere, usually back in the village but not infrequently in another part of Moscow itself. The compilers of the 1882 census frequently made unfavorable comparisons between Moscow and other European cities, notably Berlin; such comparisons are particularly revealing in the area of households. While more than three-quarters of all Berliners lived as part of a nuclear family (head of household, spouse, or child), less than one-third of all Muscovites did so. All family members (including lateral relatives) comprised 82.7 percent of Berlin's population, more than twice the proportion of Moscow's.[22]

Although an increasing number of skilled workers were settling in Moscow with their families, professionals regarded workers' lives as family-less. According to the economist A. P. Chuprov, "The tremendous growth of the tavern trade in Moscow provides the only shelter for the large number of working people without families who, in the absence of other shelter, find refuge in the inns and drinking parlors."[23] A discussion of garden settlements for Moscow's workers stated that "measures to improve the life of the workingman are tied most closely to the opportunity for a family life and a necessary prerequisite for the latter is some kind of comfortable and inexpensive home (*ochag*)."[24]

Not surprisingly, illegitimacy and high mortality were facts of life among the laboring population and causes of great concern to reformers. According to data supplied by zemstvo statistician P. I. Kurkin, during the ten-year period 1888–97, 56,631 out of 250,256 births in Moscow were illegitimate. Even allowing for the immigration of pregnant women from the countryside, at 22.6 percent, the illegitimacy rate in the city compared badly with a rate of 2.4 percent in Moscow province.[25] Of equal concern to the authrorities was the high rate of infant mortality and the slow drop in the overall death rate, from 27.1 per 1,000 population in 1870 to 24.2 forty years later. Altogether, in the half century between 1862 and 1912, the death rate dropped less than four per 1,000, hardly a precipitous decline. Throughout the 1870s and 1880s, the death rate almost equaled the birth rate and in one year (1871) actually exceeded it. Moscow's record lagged behind not only that of major European cities but that of St. Petersburg, hardly a model of a healthy city.[26]

A myriad of reports on the housing question as well as data extracted from the censuses point to an overall deterioration in the physical environment in general and in housing conditions in particular: the growth in housing stock could not keep pace with population growth; rents increased sharply at the end of the century, causing increased subdivision and overcrowding; families found it difficult to live together; and a growing number of flophouses catered to a homeless casual labor force. On the outskirts "nested wild and criminal paupers" and in central neighborhoods the scruffy skid rows around Sukharev Tower, Smolensk Market, and the infamous Khitrov Market became eyesores that received mounting publicity.[27] The authors of a 1913 compendium on municipal administration widely used by historians of the city summed up the different rates of change in housing:

> Moscow has notably changed in appearance: New, multistoried buildings are going up where once stood wooden homes with gardens and overgrown yards; gardens disappear and courtyards became smaller. And these properties at least have plumbing and sewer lines and the buildings have electricity, telephones, indoor toilets and gas stoves. Naturally all of this is available for those who can pay a handsome price for an apartment. The mass of the propertyless population of course lives as it always has.[28]

Yet it would be an oversimplification to say that there were no improvements at all, even for the laboring population. Despite the tenuousness of family ties, the continued importance of communal living arrangements, and the continued subdivision and overcrowding of units, more Moscow residents were becoming independent in their housing arrangements and an element of choice was increasingly entering the determination of housing. The decline in the number of persons dependent upon institutions or their employers for housing, and the increase in the number renting housing from private landlords, showed that a part of the laboring population was becoming free from at least one form of social control by the employer. Such independence may have been worth the price of the overly subdivided private apartments that were arguably worse than the best company housing. A striking factory worker who lived outside the company gates had less fear of losing the roof over his head as well as his wages or job than did his brothers living in factory dormitories. Likewise, despite the increased subdivision of private housing space, a recent Soviet study has documented that more of the better paid workers and their families were able to rent an entire room for themselves rather than merely a "cot" or "corner." The proportion of the factory worker's budget allotted for food decreased, per capita meat consumption increased, and more and more workers ate with their families at taverns and cafeterias rather than in company canteens.[29] Responsible for both deterioration and improvement in living conditions were the expanding but erratic economy and structural changes in the labor force.

THE ECONOMY AND THE LABOR FORCE

Although Moscow and its hinterland, Russia's oldest manufacturing region, grew less rapidly than newer industrial centers during the boom of the 1890s, in the half century prior to World War I the Moscow region remained the Empire's largest industrial region. Textiles had long been the major industry of Moscow and its hinterland, and the towns of Orekhovo, Shuia, Ivanovo-Voznesensk and Bogorodsk were synonymous with the nation's textile industry. In addition to supporting large textile mills, Moscow's hinterland sustained a lively cottage industry. Though cottage industries faced increasing competition from cheap, mass-produced and mass-marketed products, putting-out centers and workshops continued to coexist with the factories because of the availability of cheap peasant labor and the proximity of the Moscow market. Moscow's huge retail market and the demand for both cheaply made goods and luxury items also attracted domestic workers and craftsmen from the villages.[30]

In "calico Moscow" approximately 150,000 persons made their living in the textile industry and in the clothing trades. In 1902 the 54,794 persons who worked in the textile factories constituted almost half of the city's factory labor force. Large factories dominated the cotton industry, and to a lesser extent the wool and silk industries. Located primarily on the outskirts, the largest cotton mills such as the Prokhorov, Tsindel', and Giubner mills combined many operations including spinning, weaving, printing, and dyeing. Such huge mills, and in particular Prokhorov, located in what became known as the "Red Presnia" district, were centers of neighborhood and workplace organizing in 1905 and 1917.[31] By contrast, the clothing industry—that is, the production of apparel, footwear, and the like for the retail market—was characterized by small workshops of tailors, seamstresses, and shoemakers, located primarily in the central wards. Though textile factories dominated the industrial skyline, the city's manufacturing base was becoming more diversified, and industries such as food processing, printing, metalworking, and machine tool were growing rapidly.

By the end of the nineteenth century, Moscow had a broad economic base not only in manufacturing but also in commerce, transport, and services. One of the fastest-growing branches of the economy was the lodging and restaurant business, employing 50,198 in 5,617 establishments by 1902. This sector included the operation of hotels, inns, furnished rooms, lodging houses, and eating and drinking establishments. The latter group included more than 600 taverns (*traktiry*), notorious establishments offering food, drink, and entertainment, usually in a series of connecting rooms. Although contemporary accounts frequently noted the sleaziness of taverns in the outer wards, taverns were scattered throughout the city. Traditionally the favorite eating and drinking places of the city's merchants, by the beginning of the twentieth century the taverns had become a major source of entertainment for skilled workers and persons holding lower-level sales and clerical positions.[32] The taverns, as well as inns and all-night tea houses, also provided shelter for a motley clientele of cab drivers, workers, newly arrived peasants, prostitutes, and thieves.[33]

Wholesale and retail trade constituted the largest branch of commerce in Moscow; in 1902 more than 92,000 people earned their livelihood in more than 19,000 shops and stores. Moscow's lively retail trade impressed Russians and foreigners alike: in 1902, 21 percent of Moscow's population was engaged in commerce, a larger proportion than in St. Petersburg or Odessa; indeed, only Paris, among the major European cities, exceeded it.[34] An 1895 economic survey noted that the annual Nizhnii Novgorod fair had become only a temporary extension of Moscow's commercial activity.[35] A British consular official stated:

> Moscow is not only the centre of the vast tea trade of Russia but is also a great warehouse in which are collected various imported and home-made goods destined for the Far East, Siberia, Turkestan and Persia. It has become a halfway house for all travellers to Eastern Siberia and the want of proper hotel accommodation is already being felt. Every day new business premises are opened and picturesque old buildings are fast being replaced by large modern edifices. . . . The population has risen to over 1,000,000 and I think this important business centre, the real commercial capital of Russia, deserves more attention from British manufacturers and capitalists than they at present bestow upon it.[36]

Although the highly mechanized factory giants attracted a large share of the labor force, a concomitant expansion of small-scale manufacture of consumer goods and the enlargement of the market and of the monied economy multiplied employment opportunities in construction, trade, transport, services, and the professions. During the last two decades of the nineteenth century, the numbers employed in retail and wholesale sales as well as in transport and communications almost doubled; the number employed in the provision of lodging, food, and drink almost tripled. In addition, functional specialization in the economy, such as the separation of business from residence, separation of sales from production, and the concentration of sales in stores, was not widespread. Manufacturing and retailing, for example, were frequently conducted at the residence of the producer or merchant. Although by the end of the nineteenth century a distinct central business district had formed, most retail sales of essential commodities to the common people were widely dispersed throughout the city in open-air markets and undertaken by peddlers and street vendors. Hawkers and vendors, according to one observer, provided an essential function: "Since Muscovites are not able to conduct their affairs in a strictly rational (*planomero*) way, they tend to chase around; this explains the abundance of traders and vendors who fill up the city's streets."[37] In fact, although the downturn in the national economy beginning in 1900 and the scarcity and high cost of credit made it more difficult for marginal businesses to survive, the second economic boom beginning in 1908 caused an increase not only in the total number of businessmen, but especially in the number of self-employed whose ranks jumped by more than 70 percent.[38] The impression that Moscow was a city of small-scale production and distribution was still valid at the beginning of the twentieth century and even beyond 1917 to the Civil War and the early years of the New Economic Policy.

Despite national trends toward bigness and concentration of enterprise, Moscow's economy sustained a variety of organizational forms from modern stores and gigantic factories to street vending and sweated apparel manufacture. Modernization in Moscow took the form of a dual economy. At the apex stood large-scale institutions of banking, credit, and insurance and industrial magnates who controlled textile empires from Samarkand to St. Petersburg and owned plants and enterprises with large numbers of wage and salaried employees. At the bottom thrived the institutions of barter, haggle, and street vending and peasant entrepreneurs who controlled the carrying and hauling trades from Tver' to Tula. The "two economies" were intertwined. Increased wealth and greater consumption at the apex of urban society stimulated production and distribution of consumer goods, often custom-made or luxury items. Increased use of money and greater purchasing power at the lower economic levels also hastened the growth of small-scale producers and retailers of ready-made articles who catered to a vast internal market of peasants in and near the city. As the national market grew, as large factories and the railroad penetrated the countryside, and as capitalism appeared to be giving the traditional economy in the village a mortal blow, the small-scale, informal economic organizations were still vital in the largest cities and, paradoxically, the metropolis was ideally suited to sustain them.

The greater advancement of European economies enabled approximately half the population of its metropolises to live as dependents. In Moscow, however, the low wages, inadequate housing, and large number of transient immigrants meant that a high and virtually unchanging proportion of the population was in the labor force. This labor force was largely male; and, as Table 2.1 shows, certain occupational categories such as sales-clerical and skilled blue collar were all but inaccessible to women. Women were in other occupations in much greater numbers, however; for example, by 1912 almost one in three factory workers was female, and women predominated in domestic service.

Structural shifts in the labor force and changing opportunities can be seen both in changes in individual occupations and in changes in white-collar and blue-collar categories. Table 2.2 shows the eighteen most common occupations in 1902 and 1912. Four of them—drivers and haulers, weavers, chambermaids, and cooks—experienced an absolute decline, particularly significant in years of rapid population growth. All four were semiskilled or menial jobs that reflected the mechanization in the textile industry, the decline in domestic service, and the modernization of municipal transport. Another group of four—shoemakers, building superintendents, cabinet makers, and governesses—showed only moderate increases that did not keep pace with the average for the entire labor force. Like the previous group, this group consisted of manual jobs, including two skilled crafts. The remaining occupations displayed greater than average increases and two—peddlers and bookkeepers—actually more than doubled in number. With the exception of the waiters, all manual workers in this group were skilled and included printers and metalworkers who were among the leaders of the union and strike movement in 1905 and 1917.[39]

The majority of these eighteen occupations were blue collar and indeed, as Table 2.1 shows, approximately 70 percent of the city's workforce held blue-collar jobs. As is readily apparent, although one-fifth of the city's self-supporting males were skilled blue-collar workers—an impressive figure by itself—more than two-fifths of the self-supporting males and two-thirds of all blue-collar workers were semiskilled or menials. Though in sheer size blue-collar workers dominated the labor force, the most rapidly growing labor category was professionals and salaried employees. In the manufacturing and commercial sectors of the economy alone, from 1882 to 1912 the number of salaried employees increased by 350 percent, reflecting the increasing sophistication and diversification of the economy.[40]

Contemporary evidence as well as peasant budget studies of the 1920s suggest that Moscow was a land of opportunity to the well-off, skilled, and motivated and a refuge to the poor, unskilled, and drifters. Given the small size and limited employment opportunities of most provincial and county towns, nowhere else within hundreds of miles were there so many opportunities for entrepreneurial ability and self-

TABLE 2.1

Structure of the Moscow Labor Force, 1902

Occupational Ranking	Men		Women		Total	
	N	%	N	%	Labor Force	% Men
Professionals	8,929	1.8	5,903	2.4	14,632	61.0
Major proprietors, managers, officials	15,948	3.2	7,802	3.2	23,750	67.1
All high white collar	24,877	5.0	15,705	5.6	38,382	64.8
Sales-clerical	43,598	8.8	4,231	1.7	47,829	91.2
Semi-professionals	8,576	1.7	7,769	3.2	16,345	52.5
Petty proprietors, managers, officials	47,332	9.5	15,520	6.4	62,852	75.3
All low white collar	99,506	20.0	27,520	11.3	127,026	78.3
Unclassified white collar	14,107	2.8	20,647	8.5	34,754	40.6
Total white collar	138,290	27.8	61,872	25.4	200,162	69.1
Skilled	112,881	22.7	21,360	8.8	133,821	84.4
Semi-skilled and service	142,237	28.6	85,348	35.2	227,585	62.3
Unskilled and menial service	71,663	14.4	45,174	18.6	116,837	61.3
Unclassified blue collar	24,034	4.8	25,136	10.3	49,170	48.9
Total blue collar	350,815	70.5	176,988	72.9	527,413	66.5
Total white and blue collar	489,105	98.3	238,860	98.3	727,575	67.2
Unclassified	8,449	1.7	4,156	1.7	12,605	67.0
Total labor force	497,554	100.0	243,016	100.0	740,570	67.2
Total population	613,003		479,307		1,092,360	

SOURCE: *Perepis' Moskvy 1902 g.* (Moscow, 1904), pt. 2, sec. i, 46–115; pt. 3, sec. iii, 170–215.

TABLE 2.2

Most Common Occupations in Moscow, 1902 and 1912

Occupation	Number employed		% Increase or Decrease
	1902	1912	
Sales clerks	20,776	33,885	63.1
Tailors[a]	20,880	33,569	60.8
Cooks, kitchen help	36,029	32,381	−10.1
Building superintendents (dvorniki)[b]	20,859	25,167	20.7
Weavers[a]	22,007	21,976	−0.1
Office clerks	14,140	22,185	56.9
Cab drivers, draymen (izvozchiki)	24,638	19,716	−20.0
Mechanics, fitters (slesari)[a]	10,935	18,524	69.4
Teachers	8,992	16,269	80.9
Metalsmiths[c]	6,888	13,262	92.5
Shoemakers[a]	10,557	12,936	22.5
Chambermaids	13,569	12,331	−8.7
Governesses, nursemaids	10,407	10,709	5.1
Printers[d]	5,493	10,141	84.6
Cabinet makers[a]	9,020	10,127	12.3
Waiters, waitresses	5,455	10,040	84.1
Bookkeepers, cashiers	4,237	9,572	125.9
Peddlers (raznoschiki)[a]	4,182	9,194	119.8

SOURCE: *Perepis' Moskvy 1902 g.* (Moscow, 1904), pt. 2, sec. i, 46–115; pt. 3, sec. iii, 170–215. *Statisticheskii ezhegodnik goroda Moskvy i Moskovskoi gubernii*, vyp. 2 (Moscow, 1927), 68–73.

[a]Includes both "self-employed" and "worker." In 1912, however, figures for self-employed weavers, mechanics, shoemakers, and cabinetmakers are not available, making percentage increase slightly smaller than it would be otherwise.

[b]Includes guards, doormen.

[c]Working non-precious metals, such as tinsmiths, wiremakers.

[d]Includes lithographers, typesetters, and other printers.

employment.[41] A large proportion of the city's employers and the great majority of its self-employed were first- and second-generation peasant immigrants. Although they appeared more frequently in the observations of contemporaries than in the advertising section of the city directory or in official listings of manufacturing and retailing establishments, these small peasant producers, retailers, builders, and carters were ubiquitous. In all branches of manufacturing except textiles, peasants were the most numerous businessmen: in 1882, peasant ownership approached 54 percent of wood-processing establishments, 58.3 percent in the food industry, and 70 percent of the construction industry. In the various branches of retailing and services, peasant ownership reached 68 percent of the business of peddling, street vending, and hawking, and 88 percent of the carrying trades.[42] A special study of the carrying trades in the mid-1890s confirmed that peasants had virtually taken over the business: of 2,595 independent haulers, 2,255 or 86.9 percent were peasants.[43] The tenacity, or perhaps more accurately the vitality, of the peasant entrepreneur in the metropolis confirms that small-scale organization was well suited to the vagaries of the Moscow market and the industrial cycle, to the demand for made-to-order and luxury items, and to the demand of a vast internal market of peasants in and around the city.

Although evidence such as structural change in the economy and peasant ownership suggests that Moscow's laborers could experience upward or at the very least lateral occupational mobility, other evidence suggesting downward mobility is too pervasive to ignore. To begin with, the indirect evidence for upward occupational mobility for some of the city's new arrivals concerns only those who stayed in Moscow. From 1882 to 1902 almost 100,000 *left* Moscow every year.[44] Those who left probably had worse occupational prospects than those who stayed, and in many cases departure signified failure. Moves that did not improve job prospects or marketable skills, or that were the result of poor job prospects and few marketable skills, brought about an aimless drifting at the lower end of the occupational scale, a source of great concern among reformers.

Occupational immobility, downward mobility, and the aimless drifting at the bottom of the occupational ladder contributed to the growth of a casual labor force. Like Paris and London, Moscow during the second half of the nineteenth century had a chronic glut of unskilled laborers, employed intermittently or casually. In every trade, the nucleus of permanently (or more or less permanently) employed was surrounded by a casual fringe which worked on the waterfront, in transport, construction, the carting and hauling trades, in the wholesale markets, and as hawkers, messengers, vendors, draymen and laborers in low-grade and unhealthy factory jobs. Although reformers at the end of the nineteenth century decried the loss of craft skills, a large, economically marginal, reserve population in every sector of the economy from manufacturing to domestic service was vital to the metropolis at this stage of development and economic organization.

A booming but volatile metropolitan economy generated a rapidly growing but volatile labor force. More brains were needed than ever before; at the same time more brawn was needed to build, move, haul, and clean. Occupational stratification was becoming more and more complex, and the difference in skill levels and working conditions for the skilled metalworkers and the common laborers was increasing. Never had opportunities been greater for the skilled and enterprising; given that the position of the unskilled laborer is more precarious in a skilled, urban society than in an agrarian society, never had the consequences of missing those opportunities been more disastrous. What did the municipal administration do to alleviate the worst aspects of the urban environment? What services did the city provide to mitigate the effects of rapid population growth, immigration, housing pressure, disease, and erratic employment opportunities?

CITY ADMINISTRATION AND SOCIAL SERVICES

The Russian city never attained the corporate autonomy and distinctiveness achieved over centuries by the European city. On the one hand, the Russian city was little more than an administrative extension of the central government, and the public services provided in the city were essentially those of the Ministry of Internal Affairs. On the other hand, the city was the permanent home of a small proportion of its residents; the majority were transients whose legal residence was in the village. Despite its size and economic importance, Moscow was no exception to this general rule. During the second half of the nineteenth century, however, the central government granted the city a measure of autonomy, and in turn the city began to assert a measure of distinctiveness from the surrounding villages. A major step in this process, of course, was the Municipal Statute of 1870.

After 1870 cities were governed by a policy-making council (duma) and an executive board (uprava); the mayor, elected by the city council for a four-year term, presided over both bodies. Many of Moscow's mayors, such as Sergei M. Tret'iakov (in office from 1876 to 1882), Nikolai A. Alekseev (1885–93), Konstantin Rukavishnikov (1893–96), and Nikolai I. Guchkov (1905–12), came from prominent merchant families. In 1905 the central government, increasingly mistrustful of liberals in local government, established the City Prefecture (Gradonachal'stvo) and the Special Office for City Affairs, which paralleled and supervised many of the functions of the city council and executive board.

The city electorate was no more trusted than were its representatives. In 1870 the franchise was restricted by a two-year residence requirement and by property qualifications—ownership of real estate and purchase of commercial or manufacturing certificates. The property qualifications were broad enough, however, to give the franchise to "any male, even a peasant, who paid any other city taxes or fees including those amounting to as little as a ruble or two for a license to set up a stall in a street market."[45] In Moscow, for example, the electorate in 1884 numbered 18,000, that is, 2 percent of the population. By raising the property qualifications to ownership of real estate valued at a minimum of 3,000 rubles or to purchase of a commercial or manufacturing certificate costing 500 rubles or more, the 1892 Statute restricted the franchise in Moscow to 6,000 persons, considerably less than 1 percent of the population.[46] But what was perhaps even more disturbing to the proponents of municipal self-government, less than one-quarter of those having the franchise in Moscow actually voted.[47] In spite of this voter apathy, Moscow was considered to have Russia's most active municipal government. Unlike St. Petersburg, whose city administration constantly operated in the shadow of a central government suspicious of local autonomy, Moscow was administered by civic-minded industrialists, businessmen, and professionals interested in expanding social services.[48] During its first fifteen years, the city council opened schools and hospitals, began municipal public works projects such as street lighting and paving, water supply, and sewerage, and considered proposals for greater involvement in many areas of public health, housing, and urban transport.

Nevertheless, important social services, agencies, and institutions, including many hospitals, the Imperial Foundling Home, and the Workhouse, remained outside the jurisdiction of the municipality. Ultimate supervision of social services rested with the Ministry of Internal Affairs. In the late 1880s the Ministry released its control over many institutions and social services, thereby accelerating the trend toward municipal autonomy.[49] Given that city officials in St. Petersburg reacted coolly to the devolution or municipalization of social services, Moscow became the leading Russian city in the movement for municipal autonomy, expansion of services, and civic vision.

The expansion of services was dramatic. Russia's biggest cities spent the largest proportion of their budgets on health, education, and welfare. In Moscow, for example, expenditures in these areas increased from one-quarter of the budget in 1894 to almost three-fifths by 1913.[50] Elementary schools and hospitals received the lion's share of these expenses; expenditures in other areas such as poor relief, housing, and slum renovation were modest. In addition, the city began to operate its own bakery, slaughterhouse, pawnshop, and transport system, and in the 1890s the corresponding services expanded notably.

The city not only gained control over and expanded many services: it began to play a more activist and reformist role in the provision of these services. For example, under municipal control the Workhouse added a vocational center and emphasized job training, industriousness and "the creation of an intelligent, sober, literate, honest workingman—a goal dear to every Russian who wants to see our industry and productivity flourish."[51] Trying to inculcate the quintessential virtues of urban, Victorian society—self-reliance and self-improvement—the Workhouse and related agencies sponsored libraries, public readings, picture shows, and concerts.[52] So publicized and controversial were these amenities that the conservative daily *Moskovskie vedomosti* described the institution as the "favorite child" of the "City Council windbags." The newspaper insisted that the Workhouse should offer

more religion and fewer plays: "Theater, theater, everywhere the theater, even in the Workhouse a theater!"[53]

In actuality the "favorite child" of the city's activist professionals
and reformers was not the Workhouse but the district guardianships of
the poor, conceived as an agency that would transform the city's poor
and the very concept of providing social services. Established in 1894,
the guardianships decentralized poor relief in a manner patterned after
the system in the German town of Elberfeld and admired by leading
European welfare reformers such as Octavia Hill.[54] The guardianships
ran almshouses, free apartments, children's shelters and nurseries,
workshops, cafeterias, a "food stamps" program, a Sunday shelter for
women laborers, and employment offices.[55] The linchpin of the system,
as both proponents and critics agreed, was the volunteer case workers
(sotrudniki), appointed by each district council, who did the real leg
work of the guardianships. The use of volunteer case workers permitted
a greater emphasis on "open" relief, that is, aid provided outside institutions such as hospitals and almshouses.[56] Defenders of the guardianships claimed that this new decentralized, grass-roots organization
had "enlisted widespread enthusiastic support" and had "rejuvenated
welfare in the city."[57] The success of the organization in Moscow was to
have a demonstrable effect, and Moscow was already becoming a model
for welfare organization for the entire Empire.

Despite greater autonomy and activism, expansion of services, and
gains in areas such as public education, Moscow's social services could
not deal adequately with the problems of all of its citizens. Like other
Russian municipalities, Moscow faced a chronic shortage of funds, a
situation exacerbated by the overall backwardness of the country. Tax-
ing powers were limited by the city statutes, and as late as 1901 Moscow's governor-general rather disingenuously noted that the city still
did not have its own income and had to rely on loans to cover not only
operating expenses but also the budget deficit.[58] In addition, some contemporaries charged that the city council, composed largely of property
owners, failed to tax real estate even to the limits made possible by the
municipal statute, but instead charged high prices for municipal services such as the bakery, stockyards, and streetcars.[59] Since the state did
not provide enough cheap credit, the city was forced to negotiate costly
foreign loans. It was perhaps inevitable that deficits should build up:
despite increased revenues from the city's streetcars, during the period
1904–13 Moscow's deficit averaged almost one million rubles annually
and reached two and three-quarter million rubles in 1913.[60] Although
the transfer of several welfare institutions to municipal management in
1888 increased the amount spent on welfare in Moscow from 51,308
rubles in 1881 to 244,432 in 1891, and again to 1,200,000 in 1913, the
proportion of the total municipal budget devoted to welfare and poor
relief barely increased.[61] Private donations to specific charitable institu-

tions somewhat compensated for the modest amount of municipal expenditures, but the city lacked discretionary powers over these funds. Moscow easily ranked first among Russian cities in welfare expenditures, but its one ruble per capita did not compare favorably with the equivalent of three and one-half rubles per capita spent in Berlin.[62]

Moreover, city officials feared that Moscow's social services would be overburdened by the needy from the villages and that easily available relief would attract immigrants. Accordingly, officials were reluctant to assume responsibility for providing relief to immigrants and limited access to certain social services. When the police proposed as early as 1863 that the city provide low-cost housing, the city council refused on the grounds that the potential beneficiaries were not "members of the city community" and were not "directly linked with the city's interest."[63] Thirty years later the statute of the guardianships of the poor limited eligibility to "those born in Moscow or Moscow province and for those who have lived in the capital at least two years so that the establishment of the guardianships will not serve to further the influx of paupers from other provinces to Moscow."[64] The attitude of *Moskovskie vedomosti* to theater in the Workhouse, cited above, reflected a widely shared conviction, even within the city council itself, that the provision of too many social services was both fiscally and politically ill advised.

On balance, by the beginning of the twentieth century, Moscow's city council had come far. Municipal expenditures increased eightfold in the forty years prior to World War I, and total expenditures outpaced population growth such that per capita expenditures tripled to twelve rubles in 1900. This still lagged behind Berlin's spending of the equivalent of thirty rubles per person,[65] but given Russia's backwardness and the fiscal constraints imposed on municipalities by the Imperial government, as well as the latter's mistrust of local autonomy, this is not an entirely fair comparison. Even the mayor of Paris, visiting in 1911, was impressed with Moscow's public works projects.[66] Moscow was considered the leader of Russian cities, and by the beginning of the twentieth century its increasingly civic-minded businessmen and professionals were more progressive than the officials of the central government in their vision of municipal improvement and reform.

TRANSFORMATION OF THE URBAN ENVIRONMENT

On the eve of the Great Reforms, Moscow, with a population of 300,000, was a placid city, bustling only by comparison with the small towns of central Russia. The city and its inhabitants were thought of in terms of associations defined by tradition, law, and service to the state:

hence the sobriquets "gentry Moscow," "merchant Moscow," "holy Moscow," and "big village." The homes of the gentry were the "gentry nests" in the Arbat and Prechistenka neighborhoods; a resident of one of these led "a patriarchal, expansive, landowner's life transferred to the city."[67] In contrast, the homes of the reclusive merchants, many of whom were of peasant origin and were still Old Believers, were the "fenced-off castles" with guard dogs on the sleepy south side of the Moscow River. Organizations and societies, such as the English Club, the Society of Russian History and Antiquities, the Literary Society, and the Society of Amateur Naturalists, were few in number and essentially private in character. The Moscow Agricultural Society, organized in 1820, did organize exhibits and conferences for farmers and create the Moscow Literary Society in 1845 to sponsor lectures and publish books, but this kind of "outreach" activity was rare at mid-century. Even important merchant organizations like the Moscow Stock Exchange Society did not exist formally until 1870.

The sanctity, serenity, solitude, and sleepiness of holy, gentry, merchant, and peasant Moscow were broken here and there by a colorful and lively street and market life. Indeed, despite the disgust that mendicants and vagrants aroused among some well-heeled Muscovites, to others such street people remained a picturesque phenomenon, relics of the "patriarchal Muscovite" past, representatives of an unkempt rural Russia still untouched by civilization, and, to writers and artists of a populist bent, valuable as objects of study, if not actually possessors of some inner Russian virtue. A. Golitsynskii, a physician, writer, and classifier of Moscow's street folk in the manner of his more celebrated English contemporary, Henry Mayhew, described one type of mendicant, the "cape woman," almost always the widow of a lower civil servant "who had worked forty years for five rubles a month and died of pauperism, alcoholism and hemorroids." The cape woman "has a strikingly supple character. The cape woman is created precisely for the proletariat: at the same time she can be a matchmaker, gossip, and make cosmetics; she is a devotee, a mourner, a sponger, a fortune-teller, a thief—everything you could want."[68] Throughout the nineteenth century rates of violent crime were lower in Moscow than in other Russian cities,[69] and therefore, at mid-century, the street people were not objects of punishment or reform, but curiosities, even subjects of celebration. The composer Modest Musorgsky described his first trip to Moscow in 1859:

> I ascended the "Ivan the Great" bell tower from the top of which I had a wonderful view. Roving through the streets I remembered the dictum "All Muscovites bear a distinctive hallmark." This is certainly true of the common people. Nowhere else in the world could beggars and rogues of the same kind be found. They have a strange demeanor, a

nimbleness of motion that struck me particularly. In short I feel as if I had been carried into a new world, the world of yore—an unclean one, but one which nevertheless impresses me most favorably. You know I was a cosmopolitan; now I feel reborn and quite close to all that is Russian.[70]

Thus Musorgsky contrasts the "simple" people of Moscow with the cosmopolitan denizens of St. Petersburg and the cities of Western Europe. He could not have imagined that Moscow itself was so soon to be "reborn" into a "cosmopolitan" city.

Ironically, artists like Musorgsky were unwittingly responsible in part for the transformation of the city at the end of the nineteenth century. The works of the national school of painters and composers were patronized by wealthy businessmen striving, as Thomas Owens argues, "to displace the gentry as the leading role in public life."[71] Such a businessman was K. T. Soldatenkov, publisher, collector of paintings, and art patron, whose suburban estate at Kuntsevo became a center for those interested in old Russian culture.[72] Similarly, Sergei Morozov patronized the landscape painter Levitan and the cottage industries of central Russia, and founded Moscow's Museum of Handicrafts. The businessmen of Moscow had a particular affinity for old Russian culture, folk themes, and native crafts during the second half of the nineteenth century, and Morozov and Soldatenkov, both Old Believers, were typical in this respect. But the man best known for his support of national themes in art and music was the railroad magnate Savva Mamontov. At Mamontov's estate of Abramtsevo, forty miles north of Moscow, gathered the leading Russian artists of the 1880s and 1890s— Polenov, Korovin, Levitan, Serov, Vrubel, Repin, and the Vasnetsovs. In 1883 Mamontov founded a private opera comany, which, at a time when the Imperial theaters were staging Italian opera and shunning Russian national themes, introduced Shaliapin and produced *Boris Godunov, Khovanshchina, Prince Igor,* and *The Tsar's Bride.*[73] It is no exaggeration to claim that by championing private initiative over bureaucratic domination and, in Alfred Rieber's words, "by combining matchless taste and generous spending, Mamontov deserves more credit than anyone else for restoring Moscow as the cultural center of Russia in the last quarter of the nineteenth century."[74]

The businessmen's successful promotion of old Russian culture and the combination of wealth, patronage, and talent in the city catapulted Moscow into a position as one of the centers of European art. A generation after Soldatenkov's collection helped revive interest in old Russian culture, businessmen Petr Shchukin and Ivan Morozov, whose private collections of Matisse, Cezanne, and Picasso were larger than any outside Paris, enabled Moscow's artists and the artistic public to gain exposure to contemporary European culture. Even better known was the art collection of the Tret'iakov brothers, given to the city in 1892 as the basis for the Tret'iakov Gallery. In the theater, a scion of the Alekseev family of business and civic leaders, Konstantin Sergeevich, adopted the stage name Stanislavsky and, with the patronage of Savva Morozov, founded the Moscow Art Theater in 1898. Nikolai Riabushinskii of the prominent Moscow textile and banking family was a patron of the Art Nouveau decorative movement, collected French postimpressionists and Russian moderns, and edited and financed a lavishly prepared art journal with silky overlays and bindings of gold thread called *Zolotoe runo* (Golden Fleece).[75] In the decade before 1914, the Russian aesthete could frequent the Free Theater and Art School, the Society of Amateur Musicians and Thespians, the Society of Free Aesthetics, and salons, clubs, and cabarets with names like the Golden Fleece, the Jack of Diamonds, the Blue Rose, the Bat, and the Bull's-Eye. Moscow challenged accepted standards and demarcations among artistic fields not only of the Imperial Academy but of European traditions, prompting Sergei Diaghilev to observe that whatever was worth looking at came from Moscow, since St. Petersburg was still "a city of artistic gossiping, academic professors and Friday watercolor classes."[76]

If changes in Moscow's intellectual and cultural life had been limited to the world of art and art patronage, a world increasingly self-conscious and elitist, the transformation of the urban environment at the turn of the century would have been confined to a thin veneer of aesthetes. But the artistic avant-garde was only the most vivid example of the profound transformation of the city from big village to cosmopolitan metropolis. Wealthy businessmen not only patronized the arts, but supported philanthropy, participated in the city council, and joined scholarly societies. In addition, professionals on the city council, like their brethren in the zemstvos, took an increasing interest in the city around them and, in the words of a leading Soviet historian of Moscow, "planned large-scale projects to improve the city radically and give it a European appearance."[77] Finally, private individuals were organizing in unprecedented numbers according to professional, occupational, and leisure interests. A brief look at Moscow's societies and associations, its civic institutions, and its educational system will illustrate the transformative functions of the city.

Professional associations and scholarly societies began to spring up during the era of the Great Reforms and rapidly increased in number at the turn of the century in response to the increasing specialization in the professions and to the needs of new fields of knowledge. For example, the medical community could look not only to the Pirogov Society of Russian Physicians, founded in 1883 and later a hotbed of liberal intelligentsia activism,[78] but also to several more specialized associations—the Society of Obstetricians and Gynecologists (1887), the Society of Dermatologists (1891), and the Society of Pediatricians (1892). By the beginning of the twentieth century, older associations of the 1860s and 1870s such as the Archaeological Society (1864), the Society of Architects (1867), the Legal Society (1863), and the Moscow section of the Imperial Society of Russian Engineers (1870) were joined by the Society of Neurologists and Psychiatrists (1891) and the Aeronautical Society. Even more important than the associations of professionals for the dissemination of learning were the many amateur societies. For example, the Society of Amateur Artists (1861) sponsored exhibits and contests and organized the first All-Russian Congress of Artists in 1894, which discussed art theory, art education, and museum work.[79] Other disseminators of urban culture were the Society of Amateur Naturalists, Anthropologists and Ethnographers (1863), the Society of Amateur Writers (*Pisateli iz naroda*, 1902), and the Society of Amateur Astronomers. The very existence of such associations in a culture not noted for its "joiners" reflected the great transformations already taking place in the city.

The effect of professional organizations was clearly felt in Moscow's labor and union movement. Though waves of strikes hit the city and its hinterland in the years 1885–88 and 1895–98, in the decade before 1905 the per capita strike rate was among the lowest in Russia, and there was more unrest in the mill towns outside the city than in Moscow itself.[80] Despite radical propaganda aimed at workers and rudimentary mutual aid organizations going back to the 1870s and 1880s, for a long time, as Robert Johnson argues, barriers separated workers from intellectuals; it was only after 1900 that the more independent, highly skilled, and craft-conscious workers such as those in the metal and printing trades were able to organize.[81] The radicalization of labor in 1905 came about in part due to the organizing activity of liberal professionals interested in building a trade union movement and the dissatisfaction of white-collar employees such as pharmacy clerks and railroad and municipal employees.[82] The Museum for Assistance to Labor, founded in 1901 by the Moscow section of the Imperial Society of Russian Engineers, became a focal point for progressively inclined professionals and representatives of craft and clerical groups, participated in the Zubatov experiment of "police socialism," and organized public lectures and workers' libraries. In 1905 the Museum sheltered the organizations and meetings of bakers, railway employees and municipal employees, organized the first All-Russian Conference of Representatives of Professional Unions, and even provided the hall for the first two meetings of what was to become the Moscow city soviet.[83]

The Museum for Assistance to Labor was only one of many museums and exhibits through which Moscow's educated classes tried to spread learning and culture to the general public. Many, such as the

Anthropology Exhibit of 1879, the Russian Exhibit of Industry and the Arts in 1882, the Historical Museum, the Museum of Cottage Industries, the Tret'iakov Gallery, and the Alexander III Museum of Fine Arts provided traditional functions of display. Others, as illustrated by the Museum for Assistance to Labor, avowedly promoted social change. Best known for its broad educational activities was the Museum of Science and Industry, built on the basis of the Russian Exhibit of Science and Industry in 1872 organized by the Society of Amateur Naturalists, Anthropologists and Ethnographers. With public lectures and Sunday tours, begun in 1878, the museum resembled an open university by the turn of the century. Indeed the Moscow Society of Free Universities, founded in 1906, ran classes on law, economics, literature, natural sciences, and medicine at the Museum; at first attended largely by the intelligentsia and lower level white-collar workers, these classes attracted more and more blue-collar workers.[84]

But it was Moscow's educational system that was most remarkable for its attempts to reach the people of the city. Although the city had several long-established private and Imperial schools, after the Education Statute in 1864 the number of public schools grew quickly. In 1867 the first five public primary schools (all for girls) opened, and three years later the first public boys' school opened. The tuition of three rubles per year was waived for children of poor peasants. In the forty years after the first boys' school opened, an average of seven public schools opened *per year*; the number of pupils increased by more than one thousand per year, and the expenditures increased from 10,000 to more than two million rubles. On the eve of World War I, public school enrollment had jumped to almost 60,000 and the budget was 4.5 million rubles; during the period 1902–1912, one of the fastest growing occupational groups was teachers.[85] Among the city's distinctions in primary education were special classes for slow learners, an innovation not yet widely practiced even in the West.[86]

Though many who finished primary school then discontinued their schooling, a study of 7,546 graduates of the three-year public schools showed that 50 percent went on for further education. The city and private societies ran a network of general, vocational-technical, and business schools, many of which also organized adult education programs in the evenings and on Sundays. For example, both the Society of Russian Engineers and the Society to Promote Technical Knowledge (founded in 1869) ran mechanics' schools and sponsored public lectures and free drafting classes. In 1893 the latter Society opened correspondence courses, modeled after British and American self-education programs.[87] The Moscow School of Engineering, which had started as a vocational school for the orphans of the Foundling Home in the 1830s, trained 1,389 engineers between 1871 and 1897 and won prizes at international exhibitions at Vienna and Philadelphia.[88] Business schools, many of which opened in the 1890s and which demonstrate the commitment to education of the business community, also contributed to the rapid expansion of secondary education in Moscow. In 1897, for example, the banker Aleksei S. Vishniakov organized the Society for Commercial Education to train clerks already employed and to prepare young students for careers in business.[89] Access to such secondary schools was by no means limited to boys, and indeed the Nicholas Business School for Women, the Moscow Business School for Women, the Arbat Vocational School, the General Courses for Women, and the Higher Agriculture Courses for Women were but a few of the growing number of institutions providing opportunities for women.[90]

Education stood for culture, opportunity, and choice. A small but extraordinary example illustrates how far Moscow had come on the eve of World War I. In 1910 the city school commission sent a questionnaire to parents with children in primary schools to find out the type of post-primary education they wanted for their children. Of 40,000 parents solicited, 34,237 responded, itself a remarkable figure. Nine of every ten parents wanted further education for their sons and daughters, though the desirability of further education for the latter was frequently qualified by such phrases as "if it is affordable," "if it is free." The desirability of vocational and business subjects was not notably high and was lower than the desirability of courses in French and German. Indeed, though one might assume that poorer families would have perceived the vocational schools as offering better job preparation, enrollments in public secondary schools nearly equaled those in vocational schools. Several answers indicated that parents wanted their children to have not narrow vocational training but liberal arts and civic education (*zhiznevedenie, grazhdanovedenie*). One's son should be a "worthy citizen" and one's daughter should raise her children "to recognize the dignity of the individual and to respect the rights of others."[91] In both the intent of the questionnaire itself and in the hopes of some of the respondents, it is hard to imagine a more liberal spirit in any city.

CONCLUSION

Like metropolises in Europe and America at the time, Moscow seemed to its educated elite to offer the best as well as the worst of the modern urban, industrial world. Economic expansion and structural shifts coupled with unprecedented population growth and mobility created a dynamic urban environment. Although the common people had many reasons to despair, it could not be denied that Moscow provided unprecedented opportunity for natives and newcomers alike. The city's rapid growth and modernization provided hope that individual initiative and enterprise could triumph over sloth and lethargy.

In the great cities, Europeanized ways could now be mass marketed and, like the watchchains and table lamps that peasants took back to their native villages after sojourns in Moscow, spread beyond the thin layer of the Russian elite to the common people. Myriad schools, agencies, and institutions were attempting to forge "an intelligent, sober, literate, honest workingman" from the raw material of the immigrant peasant. Reformers believed that such a self-reliant workingman would resist the appeals of demagogues of the right and the left, enabling the city to avoid class strife.

In the mid–nineteenth century Moscow had been essentially a fragmented city of isolated communities separated by tradition, legal status, and service to the state. The city's sobriquets—"the gentry nests," "merchant Moscow," "holy Moscow," "big village"—aptly characterized these communities and suggest the nature of the barriers between them. The Great Reforms began to dismantle these divisions, and the boom in economic and cultural life beginning in the 1890s hastened the process. At the same time, new communities were evolving, based on profession, craft, workplace, and culture. In these emerging communities the older concept of corporate loyalty was combined with a new sense of individual dignity, self-worth, and autonomy. Daily life in the urban environment offered new opportunities for individual growth and development: wealthy businessmen patronized the arts and joined scholarly societies; artists rejected academic canons and began to experiment with light and color; professionals sought to spread education and culture among the lower classes; and skilled workers expanded their horizons through study groups and contact with the city's cultural life. An element of choice more and more entered daily life.

Not having been created by the state, the new urban groupings became increasingly resentful of the state's efforts to stifle initiative, limit choice, and circumscribe individual autonomy. The civic spirit was aimed at breaking down barriers among social and economic groups, not reinforcing them. Artists like Stanislavsky and patrons like Mamontov, Morozov, and Nikolai Riabushinskii fostered cooperation among the arts; the newspaper Utro Rossii and the Progressist Party, both funded by Pavel Riabushinskii, sought to encourage contact among political and economic sectors; and the Museum of Science and Industry and the Museum for Assistance to Labor worked to bring the educated classes and the workers into contact with each other. This new-found sense of community and purpose gained momentum until it was stifled by the arbitrary constraints imposed by the central government following the revolution of 1905.

In the half century after the Great Reforms, the burgeoning population of Moscow experienced the breaking down of traditional barriers between older communities, the emergence of new groupings along occupational or special-interest lines, and a growing spirit of independence on the one hand and community participation on the other. To be sure, just as the Imperial government retained a suffocating bureaucracy and arbitrary police, Moscow, too, retained some of its old boorishness, backwardness, and dreariness (particularly on the outskirts), and its atmosphere of village solitude. Still, by 1914, an expanding economy and labor force, wealthy businessmen, avant-garde artists, an activist city administration, progressive professionals, and skilled workers had transformed provincial and parochial Moscow into a cosmopolitan and civic-minded city. The big village had become a metropolis.

NOTES

1. Karl Baedeker, *Russia with Teheran, Port Arthur, and Peking* (London, 1914), 277.
2. I. F. Gornostaev and Ia. M. Bugoslavskii, *Putevoditel' po Moskve i ee okrestnostiam* (Moscow, 1903), 36; M. P. Zakharov, *Putevoditel' po Moskve*, 3rd ed. (Moscow, 1868), 3.
3. Akademiia nauk SSSR, *Istoriia Moskvy*, 6 vols. (Moscow, 1952–1959), I:24; David Hooson, "The Growth of Cities in Pre-Soviet Russia," in R. P. Beckinsale and J. M. Houston, eds., *Urbanization and Its Problems: Essays in Honour of E. W. Gilbert* (Oxford, 1970), 269.
4. M. Gol'denberg and B. Gol'denberg, *Planirovka zhilogo kvartala Moskvy XVII, XVIII, XIX vv.* (Moscow-Leningrad, 1935), 11, 30; V. A. Nikol'skii *Staraia Moskva: Istoriko-kul'turnyi putevoditel'* (Moscow, 1924), 114–115; G. G. Antipin, *Zariad'e* (Moscow, 1973), 7–15.
5. A. Golitsynskii, *Ulichnye tipy* (Moscow, 1860), 43–45.
6. G. Vasilich, "Ulitsy i liudi," I. E. Zabelin, ed., *Moskva v ee proshlom i nastoiashchem*, 12 vols. (Moscow, 1910–1912), XII:6.
7. Gol'denberg, *Planirovka*, 29, 58–60.
8. Moskovskaia gorodskaia uprava, *Torgovo-promyshlennye zavedeniia goroda Moskvy za 1885–90 gg.* (Moscow, 1892), 46–48, hereafter cited as *TPZ*. See also Moskovskaia gorodskaia uprava, *Sovremennoe khoziaistvo goroda Moskvy* (Moscow, 1913), 11. Additional descriptive material on the city's districts may be found in any of the books by P. V. Sytin. See, for example, *Iz istorii moskovskikh ulits* (Moscow, 1958); *Otkuda proizoshli nazvaniia ulits Moskvy* (Moscow, 1959); and *Proshloe Moskvy v nazvaniiakh ulits* (Moscow, 1948).
9. A. G. Rashin, *Naselenie Rossii za 100 let, 1811–1913* (Moscow, 1956), III, 133.
10. Ibid.; B. P. Kadomtsev, *Professional'nyi i sotsial'nyi sostav naseleniia Evropeiskoi Rossii po dannym perepisi 1897 g.* (St. Petersburg, 1909), 73; Moskovskaia gorodskaia uprava, Statisticheskii otdel, *Perepis' Moskvy 1882 g.* 3 vols. (Moscow, 1885), II, pt. 1, 66–77, and *Perepis' Moskvy 1902 g.* (Moscow, 1904), pt. 1, i, 2–4, 12–13, hereafter abbreviated *PM 1882* and *PM 1902*, respectively; *Statisticheskii ezhegodnik goroda Moskvy i Moskovskoi gubernii*, vyp. 2 (Moscow, 1927), 68–74, hereafter abbreviated as *SEMMG*.
11. *PM 1882*, II, pt. 2, 31–34; *PM 1902*, pt. 1, i, 8–11. On January 31, 1902, for example, the census counted 781,067 immigrants out of a population of slightly more than one million. This figure, of course, represents the net migration, that is, those who had moved in all previous years to the city and stayed

long enough to be counted on January 31. Those who had moved to the city but had escaped being recorded by the census takers, died, or had left were not counted. The censal figure for the number of residents in the city less than one year (though in itself also a net figure) is the closest approximation to the total number of immigrants in one year.

12. *PM 1882*, II, pt. 1, 49–50; *PM 1902*, pt. 1, i, 8. See also my *Muzhik and Muscovite: Urbanization in Late Imperial Russia* (Berkeley, 1985), chapter 4.

13. Moskovskaia gorodskaia uprava, *Glavneishie predvaritel'nye dannye perepisi goroda Moskvy 1902 g.*, 6 vols. (Moscow, 1902–1907), IV:22, hereafter cited as *GPD 1902*. See also my "Patterns of Peasant Migration to Late Nineteenth-Century Moscow: How Much Should We Read into Literacy Rates?" *Russian History*, 6, pt. 1 (1979):22–38.

14. *PM 1882*, II, pt. 1, 51–52; *PM 1902*, pt. 1, i, 6–8.

15. Tsentral'nyi statisticheskii komitet, *Pervaia vseobshchaia perepis' naseleniia Rossiiskoi imperii 1897 g.* (St. Petersburg, 1897–1905), hereafter abbreviated as *PVP*, 24a, pt. 2, xiii; Moskovskaia gorodskaia duma, *Sbornik ocherkov po gorodu Moskve* (Moscow, 1897), 4.

16. See Robert E. Johnson, *Peasant and Proletarian: The Working Class of Moscow in the Late Nineteenth Century* (New Brunswick, N.J., 1979).

17. *Moskva: Putevoditel'* (Moscow, 1915), 117.

18. Moskovskaia gorodskaia uprava, *Statisticheskii ezhegodnik g. Moskvy za 1913–14* (Moscow, 1916), 48, hereafter abbreviated *SEM*.

19. Moskovskaia gorodskaia uprava, *Glavneishie predvaritel'nye dannye perepisi g. Moskvy 1912 g.* (*Trudy Statisticheskogo otdeleniia Moskovskoi gorodskoi upravy*, vyp. 1, Moscow, 1913), 8, hereafter cited as *GPD 1912*.

20. *PM 1882*, I, pt. 2, 1–4; *GPD 1912*, 30, 34–37.

21. *PVP*, 24:4–7.

22. *PM 1882*, I, pt. 2, 75–76.

23. A. I. Chuprov, *Kharakteristika Moskvy po perepisi 1882 g.* (Moscow, 1884), 39. See also Slonov, *Iz zhizni torgovoi Moskvy* (Moscow, 1914), 165; and Vasilich, "Ulitsy i liudi," 10.

24. "Rabochii poselok pod Moskvoi," *Izvestiia Moskovskoi gorodskoi dumy*, 1906, no. 9:4. Hereafter cited as *IMGD*.

25. P. I. Kurkin, *Statistika dvizheniia naseleniia v Moskovskoi gubernii, 1883–97 gg.* (Moscow, 1902), 150–51, 166, 535.

26. P. I. Kurkin and A. A. Chertov, *Estestvennoe dvizhenie naseleniia goroda Moskvy i Moskovskoi gubernii* (Moscow, 1927), 23; *Sovremennoe khoziaistvo*, 12–13; Z. Frankel', "Neskol'ko dannykh o sanitarnom sostoianii Moskvy i Peterburga za 1909 g.," *Gorodskoe delo*, 1910, no. 20:1405–1407. The percentage decrease in the death rate from 1881 to 1910 was only 17.1 percent in Moscow; it was 22.3 percent in St. Petersburg and 28.3 percent in Paris; all other major European cities registered decreases of at least 30 percent. For comparisons with death rates in Europe, see V. V. Sviatlovskii, *Zhilishchnyi vopros s ekonomicheskoi tochki zreniia*, 5 vols. (St. Petersburg, 1902), IV:65; and S. K. Alaverdian, *Zhilishchnyi vopros v Moskve* (Erevan, 1961), 69.

27. E. D. Maksimov, *Proiskhozhdenie nishchenstva i mery bor'by s nim* (St. Petersburg, 1901), 72. See also my " 'Once You've Eaten Khitrov Soup You'll Never Leave!': Slum Renovation in Late Imperial Russia," *Russian History* (in press).

28. *Sovremennoe khoziaistvo*, 18.

29. Iu. I. Kir'ianov, *Zhiznennyi uroven' rabochikh Rossii (Konets XIX–nachalo XX v.)* (Moscow, 1979), 257–58. See also my review in *Kritika*, 17, no. 2 (1981):87–103.

30. At the turn of the twentieth century the Ministry of Internal Affairs estimated that four-fifths of the adult men and one-half of the adult women of Moscow's hinterland were employed in cottage industries (Tsentral'nyi gosudarstvennyi istoricheskii arkhiv, fond 1284, opis' 194, delo 79, list 3–4. Hereafter TsGIA). See also V. P. Semenov (Tian-Shanskii), *Rossiia: Polnoe geograficheskoe opisanie nashego otechestva*. Vol. I: *Moskovskaia promyshlennaia oblast' i verkhnee povolzh'e* (St. Petersburg, 1899), 148; M. Tugan-Baranovskii, *Russkaia fabrika v proshlom i nastoiashchem* 3d ed.. (Moscow, 1907), 347, 360, 378; V. P. Vorontsov, *Ocherki kustarnoi promyshlennosti v Rossii* (St. Petersburg, 1886), 7.

31. *PM 1902*, pt. 2, i, 116–59; *GPD 1902*, VI:66; Laura Engelstein, *Moscow, 1905: Working-Class Organization and Political Conflict* (Stanford, 1982), 43.

32. *PM 1902*, pt. 2, i, 162–63; *TPZ*, 6–25. See also the descriptions in Slonov, *Iz zhizni*, 140–41; *Ushedshaia Moskva* (Moscow, 1964), 147–48; Vasilich, "Ulitsy i liudi," 10; Vladimir Giliarovskii, *Moskva i Moskvichi* (Moscow, 1968), 307–36; and *Sputnik Moskvicha* (Moscow, 1890), 157.

33. V. D'iakonov, et al., "O postoialykh dvorakh v Moskve," *Otchet o deiatel'nosti Moskovskoi gorodskoi upravy za 1885* (Moscow, 1887), 165–78. For a fictional description see S. T. Semenov, "Dva brata," in *V rodnoi derevne* (Moscow, 1962), 38–39.

34. *PM 1902*, pt. 2, i, 160–73; *GPD 1902*, VI:76.

35. N. A. Komarov, *Voenno-statisticheskoe opisanie Moskovskoi, Vladimirskoi i Nizhegorodskoi gubernii* (Moscow, 1895), 276–77.

36. "Report for the year 1898 on the Trade and Agriculture of the Consular District of St. Petersburg," Great Britain, *Parliamentary Papers: Diplomatic and Consular Reports*, No. 2343 (1899), 54.

37. Vasilich, "Ulitsy i liudi," 10.

38. *PM 1882*, II, pt. 2, 131–34; pt. 3, 101–340; *PM 1902*, pt. 2, i, 116–97; *SEMMG*, 68–73; *TPZ*, 2–5.

39. See Victoria Bonnell, *Roots of Rebellion: Workers' Politics and Organizations in St. Petersburg and Moscow* (Berkeley, 1983), Engelstein, *Moscow, 1905*; Diane Koenker, *Moscow Workers and the 1917 Revolution* (Princeton, 1981).

40. *PM 1882*, II, pt. 2, 101–340; *PM 1902*, pt. 2, i, 116–59; *SEMMG*, 168–73.

41. Tsentral'nyi statisticheskii komitet, *Sbornik svedenii po Rossii za 1884–85* (St. Petersburg, 1886), 2–9; *Obshchii svod po imperii rezul'tatov razrabotki dannykh pervoi vseobshchei perepisi naseleniia 1897 g.* (St. Petersburg, 1905), I:6; Kurkin, *Statistika*, 22–23; Rashin, *Naselenie*, 101.

42. *PM 1882*, II, pt. 3, 303–16; *TPZ*, 16–18.

43. *Nekotorye svedeniia o lomovom izvoze v Moskve* (Moscow, 1896), 14.

44. *PM 1882*, II, pt. 2, 31–34; *PM 1902*, pt. 2, i, 8–11. See also Johnson, *Peasant and Proletarian*, 43–44.

45. Walter Hanchett, "Tsarist Statutory Regulation of Municipal Government in the Nineteenth Century," in Michael Hamm, ed., *The City in Russian History* (Lexington, Ky., 1976), 99–100.

46. Ibid., 111.; *Istoriia Moskvy*, 4:494–95, 512.

47. Gornostaev and Bugoslavskii, *Putevoditel'*, 296–97.

48. James Bater, "Some Dimensions of Urbanization and the Response of Municipal Government: Moscow and St. Petersburg," *Russian History*, 5, pt. 2 (1978):46–63.

49. *Polnoe sobranie zakonov Rossiiskoi imperii*, 3d ser., VII (1887), No. 4554; and XII (1892), No. 8708. See also *Sbornik ocherkov*, 1–7; "Doklad Komissii o pol'zakh i nuzhdakh obshchestvennykh," *Doklady Moskovskoi gorodskoi upravy* (Moscow, 1891), 27, 35, 39–40.

50. *Sbornik ocherkov*, 95, 138; Sobstvennaia ego Imperatorskogo Velichestva Kantseliariia po uchrezhdeniiam Imperatritsy Marii, *Blagotvoritel'nost' v Rossii*, 2 vols. (St. Petersburg, 1907), I:137–38.

51. Obshchestvo pooshchreniia trudoliubiia v Moskve, *Letopis' pervogo dvadtsatipiatiletiia* (Moscow, 1888), pt. 1, 276–77.

52. See my "The Moscow Workhouse and Urban Welfare Reform in Russia," *Russian Review*, 41, 4 (1982):427–44.

53. [Omega], "Liubimoe detishche upravy," *Moskovskie vedomosti*, September 25, 1902, 2.

54. "El'berfel'dskaia sistema prizreniia bednykh," *IMGD*, 1905, no. 1:17–36. A recent discussion of the guardianships is Adele Lindenmeyr, "A Russian Experiment of the Poor, 1894–1914," *Jahrbücher für Geschichte Osteuropas*, 30 (1982):429–51.

55. *Deiatel'nost' Moskovskikh gorodskikh popechitel'stv o bednykh v 1900 g.*, 9–13; *Otchet Moskovskoi gorodskoi upravy za 1901*, 259; and *za 1908*, 224; *Spravochnaia kniga po Moskovskomu gorodskomu obshchestvennomu upravleniiu* (Moscow, 1904), 439.

56. *Otchet Moskovskogo gorodskogo popechitel'stva o bednykh Prechistenskoi chasti* (Moscow, 1895), 4–12; E. Sabashnikova, "Iz deiatel'nosti moskovskikh gorodskikh uchastkovykh popechitel'stv o bednykh za 1897 g.," *IMGD*, 1899, no. 1:5.

57. *Sbornik ocherkov*, 28; N. V. Nesmeianov, "Material'nye zatrudneniia krupnykh gorodov v dele prizreniia bednykh i mery k ikh ustraneniiu," in *Trudy s"ezda po obshchestvennomu prizreniiu, sozvannyi Ministerstvom vnutrennikh del* (St. Petersburg, 1914), 2:447; Moskovskoe gorodskoe uchastkovoe popechitel'stvo o bednykh v 1895 (Moscow, 1895), 33; I. L. Goremykin, then Minister of Internal Affairs, in a circular of 1898, quoted in P. N. Litvinov, "O lichnom sostave gorodskikh popechitel'stv," *Trudy s"ezda po obshchestvennomu prizreniiu*, 2:248. See also V. I. Ger'e, "Russkaia blagotvoritel'nost' na Vsemirnoi Vystavke," *Vestnik Evropy*, 35, no. 8 (1900):509.

58. TsGIA, f. 1284, op. 194, d. 128 l. 4.

59. *Sbornik ocherkov*, 7, 26–30; V. G. Mikhailovskii, *Materialy k voprosu ob usilenii sredstv goroda Moskvy* (Moscow, 1911), 60; Moskovskaia gorodskaia uprava, *Deiatel'nost' Moskovskoi gorodskoi upravy za 1913–1916* (Moscow, 1916), 4.

60. Michael Hamm, "The Breakdown of Urban Modernization: A Prelude to the Revolutions of 1917," in Hamm, ed., *The City in Russian History*, 184; *Gorodskoe delo*, 1914, no. 3:166.

61. *Sbornik ocherkov*, 42, 112–13; *Otchet Moskovskoi gorodskoi upravy za 1908* (Moscow, 1909), 314; *Deiatel'nost' Moskovskoi gorodskoi upravy za 1913–1916*, 11.

62. *Sbornik ocherkov*, 34–38, 42, 112–113; Moskovskaia gorodskaia uprava, *Sbornik statisticheskikh svedenii o blagotvoritel'nosti Moskvy za 1889* (Moscow, 1891), xi.

63. Moskovskaia gorodskaia duma, *Doklad ob ustroistve i soderzhanii kvartir dlia nochlezhnikov* (Moscow, 1866), 6.

64. Tsentral'nyi gosudarstvennyi arkhiv g. Moskvy, f. 184, op. 2, d. 852, l. 57. Additional problems presented by the residency requirements are discussed in Sergei Speranskii, "O proekte reformy obshchestvennogo prizreniia v Rossii," *Trudovaia pomoshch'*, I, 7 (May 1898):37–40.

65. Gornostaev and Bugoslavskii, *Putevoditel' po Moskve*, 300.

66. TsGIA, f. 1284, op. 194, d. 106, l. 8.

67. Apollon Grigor'ev, quoted in Robert Whittaker, "'My Literary and

Moral Wanderings': Apollon Grigor'ev and the Changing Cultural Topography of Moscow," *Slavic Review*, 42, no. 3 (1983):397.

68. Golitsynskii, *Ulichnye tipy*, 8–9.

69. See Mikhail Gernet, *Prestupnyi mir Moskvy* (Moscow, 1924), 17–22; Moskovskoe gradonachal'stvo, *Obzor po gorodu Moskve*, 5 vols. (Moscow, 1906–1910).

70. M. D. Calvocoressi, *Modest Mussorgsky: His Life and Works* (Fair Lawn, N.J., 1956), 32–33.

71. Thomas Owen, *Capitalism and Politics in Russia: A Social History of the Moscow Merchants, 1855–1905* (Cambridge, 1981), 147.

72. Alfred Rieber, *Merchants and Entrepreneurs in Imperial Russia* (Chapel Hill, N.C., 1982), 166; Owen, *Capitalism and Politics in Russia*, 51.

73. Janet Kennedy, *The Mir Iskusstva Group and Russian Art, 1898–1912* (New York, 1977), 135. See also Stuart Grover, "The World of Art Movement in Russia," *Russian Review*, 32, 1 (1973):28–42.

74. Rieber, *Merchants and Entrepreneurs*, 169. See also John Bowlt, *The Silver Age* (Newtonville, Mass., 1979), 88.

75. Rieber, *Merchants and Entrepreneurs*, 291; *Istoriia Moskvy*, 5:636–39. See also Jo Ann Ruckman, *The Moscow Business Elite: A Social and Cultural Portrait of Two Generations, 1840–1905* (DeKalb, Ill., 1984). The most widely used memoir of merchant life is P. A. Buryshkin, *Moskva kupecheskaia* (New York, 1954).

76. Quoted in Grover, "The World of Art Movement," 34. See also Robert Williams, *Artists in Revolution* (Bloomington and London, 1978), 114–16.

77. Sytin, *Kommunal'noe khoziaistvo: Blagoustroistvo Moskvy v sravnenii s blagoustroistvom drugikh bol'shikh gorodov* (Moscow, 1926), 34.

78. *Istoriia Moskvy*, 5:429–38; Nancy Mandelker Frieden, *Russian Physicians in an Era of Reform and Revolution, 1856–1905* (Princeton, 1981), 179–99, 231–61.

79. *Istoriia Moskvy*, 5:522, 535.

80. Johnson, *Peasant and Proletarian*, 124–25, 146.

81. Ibid., 104, 115–16. Moscow's first craft union was the Union of Printers, formed in 1903.

82. Engelstein, *Moscow, 1905*, 13, 100, 116.

83. Ibid., 81, 100, 116, 156, 163.

84. *Istoriia Moskvy*, 4:636; 5:469–70.

85. *Sovremennoe khoziaistvo*, 26–34.

86. Ibid., 24.

87. *Istoriia Moskvy*, 4:662.

88. Ibid., 4:664.

89. Owen, *Capitalism and Politics*, 153.

90. *Istoriia Moskvy*, 5:372.

91. *Sovremennoe khoziaistvo*, 79–80.

BIBLIOGRAPHICAL NOTE

A myriad of publications of the Moscow City Council and Executive Board present a wealth of information on all aspects of city life. Of the five censuses taken at the turn of the century, the 1882 and the 1902 censuses, as well as the two volumes of the 1897 census pertaining to Moscow, are remarkably detailed. In addition, the 1902 census was accompanied by a six-volume analysis of various aspects of city development from housing construction to literacy. Unfortunately, the final results of the 1912 census were never published, though parts are available in the *Trudy Statisticheskogo otdela Moskovskoi gorodskoi upravy*, in *Statisticheskii ezhegodnik goroda Moskvy*, and in *Statisticheskii ezhegodnik Moskvy i Moskovskoi gubernii*, a statistical yearbook of the city and province published in 1927.

In addition to publishing the city censuses, the city council and executive board published statistical yearbooks, monthly bulletins, compilations of vital statistics, censuses of commerce and manufactures, surveys of public health, welfare institutions and housing, and the annual reports of institutions managed by the municipality. Several publications came out serially, and many studies appeared in the organ of the city council, *Izvestiia Moskovskoi gorodskoi dumy*, published monthly in several parts from 1877 to 1917 (with a cumulative subject index published in 1909). Through these sources the historian can learn not only about municipal services, public health, housing and working conditions and poor relief, but also about the attitudes of the authorities and professionals toward social issues of the day. For the student who is unable to wade through all of the specialized municipal studies, two compilations of the city council provide an excellent introduction to municipal services: *Sbornik ocherkov po gorodu Moskve* (1897) and *Sovremennoe khoziaistvo goroda Moskvy* (1913).

The city's economy and its population had a close relationship with its hinterland, and studies of the Moscow provincial zemstvo as well as nationwide surveys illuminate this relationship. Particularly valuable are the *Statisticheskii ezhegodnik Moskovskoi zemskoi upravy* and the series *Sbornik statisticheskikh svedenii Moskovskoi gubernii*. Particularly useful are P. I. Kurkin's population study, *Statistika dvizheniia naseleniia v Moskovskoi gubernii* (1902), A. A. Bulgakov's study of peasant mobility, *Sovremennoe peredvizhenie krest'ianstva* (1905), D. N. Zhbankov's ethnographic study of urban-rural relations, *Bab'ia storona* (1891), and V. P. Semenov-Tian-Shanskii's rich survey of Moscow's hinterland, *Moskovskaia promyshlennaia oblast' i verkhnee povolzh'e* (1899).

Although statistics and municipal reports give much valuable information, they do not give an impression of daily life. Descriptive, memoir, and fictional accounts bring the city to life. Old guidebooks and handbooks provide colorful descriptions of the city, walking tours through neighborhoods, and historical sketches of the city's development. The most comprehensive were *Moskva: Putevoditel'* and *Po Moskve*, published in 1915 and 1917 respectively. Equally rich is the handsome twelve-volume chronicle *Moskva v ee proshlom i nastoiashchem* (1910–1912), compiled by the dean of prerevolutionary historians of the city, Ivan E. Zabelin. *Iz zhizni torgovoi Moskvy* (1914), the memoirs of Ivan Slonov, an upwardly mobile Moscow businessman, describes the world of retailing in the 1870s and 1880s. The 1915 autobiography of Sergei T. Semenov, a peasant from Volokolamsk, *Dvadtsatpiat' let v derevne*, gives us occasional glimpses of the interaction between the urban and rural worlds. Skilled metal workers Semen Kanatchikov (*Iz istorii moego bytiia*, 1929) and P. Timofeev (*Chem zhivet zavodskii rabochii*, 1906) left equally valuable accounts of the workaday world. Fiction and the "journalism of the streets" complement the picture of old Moscow and the daily lives of its laboring population. Best known are Vladimir Giliarovskii's *Moskva i Moskvichi* and *Trushchobnye liudi* (various editions); but also worthy of mention are the sketches of A. I. Levitov and M. A. Voronov, *Moskovskie nory i trushchoby* (1866); S. T. Semenov's short stories; S. P. Podiachev's novella *Mytarstvo* (1903); and N. A. Leikin's novel *Na zarabokakh* (1891). The latter, although set in St. Petersburg, provides valuable insight into the lives of common laborers in the big city. Those prosaic aspects of city life which Muscovites took for granted often stood out in the eyes of foreigners, then as now, and the accounts of foreign travelers provide suggestive impressions of Moscow.

Several standard contemporary works provide introductions to laboring Russia: M. Tugan-Baranovskii's *Russkaia fabrika v proshlom i nastoiashchem* (1899 and 1907); A. Svavitskii and V. Sher's *Ocherk polozheniia rabochikh pechatnogo dela v Moskve* (1909); P. M. Shestakov's *Rabochie na manufakture T-va Emil' Tsindel' v Moskve* (1900); E. A. Oliunina's *Portnovskii promysel v Moskve i v derevniakh Moskovskoi i Riazanskoi gubernii* (1914); Gerhardt von Schulze-Gävernitz's *Volkswirtschaftliche Studien aus Russland* (1899); and Ivan Ianzhul's *Fabrichnyi byt Moskovskoi gubernii* (1884) and *Moskovskii fabrichnyi okrug* (1886). Useful introductions to Moscow's business elite and to the city government are P. A. Buryshkin, *Moskva kupecheskaia* (1954) and M. P. Shchepkin, *Obshchestvennoe khoziaistvo goroda Moskvy v 1863–92 gg.* (1895). Among the contemporary journals, particularly valuable has been *Trudovaia pomoshch'*, a monthly devoted to welfare problems. The six-volume Soviet *Istoriia Moskvy* (1952–1959) provides an encyclopedic chronicle of the city.

The student interested in recent English-language books on Moscow should turn to my own book as well as to the studies of labor and politics by Koenker, Johnson, Engelstein, and Bonnell and to the studies of city government, businessmen, and the economy by Rieber, Owen, Ruckman, Hanchett, Gohstand, and Thurston, all listed in the general bibliography.

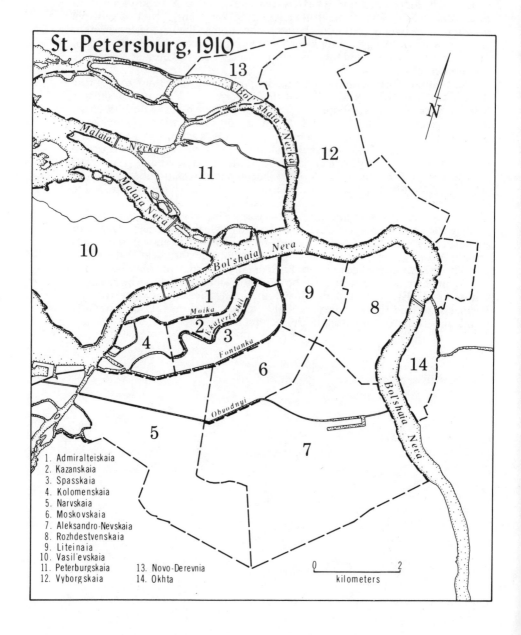

St. Petersburg, 1910

13

12

N

Bol'shaia Nevka

Malaia Nevka

11

Malaia Neva

10

Bol'shaia Neva

1

Moika

9

8

Ekaterinskii

2

3

Fontanka

4

6

14

Obvodnyi

Bol'shaia Neva

5

7

1. Admiralteiskaia
2. Kazanskaia
3. Spasskaia
4. Kolomenskaia
5. Narvskaia
6. Moskovskaia
7. Aleksandro-Nevskaia
8. Rozhdestvenskaia
9. Liteinaia
10. Vasil'evskaia
11. Peterburgskaia   13. Novo-Derevnia
12. Vyborgskaia   14. Okhta

0   2
kilometers

3.

Between Old and New

St. Petersburg in the Late Imperial Era

JAMES H. BATER

St. Petersburg, founded 1703 and capital of the Russian Empire from 1712 to 1917, occupies a special place in the history of Russia. Planted on the marshy delta of the Neva River as a symbol of Peter I's determination to modernize an Empire that stood very much outside the mainstream of European economic, political, social, and intellectual development, St. Petersburg was essentially an experiment in physical and social engineering. However, rapid economic development, especially during the late nineteenth century, transformed this planned administrative city into the Empire's leading port, a major railroad terminus, and the single largest center of industry and commerce. In the process, unprecedented pressure was brought to bear on the physical and administrative structures designed to accommodate and manage the capital's population. By the early 1900s St. Petersburg had acquired the dubious distinction of being the most expensive and the least healthy of all European capitals. For these and other reasons discontent among the masses rose. It was manifested in the abortive uprising of 1905 which sent tremors throughout the social system. Barely a dozen years later the whole structure came tumbling down during the massive upheaval of the October Revolution. Clearly, one can hardly ascribe to the city a deterministic role in history. Yet the rather intriguing question persists—did the urban environment contribute in some way to these events? It is the purpose of this chapter to explore this question and to offer a few, albeit tentative, suggestions as to the possible links between the nature of the urban environment and sociopolitical change.

IMAGE AND REALITY

The overriding impression of St. Petersburg during the eighteenth and early nineteenth centuries was one of orderliness. It was a new town and one that had developed more or less in accordance with prescribed plans. This was particularly true of the central city, where broad thoroughfares, magnificent architectural set pieces, setback requirements, uniformity of building materials, and the like all served to demonstrate the impact of the planning process on the physical fabric. Life itself was orderly. Residence in the capital more often than not was a requirement or a privilege, and to this end a vast bureaucracy supervised the activities of the inhabitants. The seasons, too, lent a certain rhythm to social and economic affairs, and both peasants and princes came and went in response to them. Within the feudalistic system that enveloped the Empire, an absolute autocracy and its underlying serfdom stood at the opposite ends of the social class continuum. Whether by rank or class, everyone in between knew his place. In a word, order prevailed.

Throughout much of the nineteenth century, images of grandeur and gentility were sustained by the legacy of grand design and Imperial munificence, by the existence of the court, and by the ostentation of the upper classes. However, it was the physical fabric of the place which usually created the most graphic first impressions.

> St. Petersburg impresses the visitor as the creation of a truly imperial mind. Massive palaces, royal monuments, stately cathedrals, immense public buildings,—all betoken unbounded wealth lavished almost recklessly upon it by its munificent rulers during the two centuries of its development.[1]

By the early 1900s many parts of the central city still reflected the architectural good taste of an earlier era (Fig. 3.1). However, the abject poverty and the material squalor of daily life and labor among the masses had come to rival the architecture as a first impression. Shoddy tenements were everywhere, especially in the central parts of the city. In the suburbs ill-constructed one- and two-story wooden houses mushroomed along streets which, while named and numbered, were unpaved (indeed, impassable at times), and, save for the occasional kerosene lamp and communal tap, largely unserviced. Factories, workshops, markets, retail stalls, peddlers—all were to be seen throughout the central city and beyond, in defiance of the zoning, land-use, and licensing controls of an earlier era. Factory chimneys now obtruded into most perspective views of the city, and the smoke they belched en-

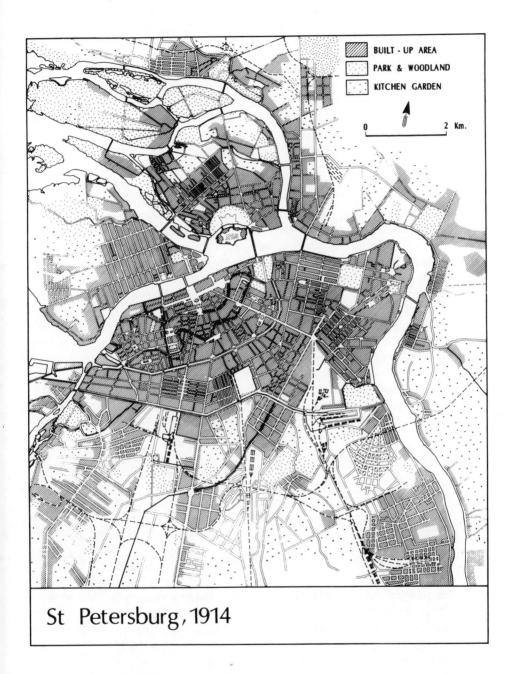

BUILT - UP AREA

PARK & WOODLAND

KITCHEN GARDEN

0   2 Km.

St Petersburg, 1914

FIG. 3.1

veloped fine architecture and jerry-built slum accommodation alike. Housing quality differences existed from one part of the city to another, and in general graded off from center to periphery just as did the level of municipal services, but for the majority of the inhabitants there was little distinction to be made. The absence of convenient and affordable public transport, the long hours of work, and the assault on real income by inflation ensured that most people lived in broadly similar and poor housing, close to, if not at, the place of work, and suffered the consequences of overcrowding and deficient municipal services.

Had St. Petersburg's population been small, the implications of its reputation as the least healthy capital in Europe would have been less serious.[2] However, with almost 300,000 inhabitants in 1800, it already ranked as a large city by European standards.[3] The emancipation of the serfs in 1861 set in motion new forces for change within society. In combination with the process of industrialization, real and perceived opportunities for people to better themselves were created, and from all corners of the Empire migrants, and especially peasants, were drawn to the city. Whether attracted by the prospect of comparatively high-paying jobs or driven by the hopelessness of rural poverty, the influx quickly gathered momentum. Between 1850 and 1914 about 1.7 million people were added to the population, bringing the total to around 2.2 million—but just over one million arrived after 1890 and nearly 350,000 came after 1908.[3] There was very little that was orderly about the human tide that swept into St. Petersburg. Images of grandeur and gentility were now anachronisms.[4]

THE URBAN ECONOMY

There is no doubt that the catalyst in the explosive urban growth of the late nineteenth century was industrial development. As the major administrative center, the city had required a host of service industries already in the eighteenth century. As the Empire's premier military center, it spawned a local complex of armaments industries. The articulation of the railroad system during the second half of the nineteenth century combined with preferential tariffs to ensure St. Petersburg a prominent place among Russian ports. From all corners of the world, and from all corners of the Empire, goods passed through the capital. A substantial portion were processed in the city, thereby adding value and employment. At mid-nineteenth century the capital's factories employed just under 20,000 workers, nearly half in textiles. The changes which occurred subsequently are outlined in Table 3.1.

The rapid expansion of the metalworking sector after 1890 is especially notable and did much to distinguish the industrial activity of St. Petersburg from Moscow, its principal competitor, where textiles still

TABLE 3.1

Industrial Employment in St. Petersburg, 1867–1913

Industrial Group	1867		1890		1913	
	N	%	N	%	N	%
Metalworking	10,160	29.4	19,160	27.5	77,816	40.0
Chemical	1,394	4.1	4,365	6.4	16,446	8.5
Food and tobacco products	4,517	13.1	12,988	18.6	20.528	10.5
Tanning, tallow, and soap	1,053	3.1	2,896	4.2	8,455	4.3
Paper and printing	3,596	10.4	6,584	9.4	23,230	11.9
Textile	12,447	36.1	22,137	31.7	43,931	22.6
Miscellaneous	1,333	3.8	1,602	2.2	4,178	2.2
Total	34,500	100.0	69,732	100.0	194,584	100.0

SOURCE: *Fabriki i zavody v S. Peterburgskoi Gubernii v 1867 godu* (St. Petersburg, 1868); P. A. Orlov, S. G. Budagov, *Ukazatel' fabrik i zavodov Evropeiskoi Rossii. Materialy dlia fabrichno-zavodskoi statistiki sostavili po ofitsial'nym svedeniiam departamenta torgovli i manufaktur* (St. Petersburg, 1894), 3rd ed.; D. P. Kandaurov, *Fabrichno zavodskie predpriiatiia Rossiiskoi Imperii (Iskliuchaia Finliandiiu)* (Petrograd, 1914).

held sway on the eve of World War I. Another distinguishing feature of St. Petersburg industry was the large scale of industrial enterprise. In 1913, for example, each factory employed, on the average, 213 people.[5] In Moscow the comparable figure was 147. In specific sectors the differences were more pronounced. For example, each of the capital's metalworking plants employed an average of 274 workers. In Moscow the equivalent figure was 113. In textiles, the comparative figures were 511 and 270. Yet Moscow was not without a complement of very large-scale enterprises. In the textile group alone, for example, nine factories there employed 1,000 or more workers. The largest, the Prokhorovskoi trekhgornoi manufaktury t-vo., which specialized in cotton spinning and weaving, had 7,400 workers on the payroll. With the equivalent of 4,800 horsepower of engine capacity, the level of mechanization in the productive process was of a tolerably high order. The largest textile mill in St. Petersburg, the Nevskoi nitochnoi manufaktury t-vo, had about the same number of employees and level of mechanization. What tended to differentiate textile production in Moscow from that of St. Petersburg was the considerable number in the former of small, usually privately owned, enterprises which had somehow or other survived the periods of economic depression and the general drift toward amalgamation and ever-larger individual plants. Even so, at the turn of the century about half of Moscow's textile workforce was employed in just eleven factories. In the capital the level of concentration of workers in large-scale factories was very much greater, and so too was the control of jointstock companies over production. In 1913 the twenty-three joint-stock textile companies in St. Petersburg accounted for 77 percent of the city's output. While some of Moscow's textile factories were certainly comparable to those in the capital in terms of labor force, mechanization, and output, the same cannot be said about its metalworking group.

Moscow's largest metalworking plant employed 2,900 people in 1913. Six other enterprises had between 1,000 and 1,500 workers. In St. Petersburg, fifty-nine fewer factories employed 39,074 more people. And several of these factories ranked among the largest enterprises in the Empire. Pride of place had long been held by the Putilov Company, which in 1913 had over 13,000 on the payroll. While only two other establishments had even as many as 5,000 workers, seventeen employed more than 1,000. Joint-stock companies controlled over half the labor force in metalworking, and accounted for nearly three-quarters of the output. In short, although the average number of workers in St. Petersburg metalworking factories was substantially below that in the textile group, economies of scale clearly played an important part in corporate decision-making. In 1913 output from St. Petersburg's metalworking plants accounted for 18 percent of the national total.[6]

The manufacture of railroad equipment, shipbuilding, and armaments in St. Petersburg was significant at the national scale. Among several of the "leading" sectors, however, output from the capital's plants was completely dominant. This was the case, for instance, in the fast-growing, recently established electrical equipment industry. Frequently financed by German money, these factories operated at a large scale from the outset. Among the most prominent of them were the Siemens and Allgemeine Elektrizität Gesellschaft establishments. The demand for electric motors, telegraph and telephone equipment, electric cable, and the like was only just being awakened in Russia, and both the potential market and the profits to be earned from supplying it were enormous. As in so many other industries, tariffs were used to foster domestic production. Out of a production valued at 56 million rubles in all Russia in 1913, roughly 40 million came from plants in the capital.[7]

Thus, industry in St. Petersburg was notable for the dominance of metalworking, the large scale of enterprise in terms of employment, the level of foreign ownership, and quite possibly, a higher level of technology than was elsewhere common, if the patchy data on use of motive power in factories can be reliably used as a guide. But it should be equally apparent that despite the singular pace of industrialization not all of those who flocked to the capital found jobs in factories. Rapid urban industrialization signaled opportunity, and as in so many other Russian cities there were wages to be earned in many other fast-growing sectors of the urban economy. For example, petty trade in St. Petersburg had not been erased in consequence of industrialization. In the early 1900s, streets were still rife with peasants hawking wares of every description, and it was through this congestion that the giants of industry and commerce had daily to pass. Indeed, taken together their entrepreneurial endeavor resulted in a trade turnover varying between 800 and 900 million rubles annually, a value in excess of that generated by industry in 1912.[8]

In 1910 over 150,000 persons gave as their occupation some form of retail trade. Included in this figure were 14,000 street traders, but this is probably an underestimate; it is likely that there were several thousand more of them among the 18,000 or so who, according to the census, had no job to their name.[9] Despite ample evidence of modernization, perhaps best reflected in the worldwide business linkages, joint-stock banks, and modern shops, there was in St. Petersburg an underlying and seemingly unchanging commercial system which operated within the framework of traditional, largely peasant, values. Peasants brought to the city their countryside manners and skills which somehow had to be adapted to, or absorbed into, the new environment. Petty commerce, transport in the form of providing droshky or hauling services, day laboring, and domestic service were common employments, for they required only minimal skills and made few demands in respect of regularity of habit, which was the first prerequisite for joining the modern industrial-commercial system. Some peasants adjusted quickly, became successful merchants and on occasion successful industrialists, and moved up in the world. While it was clearly the case that a rapidly growing segment of the peasantry was settling permanently in the city and becoming "urbanized," among the huge numbers of migrants there remained many who sustained the traditional peasant economy right up to the First World War. Put simply, there was a dual economy at work in the city.

At the opposite end of the retail scene from the peasant hawkers were department stores like the Passazh, located on the Nevskii Prospekt. The four-storied Passazh housed approximately sixty retail businesses specializing in the sale of high-quality men's and women's clothing, jewelery, and various luxury items. In between this type of operation and peasant street traders were close to 20,000 retail shops, a number nearly three times greater than it had been in 1869 and roughly consonant with the increase in population. About two-thirds of these sold foodstuffs amounting to about half the retail turnover.[10] By no means all retail trade was channeled through individual shops, for the city's markets were capacious and popular with ordinary people and nobility alike; in 1912 there were 3,081 shops or stalls located in the eighteen markets scattered throughout the city. The largest was the Aleksandrovskii novyi rynok, fronting on the Fontanka Canal in Spasskaia borough, whose 765 outlets dealt primarily in manufactured wares. Nearby on Sadovaia Street was the Apraksin market, with 478 stalls selling everything from clothing and furniture to fruit and vegetables. The Gostinii dvor still claimed the lion's share of business even though it had fewer outlets than the Aleksandrovskii market. This resulted from the more specialized nature of its 500 or so outlets, where the emphasis was on the higher-priced luxury end of manufactured consumers' goods and handcrafted wares. Having almost doubled the number of vendors since the 1860s, this complex had encroached on the adjoining streets. A short distance up Sadovaia Street, past both the Aleksandrovskii novyi rynok and Apraksin, was the city's fourth largest market, the Sennoi, which had 262 stalls concentrating on the sale of foodstuffs.[11]

By far the largest proportion of hired labor was found in construction, transport, handicraft, institutional, and personal service on the eve of the First World War. Including day laborers, in total about 350,000 people were involved, nearly twice the number of factory workers. The yardkeepers or *dvorniki*, coachmen, domestic servants, and the like who were employed by government institutions or private persons were the largest group and numbered about 200,000. Nearly 80,000 worked in transport, while construction, handicraft, and day-laboring activities absorbed the remainder.[12] Actually, the construction and day-laboring group was rather larger than the December census indicates, for during the summer workers came by the tens of thousands to work in the building trades, at the docks, or repairing the winter-ravaged streets. The 100,000 or so who arrived for the summer nearly equaled the number of peasants who left for the countryside. According to their trade, they continued to migrate to specific parts of the city: building tradesmen, carpenters, and bricklayers to Okhta, teamsters to Aleksandro-Nevskaia and adjacent boroughs, dock workers to Narvskaia, and day laborers to the central-city boroughs like Spasskaia and Moskovskaia where the hope of a job was highest among the multifarious workshops, markets, or factories.

If ten- to twelve-hour workdays in factories seemed inordinate, they were nonetheless very agreeable in comparison to the plight of hired workers generally. In late June it was sufficiently light in Petersburg to permit construction twenty hours of the day; during this period sixteen-hour workdays were quite usual. In dingy workshops, production continued whether there was natural light or not. For instance, in the several hundred small bakeries, employees were on the job sixteen to nineteen hours, the remainder of the day usually being spent sleeping somewhere on the premises. Shoemakers toiled about fifteen hours daily, and so it went, throughout the handicraft and petty retail trades. An eight-hour day remained a utopian notion.

While by Russian standards wages in the capital were comparatively good, the inordinately high cost of food and lodging ensured that they did not go far. For most factory workers only a bare existence was possible, and contemporary budget studies indicate that between 600 and 700 rubles per annum were needed to maintain a tolerable standard of living for a family. Only a very small proportion of workers reached this level, and in other sectors of the urban economy even fewer workers were so highly paid. Moreover, the cost of living during the early 1900s was rising faster than wages. Small wonder that trade unionism and revolutionist and anarchist movements, advocating a radical change in society, found fertile ground among workers. In 1905, of course, the dissatisfaction bubbled over into revolution, of which the "Bloody Sunday" confrontation was but one episode. Still, the realization that massive demonstrations and strikes were powerful political weapons was instilled in the minds of many workers. Confronted with serious inflation during the economic boom following 1908, labor unrest was increasingly manifested through strikes. Conditions in the workplace were customarily difficult. Life was made more difficult still because of the quality of the urban environment, fast deteriorating in the face of unprecedented in-migration.

SOME DIMENSIONS OF URBAN GROWTH

By the late 1860s a surge in the number of newcomers was already apparent. Although it is not possible to know for certain why this occurred, it is reasonable to suppose that the buoyant economy, the depressed state of agriculture, and the new demands placed on peasants by the emancipation worked in concert to stimulate rural-urban migration. Of course, not all those coming were peasants. Representatives of all classes and groups were to be found among the human tide sweeping into the city. But peasants were the most visible constituents, and during the years from 1870 to 1914 they became increasingly conspicuous. In 1914 nearly three-quarters of the capital's 2.2 million inhabitants were peasants, as compared with fewer than a third half a century before. The socioeconomic composition of urban growth was one matter; its sheer scale was another.

During the period from the mid-eighteenth to mid-nineteenth century, the city's population increased on the average by less than 4,000 persons per year. Between 1850 and 1870, the average annual increase more than doubled. Growth was rapid during the economic surge of the 1870s, declining somewhat with the depression of the 1880s. Overall, annual increases averaged about 15,000 people. The economic boom of the nineties signaled the onset of growth not before experienced. Between 1890 and 1914 the capital's citizenry grew each year by an average of 50,000 inhabitants, and this included a period of depression during the early 1900s when there was a perceptible brake on the rate of growth. Still, during the years of depression more than 40,000 were added to the population each year. With a resurgent economy after 1908, population growth was rapid, peaking in 1913 when the number of inhabitants increased by 107,000, nearly 22,000 more than the record set the preceding year.[13] By any standard of comparison the change was of considerable dimension.

Deaths customarily exceeded births; indeed, during the hundred-year period up to the mid-1860s, the differential was in excess of 140,000. The city therefore grew by immigration, not by natural means. For the first few years of rapid urban industrialization this trait continued. The turning point came in the early 1880s when the death rate plummeted. The reasons for this development are not clear.[14] Some improvements in public sanitation, material progress of the working classes, and a greater awareness of the need for higher standards of personal hygiene have all been cited as possible explanations. In any event, the declining death rate was a relative thing. Epidemics continued to take a heavy toll on a regular basis, and overall the capital fared very badly when the death rate was set against that prevailing in other European capitals. And, of course, within the city disease and death did not afflict all areas and all groups with equal severity. But whatever the explanation, from the mid-eighties on, births were ascendant and helped to swell the numbers added to the population.

Traditionally, migrants were mostly men aged twenty to forty, and of the peasant class. In 1869 the composition of the city's population revealed just these characteristics. Ensuing urbanization modified some of these features. For instance, by 1910 the share of females had risen from 43 to 48 percent, a greater proportion of married workers lived with their families, and the percentage of the total population actually born in the city had similarly increased. While all of this was indicative of a greater degree of stability, several things should be borne in mind. The population remained predominantly single, far more so than the average for the Empire as a whole, and, among European capitals, St. Petersburg had a particularly low per-capita ratio of married inhabitants.[15]

According to the 1910 census, 125,000, or roughly 10 percent of the peasant population, were intending to return to the countryside the following summer, and there were many others who retained the option of retreating to the village in the event of difficult times.[16] Transience clearly had not disappeared in the wake of urbanization. Moreover, such peripatetic habits were by no means restricted to the peasantry. While the huge number of peasants the cities had to absorb each year posed one set of problems for civic administration, the high proportion of transients among all inhabitants posed yet others. But just what were the dimensions of transient behavior in St. Petersburg? Censuses and city directories help shed some light on this important behavioral trait.

The dimensions of seasonal migration were not accurately established until the late 1880s, when summer and winter population counts began to be taken by the police. What they discovered was a huge difference in the number of residents. Between December 1888 and July

1889, for example, the population of the city dropped by 183,000.[17] This represented more than a fifth of the total number of inhabitants. Among the social elite the season to be seen in St. Petersburg was the winter, and all those who could manage to leave during the summer did so. Peasants departed for different reasons, but they helped to swell the exodus nonetheless. For the urban area as a whole, the net loss was diminished a little by an influx of seasonal workers, many of whom resided in the outlying suburbs. In the summer of 1889 they numbered 35,000, the majority being peasants who worked in the building trades, street repair, and the like.[18] All told, the season "deficit" for the urban area in that year was about 150,000.

The pattern persisted after the turn of the century. For example, the share of the total population actually born in St. Petersburg remained small. In 1900 it comprised about 32 percent of the 1.4 million inhabitants; in 1910 it accounted for about the same proportion of the citizenry, which now numbered 1.9 million. Moreover, as the censuses reveal, a large proportion of this massive in-migration did not put down permanent roots in the city. The number of migrants who, in 1900, had lived in St. Petersburg for five or fewer years totaled 414,951. This same group appears in the 1910 enumeration in the category of eleven to fifteen years' residence in the city; that is, they had arrived in the capital some time between 1896 and 1900. But in 1910 this group had been reduced from 414,951 to 143,591. Apparently 65 percent of this migrant category had departed the city or died during the 1900–10 period. Given the usual age of migrants it is probable that most had departed the capital under their own locomotion.[19]

Of course, the suspicion is that migrant peasants accounted for the greatest number of departures. Since the St. Petersburg census separates peasants from *meshchane*—that rather amorphous estate (*soslovie*) encompassing elements of the urban middle bourgeoisie—an examination of the general dimensions of transience can be carried a little further (see Fig. 3.2). A comparison of the number of peasants who had lived in the city for five years or less in 1900 with the eleven to fifteen years' residence category in the 1910 census indicates an absolute drop in number from about 325,000 to 115,300. Once again, about 65 percent of the group had departed or died. Though the *meshchane*, who comprised 15.5 percent of the total population in 1910, were ostensibly more urban oriented, and thus less transient in behavior, more than half their number had migrated to the capital. Using the same procedure as applied to the peasant estate reveals that nearly 60 percent of the group arriving in the 1896–1900 period were no longer resident in the city in 1910. The census data thus intimate that transience was widespread, and this is borne out by some data drawn from the city directories.[20] A random sample of 1,500 males was drawn from the 1909 St. Petersburg directory and traced in the 1912 edition. At the end of the three-year

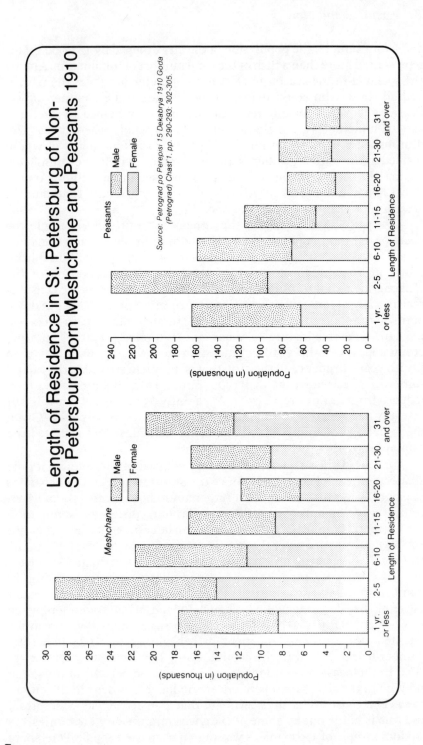

FIG. 3.2

period 553 (36.9 percent) were still at the same address; 448 (29.9 percent) were living elsewhere in the city; and 499 (33.2 percent) could not be traced, apparently having either departed the city or died. It is unlikely that very many died in such a short timespan. While it is possible that some of these seemingly transient individuals were simply omitted from the 1912 directory, it probably could not have been a very large number, for each year witnessed a sizable increase in the coverage.[21] Indeed, it would seem that being listed was growing not just in popularity but in importance as well, since directories were arguably now an indispensable feature of urban life. In short, even among the ostensibly more stable element of the population—that which was listed in the city directory and which tended to be strongly biased toward the top rather than the bottom of the social class hierarchy— transience was an ingrained habit. Moreover, among those who could be traced, moves from one residence to another within the city were common; indeed, some of these would have changed their address more than once during the three-year period.[22] Such mobility was facilitated by the low level of home—or, more accurately, apartment—owner- ship,[23] and among the social elite it was perhaps further encouraged by a good supply of furnished apartments available for rent at the luxury end of the market.[24] Thus during the early 1900s it is evident that the urban growth process was one in which transience of one kind or another had an important part to play.

The principal implication to be drawn from all this is that for people from all classes the ties to St. Petersburg in particular, and in some cases perhaps to urban life in general, were not strong.[25] No doubt for a great many inhabitants of St. Petersburg the following recollection would have struck a familiar chord:

> Every summer we went south, and the last glimpse of St. Petersburg is very clear in my mind, because I always made it a point to cast back a farewell glance as the train pulled off from the glass roofed *Nikolaevsky* [Station] . . . and in a few minutes my city would be nothing but a forest of factory chimneys under clouds of gray smoke.[26]

To the extent that people of whatever background and socioeconomic status had limited or no attachment to the city, the management of urban affairs was bound to be rendered more difficult. Those who did stay had to shoulder a disproportionate share of the burden: the social costs associated with rapid urban industrialization.

SOME SOCIAL COSTS OF RAPID URBAN GROWTH

We have already noted the huge numbers of immigrants who had to be absorbed each year. These figures suggest that congestion increased substantially. We might well ask, to what extent, and more to the point, with what consequences?

In 1869 only the notorious third ward of Spasskaia borough in the central city had more than 70,000 people per square kilometer. Living conditions within the borough were widely acknowledged at the time to be intolerable. There had indeed been some reconstruction in the central city since then, but in 1910 the adjacent second ward of Kazanskaia borough had achieved the same population density, and within the central city there were now six other wards in the 51,000 to 70,000 range. Together these wards encircled the lower-density Admiralteiskaia borough, where high rents and pockets of first-class residential properties had checked population growth, and the prime commercial area around the lower Nevskii Prospekt, where residential uses often gave way to commercial ones. While population densities graded off toward the periphery, they were in fact still high. Indeed, population density increased in virtually every ward of the city from the 1860s to 1914.[27]

What the rising population densities meant very much depends on the stratum of society being examined. All had to contend with growing congestion. For the privileged, this was at most an annoying inconvenience. For the masses, competition for housing intensified, rents rose rapidly, and their situation deteriorated accordingly. A housing crisis loomed, arrived, and deepened. Housing conditions for the masses quickly became a scandal. The 1860s had already witnessed the large-scale conversion of cellars—space which previously had remained empty or had been used for storage owing to regular flooding—into apartments. Rooms of all kinds were subdivided again, giving rise to the *ugol* or corner habitation for single persons and families alike. The *ugol* soon became so widespread as to warrant being designated a national specialty. Overcrowding in these denlike quarters reached incredible levels. Official surveys were regularly turning up cases of fifteen or more people per apartment, ten or more to a room, and five or more per bed.[28] The sanitary doctor responsible for Vasil'evskii Island in the mid–1890s, for example, observed that among sixty-eight apartment buildings, housing some 5,500 of the working poor, "there is scarcely a corner of an apartment where workers would not be sleeping two to a bed. Married men with wives and children slept together with single [workers] in one and the same rooms."[29] And these conditions were characteristic of a district in no sense "distinguished" for its degree of overcrowding! In some of the central city boroughs like Kazanskaia, Moskovskaia, and parts of Narvskaia, the situation was generally worse. With at least 10 percent of the population obliged to live in an *ugol*, it is small wonder that by the turn of the century there were twice as many people per apartment as in Berlin, Vienna, or Paris.[30] Indeed, increasing numbers were unable to rent permanent accommodation of any kind, no matter how tiny. And not all of these people were indigent. Studies of the *nochlezhnie doma*, or doss-houses, which sprang up to meet the demand for temporary shelter revealed that large numbers of the regularly employed were having to take beds there on a more or less permanent basis.[31] The irregular incomes of thousands more dictated that a bed be sought in one of these overcrowded and pestilent doss-houses each night. Authorities expressed grave concern over the fact that each year brought an increase in the homeless population, a group which knowledgeable obervers reckoned to be one percent of the total population.[32] Crammed into temporary shelters in ever greater densities, the homeless population simply made worse the already shocking levels of overcrowding.

Clearly, public transport developments in other cities had helped to alleviate overcrowding by permitting decentralization. In St. Petersburg this had not happened. We might at this point briefly explore why.

Unlike many municipal governments in the nineteenth century, that of St. Petersburg was far from being enthusiastic about technological innovations in public transport.[33] The horse tram did not appear on city streets until 1864, and it took a full decade of petitions and discussions before the city council agreed to permit expansion of the system. The reasons were numerous, but figuring prominently among them was the potential negative impact of such technology on the many thousands of private cabs, whose owners collectively paid a sizeable amount of money to the city in the form of licenses. The income derived from the concession granted to the one company running the limited horse-tram service was very much less. The results were obvious. Few people rode the horse cars, fewer still could afford to hire a private conveyance, and on the whole, spatial mobility was severely restricted.

By the mid-1870s the city council had at last been convinced of the benefits of a more extensive horse-tram system within the city and agreed to allow two other companies to expand the network and improve the service. The city, in return for granting the concessions, was to receive a small share of the gross returns—and a small share it was; out of gross receipts of nearly 3 million rubles, for the three companies concerned, only 86,000 rubles found their way back to the city.[34] Other modes of public transport withered in the face of competition from the horse trams. Traffic on the canal boats steadily declined and, except for the summer months, so too did traffic on the remaining omnibus routes. The omnibus garnered a sizeable volume of traffic in the summer simply because it provided links with popular suburban areas for summer houses (*dachi*), something which the horse tram did not do very well and which the steam railway did barely at all.[35] By 1890 public transportation service was essentially a city, as opposed to a suburban, phenomenon. It was to remain so.

In response to widespread dissatisfaction with service and income, the city council in the early 1890s decided to take over the system.[36] The obvious room for improved service to the public, and the seeming ease with which a reasonable rate of return on investment could be realized, served as catalysts in the decision. But concession holders resisted takeover, and complete control of the system did not come until the early 1900s.

The urgent need to decentralize the population was the overriding, publicly stated objective of the city-owned public transportations system. Plans were prepared for expanding the network, especially to the periphery of the city and even beyond; cheap fares were to be introduced; and an alternative to the horse car—the electric tram—was proposed. Though the city acquired control of the system in 1902, five years were to elapse before electric traction was introduced. By this time there were electric trams even in a number of provincial towns in Russia; thus the capital was in no sense an innovator. Furthermore, it should be noted that at the time the electric tram was the major development in St. Petersburg, the fifth largest city in Europe, places like Paris and London were moving ahead with underground public transportation systems.

By 1914 the objectives set forth at the time of the takeover had not been met. Though traffic had increased, it was still comparatively low. At 150 trips per capita, it was less than Moscow with its 165 trips per capita.[37] Service did not begin until 8:00 A.M., which did not help the working classes. Fares were relatively high, with no system of cheap workingmen's fares. Few lines penetrated the suburbs, and most of those that did remained the province of the very much slower horse-drawn trams. It is not clear why more effort was not expended in providing public transport in the suburbs, though there are recurring suggestions that property-owning cliques on St. Petersburg's council opposed the idea, desiring to maintain at artificially high levels central-city land values and rents. Once the extension of electric tram service did begin, accusations arose of route manipulation to benefit certain property-owning members of council.[38] Whatever the reasons, the consequences of this failure, in terms of heightened congestion in particular, and the state of public health in general, were serious. Unable to move freely within or into the city, the inhabitants of St. Petersburg in the early 1900s labored and lived within a rapidly deteriorating environment. Few places were so hazardous to live in, a claim which the incidence of death and disease verified right down to the First World War.

Disease of all descriptions had always flourished in St. Petersburg. The deltaic site and regular flooding, combined with inadequate facilities for water supply and waste disposal and an increasingly acute housing shortage, served to create an ideal environment for assisting the spread of disease. Outbreaks of cholera and typhus were almost annual occurrences; reporting on the severity of the epidemics was one of the regular tasks of the various diplomatic missions in the city. Especially severe outbreaks were just as certain to prompt European governments to send special representatives scurrying to St. Petersburg for detailed first-hand reports as they were to bring about a dramatic increase in deaths. Infectious diseases accounted for roughly 38 percent of all deaths during the epidemic-ridden years from 1886 to 1895. In 1908, during the height of yet another outbreak of cholera, they accounted for 47 percent.[39] There were few who would contest the assertion of the British Consul the following year that "St. Petersburg, compared with large cities of Europe, and even of Russia, has the highest rate of mortality in general and the highest deathrate from infectious diseases."[40]

Though expansion of municipal services like water and sewerage took place at an unparalleled pace after 1890, the demand for such services always outran the supply. On the eve of World War I, at least a quarter of the city's apartments did without the benefits of running water or water closets. And, of course, disparities existed within the city. Peripheral regions experiencing rapid population growth frequently had neither municipal water nor sewage systems. Suburbs outside city boundaries, of course, were under a different jurisdiction— the gentry-dominated zemstvo—which rarely provided such services. It would be misleading to assume, however, that residing in the central city where there was a municipal water service would necessarily be safer than in the suburbs. The reason for this was outlined once again by the British Consul:

> A part of the town is still supplied with quite unfiltered water, and latest statistics show that this part is less affected by cholera and typhoid than the parts of the town in which filtered water is used. Recent analyses have proved that the filters themselves are contaminated.[41]

Diseases like cholera and typhoid had been traced back to an impaired water supply so often by the city's medical staff that, scientifically, it was no longer possible to attribute such scourges solely to ill-defined environmental factors like the damp climate and marshy site. The inhabitants were dependent upon the Neva River, its tributaries, and the city's canals for drinking water. None was free from contamination. As the *Times* correspondent noted:

> One fails to understand how it could ever have been supposed that the water would be anything else but contaminated if taken out as it is at present, from a part of the River Neva within the city bounds, where the dirt and refuse from the mills, factories, villages, cemeteries, and

barges are floated down from upstream, right over the intake in front of
the waterworks.[42]

But knowing what the problem was was one thing: doing something
about it was quite another.

Over the years there had been no shortage of proposals for a proper
drainage and water supply system. Obviously drainage and water supply
went hand in hand. Yet, as the Moscow daily newspaper, *Russkiia
vedomosti*, pointed out, in some parts of the city supplied with water
from the municipal system, raw sewage was still gathered up in carts
each night from the courtyard cesspools and dumped into the nearest
waterway, polluting both air and water in the process.[43] Those parts of
the city still only minimally serviced by the municipal water system
drew drinking water from those very same rivers and canals. There were
plenty of schemes to ameliorate the situation: by the early 1900s there
had been at least forty different proposals for drainage improvement
alone.[44] But money was short and the city council was reluctant to incur
debt; hence all were stillborn. It was only when the question of public
health in St. Petersburg was made a national as opposed to a local issue
that things began to happen:

> . . . thanks to Prime Minister Stolypin the sanitary reform of St. Peters-
> burg is no longer "beyond the hills," as the Russian expression
> goes. . . . The only drawback to the prospect is the enormous expense
> which the work will entail. To begin with, a small loan of 100,000,000
> roubles—about three and a quarter times more than the annual
> budget—will be required, which will have to be paid off by the citizens
> in the shape of fresh and increased taxation, and this can only tend to
> make living in the Russian capital more expensive than ever.[45]

Even with the public indictment of the city council for having let
matters deteriorate so far, the central government action did not bring
about an immediate response. A plan had to be decided upon and in the
end a pipeline to bring water from Lake Ladoga, thirty-five kilometers to
the southeast, was accepted as a logical solution.[46] But construction did
not begin until 1914, five years after the direct involvement of the
central government.

Daily life and labor among the masses who had descended upon St.
Petersburg were harsh enough in economic terms. The quality of the
urban environment in terms of overcrowding, public health, and sanitation clearly presented other problems. Responses varied. Some peasants
who retained a real link with the village might seek refuge there from
time to time. Others simply endured conditions as they found them.
Some public-spirited individuals and organizations offered assistance of

one kind or another, and had done so for decades. For example, in the 1860s at least five charitable organizations provided subsidized housing for the poor. Two provided extremely cheap accommodation for Finns and Estonians, while the Orthodox Church ran yet another housing program. Chief among them, however, was the Society for Providing Low Cost Apartments and Other Assistance to the Needy Population in St. Petersburg. Founded in 1861, it owned 140 lodgings in 1869.[47] But the efforts of these organizations over the years paled in relation to the demand. By the 1890s the city itself was providing some accommodation for the homeless. Where charitable and municipal efforts were found inadequate, commercial interests stepped into the breach. By the early 1900s there were a good number of apparently highly profitable flophouses offering a bed for the night and morning tea to those who could not find permanent, affordable housing. And as we have already noted, the homeless were now reckoned to account for one percent of the total population, that is, more than 20,000 people in 1914.

By the turn of the century there were a great many charitable and professional organizations attempting to ameliorate the plight of the poor. As well, there were numerous scientific and educational institutions in St. Petersburg whose nominal concerns embraced the quality of the urban environment. For example, medical doctors and veterinarians were trained in the capital, and indeed many in fact used the city as a laboratory for academic inquiry. Dissertation after dissertation provided hard statistical data on one facet or another of morbidity and mortality. And, of course, there was also the city's sanitary inspectorate, which produced volumes of data on the relationship between overcrowding, municipal services, and public health. All told, there was no shortage of information as to what was occurring in St. Petersburg. But the responsibility for the health and well-being of the capital's inhabitants did not rest on the shoulders of charitable or professional organizations; it was the mandate of municipal government. We have already noted the rather tardy response of the city council to public transport and water and sewage problems. The questions arise, who sat on council, and in a general sense, how did council conduct its affairs?

THE MUNICIPAL RESPONSE TO CHANGE

As Table 3.2 indicates, from 1870 to 1912 the composition of St. Petersburg's city council underwent two notable changes: the long-dominant mercantile elite were reduced in number; and the professional category increased their representation. There were more professionals on the council in 1912 largely because the 1903 Municipal Statute, which pertained only to the capital, permitted a portion of the

TABLE 3.2

**Socioeconomic Composition of St. Petersburg's City Council,
1873–1912**

Socioeconomic Group	1873		1893		1912	
	N	%	N	%	N	%
Merchants and honored citizens	120	47.6	79	49.3	51	31.9
Nobility (without occupation)	8	3.2	8	5.0	10	6.3
Military officers	18	7.1	8	5.0	9	5.6
Government employees (excluding military)	71	28.2	22	13.8	26	16.3
Professional	6	2.4	19	11.9	41	25.5
Others	29	11.5	24	15.0	23	14.4
Totals	252	100.0	160	100.0	160	100.0

SOURCE: S. P. Luppov, "Gorodskoe upravlenie i gorodskoe khoziaistvo," *Ocherki istorii Leningrada* (Leningrad, 1957), 816; "S. Peterburgskoe gorodskoe obshchestvennoe upravlenie v 1893 godu," *Otchety S. Peterburgskikh Gorodskoi upravy i ustavnovlenii . . . za 1893 g.* (St. Petersburg, 1893), xi–xiv, xxix–xxxv; *Ves' Peterburg na 1912* (Petrograd, 1914), pt. 1, 308 passim.

rentier class to stand for election. But while the socioeconomic complexion of the council changed, long-standing patterns of civic administration did not.

As in most Russian cities the electorate comprised a tiny fraction of the total population. In St. Petersburg it was less than one percent. Yet few bothered to vote; and those elected had long had a well-deserved reputation for minimal involvement in council affairs. The membership of the council already had been dropped from 252 to 160 and quorum reduced from two-thirds to one-half in 1892 as a result of this indifference.[48] The opportunity for manipulation of policy and practice was clearly present.

The 1870 Municipal Statute had given city government a freer hand in raising revenues, with some unforeseen consequences. In the capital, direct taxes and fees comprised 70 percent of city revenue. Two decades later the share had been reduced to less than one-half. By 1913 it had been eroded still further. In their stead, profits from municipal enterprises came to dominate the income side of the ledger. From slaughterhouse to water supply to public transport, municipalization had proceeded steadily from the 1880s on. Monies from city-owned businesses comprised barely 10 percent of income in 1870; by 1913 they amounted to nearly two-thirds. In management of municipal enterprises emphasis was on maximizing profits and minimizing the per-capita debt. Such conservative management was perhaps wise. But the quality of service, as we have seen, was rather less than adequate. At the same time, property taxes, which were known to be easily administered and potentially remunerative, were rejected by the city fathers without trial.[49] Was there a link between the socioeconomic complexion of the council and these taxation policies? Before exploring this matter we might briefly examine how the St. Petersburg city council responded to some other important areas of responsibility.

In Table 3.3 several categories of municipal expenditures are presented for 1883 and 1908. From these data it is apparent that great relative gains were made during the twenty-five year period. But the significance of the changes obviously depends upon starting positions. Take education, for example. In the early seventies there was very little in the way of city schools to meet the obvious need to educate the populace. By the early nineties, however, there had been some progress in filling the educational void: more than 300 city-run primary schools, and an additional 180 or so private and church-supported institutions. Total enrollment was nearly 30,000 students. By the turn of the century more money than ever had to be directed toward educational needs. Over 50,000 children were now in school; however, fully a third of the eight-to-eleven age group were not.[50] And for the population as a whole, illiteracy was still about 38 percent. According to the 1910 census, illiteracy had been reduced to 31 percent. But this meant that well over 600,000 people could still not read. There simply was not enough money to educate the population, and some felt that the money spent was not being allocated wisely. This criticism arose from the financial

TABLE 3.3

St. Petersburg's Municipal Expenditures, 1883–1908

Category	1883 (millions of rubles)	1908 (millions of rubles)	Percentage Change
Health and sanitation	0.295	4.801	1,627
Education	0.409	2.553	624
Charitable services	0.393	1.146	292
Maintenance of various government agencies, police & fire service	1.971	3.003	152
Civic Works	0.594	1.975	332
Maintenance of municipal government	0.712	1.702	239

SOURCE: M. Fedorov, "Finansovoe polozhenie Peterburga," *Gorodskoe delo* (1909), no. 1:13.

support accorded the upper years of the school system at a time when
there were thousands of children who could not attend primary school
owing to a lack of places. How limited the funds were is easily appreciated from a comparison with municipal expenditures on education in
other cities. In 1907 the educational fund was equivalent to 1.62 rubles
per capita, admittedly a vast improvement over the 0.03 figure for 1872.
But it still ranked well behind the 5.40 rubles spent on all Berliners in
1903, the 4.65 on all Viennese, and the 4.23 for each man, woman, and
child in Paris.[51] Using even the lower Paris figure as a basis would have
generated over six million rubles for education instead of the 2.5 million
actually spent in St. Petersburg.

Accusations of manipulation of council policies in St. Petersburg
are not uncommon. Given the quality of municipal services, there is
certainly justification for the widely held view among contemporary
observers that a sizable portion of the financial burden of running the
city had been taken off property owners and intentionally placed on the
populace at large. Contemporaries familiar with the administration of
civic affairs vary only in the severity of their condemnation. The com-
ments of Harold Williams are typical not just of the outsider's point of
view, but also of those Russians who were trying to bring about change:

> It is only during the last few years that St. Petersburg has begun to show
> something like civic spirit. A prominent building on the Nevsky is that
> of the City Duma or the City Council. This building has a shabby,
> neglected look, and its appearance is typical of the state of the adminis-
> tration of the city. No big European capital is so badly managed as St.
> Petersburg is. The city has a Governor or Prefect, called the Grado-
> nachalnik, who is the Chief of Police and is responsible for the mainte-
> nance of order. But the administration of economic affairs is in the
> hands of an elective council. Under the Municipal Law the chief elec-
> toral power is in the hands of the wealthier property-owners, and for
> very many years the big house and property-owners in St. Petersburg,
> who are mostly well-to-do merchants or retired officials, formed in the
> Council a close and powerful coterie and managed the affairs of the city
> in their own interests. The privileged position of this coterie added to
> the constant intersection of the competency of the Council by that of
> the Gradonachalnik and the Government fostered corruption and
> checked development. . . . All imaginable defects of city government
> are, in fact, well represented in St. Petersburg.[52]

THE SOCIAL FABRIC OF THE CITY

Ostentatious life styles as well as architectural magnificence
helped to shape the image of grandeur traditionally associated with St.
Petersburg. But only a small segment of urban society was by custom

inclined to engage in the conspicuous consumption of wealth. The growing affluence of the merchant class, for example, was for a long time quite inconspicuous, as the "richest tradesmen" lived "poorly and wretchedly."[53] There were many reasons for this. Among them was the fact that social mobility depended as much upon civil or military rank as it did upon wealth; and in the tightly knit world of position and privilege the status of a merchant had normally counted for relatively little. This was quite different from the situation in Moscow, or for that matter most other Russian cities, where the entrepreneurial elite was not only accepted but usually set the tone among the upper classes.[54] By the turn of the century, industrialization and all that it stood for in terms of modernization had clearly transformed much of city life, and businessmen could now be found at levels of the hierarchy which they could not previously have aspired to. Yet many of the old values had survived more or less intact, and commerce and industry still did not constitute wholly acceptable occupations for those who set great store by social position. Thus, just as in the past, "the sons of considerable merchants are pretty sure to be found abandoning the business of their sires in order to take to scribbling in some Government department."[55] Certainly there was a slowly emerging, rather ill-defined middle class. Indeed, it was frequently the case that the expense of a large home, lavish entertainment, and a complement of domestic servants was more easily assumed by its members than many who belonged to the social elite. Nonetheless, St. Petersburg society continued to be strongly influenced by an often profligate and sometimes penurious nobility, a parasitic bureaucracy, and the resident military personnel than by the bankers, brokers, industrialists, and others who contributed to the city's economic viability.

For those who had the requisite social position, as well as the financial means, there was a vast cultural life to enjoy. Opera, ballet, theater—all were world class. Orchestra, ensemble, cafe violinist, singer—all existed in abundance. Not only did the Imperial court sustain many such activities, it was not uncommon for the nobility to have a retinue of musicians as part of the domestic scene. The social life was lavish and required a considerable measure of endurance. Dances at private homes frequently began in the late afternoon and concluded early the following morning, with a sumptuous, if not extravagant, banquet in between. The winter's cultural fare and social round served as a magnet for provincial folk with social aspirations. Even the poor were provided with a reasonable variety of musical and other theatrical entertainments free of charge. Not all of the lower classes preferred the traditional, simpler pleasures such as watching (and betting on) the illegal fist fights which took place on the islands, or drinking in one of the city's numerous dingy taverns. But it seems that most did. Not only did the economy of the city reflect the different worlds of modern industry and commerce and the bazaar mentality of the semiliterate peasant peddler, so too did the culture of the city. The very fabric of St. Petersburg was shaped accordingly.

The general configuration of the city's social class structure in 1910 is presented in Table 3.4. The complete dominance of the peasant *soslovie* is clear. Given the huge influx of peasants and the deteriorating state of the urban environment, how did the social elite respond? In broadly similar circumstances in the cities of Europe and America, one common defensive strategy had been the creation of socially homogeneous residential enclaves. But this was often predicated on the existence of adequate public transport, and we have already noted the absence of such in the Russian capital. The relationship between residential segregation and class identity, while perhaps tenuous, is nonetheless of possible importance to the history of St. Petersburg.

Contemporary descriptions suggest that certain socioeconomic groups or classes preferred to live in particular parts of the city. The nobility, for example, was associated with the central city and not the peripheral boroughs. Merchants and other business people gravitated to places of commerce; for instance, Vasil'evskii Island near the Stock Exchange and warehousing complex, or the central city near the various markets. While certain socioeconomic groups may have been associated with particular city regions in the minds of contemporaries, available data on residential locations suggest that segregation was limited.

The indices in Table 3.5 reveal the percentage of each estate or *soslovie* which would have had to shift residence in order to make the distributions over all thirty-eight census wards identical.[56] It is notewor-

TABLE 3.4

Social Structure in St. Petersburg, 1910

Estate	Number	Percentage
Hereditary nobility	74,812	3.9
Personal nobility	63,103	3.3
Clergy	9,325	0.5
Honored citizens	77,239	4.1
Merchants	13,580	0.7
Meshchane	294,864	15.5
Peasants	1,310,449	68.6
Foreigners	22,901	1.2
Finns	17,401	0.9
Others	20,468	1.1
	1,905,589	100.0

SOURCE: *Petrograd po perepisi 15 Dekabria 1910 goda* (1914), pt. 1, sec. 2, 12–13.

TABLE 3.5

Indices of Residential Dissimilarity among St. Petersburg's Estates, 1910 and 1869

Estate	Index 1910	Index 1869
Hereditary nobility	22.1	21.2
Personal nobility	18.4	18.1
Clergy (black)	60.1	
Clergy (white)	19.1	
Honored citizens	11.0	
Merchants	22.0	15.7
Meshchane	20.4	
Finns	30.0	22.1
Peasants	15.6	16.7
Foreigners	26.2	27.7

SOURCE: James H. Bater, *St. Petersburg: Industrialization and Change* (1976), 197, 376.

thy that there is little evidence of spatial segregation according to where these ten categories of St. Petersburg's population lived. The only exception was the regular, or so-called black, clergy. There were only 360 black clergy, a sizable number of whom seem to have lived within the walls of the Aleksandro-Nevskii Monastery. Nearly a quarter of the people belonging to the Finnish estate, the next most segregated group, lived in Vyborgskaia borough. Many no doubt arrived in St. Petersburg by train and thus disembarked at the Finland Railroad Station located in this borough. That they should have lived nearby is therefore not surprising. Moreover, a good number of Finnish migrants actually worked for the railroad and lived in company housing near the Finland Station.[57] But their concentration was relative since about 30 percent of St. Petersburg's Finnish population would have had to change residence in order to balance the distribution across all wards.

Comparison of indices for 1910 with 1869 cannot be taken too far since there were some minor changes in ward boundaries. However, it is apparent from Table 3.5 that there were more similarities than differences. For example, in 1869 the index for foreigners was 27.6; in 1910 it was 26.2. Many lived in Vasil'evskaia borough and among them Germans were traditionally quite prominent. Indeed, German was still heard on the streets, in the shops, and in the numerous beer houses. In this respect, Vasil'evskii Island retained something of its earlier image of a center of foreign business endeavor and cultural life. However, other boroughs had just as many, or more, foreign residents. If we can draw any conclusion from the indices presented in Table 3.5, it is that despite rapid urban-industrialization and its attendant social and environmen-

tal disorders, residential segregation among these ten broad socioeconomic groups was as weakly developed in the early 1900s as it was in the
1860s.

Another way of determining who lived where is to cull from the
city directory information about the inhabitants of particular streets.[58]
Eight streets, ostensibly representative of different social class areas,
according to contemporaries, have been selected.[59] Included are Galernaia and Millionnaia, both in Admiralteiskaia borough and representative of an exclusive and high rent district. The Second Line on
Vasil'evskii Island was in some respects similar. It was close to the
Exchange and University; most of its residents lived in the first ward
which had the highest rent in the borough. Srednaia meshchanskaia
Street was in the second ward of Kazanskaia, a densely populated petty-
trade and handicraft area. The ostensibly lower-class streets chosen as
examples are Svechnoi pereulok in the second ward of Moskovskaia, the
Seventh Rozhdestvenskaia Street in the second ward of Narvskaia, and
Guliarnaia Street in the first ward of Peterburgskaia borough (see map).[60]

Among the few representatives of the nobility (without specified
occupation) all but three lived on either Millionnaia or Galernaia
Streets in 1867 (Table 3.6). While both of these streets also had a sizable
roster of residents from the professions and government service, they
were not so exclusive as to be devoid of craftsmen, or indeed, of laborers
and factory workers. As well, there would have been many domestic
servants. The Second Line on Vasil'evskii Island had the largest number
of residents who could be identified as members of the merchant class.
Given the Island's port and related functions, this is not unexpected.
Streets in ostensibly working-class areas did reveal a higher proportion
of residents in trade and industry, but as the data in Table 7 reveal,
separation of socioeconomic groups was far from exclusive.

By 1912 there had been a number of changes in the social geography
of these streets (Table 3.7). Members of the nobility (without specified
occupation) were now to be found on all streets, save for Second Line. In
some cases they were living in what were traditionally regarded as
working class boroughs. Of course, since title and wealth were by no
means synonymous in Russian society, this is not necessarily of great
moment. At the other end of the social class continuum, there were still
to be found elements of the working class on supposedly high-status
streets. Clearly some craftsmen were both highly specialized and highly
paid. But not all of those craftsmen who lived on Millionnaia, Galernaia,
and Second Line were in that category, to be sure. Guliarnaia, which was
only sparsely developed in 1867, could now boast a fairly varied socioc-
cupational profile, including a good number of artists. On balance, it is
apparent that neither directory nor census sources show much tendency
for residential segregation during the late Imperial era.

The point really is that within a fairly rigid social class sytem,

TABLE 3.6

Socioeconomic Composition of Selected Streets in St. Petersburg, 1867

	Galernaia		Millionnaia		Second Line		Meshchanskaia		Svechnoi		7th Rozhdestvenskaia		Zarotnaia		Guliarnaia	
	N	%	N	%	N	%	N	%	N	%	N	%	N	%	N	%
Nobility[a]	8	1.8	11	3.6	2		0		0		0		0		1	1.6
Banker	3		0		0		2		0		0		0		0	
Merchant	49	11.1	26	8.6	80	24.2	64	15.1	16	19.0	15	14.2	2	3.1	3	4.8
Manufacturer	1		0		0		1		0		0		0		0	
Craftsman	43	9.7	26	8.6	52	15.7	165	38.8	20	23.8	19	17.9	19	29.2	11	17.7
Laborer/Factory Worker	14	3.2	4		12	3.6	35	8.2	8	9.5	8	7.5	5	7.7	1	1.6
Tutor/Teacher	23	5.2	14	4.6	14	4.2	10	2.4	2	2.4	0		3	4.6	2	3.2
Doctor	5	1.1	0		3		7	1.6	0		1		1	1.5	0	
Engineer/Architect	3		2		2		1		0		0		0		0	
Artist	12	2.7	6	2.0	10	3.0	18	4.2	3	3.6	1		3	4.6	0	
Other Professional	24	5.4	11	3.6	7	2.1	16	3.8	4	4.8	1		1	1.5	4	6.5
Military	1		5	1.7	0		0		1	1.2	1		0		0	
Govt. Service	84	19.0	83	27.4	54	16.3	31	7.3	9	10.7	25	23.6	14	21.5	17	27.4
Clergy	10	2.3	1		2		3		0		1		0		1	1.6
Student	9	2.0	8	2.6	28	8.5	8	1.9	1	1.2	0		0		0	
Not Specified	154	34.8	106	35.0	65	19.6	64	15.1	20	23.8	33	31.1	17	26.2	22	35.5
Total	443		303		331		425		84		106		65		62	

SOURCE: *Vseobshchaia adresnaia kniga S. Peterburg* (1867–68).

NOTE: Percentages have been rounded off; only those over 1% are shown.

[a]Without specified occupation.

TABLE 3.7
Socioeconomic Composition of Selected Streets in St. Petersburg, 1912

	Galernaia		Millionnaia		Second Line		Meshchanskaia		Svechnoi		7th Rozhdestvenskaia		Zarotnaia		Guliarnaia	
	N	%	N	%	N	%	N	%	N	%	N	%	N	%	N	%
Nobility[a]	11	8.4	8	8.2	0		1	1.3	3	8.6	8	6.3	1	1.4	3	2.4
Company Director	6	4.6	7	7.2	0		2	2.6	0		6	4.8	3	4.2	0	
Banker	1		1	1.0	0		2	2.6	1	2.9	1		0		3	2.4
Merchant	16	12.2	5	5.2	8	12.7	12	15.8	6	17.1	13	10.3	17	23.6	14	11.3
Manufacturer	0		1	1.0	2	3.2	2	2.6	0		2	1.6	0		0	
Craftsman	3	2.3	4	4.2	8	12.7	6	7.9	0		6	4.8	0		2	1.6
Laborer/Factory Worker	0		2	2.1	0		3	3.9	0		6	4.8	2	2.8	4	3.2
Teacher	2	1.5	1	1.0	3	4.8	2	2.6	1		1		2	2.8	1	
Professor	0		0		3	4.8	0		0		0		0		0	
Doctor	5	3.8	1	1.0	2	3.2	0		0		2	1.6	1	1.4	3	2.4
Engineer/Architect	1		2	2.1	1	1.6	1	1.3	0		1		1	1.4	1	
Artist	1		0		0		1	1.3	1	2.9	3	2.4	0		10	8.1
Other Professional	2	1.5	2	2.1	0		0		4	11.4	2	1.6	0		0	
Military	9	6.9	15	15.5	4	6.4	1	1.3	0		9	7.1	7	9.8	6	4.9
Govt. Service	29	22.1	26	26.8	7	11.1	4	5.2	5	14.3	28	22.2	11	15.4	22	17.9
Clergy	2	1.5	1	1.0	1	1.6	0		0		1		0		2	1.6
Student	5	3.8	1	1.0	1	1.6	0		1	2.9	2	1.6	0		1	
Not Specified	38	29.0	20	20.6	35	55.5	39	51.3	13	37.1	35	27.8	27	37.6	51	41.4
Total	131		97		63		76		35		126		72		123	

SOURCE: *Ves' Peterburga na 1912 g.* (St. Petersburg, 1912).
NOTE: Percentages have been rounded off; only those over 1% are shown.
[a]Without specified occupation.

especially where the values at the top changed only very slowly, it may not have mattered so much precisely where one lived in the city, as compared with other cities where wealth was more nearly synonymous with position in society. That is, recognition came in a more personal way and need not have been reinforced by the development of elite residential neighborhoods. To be sure, there were parts of the city recognized as "upper class," but as has been demonstrated by the directory data for the 1860s and 1900s these were not to be thought of as exclusive enclaves. Simply put, the situation seems not to have altered much during the decades of rapid industrialization. If anything, there are grounds for arguing that the admixture or heterogeneity increased. Suburban residential districts catering to the "elite" or middle classes, however defined, were not much in evidence. The urban poor, on the other hand, were literally everywhere, having intruded into what were formally more segregated areas. Ability to pay therefore seems to have been reflected in the size of the apartment and the manner in which it was fitted out as much as in location. Lavish decoration of living space insulated elites from the lower orders, who sometimes lived in squalor in the garrets above and in the cellars below (creating in the process a kind of three-dimensional segregation), and from the deteriorating quality of the urban environment in general. On the streets, personalized symbols of rank and status had long proclaimed one's place in society, though by the early 1900s such symbols no longer guaranteed a deferential response from the burgeoning masses. Still the decorative paraphernalia that went with rank or *chin* in the civil and military service continued to add a sense of occasion to street life right to the end of the Imperial era.

Appearance also designated one's place in the world of artisans, skilled workers, and overseers. Memoirs of St. Petersburg workers include reference to the importance of dress in determining the nature of the relationship with factory management. Skilled workers in the better-paying industries such as metalworking could afford decent clothes, and when so attired were spoken to more politely. As a rule, on the shop floor and on the street members of the working class were addressed by their superiors in the familiar, that is by *ty* and not the formal *vy*. Such nuances in dress and verbal communication were by no means restricted to the relationship between workers and employers. Within the working class world, the form of social interaction was very much conditioned by one's appearance.[61] Differences in status were especially palpable on Sundays and holidays when all who could paraded their finest. The recently arrived peasant in his calico shirt and high boots stood out clearly on such occasions. He was all too readily ridiculed by those who could afford a few of the affectations of the urban world, even if in vocabulary, accent, and behavior the village affiliation of the former was no different than the latter.

In summary, the social fabric of the city was shaped by the perpetuation of traditional values which placed as much store on personal appearance as residential location. While such values were by no means exclusive to the social elite, being evident as well among workers, it was the former who had the economic power to change the physical form of the city most substantially through residential segregation. It is perhaps somewhat surprising that there was no marked segregation of this sort, given the actual state of the urban milieu. Social unrest was rife and manifested itself in the 1905 uprising, in the growing incidence of strikes, and more generally in increasing crime of every description. Robberies, murders, suicides—all might be said to have reflected the underlying malaise. Some extreme antisocial behavior was no doubt prompted by the hopelessness of individual and family affairs. The cost of living, as we have noted, was escalating and it was more difficult each year for the average worker to keep abreast of day-to-day needs. Anarchist and revolutionary ideas lodged more and more easily in receptive minds. Political assassinations grew in number. Respect for place and privilege was being eroded. Such unrest had prompted unease in other European cities, where the response, for those who could afford it, had been to relocate in districts within the city that possessed a more recognizable class homogeneity—more often than not a suburban sanctuary—resulting in a very marked degree of segregation. In this respect, as in the areas of sanitation, education, and transportation and much else besides, the Russian capital was out of step with other major urban centers of the time.

BETWEEN OLD AND NEW

It has been argued that class segregation was one of the principal features that distinguished the industrial city from its commercial antecedent.[62] As handicraft activities and petty commodity production withered, as petty trading was displaced by modern commerce, as workplace and residence became physically separate, so the fabric of the city changed. Clearly the urban environment is a reflection of the values and technology of the time. In bringing about change, it may well be that the urban environment itself is not simply a passive agent. For example, research on other cities has suggested a relationship between the residential segregation of industrial workers and the rise of class consciousness and a sense of solidarity.[63] In the case of St. Petersburg, the particular spatial organization of the city and the general quality of the environment may also have played some part in the processes of social and political change, and on this topic we might briefly speculate.

From the foregoing discussion it is clear that while industrialization did not entirely displace the traditional economy, it did change the face of the city, and usually in entirely undesirable ways. Of necessity, some traditional management practices were altered. For instance, the customary paternalistic relationship between factory owner and workers did not survive intact into the 1900s. Thus, growing numbers of workers were obliged to seek their own housing, as opposed to residing in company-owned accommodation (still more common in Moscow after the turn of the century).[64] As a result they were less easily controlled, less easily subjected to surveillance during their non-working hours. In St. Petersburg the freedom to seek accommodation on the open market had a "cost," both in terms of the actual price of housing and in terms of its quality. But there may have been unanticipated "benefits." One potentially important one is that being out from under the thumb of owner and overseer may have facilitated the emergence of class consciousness and trade unions. Further research on this theme may prove especially insightful.

In St. Petersburg residential segregation was apparently limited. To the extent that workers dominated certain parts of the city, there may have been forged a greater sense of class consciousness. But insofar as heterogeneity as opposed to homogeneity of city streets and districts reflects the reality of the times, this facet of the urban environment may also have worked to exacerbate tensions and conflicts in society. The very fact that rich and poor were so intermingled, that they lived in such close proximity during a time when the values underpinning society at large were increasingly being questioned and challenged, perhaps sharpened awareness of the enormous gulf between classes and thereby heightened resentment.

Many of the trappings of modernization had only with difficulty been grafted onto Russian society. Much in St. Petersburg testified to these contradictions between old and new. Deficient municipal services and retarded technology in public transport hindered the creation of bucolic suburban enclaves for the elites and the emerging middle classes, thus limiting use of the defensive strategy against perceived urban ills commonly employed by elites in cities throughout Europe and America.[65] Even the prevailing values of decision-makers on the city council seem to belong to an earlier, more tranquil era, an era in which order and stability were ensured by means of Imperial fiat. The lack of resolve on the part of the city council clearly exacerbated the already difficult task of coping with rapid urban industrialization. The quality of the urban environment deteriorated, adding to the misery of the poor and not so poor alike. The link between morbidity and public unrest is no doubt there, although direct evidence is lacking. Still, to judge from the perpetuation of seasonal residence in the Imperial capital on the part of large numbers of the social elite, St. Petersburg cannot have been especially attractive during the spring and summer months. Those who were obliged to stay in this pestilential environment, working long hours for little money, were not all so naive as to miss the connection between political power and improved quality of life.

The many concessions which the revolution of 1905 was instrumental in wringing out of a shaken autocracy simply reinforced the perception among the masses that change was perhaps possible, especially if confrontation occurred on a large scale. In the years down to the First World War there was reason for still more change, for more accommodation to the aspirations of the masses. Conditions in the city, in the workplace, in the home were little improved—indeed, frequently deteriorated further—as each year witnessed still larger numbers of people to be absorbed somehow or other. Higher levels of literacy, rising expectations, and growing recognition of the inequalities produced by the autocracy's felt need to perpetuate the status quo all served to underscore the need for change. The urban environment itself clearly spoke to such a need as well.

Put simply, by the early 1900s the old order was no longer so readily accepted. Indeed, for a growing proportion of the urban population the demise of the old order was acknowledged as essential for the economic, social, and political well-being of the Empire and its millions of inhabitants. For the hundreds of thousands who had migrated to the capital to escape the poverty of life in the village, the harsh reality of urban existence must surely have sharpened their awareness of inequity. In the event, with the chaos produced by World War I, the fabric of urban society began to come apart. What happened in 1917 perhaps cannot be directly tied to the urban environment, but neither can it be ignored when interpreting the currents of change that culminated in a new ideological blueprint for society.

NOTES

1. Jared W. Scudder, *Russia in the Summer of 1914* (Boston, 1920), 109.

2. G. L. von Attengofer, *Mediko-Topograficheskoe opisanie Sankt-peterburga, glavnago i stolichnago goroda Rossiiskoi Imperii* (St. Petersburg, 1820), 107.

3. E. E. Kruze, D. G. Kutsentov, "Naselenie Peterburga," in *Ocherki istorii Leningrada* (Moscow-Leningrad, 1956), Vol. III, 105.

4. For a full discussion of the impact of industrialization, see James H. Bater, *St. Petersburg: Industrialization and Change* (London and Montreal, 1976).

5. Factory employment data are drawn from D. P. Kandaurov, *Fabrichno-Zavodskie predpriiatia Rossiiskoi Imperii (iskliuchaia Finliandiiu)* (Petrograd, 1914).

6. E. E. Kruze, "Promyshlennoe razvitie Peterburga v 1890kh–1914 gg." in *Ocherki istorii Leningrada*, 15.

7. "Elektricheskaia energiia, i elektrotechnicheskaia promyshlennost' v Rossii," *Promyshlennost' i torgovlia*, 1913, no. 2:61–64.

8. E. E. Kruze, "Transport, torgovlia, kredit," in *Ocherki istorii Leningrada*, 73.

9. *Petrograd po perepisi 15 Dekabria 1910 goda* (Petrograd, 1914), Part 2, Section 1.

10. Kruze, "Transport, torgovlia, kredit," 79.

11. *Ves' Peterburg na 1912 g.* (St. Petersburg, 1912).

12. E. E. Kruze, "Rabochie Peterburga v gody novogo revoliutsionnogo podema'," *Istoriia rabochikh Leningrada* (Leningrad, 1972), Vol. 1, 390.

13. Kruze, Kutsentov, "Naselenie Peterburga," 105.

14. *Entsiklopedicheskii slovar* (St. Petersburg, 1900), Vol. LVI, 314–16.

15. L. Kupriianova, "Rabochii Peterburga," *S. Peterburg i ego zhizn'* (Petrograd, 1914), 185–86.

16. *Petrograd po perepisi*, 290.

17. "Ischislenie naseleniia S. Peterburga 15 Iiulia i 15 Dekabria 1888 goda," *Statisticheskii ezhegodnik S. Peterburg* (1888):7–59 and (1889):6–25.

18. "Ischislenie naseleniia," 7, 51.

19. *Petrograd po perepisi*, 16–25; *S. Peterburg po perepisi 15 Dekabria 1900 goda* (St. Petersburg, 1903), Vol. 1, 32, 33.

20. Although use of city directories for the purpose of establishing levels of transience is problematic, it is of interest that the pattern established by the census is confirmed. The major problem associated with the use of the city directory is that it speaks to such a small percentage of the total population. Unlike the published census, however, it is possible to trace the duration of residence in the city of specific individuals. Because of the Russian practice of listing persons according to family name, abbreviated first name, and patronymic, possible confusion among individuals with the same family name is minimized. In the census, of course, we are dealing with aggregates. For discussion of the nature of the difficulties raised in tracing individuals in the absence of such information, see C. Pouyez, R. Roy, and F. Martin, "The Linkage of Census Name Data. Problems and Procedures." *Journal of Interdisciplinary History*, XIV, no. 1 (1983):144–52. For discussion of sampling procedures, see James H. Bater, "Transience, Residential Persistence, and Mobility in Moscow and St. Petersburg, 1900–1914," *Slavic Review*, 39, no. 2, (1980):239–54.

21. For instance, in the 1909 to 1912 period listings rose from 186,000 to 210,000 individuals. The systematic sample was drawn from *Ves' Peterburg na 1909 g.* (St. Petersburg, 1909) and traced in *Ves' Peterburg na 1912 g.* (St. Petersburg, 1912).

22. Owing to the infrequent street name changes and consistent house numbering in the early 1900s, we can be reasonably certain that we are here dealing with actual relocations.

23. In 1900, for example, nearly 90 percent of the 1.275 million inhabitants lived in apartments or rooms located in fewer than 16,000 buildings. The number of property owners was smaller than the number of buildings. *S. Peterburg po perepisi 15 Dekabria 1900*, Part 3, Section 2, 677.

24. See for instance *Journal de St. Petersbourg*, December 9, 1893, 4.

25. For some related examples, see S. Thernstrom, Peter Knights, "Men in Motion, Some Data and Speculation about Urban Population Mobility in Nineteenth Century America," *Journal of Interdisciplinary History* (Autumn 1970):7–36; M. Anderson, *Family Structure in Nineteenth Century Lancashire*, (Cambridge, 1971); Howard Chudacoff, *Mobile Americans: Residential and Social Mobility in Omaha, 1880–1920* (New York, 1972); S. Thernstrom; *The Other Bostonians, Poverty and Progress in the American Metropolis* (Cambridge, Mass., 1972); M. Katz, *The People of Hamilton, Canada West: Family and Class in a Mid-Nineteenth Century City* (Cambridge, Mass. 1975); C. G.

Pooley, "Residential Mobility in the Victorian City," *Transactions of the Institute of British Geographers*, IV, no. 2 (1979):258–77.

26. Tatiana W. Boldyreff, *Russian Born: A Pageant of Childhood Memories* (Boston, 1935), 42.

27. Bater, *St. Petersburg*, 166–68, 319–20.

28. K. Pazhitnov, "Zhilishchnaia politika gorodskoi dumy gor. Petrograda," *Izvestiia Moskovskoi gorodskoi dumy*, 1914, no. 10:29–53.

29. Iu. M. Fridval'd, "K Voprosu o zhilishchakh Peterburgskikh rabochikh," *Izvestiia Movskoskoi gorodskoi dumy*, November 1895:13.

30. D. Polupanov, "K kvartirnomy krizisu Pcterburga," *Gorodskoe delo*, 1913, no. 5:1350–57.

31. K. L. Karaffa-Korbut, "Nochlezhnie doma v bol'shikh Russkikh gorodakh," *Gorodskoe delo*, 1912, nos. 11 and 12:691–712.

32. Pazhitnov, "Zhilishchnaia politika," 33, 35.

33. James H. Bater, "The Development of Public Transportation in St. Petersburg," *Journal of Transport History*, N.S. 1, No. 2 (1973):85–102.

34. S. P. Luppov, "Gorodskoe upravlenie i gorodskoe khoziaistvo," *Ocherki istorii Leningrada* (Moscow-Leningrad, 1957), Vol. II, 810–44.

35. *Spravka k voprosu ob uluchshenii sposobov peredvizheniia naseleniia S. Peterburga* (St. Petersburg, 1901).

36. "Po voprosu o vykupe predpriiatiia 2-go aktsionernago obshchestva konno-zheleznykh dorog v S. Peterburge," *Izvestiia S. Peterburgskoi gorodskoi dumy*, 1895, no. 20:353–62.

37. "Gorodskiia zhelezniia-dorogi v Peterburge i Moskve," *Izvestiia S. Peterburgskoi gorodskoi dumy*, 1914, no. 26:2968–69.

38. See, for example, A. Zhuravlev, "K voprosu o finansovoi politike v oblasti munitsipal'nykh predpriiatii," *Gorodskoe delo*, 1909, no. 6:233–43; G. Dubelir, "Planirovki gorodov," *Gorodskoe delo*, 1910, no. 10:648–49; Harold W. Williams, *Russia of the Russians* (New York, 1915), 419.

39. "Kak khvoraet i umiraet stolitsa," *Gorodskoe delo*, 1909, no. 11:544–47.

40. A. W. Woodhouse, "Report," *British Parliamentary Papers: Diplomatic and Consular Report 1909*, XCVII, 943.

41. Woodhouse, "Report," 943.

42. G. Dobson, *St. Petersburg* (London, 1910), 109.

43. *Russkiia vedomosti*, January 17, 1909.

44. N. N. Petrov, "Gorodskoe upravlenie i gorodskoe khoziaistvo Peterburga." *Ocherki istorii Leningrada* (Moscow-Leningrad, 1956), vol. 3, 901.

45. Dobson, *St. Petersburg*, 110.

46. M. Shokotov, "S. Peterburgskaia gorodskaia zhizn," *Izvestiia Moskovskoi gorodskoi dumy*, 1903, nos. 11 to 13:72–81.

47. *Gorodskoe delo*, 1909, no. 11:544–47.

48. G. T. Shreider, *Nashe gorodskoe obshchestvennoe upravlenia* (St. Petersburg, 1902), 66, 80, 169.

49. P. Sorskii, "Biudzhet Peterburga," *Izvestiia Moskovskoi gorodskoi dumy*, 1907, no. 5:17–33.

50. "Resul'taty revizii S. Peterburgskago gorodskogo upravleniia, *Izvestiia Moskovskoi gorodskoi dumy*, 1903, no. 3:125; S. S. Volk, "Prosveshchenie i shkola v Peterburge" *Ocherki istorii Leningrada*, 356.

51. Sorskii, "Biudzhet Peterburga," 18.

52. Williams, *Russia of the Russians*, 419–20.

53. *Recollections of Russia During Thirty-Three Years' Residence* (Edinburgh, 1855), 157.

54. See Alfred Rieber, *Merchants and Entrepreneurs in Imperial Russia* (Chapel Hill, 1982), 85–87, 147.

55. Dobson, *St. Petersburg*, 98.

56. Clearly the higher the proportion having to move, the greater the degree of spatial segregation. For a discussion of the methodology involved see Bater, *St. Petersburg*, p. 433.

57. Proximity of workplace and residence was common in St. Petersburg in the late Imperial era, though company housing had declined appreciably in importance since mid-nineteenth century. See James H. Bater, "The Journey to Work in St. Petersburg, 1860–1914," *Journal of Transport History*, N.S. III, no. 2 (1974):214–33.

58. As noted earlier, the directory provides supplementary information of a socioeconomic kind for about two-thirds of the entries; it is possible to draw a rough profile of the socioeconomic "complexion" of individual streets. It should be borne in mind, however, that the directory coverage is far from complete, that it is biased toward the upper echelons of urban society, that our selection of streets is necessarily arbitrary, and that the assignment of individuals to particular socioeconomic categories is not without its pitfalls.

59. All residents are included in the 1867 survey, but owing to the nearly threefold increase in the city's population between 1867 and 1912 we have drawn a systematic sample for the latter year. The first column of each of the 1,065 pages in the 1912 directory was surveyed for residents of the selected streets. Each page has four columns. We are therefore dealing with about a one-quarter sample which, given the nature of the city directory, has the characteristic of a random sample.

60. For further discussion of these streets and boroughs see Bater, *St. Petersburg*, 373–75.

61. Victoria E. Bonnell, ed., *The Russian Worker* (Berkeley, 1983), 10–14.

62. See for example, M. Ball, "The Development of Capitalism in Housing Provision," *International Journal of Urban and Regional Research*, 5 (1981):145–77; James E. Vance, "Housing The Worker: The Employment Linkage as a Force in Urban Structure," *Economic Geography*, 42 (1966):294–325.

63. For instance, see G. Stedman Jones, *Outcast London: A Study in the Relationship Between Classes in Victorian Society* (London, 1971).

64. See James H. Bater, "The Industrialization of Moscow and St. Petersburg," in James H. Bater, R.A. French, eds. *Studies in Russian Historical Geography* (London and New York, 1983), Vol. 2, 291–301.

65. See for example, Sam Bass Warner, Jr., *Streetcar Suburbs: The Process of Growth in Boston, 1870–1900* (Cambridge, Mass., 1962).

BIBLIOGRAPHICAL NOTE

There are bountiful sources available for those interested in the history of St. Petersburg. From the writings of Pushkin and Dostoevsky to guidebooks and memoirs there is much that can be gleaned to add to an appreciation of what the capital of the Russian Empire was like. Among secondary scholarly works a number are deserving of recognition, some of which have been cited in this study. Certainly the most useful general reference is the *Ocherki istorii Leningrada* (Moscow-Leningrad, 1955–). The six volumes of this monumental study published by the Soviet Academy of Sciences cover the history of St. Petersburg from its founding in 1703, through its period as Petrograd from August 1914 to

Lenin's death in 1924, after which it was again renamed, to the post–Second World War years. Over the past fifteen years or so, there has been a spate of more specialized studies on the history of St. Petersburg in the latter part of the Imperial era. Notable among them is Reginald Zelnik's *Labor and Society in Tsarist Russia: The Factory Workers of St. Petersburg, 1855–1870* (Stanford, 1971), and on a broadly similar theme the author's *St. Petersburg: Industrialization and Change* (London, 1976). The welcome appearance of several volumes covering aspects of St. Petersburg's social and political history has done much to further our understanding of the city during this period. One might count among these recent efforts Victoria E. Bonnell's *Roots of Rebellion: Workers' Politics and Organizations in St. Petersburg and Moscow, 1900–1914* (Berkeley, 1983), S. A. Smith's *Red Petrograd: Revolution in the Factories, 1917–18* (Cambridge, 1983), and Rose Glickman's *Russian Factory Women: Workplace and Society 1880–1914* (Berkeley, 1984). On the growth of St. Petersburg and its migration field, Max Engman's *St. Petersburg och Finland. Migration och Influens, 1703–1917* (Helsingfors, 1983) is a major contribution. And of course, in the journals there is a steadily growing body of more specialized scholarship available, most notably in English, German, and Swedish.

There is a wealth of sources available to those with a command of the Russian language. For example, there is much of value on the history of St. Petersburg which can be culled from the newspaper literature. Of particular interest are *S. Peterburgskiia vedomosti*, published daily and available in the Slavic Collection of the Helsinki University Library from 1891 and the *Journal de St. Petersbourg* available from 1881 in the British Library. Many other pertinent newspapers such as *Novoe vremia, Russkiia vedomosti,* and *Moskovskii vestnik* carried articles on St. Petersburg and are available on microfilm. Current runs and locations are listed in standard references on newspaper holdings. Of the many Russian journals of value for the study of urban history in the late imperial era one stands out—*Gorodskoe delo*. First published in 1909, it is an indispensable guide to the urban scene in the early 1900s. Reports on the management of civic affairs in the capital are of particular value since they tend to counterpoise the argument in some official city documents. It should not be thought, however, that the reports and discussion in the *Izvestiia S. Peterburgskoi gorodskoi dumy*, the official city council publication which began in 1863, were typically uncritical, for this was certainly not the case. The *Arkhiv sudebnoi meditsiny i obshchestvennoi gigiyeny* or Archive of Forensic Medicine and Social Hygiene began publication in 1865 and ran for the better part of a decade. Like the medical doctoral dissertation series, which started around 1890, and the Pirogov Society publications, it provides a wealth of information on the sanitary conditions within the city. Yet another perception of the St. Petersburg scene may be obtained from reading the sundry British, French and American diplomatic reports. While their main focus is on political and economic affairs in the Empire, they frequently include reports on life in the capital itself.

There is simply a mountain of primary sources available in published form, much of it little used. From census statistics to maps and plans to city directories to factory statistics—the list rolls on. A detailed discussion of a number of these sources may be found in *St. Petersburg: Industrialization and Change*, referred to above. Of still greater volume are the archival sources which are described in detail in numerous publications and to which we can here do no more than make passing reference. Suffice it to say that for the enthusiast of things both Russian and urban, there are innumerable avenues still open to inquiring minds. Much has been written about St. Petersburg to be sure, but there is much that remains to be built upon the body of existing scholarship.

4.

Continuity and Change in Late Imperial Kiev

MICHAEL F. HAMM

As the organizing center of ancient Rus' and the early citadel of Russian Christianity, Kiev has always held a special place in Slavic history. Kiev's princes brought the Eastern Slavic tribes under their control and came to rule a state which, at its zenith in the mid-eleventh century, stretched from the Baltic to the Black Sea. Kiev may have housed 30,000 or more inhabitants at this time, making it one of Europe's largest towns.[1] In the nineteenth century historian Mikhail Pogodin (1800–1875) still thought of Kiev as "a treasure . . . a wonder! Russians can only be enchanted upon seeing it for the first time!" For Emperor Alexander II (1818–1881), Kiev was "the Jerusalem of the Russian lands."[2]

The Mongols destroyed Kiev in 1240 and controlled the city and the Russian lands for the next century and a half. In the fourteenth century Lithuanian princes extended their control over Kiev and much of the Ukraine. Though the city was refortified, it was ravaged by Crimean Tatars in 1416 and again in 1482. The Lithuanians extended the Magdeburg Rights (which allowed self-government for certain towns) to Kiev at the end of the fifteenth century. Poles came to dominate the Lithuanian state, and in 1569 the Union of Lublin provided for a common Polish-Lithuanian sovereign and diet. Polish Catholic influence spread throughout the Ukraine, helping to spark a series of revolts which in 1654 left the Ukraine divided between Muscovite Russia and Poland, essentially along the Dnepr River. The Kievan Brotherhood, founded in 1615 in Kiev's Bogoiavlensk

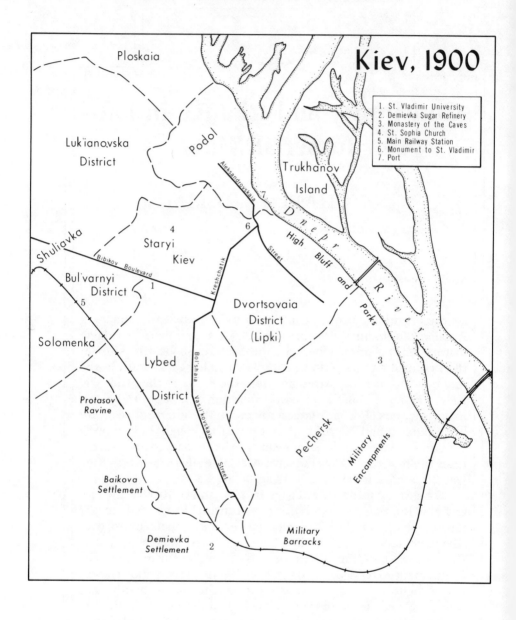

Kiev, 1900

1. St. Vladimir University
2. Demievka Sugar Refinery
3. Monastery of the Caves
4. St. Sophia Church
5. Main Railway Station
6. Monument to St. Vladimir
7. Port

Ploskaia

Luk'ianovska District

Podol

Trukhanov Island

Dnepr

Shuliavka

Staryi Kiev

4

Bibikov Boulevard

1

Aleksandrovskaia

7

6

High Bluff and Parks

River

Bul'varnyi District

5

Kreshchatik

Dvortsovaia District (Lipki)

Street

Solomenka

Lybed District

Bol'shaia Vasilkovskaia

3

Protasov Ravine

Pechersk

Military Encampments

Baikova Settlement

Street

Demievka Settlement

2

Military Barracks

Monastery, was one influential proponent of joining forces with the Russians against the Poles, but Kiev may also have become an important center of emerging Ukrainian consciousness by this time. The eminent Ukrainian historian Mykhailo Hrushevskyi (1866–1934) maintains that Kiev was already "the center of Ukrainian national life."[3]

Located on the "right bank" (or west bank) of the Dnepr, Kiev was formally annexed by Russia in 1686. The rural right-bank Ukrainian provinces (Kievskaia, Podolskaia, and Volynskaia in Russian) remained with Poland until the partitions of 1772, 1793, and 1795 ended that country's existence as an independent state. Russia annexed nearly all of the Ukraine during the partitions, and Kiev became the main administrative center for Russia's new "Southwest Region."

Throughout these centuries Kiev remained a series of small settlements separated from one another by hills and ravines. From the eighteenth century the city did grow, however; its population, estimated at 10,000 in the 1720s, reached 30,000—probably for the first time since before the Mongol invasions—by the 1750s. Great monasteries, particularly the Monastery of the Caves (Pecherskaia lavra, founded in 1073), and a fortress which grew in importance as Russians battled Poles, Ottoman Turks, and Crimean Tatars for control of the Ukraine, dominated the city and its economy. The number of troops deployed in the garrison was one factor which caused the city's population to rise and fall. Another was the perennial problem of epidemics. In 1770–71, for example, plague killed 6,000 Kievans and caused many others to flee. By 1786 Kiev had 42,000 people, though it probably continued to experience periodic fluctuations in population, at least until the 1820s or 1830s.[4]

Trade was always important to Kiev's economy. Land and water routes to Poland, Hungary, Persia, and the Ottoman Empire passed through the city, and salt and other commodities came from the Urals via the Dnepr and Volga trade networks. The monasteries attracted thousands of pilgrims to the city. "They appear as *the* people of Kiev, for whose sake the city stands . . . bringing their smell of sweat and poverty, their infirmities and sorrows, into an atmosphere already gutted with incense and mustiness," one German traveler wrote.[5] Monasteries were also prominent in the two most important local trades, milling and distilling. Monks from the Monastery of the Caves had fourteen taverns in Pechersk District in the 1750s, one on each street.[6] In 1766 it seemed to one observer that "the making of vodka and other drinks was the main, if not the only, form of production in Kiev."[7] For all of the city's "miracle-working icons," went an eighteenth-century lyric, "its men, though charitable to the poor, are in the end destroyed by its taverns. They become stingy: good men become bad."[8]

Kiev's growth was spurred by Russia's annexation of the Black Sea littoral and the opening of Odessa's port in 1794. The Contract Fair was moved to the city from Dubno in 1797: it brought up to 7,000 traders in agricultural commodities to Kiev each winter, some from as far away as England. In the nineteenth century the Fair became the organizing center of Russia's burgeoning beet sugar industry. The Great Ball that accompanied the Fair became the high point of Kiev's social calendar.[9]

Kiev's importance as a center of learning should not be overlooked, for its monasteries helped introduce Western ideas into seventeenth and eighteenth-century Russia. From 1616 the Monastery of the Caves operated a press which contributed greatly to the development of book-printing in the Empire.[10]

But while it grew in size and importance, Kiev still impressed a visitor in 1800 as "three separate settlements"—Pechersk, Staryi Kiev (Old Kiev, sometimes called High City), and the Podol. There were no paved bridges, and communication between one settlement and another was "difficult." Each was fortified with at least earthen walls, and each gave the appearance of a "village." In the words of the visitor, "Kiev hardly deserved to be called a city at all."[11]

Pechersk stood high above the Dnepr and included the Monastery of the Caves, whose great domes provided a magnificent silhouette for the city, and the main fortress, which was expanded several times, in the 1830s for the final time. Pechersk lost importance in the nineteenth century, for industry and commerce located elsewhere. In 1900 Pechersk could still be described as an odd amalgam of soldiers, monks, and pilgrims, a kind of window to Kiev's past.

Staryi Kiev was also located on high ground, but away from the Dnepr. The site of St. Sophia church (Sofiiskii sobor) and the ruins of the Great Gate, it had been the most heavily populated part of ancient Kiev. It grew rapidly in the nineteenth century as a commercial and residential district. St. Vladimir University was founded here in 1834. Some of Kiev's most fashionable neighborhoods also developed in this district, but more typical, perhaps, was Sviatoslavskaia Street, the boyhood home of the writer Konstantin Paustovsky (1892–1968), who recalled a muddy street "filled with ugly apartment houses and pavements made of yellow brick . . . which led across a vast wasteland cut by ravines."[12]

The Podol, Kiev's "low city," lay along the Dnepr. Mentioned in manuscripts as early as 1111, it remained the largest of Kiev's settlements in population until the mid-nineteenth century. The Podol had all the color of a river port and commercial hub. Its open-air markets were among the oldest and largest in the city. The Contract Fair was held there, and a great hall built to accommodate it. Still, around 1800, a visitor could write that the Podol "didn't have the appearance of a city." Stone buildings were rare; there was "no order to the buildings or architecture." Its low wooden huts were hidden from view by churches and monasteries. Its unpaved streets were so narrow that "two carriages could barely pass," and residents were "choked with dust."[13]

Beginning in the 1820s Kiev apparently grew steadily, reaching 65,000 inhabitants and soldiers by 1861, the year of the emancipation of the serfs which set the stage for five decades of explosive growth. By 1874 Kiev had 127,251 people; by 1897, 247,723; and by January 1, 1914, 626,313.[14] The open spaces between Kiev's historic districts filled in. Dvortsovaia (Palace) District, also called Lipki, named for the royal palace built there by Elizabeth Petrovna (1709–1762) for use during royal visits to the city, grew between Pechersk and Staryi Kiev and became the premier high-rent neighborhood. Near the palace were Marinskii Park, in Paustovsky's description, "with walls of pink and white lilacs three times a man's height," the Tsarist Garden, and Merchants' Park. They stretched high above the Dnepr and the Podol.

> The entire population was proud of this view. A symphony orchestra used to play all summer in the Merchants' Park. There was nothing to interfere with the music except the drawn-out whistling of the steamboats, carried up from the Dniepr. The last part on the Dniepr bank was on Vladimir hill. The monument to Prince Vladimir stood there, holding a bronze cross in his arms. Electric lights, wired to the cross, were lighted at night, and the blazing cross hung high in the sky over the slopes of Kiev.[15]

As if symbolically, Kiev's hills were crisscrossed by ravines, where life at its lowest often could be found. The *yar* (ravine) on Sviatoslavskaia street fascinated the young Paustovsky who later recalled its shanties made from scrap metal, broken crates, and shredded mattresses. "Dirty sacks hung in place of doors."

> Bareheaded women in rags sat beside the fireplaces. They called us "young masters" or asked for a drink of vodka. Only one of them, a shaggy, gray old woman with a lioness's face, smiled at us with her single tooth.
>
> She was an Italian beggar who was well known in Kiev. She used to walk from courtyard to courtyard and play the accordion. For an extra payment she would play the "Marseillaise." When she did this, one of the little boys would be sent to give warning in case a neighborhood policeman should appear. The beggar ... would also sing it in a piercing, raucous voice. She made the song sound like an angry challenge, like a curse of all the inhabitants of the Svyatoslavskaya *yar*.
>
> Among those who lived in these shanties we recognized old acquaintances. There was Yashka Padushi, a beggar with white, vodka-like eyes.... He would drink a quarter liter of vodka in one swallow, hit himself on the chest with all his strength, and howl tearfully: "Come unto me, all who are suffering or overburdened, and I will give you peace!"

There was a bald old man who peddled toothpaste on Fundu-
kleyevskaya Street near the Francois Cafe, and a hurdy-gurdy man with
a parrot.[16]

Ravines were filled in: endless convoys of dirt-filled wagons and
constantly muddy streets became part of the urban scene. The city
spread and new districts developed. Ploskaia (Flatlands), called Bolon'e
or Obolon in ancient manuscripts, grew outward from the Podol. Sometimes it was called Meshchanskaia for the *meshchane* (mainly artisans)
who came to predominate there. Spring in Kiev always began with the
flooding of the Dnepr, and Ploskaia was particularly susceptible to
flooding, and to cholera. New areas grew along the railroads, which were
begun in the 1860s: Bul'varnyi and Lybed Districts, Luk'ianovka, Shuliavka, Solomenka, and Demievka. They absorbed many of Kiev's pro-
letarians, the peasants and artisans who came by the thousands in
search of work.

By 1900 Kiev had resumed its ancient role as one of Europe's great
cities, and a valley of a different sort, the Kreshchatik, had become the
new symbol of the city's burgeoning commercial, industrial, and financial vitality. Named for the Kreshchatoi Valley, itself crossed by
ravines, the Kreshchatik had been a series of dirt paths, wooden huts,
and distilling shacks connecting Pechersk to the river landing in the
Podol. Kievans had begun to relocate there after 1811, when a great fire
destroyed much of the Podol, and during the 1830s, when the Pechersk
fortress was expanded. In the 1800s the Kreshchatik was still dotted
with small wooden homes, restaurants, and beer halls, including the
Krantsa, where the skittles alley became a favorite among the city's
Germans. Russians and Germans dominated the trading establishments on the Kreshchatik at this time: there were no Jewish traders, a
fact which would change markedly by 1900. The Kreshchatik changed
as rapidly as Kiev grew. Four and five-story stone and brick buildings
became common. City Hall was located there, as were the great banks,
hotels with names like Belle-vue and Grand-hotel, fine shops, and
corporate headquarters. Thus evolved the Kreshchatik, aside from St.
Petersburg's Nevskii Prospekt probably Russia's most famous Main
Street and the symbol of Kiev still today.[17]

KIEV'S ECONOMY: CONTINUITY AND CHANGE

Agricultural products, armaments, and various consumer items
had traditionally been the mainstays of Kiev's economy. At the time of
the Emancipation, the armaments plant known as the Arsenal (founded
1764) was the city's largest employer, and the city had some thirty
workshops employing silversmiths, twenty-eight printshops and bind-

eries, thirteen engraving shops, and eleven clock and watch makers.[18] In 1914, after five decades of spectacular growth, food processing and the making and purveying of consumer goods and services still dominated the city economy. New industries had become prominent during these decades, particularly machine building and metallurgy, but they developed largely in response to the demand created by Kiev's agricultural industries, and above all by the beet sugar industry.

Sugar had been imported by Russia and refined near St. Petersburg and Riga, the ports of entry, until the blockade of the Napoleonic Wars and the high tariffs of Alexander I encouraged Russian scientists to introduce the crop locally. By the mid–1850s, Kiev Province accounted for half of Russia's beet sugar production. Entrepreneurs such as Israel Brodskii (who became one of Kiev's leading industrialists and philanthropists) brought in new equipment and refining techniques from the West, and by 1860 60 percent of the workers of the Ukraine and 13 percent of all workers in the Russian Empire were employed in the sugar industry. Kievskaia and adjacent Podolskaia Provinces still accounted for 54 percent of Russia's production in 1914.[19] One syndicate, founded in 1887 and centered in Kiev, came to control 203 of the 244 refineries in the country.[20] By the 1890s Kiev served as the corporate headquarters for seventy refiners; by 1912, 117.[21] The city's largest refining facility was the Aleksandrovskii Refinery (founded 1868), better known as the Demievka Refinery, for it was actually located in the outlying settlement of Demievka. It employed 1,200 workers in 1897 and 1905 (400 of them women), and 2,000 in 1913.[22]

Other agricultural-products industries grew as well. The Solomen Kogen tobacco plant was founded in 1861; it had at least 300 workers in 1905, making it one of the largest employers in the city. By 1885 there were nine tobacco plants in the city, and by 1900 there were 1,650 tobacco workers. Eight brewers of beer or mead were operating in Kiev by 1900, and by 1913 the food, beverage, and tobacco industries accounted for 4,842 of the city's workers.[23]

These industries, and especially sugar, brought large amounts of capital into the city, thereby stimulating the growth of its financial sector. In 1867 the only bank in Kiev had been an office of the State Bank; in the 1890s more than thirty financial and credit institutions were in operation.[24]

A substantial machine-building and foundry sector also developed in response to new demands for processing, refining, and farm equipment. The largest of these new industries were the South Russian Machineworks, founded in the late 1880s, and the Greter Machine and Boiler Works, established in 1881, which became Greter & Krivanek via merger in 1890. In the 1890s Greter and Krivanek expanded its output by five times and doubled its work force to nearly 1,000. By 1913 Kiev had eighteen machine works subject to factory inspection, with 2,768 workers, and seventeen metallurgical operations, with 897 workers. Together they accounted for about one-fifth of Kiev's industrial output and one-quarter of its factory proletariat.[25]

Railroads played a major role in the growth of Russia's cities from the 1860s, and Kiev proved no exception. Its line to Moscow, via Kursk, was built from 1863 to 1868, and from 1868 to 1871 its rail link to Odessa, via Balta, was completed. The Kovel and Poltava lines were finished in 1901–1902. In the 1880s the Southwestern Railroad threatened to move its headquarters to Odessa if Kiev's city council refused to donate a large tract of free land. The council gave in, and near the main terminal in Bul'varnyi District the railroad built Railway Colony, a settlement for its employees which included stone barracks, a hospital, a school and technical institute, and an elevated bridge over the tracks to the city.[26] The number of railway employees remained at about 2,500 in the 1890s and in 1905, but dropped to 1,600 by 1913.[27]

The Dnepr had always been important to Kiev's economy, and barge traffic increased greatly after the 1860s. Kiev's council delayed for years a much-discussed plan to build a rail spur from the main terminal to the river port, however. Nearby Cherkassy had built such a spur and could boast an industrial output 60 percent that of Kiev's, though it had only 10 percent of Kiev's population.[28] Just before the First World War, Kiev's council finally approved the plans for a rail spur, but years of indifference to the project indicate that local civic leaders had little interest in promoting heavy industry in the city.[29] Much of Kiev's freight continued to be hauled about by hand- or animal-pulled conveyances. About 9,000 Kievans (including dependents) relied on carting and hauling to earn a living, according to the 1897 census.[30]

The growth of the printing industry also deserves mention, for by 1900 there were twenty-one major print shops, with about 1,200 workers; by 1913 there were 1,579 print workers, about 10 percent of Kiev's "factory" labor force. Many small shops also existed, often in basements. Workdays of eighteen or twenty hours were still common in the printing industry in the early 1900s, and workers from the print shops were among the most militant in Kiev by the turn of the century.[31]

Thus, by the end of the nineteenth century, the leading sectors of Kiev's industrial economy had been delineated. During the Empire-wide economic slump of the first decade of the twentieth century, Kiev's economy grew very slowly. The recovery that began in 1909–10 had a significant impact, as Table 4.1 shows.

Kiev had about 15,000 industrial workers in 1912 (21,000 in 1916 when wartime production was in full gear), but it was not a factory town. In Moscow and St. Petersburg one-third of the huge factory labor force worked in plants with 1,000 or more employees, but in Kiev only the Demievka Refinery and the Main Railway Shop had this many employees. In 1912 Kiev had only six enterprises with at least 500

TABLE 4.1

Growth in the Number of Major Enterprises, Employed Workers, and Product in Kiev, 1901–1913

Year	N Major Enter- prises	N Employed Workers	Product, in Millions of Rubles
1901	117	8,756	18.8
1905	118	9,076	19.4
1910	128	10,377	28.3
1913	177	15,220	37.5

SOURCE: *Istoriia gorodov i sel Ukrainskoi SSR. Kiev* (Kiev, 1979), 154. After 1905 annexation of outlying neighborhoods added some enterprises and workers to the city, but the exact numbers are difficult to determine.

employees, twenty-nine from 200 to 500, eighty-seven from fifty to 200, and 1,660 with fewer than fifty.[32] Artisans, service personnel, and day laborers continued to form the backbone of the city economy. Thousands worked in the building and hauling trades. Hundreds crafted specialty items—"the flat-iron, the ice cream freezer, and the folding mirror" that amazed and delighted Paustovsky's grandfather, who lived in a nearby village. "All the things we had brought from Kiev astonished him . . . . 'There's a tool for everything,'" the old man exclaimed.[33] Nearly 10 percent of all Kievans worked in the apparel trades in 1897, mostly in small shops.[34] The 1902 city directory lists at least 620 shops trading in clothing, about 230 craftsmen of shoes and boots, more than 100 haberdashers, and dozens selling specialty items like ties and corsets.[35] Hundreds served the needs of an estimated 900,000 yearly visitors to the city, including 150,000 to 250,000 religious pilgrims. Kiev's memoirist, Starozhil, recalls that trade in incense did a booming, year-round business, and that some Kievans were ruthlessly honest in listing their occupations when an Address Table (the precursor to the modern telephone directory) was opened in 1889. Under occupation one wrote, "wanted to be a doorman but was too lazy"; another considered himself a "sponger," while a merchant's wife listed her job simply as "fulfilling wifely duties."[36]

In 1914 39 percent of Kiev's population was legally classified as *meshchane*, a category that included artisans, clerks, domestics, and a variety of other urban skills. This figure was very similar to that of 1845 (44 percent) and 1897 (40 percent).[37] Peasants comprised only 33 percent of Kiev's 1914 populace; they comprised at least 70 percent of more heavily industrialized Moscow, St. Petersburg, and Riga. Artisans could work anywhere, including factories, but in Kiev most worked independently or in small shops. Perhaps the most striking change came in the ethnic composition of the *meshchane*. In 1860 most were Russian or Ukrainian; by 1914 the group included thousands of Jews.

KIEV'S CHANGING ENVIRONMENT

The wonders of modern technology did not go unnoticed in Kiev. Great interest was created in 1887 when a local engineer built a model of an airplane; he died, impoverished, before his expectations for the craft could be realized. By 1914, however, Kievans were reading about Captain Nesterov, who had managed to fly from Kiev to Odessa in only three hours and eight minutes (8 1/2 hours was the record from Kiev to St. Petersburg). Nesterov also helped make aerial films of Kiev for use in the city's early film industry, which began around 1897. (The first cinema, Illiuziony, opened in the early 1900s.)[38] Automobiles were also making news. In 1914 an auto club, using Fords, Opels, and Mercedes, among other models, drove from Moscow to Kiev in sixteen hours, excluding stops. Officials in Kiev and Smolensk Provinces were quick to help the motorists, but the residents of Moscow Province were hostile, according to a newspaper report.[39]

Inside the city new modes of transportation also made their appearance. Horse-drawn trams were discussed as early as 1869 and finally introduced in 1890. Russia's first electric streetcar began to operate from the Podol along the Kreshchatik in 1892, despite the protestation of councilman Dobrynin, himself an engineer, that electricity could pull nothing more than a toy carriage. In 1911 a private bus company was permitted to open eight lines to compete with the notorious "murder-buses," Kiev's carts and carriages whose drivers' "slovenly appearance and insufferable insolence" had long been a scandal. ("They're the talk of the town: one uses them only in cases of extreme need," it had been noted as early as mid-century.)[40] The council also permitted motorized taxis and required older carriages to add roofs and rubber tires in 1913. Meters were installed, ending the age-old practice of haggling over fares. These measures were designed to curb wear and tear on local bridges, always a budgetary burden in ravine-filled Kiev, reduce noise, which was said to be harmful to those with nervous disorders, and assuage midwives, who were convinced, reformers noted, "that a great many female ailments are caused by walking along rutted bridges."[41]

Kerosene streetlamps made their appearance in 1869, and the hazardous practice of igniting wooden splinters for lighting became less common. Gaslights appeared on the Kreshchatik in 1872, and electric streetlights began to be installed around 1900.[42] Kiev's council remained reluctant to utilize the great income potential of electricity and motorized transport, however, and the city continued to rank among the slowest of Russia's cities to develop a substantial sector of city-run, revenue-producing services and utilities.

The poor quality and, at times, inadequate quantity of water contributed to public health problems in Kiev right up to the Revolutions of 1917, and probably beyond. Cholera, transmitted through impure water and improper sanitation, made at least eleven appearances between its first recorded visit in 1830 and 1872, killing up to 15 percent of the urban population during particularly severe epidemics.[43] The crowded, sometimes flooded, Podol was often hard-hit, as were the poorer districts throughout the city. During the outbreak of 1830–31, Kievans were warned by their dutiful, if puzzled, Military Governor not to eat plums, cherries, gooseberries, or virtually any fruit, especially if it was spoiled or unripe. Mulberries were said to be especially dangerous, and mushrooms were also to be avoided. Police were instructed to check the markets for spoiled or unripe fruit, and Kievans were cautioned, more wisely than anyone realized, to drink only vodka, tea, or *sbeeten* (a drink made of boiled water, honey, and spices), but not water, especially after eating fruit or salted fish.[44]

Underground wooden pipes had been laid as early as the 1770s, though most Kievans continued to rely on wells. Rapid population growth forced the city to begin to draw water from the Dnepr in 1871, but in the 1880s water sellers were still common on Kiev's streets, partly because of an inadequate number of taps accessible to the public.[45]

In the 1890s, the city battled with the privately owned water company over rates, extension of service, and the need for new filters. The battles continued into the twentieth century, until a cholera epidemic in 1907, which produced 1,091 confirmed cases and 389 deaths, forced the city to shut the system down and rely on artesian wells. Complaints about shortages flowed into city hall almost daily, but the council refused to approve proposals to build a new pumping station, extend the system to the city's outskirts, or even make a detailed study of the potential of the network of artesian wells which reportedly stretched into Voronezh Province. In 1914 at least 2,900 of Kiev's 7,000 homes lacked piped water; some schools had no water at all and had to close temporarily.

Finally, on March 20, 1914, the council formally agreed that a shortage existed and resolved to buy the water company. It did not act on another proposal to build an auxiliary system which would pump water from the Dnepr for fire protection and sanitary use. Paris and Vienna had built similar systems, encouraging one Kievan to note sourly that although "Kiev is certainly not Vienna, its inhabitants do want water."[46]

Inaction on the critical issue of water resulted from many factors, but two predominated. First, many property owners who sat on the council preferred cheap water to pure water; one particularly conservative and powerful faction signed the initial contract tying the city's hands to the advantage of the water company. When the contract came up for renewal in 1895, instead of addressing the issues of quality and quantity, it extended the contract in return for a 33 percent reduction in rates.[47]

Second, those hurt most from shortages, high rates, and poor quality lived in "the desperate outskirts" and had virtually no representatives on the council. Here water carriers plied their trade, sometimes at prices eight times higher than the price of tap water in the central districts.[48] Area residents hence used river water or water that accumulated in pools or ravines. Cholera epidemics often started in these neighborhoods.

Progress was made in other areas of public health, though at a slow pace. In the 1880s pig-breeding was still common in Kiev, and cattle were slaughtered throughout the city. Animal aromas blended with stagnant water and waste-filled ravines to befoul the air. Dogs roamed by the thousands, finally forcing authorities to hire a dog-warden; in his first week on the job alone, he killed 500 itinerant canines. Only two sanitary inspectors, each with advisory authority only, worked for the city at this time. Starozhil recalls that hygienic standards were enforced mainly when city officials heard reports of epidemics elsewhere in Russia and feared they might spread to Kiev.[49]

In 1894 a sewage system was built by a private concessionaire. In 1909 the city council municipalized the system and announced that "the whole city now has sewers."[50] By this it meant the historic districts, such as the Podol and Staryi Kiev, and affluent new districts such as Dvortsovaia. Shuliavka, Solomenka, and other outlying areas, it seems, were only peripherally regarded as part of the city. The council applied for loans to extend the system, but newspaper reports from 1914 indicate that Kiev was still dumping untreated sewage into inlets in the outskirts, and in turn was being sued by residents there.

Public health issues thus remained major and only partly resolved concerns right up to 1917. Kiev did have a large number of doctors compared with other Russian cities: one per 701 inhabitants in 1904. Khar'kov had one per 521, Moscow and Odessa one per 837, Riga one per 896, Nikolaev one per 1,375, Saratov one per 2,082, nearby Zhitomir one per 3,175, Baku one per 3,546, and Samarkand one per 16,340.[51] Merchant E. G. Popov opened an eye clinic in 1887 which utilized the services of university medical Professor Karavaev and became regionally renowned. Eye disease was particularly rampant in the city and the region. In the 1870s an estimated one-third of all Kievans suffered from venereal disease.[52] Blindness, one side effect of advanced syphilis, still accounted for 11 percent of all rejections for military service in Kiev

Province from 1905 through 1912.[53] But doctors and clinics could not do much to combat epidemics spawned by congested housing, foul water, and inadequate waste removal. Survival in Kiev depended somewhat upon where one lived. From 1895 to 1899, for example, Dvortsovaia had 490 deaths per 1,000 births, poorer Luk'ianovka 635, and outlying Demievka and Kurenevka 817 and 882 respectively.[54] Solomenka, a hilly, ravine-filled area annexed by Kiev in 1910, had but two streets that were passable year-round. Solomenka's garbage was collected only in summer and winter, and at high cost. Waste and water filled its ravines. In 1913 its 30,000 inhabitants still had no doctor, hospital, or organized medical services. Three schools served only 350 children. "Hooligans" roamed the unlit streets, and after 9:00 P.M., "life on the streets stood still."[55] In Shuliavka, partly annexed to the city and the site of Greter & Krivanek, other large factories, and the Kiev Soviet in 1905, angry residents complained about the absence of schools, streetlights, medical facilities, and decent water. Epidemics brought this anger to a boil. Asked one resident in an open and rhetorical letter during the cholera epidemic of 1907: "Do the authorities even know where Shuliavka is?"[56]

MULTINATIONAL KIEV

Booming Kiev had its exotic elements. The flamboyant and despotic millionaire I. A. Tolli, who became mayor in 1884, was the son of Greeks who had migrated to Odessa during the reign of Catherine II (1762–1796). Stundists, some from Austria, established a flourishing community in Demievka. Preaching the virtues of baptism, they worked the markets of the Podol, converting many peasants and stirring up many controversies.[57] A May 4, 1914, issue of *Kievskaia mysl'* (Kievan Thought) described some 200 pigtailed, "smiling" Chinese who periodically came to the city to peddle silk, shawls, and trinkets on its street corners. The city directory records a "Gypsy Alley" in Ploskaia, indicating the probability of a gypsy encampment somewhere close. But Kiev was mainly a city of four national groups, whose numbers are listed in Table 4.2.

Among the most interesting generalizations that can be drawn from the data is that Kiev had become one of Russia's most important centers of Jewish life, even though it was not formally part of the Pale of Settlement, the surrounding territory that stretched from the Empire's Polish and Lithuanian lands through much of the Ukraine where Jews had been required to live. By January 1914 there were 81,250 Jews officially in Kiev, and probably hundreds of others who had escaped detection. Jews, in fact, had come to outnumber Ukrainians, if the size of the latter group is measured by language usage. Judeophobia became a

TABLE 4.2

National Groups in Kiev, 1874–1917

	March 2, 1874		Jan. 28, 1897		Sept. 11–16, 1917	
	N	%	N	%	N	%
Ukrainians	38,533	30.3	54,673	22.1	76,792	16.7
Russians	58,173	45.7	130,931	52.9	231,403	50.3
Poles	7,863	6.2	16,579	6.7	42,821	9.3
Jews	13,803	10.9	32,093	13.0	87,246	19.0

SOURCE: M. V. Ptukha, *Naselenie Kievskoi gubernii* (Kiev, 1925), table 13.

central issue in city politics, though after 1892 Jews could not vote and none, to my knowledge, served on the city council. In 1881, 1904, and 1905, communal relations were deeply scarred by pogroms.

Jewish settlement in Kiev goes back at least to 1794. In 1809 there were twenty-five households with 452 members in the city. Many were apparently coppersmiths. Settlement was banned in 1827, as were traditional clothing and customs such as the shaving of the bride's head upon marriage, but Jews could circumvent these prohibitions by paying special taxes.[58]

Beginning in 1856 Alexander II provided opportunities for prominent Jewish merchants, artisans, and university graduates to live and trade outside of the Pale. Kiev's Jewish community grew accordingly, and in the 1880s, if not earlier, ran its own postal service (with branches in Zhitomir, Berdichev, and other nearby towns), until state officials, jealous of its success, shut it down.[59] A court ruling permitted the most prosperous (first guild) Jews to buy property anywhere in Russia; Kiev's Jews thus moved about the city, settling even in fashionable Dvortsovaia. City directories indicate that by 1900 Jews owned homes and shops along the Kreshchatik,[60] while property tax rolls for 1913 reveal that at least 521 Jews were members of the city's economic elite.

Most of Kiev's Jews were, of course, not affluent. Most were artisans and peddlers whose commercial endeavors lent "a certain feverish vitality, running, bustling, making deals, accompanying each word with rapid gestures; everywhere, their quick, guttural speech; everywhere, with each step, they stop visitors with offers of goods."[61] On Aleksandrov Street, in the garment district that grew in the Podol, Jewish traders so aggressively wooed potential customers that it took a "special heroism" to wander down the street.[62] Ploskaia also had many Jews, but by 1900 Lybed District seemed to be the center of Jewish life in the city. Lybed grew by 155 percent from 1896 to 1912 (compared with 106 percent for Kiev as a whole), at least in part because of an ongoing flow of migrants from the desperate quarters of the Pale.[63]

Few of these Jews could feel secure about their residence in Kiev. The May Laws of 1882 initiated a long series of often ambiguous and conflicting decrees and judicial "clarifications" which were intended to restrict as many Jews as possible to the Pale. Interpretation and enforcement of this morass of regulations fell mainly upon the local police. Thus, Kiev's memoirist Starozhil recalls that bribery and payoffs became "the main source" of income for many a police official who had the power to determine which Jews could buy a place in one of Kiev's schools, or a permit to ply their trades. Police chief Mastitskii enforced the regulations strictly in 1882, and allowed only 3,263 Jews to remain in the city. By 1887, under the less scrupulous Zhivogliadov, some 16,000 Jews had managed to earn or purchase a residence permit. At the precinct level, some officials "lived honestly, strictly from their salaries," while others preyed on Jews. Captain Mikhailov "believed in equality." From Jews he extracted money, while on market day he confiscated goods of all kinds from Russian and Ukrainian traders until he could find no more room in his carriage. Equality earned the brazen Mikhailov a conviction in court. A certain Zbarskii, himself a Jew, was hired to search the Pale for Jews who were willing and able to buy their way into Kiev. Meanwhile street policeman sought assignments in Jewish neighborhoods, where the potential for income was high. Some extracted money from Jews "to protect" their thatched roofs from catching on fire.[64] The attitudes and character of the city police thus determined which Jews could live in Kiev and under what terms. As the War approached police were cracking down. *Kievskaia mysl'* reported "nightly round-ups" and noted that at least 30,000 Jews were being threatened with expulsion, including many who had been in the city for decades.[65]

Communal relations in Kiev were apparently peaceful: the only pogroms prior to 1881 occurred in Odessa. But in 1881, after the assassination of Alexander II, some 225 pogroms left an estimated 20,000 Jews homeless throughout Russia. In Kiev an undetermined number of Jews were victimized by crowds estimated at 4,000.[66]

In September and October 1904, anxious soldiers awaiting departure for the Japanese front perpetrated violence against Kiev's Jews. In July 1905 100 Kievan Jews were killed, 406 were injured, and 100 homes were looted. A three-day pogrom at the end of October caused at least sixty deaths and 369 injuries. Some 7,000 families were affected, and at least 2,000 shops were looted. In Odessa the conflict was worse: reports vary, but 500 to 800 were killed and 5,000 wounded there. In both cities Jewish defense leagues, probably composed largely of students and youths, acted heroically. In Kiev most of the casualties were members of the defense organizations. In Zhitomir Jewish self-defense was so active that the number of Christian deaths exceeded the number of Jewish deaths.[67]

The details of these pogroms are very scarce. Vasilkovskaia, a neighborhood in Lybed District, was certainly one area where tensions were high. The horrible screams of this area's pogrom victims haunted the memories of Paustovsky years later. There were actually two Vasilkovskaia streets in Kiev. Little (Malo-) Vasilkovskaia was the site of the city's synagogue. Big (Bolshaia) Vasilkovskaia began to develop in the 1830s as an extension of the Kreshchatik. It was still unpaved in the 1890s. A sanitary doctor discovered thirty-two people, twenty-six of them teenagers, living in a single room at the Val'ker Machineshop on Bolshaia Vasilkovskaia in 1878; in 1902, 1,400 copies of the illegal Bolshevik newspaper *Iskra* were seized in one of the street's warehouses.[68] Additional information about the area is hard to find, but it would seem that Vasilkovskaia, with its synagogue, was the center of Jewish communal life in Kiev, and that surrounding Lybed District housed large numbers of Jews, many of them poor and some of them active, no doubt, in revolutionary causes.

In many cities police and soldiers joined the pogromists. Kiev's police were allegedly told in 1905 that they could beat up Jews but could not plunder their shops.[69] Recent arrivals from the countryside no doubt retained the traditional view of the Jew as a moneylender, land-leaser, vodka-seller, exploiter. Trotsky describes the pogrom crowd as the "small shopkeepers and ragamuffins . . . the professional thief and the amateur robber, the small artisan and the brothel doorman, the hungry and ignorant *muzhik* (peasant) and the one who just yesterday left the village for the deafening din of the factory machine."[70] Apartment-building doormen pointed out Jewish flats, and there were plenty of "Black Hundred" organizers who could incite the crowd. When Prime Minister P. A. Stolypin was assassinated in Kiev in 1911, Black Hundreds called for pogroms, but none occurred, probably because Nicholas II was visiting the city. In Kiev a group of nationalist hooligans called "Two-Headed Eagle" seemed the most willing to perpetrate violence. Mainly youths, some of whom wore their school uniforms while commiting acts of terror, they followed V. S. Golubev under whose leadership "everything was permitted."[71] Kiev's nationalist newspaper, *Kievlianin* (Kievan), identified the Jews as the enemies of Christ and Tsar. In Zhitomir photographs of intended victims were carried by pogromists, indicating that within the mob there were organized elements. Whatever the details, the images left by Paustovsky of a Kiev pogrom are chilling:

I . . . suddenly froze—from far away in the direction of Vassilkovskaya [sic] Street, pouring over the whole city closer and closer . . . came a many-voiced scream of terror, the death cry of a large number of people. You could not hear a single separate voice. . . .

The ring of these pogroms had been tightening around Kiev and finally . . . the first night pogrom began on Vassilkovskaya Street. The thugs surrounded one of the big buildings but did not succeed in breaking into it. In the dark, quiet building, shattering the evil silence of the night, a woman screamed, piercingly, in terror and despair. She had no other way to defend her children—nothing but this unbroken, unwavering shriek of fear and helplessness.

Suddenly the woman's single scream was answered by an exactly similar cry from the whole building, all the way from the ground floor to the roof. The thugs could not stand it, and started to run. But there was no place for them to hide; outstripping them, all the buildings along Vassilkovskaya Street were now screaming, and all along the little lanes which led away from it.

The cry grew like the wind, covering block after block. The most frightening thing about it was that it was coming from dark buildings, which seemed uninhabited, and that the streets were all deserted and dead with nothing but an occasional dull street lamp seeming to light the way for the quivering, wailing scream. . . .

. . . By now Podol was screaming, and Bessarabka, and the whole enormous city. The cry must have been heard far beyond the city limits . . . a cry for mercy and compassion. . . .

I had heard individuals cry in fear, and even crowds of people, but never before had I heard an entire city cry.[72]

Polish influence in Kiev was particularly strong between the Union of Lublin in 1569 and the uprisings of 1648–54. Polish influence in the surrounding provinces of the right-bank Ukraine remained strong even under Russian rule, for Poles owned much of the land and many of the food-processing industries. As late as 1910 perhaps 40 percent of all Ukrainian sugar refineries were owned by Poles.[73]

In the nineteenth century many of Kiev's Poles were wealthy and influential "members of the privileged classes."[74] The sugar magnate Branicki lived in Kiev, and the city's largest brewery was owned by a Pole. Table 4.3 shows that in 1913 nearly 10 percent of Kiev's property-owning elite were Poles.

In the 1850s Kiev was the major center of the Polish national movement that culminated in revolt against Russian rule in 1863. More than half of the students at St. Vladimir University from 1834 to 1863 were Poles.[76] The University was closed for a year in 1839 after unrest followed the execution of Polish nationalist Szymon Konarski in Vil'na. In the 1850s a nationalist organization called Trinity emerged among Kiev's Polish students. It established contact with other Poles within and outside the Empire and by 1859 helped ignite the simmering discon-

TABLE 4.3

Ownership of Income-Producing Property in Kiev, 1913

Assessment	Total	Orthodox	German	Polish	Jewish	Armenian-Tatar	Other
Below 1,500 rubles	4,372	4,022	48	209	69	3	21
Above 1,500 rubles	4,916	3,730	157	474	521	1	33

SOURCE: Tsentral'nyi gosudarstvennyi istoricheskii arkhiv Leningrada, fond 1288, opis 5, delo 170 (1914), list 130. "Orthodox" includes Russians and Ukrainians. 1,500 rubles of assessment was the cut-off point for voting eligibility in city elections for the non-Jewish property owners.

tentment in Warsaw. Several poorly armed detachments of Poles left Kiev to fight in 1863; at least forty were killed.[77] After the insurrection was crushed, Kiev's importance as a center of Polish nationalism declined sharply. Warsaw's "Main School" became a university in 1869, and by the 1870s less than one-fifth of the 800 students at Kiev's university were Poles.

By 1897 half of Kiev's Poles were employed in manufacturing, day labor, or the service trades, and about 10 percent were merchants and traders. From 17,000 in 1897, the number of Poles grew to an estimated 60,000 by 1914.[78] About 5,000 lived in the Podol, and plans were being made to build a second Catholic church there. The existence of some twenty-five city affiliates of the Polish youth movement in the 1890s and three Polish newspapers (one a trade union paper) by 1905 indicates that Kiev's Poles maintained a high level of cultural awareness and political activism.[79] Spoken Polish may have lost some of its purity in the city, however. While in Poland during the First World War, Paustovsky recalled "that frightful Polish-Russian-Ukrainian jargon which we in Kiev used to think was the Polish language."[80]

Not surprisingly, Polonophobia continued to be a major element in the municipal politics of Kiev right up to the Revolutions of 1917. The Nationalist Party, led by State Duma delegate A. I. Savenko, made particularly vitriolic anti-Polish statements. It was rabidly anti-Semitic as well, and undoubtedly raged against Ukrainian nationalism, though I could find no particular instances of this in my study of Kiev's 1910 municipal election. Many factors probably contributed to Polonophobia in Kiev: the wealth of many local Poles; competition for jobs with a rapidly growing number of Polish migrants; the activism of the city's Polish community in the 1863 revolt and of the Polish Social Democrats in the turbulence of 1905. Unlike the Jews, who were disenfranchised in 1892, property-owning Poles could vote. They comprised about 10 percent of Kiev's electorate, enough to swing a close vote away from the Nationalists who sought to control the city council. Poles had done just that in a 1914 election in Zhitomir, though state officials, disturbed by the outcome of the election, overturned its results on a technicality. Kiev differed from Minsk and Vil'na, however, in that Poles controlled *most* of the property, and hence the electorates, in the latter cities. In Minsk, where Russians outnumbered Poles two to one in the general populace, Polish control of the council led some Russians to boycott city elections.[81] It is worth noting, too, that Polonophobia in Kiev may have resulted simply from the general fear of Polish nationalism in a vulnerable multinational Empire and of alleged Habsburg designs on the Ukraine, concern over which was often expressed in Russian nationalist circles, rather than from local conflicts.

Kiev's location in the Ukraine (2,819,000 Ukrainians lived in Kiev Province alone in 1897)[82] makes the small number of Ukrainians in the city's population and the decline of Ukrainians in total city population from 30 percent in 1874 to 17 percent in 1917 surprising. Many Ukrainian peasants who moved to Kiev probably learned to speak Russian (a language that after all is very close to Ukrainian) and counted themselves or were counted as Russians in the census. Russian was the language of Kiev's administration, industry, schools, and undoubtedly much of its commerce. Ukrainian was banned in the schools in 1876, and even original Ukrainian literary works had to use the Russian orthography. One can draw a parallel with Lemberg (Lvov, Lviv), the urban center for the Habsburg Province of Galicia, which had many Ukrainians. Poles predominated in Lvov, and even though the city was the most important center of the Ukrainian national movement at that time, more than half of Lvov's ethnic Ukrainians were linguistically Polonized in 1890, and in 1900 barely 5 percent of its artisans declared Ukrainian to be their language of intercourse.[83]

Kiev did become an important center for the study of the Ukrainian heritage, however. At St. Vladimir University, historians V. B. Antonovich (1830–1908) and V. S. Ikonnikov (1841–1923) aided the Ukrainian movement by lecturing and publishing widely on the region's heritage. M. S. Hrushevskyi, perhaps the best-known national historian of the Ukraine, studied under Antonovich at St. Vladimir. M. Dragomanov helped pioneer the study of Ukrainian literature, and P. I. Zhitetskii (1836–1911) helped lay the foundation for the scholarly study of the Ukrainian language.[84] Hromada, an organization dedicated to promoting the Ukrainian heritage, was active in Kiev, and while Ukrainian-language publications were banned after the Polish Revolt of 1863, Hromada helped establish a press "if not Ukrainian in language, then at least Ukrainian in spirit."[85] *Kievskii telegraf* (Kiev's Telegraph, 1859–76) and *Kievskaia starina* (Kievan Antiquities, 1882–1907) were the most important products of this effort. The Kiev Historical Society and the Southwest Branch of the Russian Geographical Society, some members of which were associated with Hromada, pursued a variety of studies, and the latter conducted the 1874 census in the city. In 1906 Ukrainian-language publications again began to appear in Kiev, though they were far more prominent in Lvov and abroad. Of the 141 Ukrainian-language periodicals published in the world in 1913, only nineteen originated in the Russian Empire.[86]

Despite restrictions Ukrainian theater achieved great success in Kiev and elsewhere. In fostering awareness of Ukrainian identity, it "came to take the place of books in serving the masses."[87] The efforts of M. L. Kropivnitskii, a Ukrainian actor, playwright, and director, are particularly notable here. Kropivnitskii's troupe drew praise even from the Russian nationalist paper *Kievlianin*, though it was not allowed to perform in Kiev between 1883 and 1895.[88]

On February 25, 1914, the hundredth anniversary of the birth of

T. G. Shevchenko (1814–61), Ukrainian poet, artist, social critic, and nationalist, Kiev's students managed to all but close down the city's higher educational institutions and stage a series of demonstrations despite an official ban. Ukrainian shops closed on this day, *Kievskaia mysl'* reported. The demonstrations brought out Cossack reinforcements and the extremist Two-Headed Eagle rowdies, who proceeded to tear down portraits of Shevchenko, harass demonstrators, and embark upon several days of window-smashing and general vandalism. Otherwise, Kiev's demonstrations were peaceful, and *Kievskaia mysl'* branded as lies reports in St. Petersburg's *Novoe vremia* that half of the city's demonstrators had been Jews, that red flags had been unfurled, and that crowds had marched to the Austrian Consulate shouting "Long live Austria; down with Russia!"[89] Students, of course, were notorious demonstrators, and it is difficult to draw conclusions about the depth of Ukrainian national sentiment in the city from this event. Ukrainian issues did not seem to be a factor in the city election of 1910, which was otherwise characterized by vitriolic attacks by the Nationalist Party against Poles and Jews. The staid city council could not have been too worried about the memory of Shevchenko, for it named a street after him, pending approval from the Ministry of the Interior, though it did make clear that it was honoring Shevchenko as an artist and not as a politician. In sum Ukrainian sentiment seemed to be a small but growing part of Kiev's political scene, but not a major source of conflict in the city.

MUNICIPAL POLITICS IN LATE IMPERIAL KIEV

The 1870 Municipal Statute gave substantial authority to the city council even though only 3 percent of Kiev's citizens could vote or serve on it. The 1892 "counterreform" brought the council more firmly under state control and further reduced the electorate to a handful of owners of income-producing properties. In 1910 about 5 percent of Kiev's merchants could vote, and in all 3,757 could participate in city affairs, about 1 percent of the total population.[90]

In Kiev ongoing problems with water dramatized the shortcomings of the system. In 1910, for example, another cholera epidemic claimed as many victims as had mid–nineteenth century epidemics.[91] The outlying neighborhoods were particularly vulnerable, but epidemics threatened all Kievans, and thus brought many highly educated voters into local politics. Noting this trend, Ekaterinoslav's newspaper, *Iuzhnaia zaria* (The Dawn of the South), asserted that "times had changed" in Russia's south.[92]

Ekaterinoslav elected forty-two councilmen (in a seventy-two-man council) in 1913 with at least some higher education. There, and in Khar'kov, where one voter sourly accused reformers of "thinking Khar'-kov could be turned into Paris," and in Kiev, poorly educated and demagogic councilmen, often from the extremist Nationalist Party or the Union of Russian People, went down to defeat. At least after 1905 doctors, engineers, and other *intelligenty* seemed to take a more active role in city affairs, perhaps in response to the revolutionary upheavals of that year.[93] The majority of Kiev's council which sat from 1906 until 1910 appeared to be led by professional people, and certainly was re-form-oriented. Though the coalition published a lengthy booklet during the 1910 election listing its developmental accomplishments, it did not identify the names or professions of its members. (Most of the candidates no doubt were well known to the small electorate.) Labelled "Kadets and Polish hirelings" by the local Nationalist Party, this coalition was said to be closest politically to the moderately conservative Octobrist Party.[94]

The main opposition came from the Nationalists, who claimed to represent "the simple people." They raged against "the *intelligenty*," and included no professional people in their slate of candidates. They managed, illegally, to disenfranchise voters who represented firms with Jewish or foreign stockholders. In 1910 their attacks against Jews and Poles were so vitriolic, they divided the Party. Many Nationalists were defeated, and the city's major progressive newspaper, *Kievskaia mysl'*, suggested that Kiev's voters had been frightened by the example of Odessa, where General Tolmachev's right-wing clique had openly terrorized voters. Odessa generally had a bad reputation among municipal progressives, and many a commentator spoke of "Odessa morals" and warned that businesses were leaving the plague-ridden, extremist-dominated city, which could no longer call itself "the Palmyra of the south."[95]

The 1910 council did have its share of extremists, of course. And it had its share of eccentrics. Nationalist F. G. Ditiatin, known as the Great Silent One, asked for the floor only once in ten years. Given the floor, he said only, "I refuse to speak." Absenteeism was also a problem. Lack of a quorum cancelled forty-one of the scheduled 100 council sessions in 1913. Nationalist N. I. Chokolov missed 314 of the 367 sessions during the previous term. "I couldn't work with the Kadets," he explained.[96]

But Kiev also had a long-time, widely respected mayor, I. N. D'iakov, who was so conscientious that he reportedly refused to cut off debate on the council floor even after receiving reports that his house was on fire.[97] The tough-minded activist D'iakov had an interesting and appropriate connection to Gustav Eisman, Kiev's strong-willed mayor from 1879 to 1884. If Louis XIV could claim, "I am the state," Eisman could claim, "I am the council," recalled one memoirist. Eisman had refused to allow his only daughter to marry a certain officer, fearing that he sought only her money. They married secretly, and when his daughter died a year later in childbirth, her distraught husband threw himself from Kiev's chain-bridge into the Dnepr. Thus convinced that the marriage had indeed been one of love, the elder Eisman showered his affections on the surviving granddaughter, who grew up to become the wife of D'iakov.[98]

Thanks to the efforts of D'iakov and others, great advances were made in many areas, including school construction and public transport. But as the water controversy indicates, the city's reluctance to municipalize utilities and services, or establish new ones, remained a major shortcoming. Kiev did take over its sewer system in 1909. It opened a slaughterhouse and a pharmacy, which made medicines available at lower cost. But in 1915 it still had no city-run bank, electric plant, gasworks, pawnshop, or transit system. While renegotiating its contract with the privately owned electric utility, it discovered shortages of 660,000 rubles over the previous decade, which implied corruption, inadequate auditing, or both. Said one local news reporter: "The city economy is run behind closed doors."[99]

In 1904 Kiev's per capita spending was calculated at 9.5 rubles, about the same as Odessa's (11.2), Khar'kov's (10.3), and Saratov's (8.6), though well behind Warsaw's (25.5) and Moscow's (17.5). By 1910 Kiev's per capita expenditures had fallen to 6.5 rubles, about half that of Odessa, Khar'kov, Saratov, or Baku, and less than one-third that of Riga, Moscow, or St. Petersburg.[100] Riga (1913: 481,950), though smaller than Kiev, had a substantially greater budget, for it earned income from a variety of city-run enterprises, including a savings bank, two dairy farms, a river boat on the Dvina, several factories, and a gasworks.

Kiev's expenditures, which barely grew at all during the first half of the nineteenth century, grew by 5 1/2 times between 1867 and 1875, and doubled again by 1885. By 1897 the city spent 1.7 million rubles, by 1904, 3.1 million. But by 1914 its outlay of 5.6 million rubles capped a mere 85 percent growth for a decade (1904–1914) in which the population had doubled.[101] While Warsaw was collecting a million rubles annually from its streetcars, Kiev was earning a paltry 55,000 rubles. Warsaw earned two million rubles per year in water revenue, Kiev nothing until it municipalized its system in 1915. Kiev paid out 130,000 rubles to light its streets. Asiatic Astrakhan (1915: 164,000) earned 67,315 rubles in profit from its streetlights. Moscow derived about 20 percent of its budget from city utilities and enterprises, tiny Chernigov (1915: 38,000) about half of its, but prewar Kiev earned only 10 percent of its income from such endeavors.[102]

Thus, it is not difficult to understand why Kiev acquired a reputation for administrative indifference among Russia's municipal reformers. Low revenue from enterprises forced a greater reliance on property taxes, but here, too, Kiev's levy was well below that of Moscow's, Warsaw's, Riga's, or Odessa's.[103] Kiev spent but 260,079 rubles on public care in 1913, and much of this came from private bequests.[104] Even these funds were often handled with indifference. The council apparently forgot about a generous grant it had received in 1900 to build and endow a tuberculosis sanitorium until 1910, when a private philanthropic group finally demanded that the money be put to use.[105] City government tended to rely on a well-established tradition of generosity among local notables such as N. O. and E. G. Popov, whose clinic for eye surgery served 1,500 patients in its first year alone. Long noted for his stinginess and greed, merchant M. P. Dekhterev nevertheless bequeathed three million rubles to charity. The sugar-baron Tereshchenko and Brodskii families were well known for their bequests. Tereshchenko founded various schools, shelters, and a free hospital for day laborers in Shuliavka. The Demievka Refinery also had a small hospital for its workers. The fact that there were about 500 free hospital beds in the city no doubt eased the consciences of the 1906 council when it raised per diem rates in the city hospitals from 30 kopeks to 1.3 rubles.[106]

The council did decide in 1914 to establish a youth club for the poor and shelterless, despite claims that such clubs would only encourage drunkenness, but it relied on the private sector to run night shelters for adults. The shelters (popechitelstva) put under its charge in 1899 simply "vegetated" from inactivity, Kievskaia mysl' complained during the First World War. "Who even knows anything about them?" it inquired.[107] In general Russia's city councils represented the narrow interests of affluent property owners, most of whom lived in the advantaged central neighborhoods. They were underfinanced, and state officials often invalidated the election or appointment of social or political activists.[108] Still, many councils pursued developmental programs with great vigor. Kiev's council at times showed vigor, but overall it seemed less energetic and responsive to human needs than some other municipal councils. And, as was true throughout Russia, the comparatively prosperous central districts drew most of the developmental benefits while the needs of the poorer peripheral areas remained largely the concern of private charity.

LABOR CONFLICT IN KIEV

Nationalist demagoguery slowed developmental progress in Kiev, for the virulent anti-Semitic and Polonophobic diatribes of the Nationalist Party poisoned public debate, deflected attention from pressing issues such as water quality, and no doubt convinced many moderate Kievans to avoid city politics altogether. But aside from the pogroms, which were to some extent the products of nationalistic fervor, bloody manifestations of national friction were well contained by authorities after 1863. National tensions, in fact, came to be over-shadowed by another form of conflict, that between employer and employee.

Strikes did not become a common occurrence in Kiev until the mid-1890s. In 1867 railway workers demanded and won concessions on housing, medical care, and wages, but from the 1860s until 1894 there were only fifteen recorded strikes; from 1895 to 1899, there were twenty-seven.[109]

The best-organized and most militant of Kiev's workers were the employees of the railways and the South Russian and Greter & Krivanek machine works. They played leading roles in the "general strike" of July 1903, waged in sympathy with strikers in Baku and Odessa; an esti-mated 12,000 to 15,000 Kievans joined this strike. South Russian's workers were the first to walk out when news of Bloody Sunday reached the city in January 1905: about 6,000 Kievans joined this conflict, the opening round of a chaotic year. Rail workers struck in January and February, while workers shut down South Russian from February 10 until March 1. Employees of these large operations had security in numbers, and many were sufficiently skilled to make it difficult to fire and replace them on short notice. They were also the special targets of leftist agitators, and Soviet historians argue that the Bolsheviks came to win predominant influence among the workers in Kiev's machine and metallurgical sectors.[110]

Tobacco workers, angered by excessive amounts of dust in their mills and by low wages, long hours, and impolite treatment, were also quick to strike, but in general workers from the city's agricultural industries were relatively passive. At the Demievka sugar refinery, for example, where many workers were seasonal and some came from as far as Minsk and Mogilev Provinces, wages were very low, but workers struck infrequently and settled quickly when modest raises were offered.

Kiev's artisans often endured more onerous working conditions than their coworkers in the factories, since they generally worked in shops too small to warrant any kind of supervision. The city passed rules on mandatory rest periods and days off, but did not enforce them. Artisans did strike: bakers, for instance, waged a massive strike in 1900, but in early 1914 many were still working nineteen-hour days, about 60 percent even longer, many round-the-clock. Most lived at their place of work and slept on crates. Confectionery workers averaged eleven-hour days at this time, but half had no break and one-third worked more than twelve hours. The confectioners' union complained that its exhausted workers had been "turned into slaves."[111]

Tailors also struck: some sixty shops, most with three to eight workers, were closed down by strikers in 1901, who listed wages and eighteen-hour workdays as their main grievances. Jews were prominent in the garment industry (proclamations were published in Russian and Yiddish during this particular strike), and so were women. Some piece workers, presumably women who worked at home, also joined this strike, while carpenters, building-trades workers, butchers, and others who were not employed in Kiev's large factories joined the great strike of 1903 on its fifth day.[112] The Kuznetsov Match Works was probably typical of Kiev's smaller factories (or larger workshops). Its seventy employees included twenty-one men, fifteen women, fifteen teenagers, and nineteen juveniles. Only the men and six of the teenagers participated in a 1902 strike.[113]

Kiev's strikes turned out impressive numbers of participants, especially in 1903 and 1905. Low wages and poor employment conditions were the main grievances, and workers from the larger factories often won concessions. Major strikes usually came in response to events elsewhere, however—to strikes in Baku and Odessa in 1903, to Bloody Sunday in St. Petersburg in 1905, or to the shooting of the Lena Goldfield workers in 1912, for example. Sometimes "solidarity" also resulted from coercion. In October 1905, for example, bands of workers and students broke into shops and schools, forcing them to close.[114]

To what extent did Kiev's urban environment contribute to political and social conflict in the late Imperial period? The question is central to urban history, and it is very difficult to answer. Large cities attracted radical intellectuals and agitators. Small, clandestine circles made contact with Kiev's workers in the early 1870s in the factories, in the Podol, and in "the desperate outskirts." Notable here was the South Russian Workers Union, which had about ten organizers, most, if not all, of noble status; three from its ranks were women, and two of the men were ex-medical students from Khar'kov University. Around 1880 the group made contact with a few workers from the railyards and the Arsenal and quickly developed an active following of about 700 to 800 workers. They met secretly with groups of about 100 workers, every night, all night, in wooded areas outside of the city. These encounters served to bring revolutionary ideas to the factories and countered the influence of local priests, who claimed to have visionary contact with the Virgin Mary and who promised workers that "days of joy and justice" were just ahead.[115] Activist Elizaveta Koval'skaia recalls that revolutionary sentiments were strong among Kiev's laborers, but so were loyalties to the Tsar. Workers were encouraged to resist searches, fines, and beatings, and to demand that their dignity as human beings be respected. One demand made by the Union in 1880—that the Arsenal put a louder whistle on its roof so that workers could get to work on time—demonstrates that Kiev was growing and that it could no longer be assumed that workers lived in the immediate vicinity of the factories.[116]

Poor living conditions contributed to discontent, particularly when severe epidemics highlighted developmental shortcomings in Shuli-avka and other disadvantaged districts. Koval'skaia was shocked by living conditions "where it was difficult to move, to breathe"; one sample showed that two-thirds of Kiev's workers with families had their own flats, but six out of ten workers without families had less than a room to themselves.[117] Sometimes "company housing" brought objec-tions. Murashko's iconostasis workshop was struck in 1902 by its fifty-two workers who disliked the housing and the cold borshch he provided (payment for which was deducted from their wages).[118] High rents were the most burdensome problem related to housing, however, for most Kievans had to rely on the private sector to find a room or a corner of a room. The exceptional growth of the city sent rents upward. In 1904 a room in the outskirts could be rented for 25 rubles per year, a good room in the central districts for 100 rubles maximum. By 1912 rooms in outlying neighborhoods averaged 180 rubles, and even the most primitive cost 100. In the center, rooms were renting for 300 to 400 rubles.[119] *Kievskaia mysl'* noted that from 1900 to 1912 the number of available apartments grew only half as fast as the population, and that apartments renting in the cheapest categories constituted a smaller percentage of the total available in 1912 than in 1900.[120] High rents and crowded conditions were not as important as low wages and long work-ing hours in promoting strikes, but they were realities for many Kievans and sometimes were listed as grievances by strikers or petitioners to the city council.[121]

EDUCATION—FORMAL AND INFORMAL—AND THE PRESS

The contributions of the Monastery of the Caves to book pub-lishing in Russia and the Ukraine underscored the historic importance of Kiev as a center of learning. Beginning in the nineteenth century, Kiev became a center of secular learning and publishing as well. The most significant milestone in this process was the founding of St. Vladimir University in 1834, but the creation of an extensive network of elementary and secondary schools, literacy societies, and peoples' clubs greatly expanded literacy, broadened intellectual horizons, and nur-tured a variety of political challenges to the regime.

In 1848 Kiev had only three primary schools; it had no public library (until 1866) and only two bookshops. By 1874 there were at least thirty-seven primary schools, by 1908 at least sixty-one. The city's first trade

school opened in 1870 to provide skilled workers for the building of the
Kiev-Odessa Railroad, and a variety of other secondary schools, including the first *gymnasium* for women, opened during that decade. By 1917
there were at least fifteen secondary schools with 1,362 male and 890
female students.[122] In 1910 about half of Kiev's 25,000 school-age youths
remained out of school, though only 1,180 were denied enrollment
because of lack of space. Many of the unschooled were apprentices (who
spent their days running after supplies and vodka and who were often
abused by supervisors, according to the local press).[123]

In 1913 there were as many university-level students in Kiev—
15,000 distributed among eight institutions—as there were workers in
factories and railyards subject to inspection by state officials. The Kiev
Polytechnical Institute (1901 enrollment: 1,050), founded in Shuliavka
in 1898, and St. Vladimir University, which grew from a few dozen
students in 1834 to 5,000 in 1914, seemed to have the greatest number of
politically active students.

Before the Polish Revolt of 1863, a majority of St. Vladimir's students were sons of noblemen (61 percent in 1861), and most were Poles.
By 1878–79 nobility (*dvoriane*) accounted for only 22 percent of the
students, many of whom were receiving financial assistance. Of 805
students, 593 were said to be Orthodox (the category for Russians and
Ukrainians), 136 Catholic (almost all Poles), and seventy-six Jewish. St.
Vladimir had notable scholars in many fields, but medicine was the
most prominent: its faculty enrolled about two-thirds of the students in
the late nineteenth century.[124]

After Polish national ferment closed the University temporarily in
1839, standards of "proper behavior" were enforced with great vigor.
Dancing and gymnastics were included in the regimen, and the halls
came to "resound with the war-like cries of the always-drunk watch-
man—'rompez!'—and the tinkling of swords and sabres."[125] Meanwhile,
Governor-General Bibikov cruised about the city with two Cossacks in
search of students not properly attired in frock coats or found to have
buttons missing. Curfews were imposed and students were banned from
Kiev's taverns.

Nevertheless, duels and orgies remained much in style; one writer
poetically recalled student activities in the 1850s:[126]

> I remember sometimes
> Merchants calling me at midnight
> Wanting to beat me up.
> But I beat the hell out of one,
> and cracked open another with a bottle.
> Like a madman, he staggered for a long time.
> I returned home, beaten but triumphant.

Recalled another about St. Vladimir in the 1850s:

> The Poles were slim and gracious, dandies with their cocked hats, thin, turned-up mustaches, and self-assured gait. The Jews, sharply featured, moved quickly and stuck closely together. They spoke quietly, but with animated gestures. Some were from wealthy homes in Odessa, and wore massive golden chains; their Russian accent was so distinct, it offended one's ears. The Little Russians (Ukrainians) were hefty, well-built, strongly featured people who spoke in loud, animated, national speech. They laughed loudly, were a bit rude, even cynical. There were only a few Russians, and they kept to the background. Poles predominated, then Little Russians, then Jews. The predominant language was Polish. Many students from all groups were well-washed and slicked-down aristocrats with English hair-dos, narrow and stylish pants, and French accents. Exactly opposite was the democratic element, well-tanned, with shabby suits and old hats and without gloves. The seminary students were a different breed. They were serious, austere, and kept to themselves.[127]

By the end of the nineteenth century, students were demanding an end to punishment cells and arbitrary suspension, greater democratization of admissions, and autonomy for the universities. The state responded by passing the "Temporary Rules" of July 29, 1899, which permitted the drafting of disruptive students into the army. In 1901, 183 students from St. Vladimir were conscripted for one- to three-year terms after a student strike.

The importance of the educational sector in promoting political change in Kiev is perhaps best illustrated by noting that the city's first Marxist circle was formed at the University (in 1889). Police frequently identified various students as local agitators. Medical student N. N. Konopatskii, for instance, helped organize a walkout at the Demievka Refinery in 1905. Autonomy was granted the universities in August 1905, and both the University and the Polytechnical Institute became "main hotbeds of disorder," according to police reports, a pattern that could also be found in Moscow and other cities. They were organizing centers of the stormy protests of October 1905, the scope and intensity of which convinced Nicholas II to make his historic concessions that included Russia's first modern parliament (duma). Crowds as large as 10,000 assembled at St. Vladimir, while the Kiev Soviet used the Polytechnical Institute as its headquarters. Students continued to make their voices heard in 1906; in October of that year, 2,500 of them struck to honor those who had been killed a year earlier. Finally, during the crackdown of 1907, 800 were suspended and many were banished from the city after protests followed government edicts curtailing the right of assembly and restricting university autonomy.[128]

Kiev's students brought an intellectual vitality to the city, an awareness of alternative world views that helped break down parochialism and ignorance. Many were active organizers. Professors, too, helped organize and educate beyond the confines of the schools. Medical professor N. A. Khrzhonshchevskii lectured widely on health and medicine and helped sponsor the semilegal Committee for a Reading Public (1882–1901). In 1901 it was given legal status as the Society to Assist Primary Education. Before his exile, political economist N. I. Ziber (1844–88) helped popularize the economic ideas of Karl Marx.[129] Along with Antonovich, Ikonnikov, and others involved in Ukrainian studies, such men opened vistas, provoked debate, challenged tradition, and helped prepare the populace for the variety of social and political alternatives that would suddenly emerge in 1917.

The impact of the informal educational and cultural organizations is difficult to measure, but clearly they disseminated ideas in a manner that came to threaten the regime. The Kiev City Directory for 1902 reveals that the city had at least three Sunday schools (which provided free training in reading, writing, and mathematics and free books and supplies for males over twelve), and five literacy schools for both sexes. The Kiev Sobriety Society ran evening classes or reading rooms in twenty locations throughout the city. The popularity of such organizations can be seen in the fact that the Committee for a Reading Public drew 160,000 people to 700 lectures between 1882 and 1900.[130]

To celebrate the anniversary of Pushkin's birth in 1899, the Literacy, Sobriety, and other societies founded the Troitskii People's Club. Completed in 1902, it contained a thousand-seat auditorium, reading rooms and lecture halls, a center for the free distribution of books to the city's literacy schools, a children's museum, and an inexpensive tearoom for workers. Union officials established an office in the Club which provided free legal advice. During its first year of operation, the library and reading rooms drew 80,000 visitors. In 1903–1904, sixty-seven lectures drew an average audience of 200 people.[131]

While the specific role of the Troitskii Club in the strikes and upheavals of 1903 and 1905 is not clear, the government found it and similar places threatening. In 1908 the Literacy Society was closed, and the city took over the Troitskii Club. The reading rooms were closed; the library was closed for four years, then reopened on a paying basis. Office space was leased (to the city sewer commission, for example) to make the building profitable. The Sobriety Society's tearoom was turned into a bar. Aware that peoples' clubs and philanthropic societies often broadened intellectual horizons and helped articulate demands for change, the government carefully curbed their activities after 1905. Thus, in 1913 for example, the 151-member Kiev Society for Self-Education held meetings, but had no members from Demievka, Shuliavka, or Luk'ianovka, and sponsored no activities in these poorer districts.[132]

By 1897 63 percent of all males and 46 percent of all females in Kiev were literate. About 75 percent of males and 60 percent of females aged 20 to 29 could read and write. By contrast, in rural Kiev District only 24 percent of the males and 6 percent of the females were literate, and in 1914 a zemstvo survey indicated that little or no progress was being made to combat illiteracy in rural Kiev Province. For every six children enrolled in elementary school, one was denied admission for lack of space. Great distances between home and school discouraged others from enrolling, and more than one-quarter of the rural students dropped out before finishing their studies. Only one-third of the eligible rural children were attending school, the study concluded.[133]

Thus, in contrast to the countryside, Kiev became a sea of printed words, an environment in which printed materials of all kinds created a great urban marketplace of ideas. In 1859 Kiev had but one "newspaper," the semiofficial *Gubernskie vedomosti* (The Gazette of the Province). In that same year *Kievskii telegraf* began to define the early goals of the Ukrainian national movement, only to be challenged, beginning in 1864, by *Kievlianin*, which was subsidized by the Imperial government and which advanced the views of Russian nationalists. By 1904 rotary presses could produce 30,000 newspapers per hour, and to meet the growing demands of the literate public, at least nine newspapers and twenty-five journals were being published in the city.[134]

In 1906 restrictions against publishing in languages other than Russian were eased, and by 1912, Kiev's Temporary Committee on Press Affairs, which served as an organ of censorship for the region, was reviewing 3,172 books, 1,380 journals, and 2,878 newspaper issues in Russian, 117 books, 155 journals, and 256 newspaper issues in Ukrainian, 62 books, 73 journals, and 349 newspaper issues in Polish, and 41 "Jewish" books.[135] Penny-papers appeared in many cities, often fanning the flames of ignorance and bigotry. (Odessa's mayor Pelikan, for example, used city funds to help print his paper, *Znamia* [Banner], which warned of Jewish designs on the blood of Christian children.) Kiev probably had similar papers, but even in the respected *Kievlianin* editor V. V. Shul'gin (a State Duma deputy) told Kievans that pogroms were a just punishment for Jewish sins against Russia.[136] In contrast *Kievskaia mysl'* wrote movingly about the plight of the disadvantaged and the persecuted. The printed word could incite hatred, bigotry, and class conflict. It could also break down class and national barriers, promote sensitivity and understanding, contribute to an urban environment more tolerant of diversity and more amenable to change, and stimulate new ways of thinking about equity, justice, and authority. In 1880 the South Russia Workers Union had tried to organize Kiev's proletariat by holding all-night, secret meetings in the city outskirts. Such endeavors were hardly necessary two decades later. During the July 1903 strike alone, 24,000 leaflets were printed and distributed, including 4,000 which were directed at the soldiers charged with keeping order.[137]

Since the eighteenth century, cultural differences between city and countryside in Russia had been unusually sharp. As 1917 drew closer the gap between the urban and the rural population may have been widening, a gap that liberals and moderates found difficult to bridge in 1917, one scholar has suggested.[138] A glance at literacy and publication in Kiev and in rural Kiev Province tends to lend credibility to this view.

CONCLUSION

Prior to the Great Reforms, Kiev grew very slowly. Its population fluctuated largely in accordance with the number of troops deployed in the garrison, the severity of local epidemics, and seasonal economic activities. In size and character Kiev in 1850 differed little from Kiev in 1750. From the 1860s to 1914, Kiev exploded into a metropolis of more than 600,000 people. Thousands of migrants found work in its railyards, sugar refineries, food-processing plants and tobacco mills. These labor-intensive industries attracted large amounts of capital to the city, and their equipment needs led to the establishment and growth of numerous foundries and machine-building operations.

But for every migrant who found factory work, many more found opportunities in the small workshops and in the construction, hauling, vending and service trades. Small enterprises continued to dominate the local economy. Only 9,288 of Kiev's 600,000 residents in 1913 owned enough income-producing property to warrant even a minimal real estate tax. Saratov, with 225,000 people, had more taxpayers, while Khar'kov, Samara, and Kishinev, each much smaller than Kiev, had nearly as many.[139] Industry had enhanced economic opportunity, but Kiev had not become a factory town. Its civic leaders, in fact, seemed barely interested in promoting heavy industrialization, postponing for decades the plans to connect the main rail terminal with the river port, for example. During the War at least one councilman still hoped that Kiev would become an industrial center, citing the new rail line to Chernigov, the projected canal from Riga to Kherson that would pass through the city, and the assumption that the textile mills in war-torn Lodz would relocate in Kiev. "The future looks bright," he suggested in 1915.[140]

As Kiev grew it spread outward along the rail lines and river low-lands, annexing nearby settlements which had also grown quickly and haphazardly. Perhaps one-quarter of the 300,000 inhabitants added to the city's population between 1907 and 1914 lived in Shuliavka,

Solomenka, or other annexed areas. Kiev also grew inward, and its separate, historic settlements—the Podol, Pechersk, and Staryi Kiev—fully fused into a single metropolis in the latter decades of the nineteenth century. The Kreshchatik, early in the century a valley of wooden huts and distilling shacks, became its Main Street, the site of its finest shops, great banks, and fancy hotels, the new symbol of its commercial vitality. By 1900 no visitor would have echoed the claim made a century earlier, that "Kiev hardly had the appearance of a city at all."

Life became easier on the Kreshchatik and in the older, central neighborhoods as electricity, running water, sewers, and paved streets became common. Such amenities enhanced the attractiveness of a city already renowned for the beauty of its hilltop parks, majestic churches, and spectacular views, but local authorities were far less willing to pay comparable attention to the needs of the cholera-ravaged "desperate outskirts." In 1910 Kiev ranked near the bottom of Russia's major cities in per capita spending; municipal reformers from elsewhere in the Empire came to regard the city as a model of archaic management, and bankers saw it as a poor credit risk. During the First World War Kiev's image suffered further when its officials were criticized for failing to cooperate with the mobilization effort and for regarding public work as "alien . . . of no concern."[141] Kiev's great entrepreneurial families had given generously to the poor in the nineteenth century, but it is difficult to find a similar tradition of beneficence and civic consciousness in the attitudes of the city council toward the poor.

Inevitably, developmental inequities rankled the disadvantaged. It is hardly surprising that in 1905 the final outburst of anger, the Shuliavka Republic, an underground counter-government that was finally suppressed on December 17, occurred in a district noted for its epidemics and poor living conditions. Complaints about crime became common, especially in the outlying districts, though data on changing patterns of criminal behavior are difficult to find. Russia's cities were described as dens of crowding, undernourishment, commercial dishonesty, "terrifying vice and social inequality . . . and neglect." In 1910 Starozhil complained that crime in Kiev was committed in the name of politics. In the 1880s people could walk anywhere at night, he recalled. If a murder occurred it was talked about for months. "Now a murder that is an outrage in the morning is forgotten by evening because some new outrage has been committed. . . . At daybreak you hardly know whether you'll see the evening. You live from day to day. You really don't live, you vegetate. You take a breath and thank God."[142]

Growth and change also produced new conflicts, from pogroms to massive strikes. Kiev remained relatively quiet after the upheavals of 1905, though events such as the shooting of workers in the Lena Goldfield brought several thousand angry protesters out on its streets. Repression had been effective, at least on the surface. In June 1914 only 207 of Kiev's 10,000 to 12,000 woodworkers and only 331 of its more militant 4,000 to 5,000 metalworkers were union members, and union officials could not find workers who were willing to work as organizers.[143] Beneath the surface, however, ideas and aspirations had been molded that would play a major role in the disruption and chaos of 1917–20.

Many subtler changes were also taking place. Some of the ancient festivals—the return of the birds on March 25, celebrated by the traders of the Podol's flea market and Poultry Row, for instance—continued to be held, but many traditions disappeared. The Festival of Candles, celebrated at least since 1700 on September 1 to mark the coming of fall's shorter days, was observed only in the Grain Market by 1910. Traditionally, employees had been given a tree decorated with fruit, nuts, and a candle on top, but the evolution of larger, more impersonal workshops and the imposition of various taxes on traders and artisans had contributed to the demise of this custom.[144]

In the 1880s men, women, and children had bathed together in the Dnepr, a practice that had apparently stopped by 1910. Perhaps this change resulted from the fact that bathhouses were available in 1910, but not in 1880, or that the growth of the city made it difficult to find a secluded spot in 1910. Starozhil suggests that morals had changed; they were "simpler" in the 1880s.[145] In the fast-growing, fast-changing urban environment, behavior that seemed natural in 1880 apparently evoked public disapproval a few decades later.

Kiev changed greatly between 1860 and 1914, and like other Russian cities came to provide myriad economic, cultural, and intellectual opportunities that stood in marked contrast to the timeless routines of village life. "I've knocked about and lived in cities," Turgenev's caricature of the rebellious intellectual of the 1860s, Eugene Vassilich Bazarov, had announced, proclaiming his worldliness.[146] Bazarov could not have foreseen how much more convincing his affectation would have been in 1914 than it seemed in the 1860s.

NOTES

I wish to thank the International Research and Exchanges Board, the Summer Research Lab at the University of Illinois at Champaign-Urbana, and Centre College for their assistance in supporting the research for this essay. Thanks also to the staff at the State Lenin Library in Moscow and the Central State Historical Archive in Leningrad for their assistance in providing materials. Among those who read this essay in its various stages of development, I wish to thank Dan Brower, Stephen Corrsin, JoAnn Hamm, John-Paul Himka, David Newhall, and Frederick Skinner for their valuable suggestions.

1. Kiev apparently had the capacity to house 50,000 residents, according to archaeologists. Paris and Constantinople were larger at this time, and Venice and Thessaloniki may have been. See P.P. Tolochko, *Kiev i Kievskaia zemlia v epokhu feodal'noi razdroblennosti XII–XIII vekov* (Kiev, 1980), pp. 89, 218.

2. Both statements are cited inside the front cover in *Kiev i ego sviatyni, drevnosti, dostopamiatnosti* (Kiev, 1900).

3. Michael Hrushevsky, *A History of Ukraine* (New York: Archon Books, 1970), pp. 283–84. For a Soviet view see Institut istorii akademii nauk USSR, *Istoriia Kieva* (Kiev, 1963), Vol. 1, pp. 138–43, and *Istoriia gorodov i sel Ukrainskoi SSR. Kiev* (Kiev, 1979), pp. 57–77, hereafter *Istoriia gorodov . . . Kiev.*

4. Early population data are inconsistent, sometimes omitting districts, sometimes including soldiers and students, sometimes not. See "Naselenie Kieva v proshlom stoletii," *Kievskaia starina,* 1888, no. 4:353–54, and I. Pantiukhov, *Opyt sanitarnoi topografii i statistiki Kieva* (Kiev, 1877), p. 119. Pantiukhov estimates that the average population over the centuries was as follows: 9th century, 9,000; 10th, 17,000; 11th, 28,000; 12th, 30,000; 13th, 13,400; 14th, 10,000; 15th, 8,500; 16th, 9,000; 17th, 10,000; 18th, 15,500 (p. 114). *Istoriia Kieva,* pp. 182–83, provides data for 1763 and 1786. For the impact of epidemics, see Pantiukhov, p. 325, and *Istoriia Kieva,* pp. 182–83.

5. Rudolph Binion, *Frau Lou: Nietzsche's Wayward Disciple* (Princeton: Princeton University Press, 1968), p. 272. This impression is from 1900.

6. *Istoriia Kieva,* p. 192.

7. I. Luchitskii, "Kiev v 1766 godu," *Kievskaia starina,* 1888, nos. 1–3:10. Of the eighty-four known farmsteads located near Kiev at this time, sixty-two were involved in distilling (p. 73).

8. Ibid., p. 74.

9. *Istoriia Kieva,* p. 254, and V. S. Ikonnikov, "Kiev v 1654–1855 gg.," Part IV, *Kievskaia starina,* 1904, no. 12:254.

10. *Istoriia Kieva,* p. 175. See also the chapter "Moscow and Kiev (1613–1689)" in Donald W. Treadgold, *The West in Russia and China,* Vol. 1 (Cambridge: Cambridge University Press, 1973).

11. These were the impressions of the poet V. Izmailov, cited in V. Gorlenko, "Kiev v 1799 godu," *Kievskaia starina,* 1885, no. 3:586.

12. Konstantin Paustovsky, *The Story of a Life,* trans. Joseph Barnes (New York: Barnes & Noble, 1979), p. 44.

13. Gorlenko, p. 586.

14. For 1874 and 1897, see M.V. Ptukha, *Naselenie Kievskoi gubernii* (Kiev, 1925), Table 8, p. 29. The 1914 figure is from the census published in *Kievskaia mysl'* (Kiev), March 25, 1914. V. S. Ikonnikov, Part IV, p. 532, gives Kiev's population of 1856 as 57,168.

15. Paustovsky, p. 58.

16. Ibid., p. 45.

17. For information on the early Kreshchatik, see Luchitskii, p. 15, and M. L. Shul'kevich and T. D. Dmitrenko, *Kiev* (Kiev, 1978), p. 73. For the 1880s, see Starozhil (Old-timer), *Kiev v vos'midesiatykh godakh* (Kiev, 1910), p. 3. See the city directories for later years. For example, see *Ves' Kiev na 1902* (Kiev, 1903), passim.

18. Ikonnikov, Part IV, p. 533, mentions that there were about 6,000 skilled workers in Kiev in 1845.

19. For the growth of the sugar industry, see R. S. Livshits, *Razmeshchenie promyshlennosti v dorevoliutsionnoi Rossii* (Moscow, 1955), especially pp. 42, 118–21, 212.

20. *Istoriia gorodov . . . Kiev,* p. 119.

21. *Istoriia Kieva*, pp. 353, 463. These refiners had fields spread among thirteen provinces.

22. For notes on the Demievka Refinery, see ibid., p. 345, *Istoriia gorodov . . . Kiev*, pp. 115, 154–55, and *Pod'em revoliutsionnogo dvizheniia na ukraine nakanune pervoi russkoi revoliutsii*, Vol. 2 (Kiev, 1955), pp. 114, 300.

23. For information on the Kogen plant, see *Pod'em revoliutsionnogo dvizheniia*, Vol. 2, Part 2, p. 145. For the 1885 and 1913 data, see *Istoriia gorodov . . . Kiev*, pp. 115 and 154, and *Istoriia Kieva*, pp. 345–46. For a profile of Kiev's labor force in 1900, see *Kiev i ego sviatyni*, p. 20.

24. In 1909 the State Bank provided 400,000,000 rubles in credit for the sugar industry. Led by the Russian-Asian Bank, St. Petersburg's banks came to control much of the capital of the Demievka Refinery, the South Russian Machineworks, and other large industries in Kiev. See *Istoriia Kieva*, p. 353, and *Istoriia gorodov . . . Kiev*, p. 155.

25. For a good survey of this sector, see *Istoriia gorodov . . . Kiev*, especially pp. 116 and 154. After the Revolution, South Russia became the Leninskaia kuznitsa plant, Greter & Krivanek the Bolshevik factory.

26. Starozhil, p. 72, implies that the railroad took advantage of a weak-willed city council. See *Kiev i ego sviatyni*, pp. 248–49, for a discussion of the railroad colony.

27. *Istoriia Kieva*, p. 344, and *Istoriia gorodov . . . Kiev*, pp. 117 and 154.

28. D. M. Kumanov, "Iz Kieva," *Gorodskoe delo* (St. Petersburg), 1909, no. 7:316.

29. The issue is discussed in *Obzor deiatel'nosti Kievskoi gorodskoi dumy za chetyrekhletie 1906–10 gg.* (Kiev, 1910), which surveyed the previous city council's accomplishments.

30. *Pervaia vseobshchaia perepis' naseleniia rossiiskoi imperii, 1897 g. XVI, Kievskaia guberniia* (St. Petersburg, 1904), pp. 198–99.

31. *Istoriia gorodov . . . Kiev*, pp. 117 and 154, and *Pod'em revoliutsionnogo dvizheniia*, Vol. 1, pp. 354, 362.

32. The Demievka Refinery had about 2,000 workers at this time, the Main Railway Shop 1,600. See *Istoriia gorodov . . . Kiev*. p. 154. Of Kiev's factories, Arsenal and Greter & Krivanek had close to 900 workers in 1905 (*Pod'em revoliutsionnogo dvizheniia*, Vol. 2, pp. 632 and 649), South Russia somewhat fewer. Kiev had no employer comparable to Khar'kov's locomotive works (4,000 workers), Nikolaev's boatyards (9,200), or the giant metallurgical operations in or near Ekaterinoslav which employed 10,000 workers in some cases. See *Rabochee dvizhenie na Ukraine v gody novogo revoliutsionnogo pod'ema, 1910–1914 gg* (Kiev, 1959), p. 3.

33. Paustovsky, p. 18.

34. *Pervaia vseobshchaia perepis'*, pp. 198–99.

35. *Ves' Kiev na 1902 g.*, pp. 553–55, 597–601, and 608–18.

36. Starozhil, pp. 202, 208–209. Starozhil estimated the pilgrim traffic at 150,000 per year. *Kiev i ego sviatyni*, p. 21, estimated the figure to be 250,000 in 1900. In the 1840s 50,000 to 80,000 pilgrims had come annually to Kiev.

37. For 1914 data, see *Kievskaia mysl'*, March 25, 1914. For 1845, see V. S. Ikonnikov, Part IV, p. 527. For 1897, *Pervaia vseobshchaia perepis'*, p. 50.

38.. Starozhil, p. 200, talks about the engineer Geshvend. *Kievskaia mysl'*, March 20 and June 8, 1914, discusses Nesterov; *Istoriia Kieva*, pp. 621–28, the city's early film industry.

39. *Kievskaia mysl'*, June 29, 1914.

40. Starozhil, p. 88, and V. S. Ikonnikov, Part IV, pp. 648–49.

41. *Obzor deiatel'nosti*, pp. 14 and 29–31. Bridges were usually paved by

using the German method of setting stone in concrete. Asphalt paving was deemed too expensive.

42. Igniting wooden splinters was a common cause of fire in Russia's heavily wooden cities. See Shul'kevich and Dmitrenko, p. 92. By 1904 Kiev had about 1,000 streetlights.

43. Pantiukhov, p. 324.

44. "Mery protiv kholery 1831 g.," *Kievskaia starina*, 11 (1903):72–73.

45. For a survey of Kiev's water problems, see *Izvestiia Moskovskoi gorodskoi dumy*, 1912, no. 2:41–42. See also Starozhil, p. 13.

46. *Kievskaia mysl'*, May 6, 1914. See also April 30 and May 3, 1914 issues. By this time this Ministry of the Interior was planning legislation to force Kiev to municipalize its water system.

47. Ibid., May 10, 1914.

48. Ibid., June 1, 1914.

49. Starozhil, pp. 6–10.

50. *Obzor deiatel'nosti*, p. 38.

51. Tsen. statis. kom. MVD, *Goroda Rossii v 1904* (St. Petersburg, 1906), passim.

52. The 1872 data was compiled by statistician Iu. Giubner and appears in Pantiukhov, p. 418. For the Popov eye clinic, see Starozhil, pp. 176–77.

53. Ptukha, p. 53.

54. *Istoriia gorodov . . . Kiev*, p. 122. Overall, deaths per 1,000 births in Kiev fell from 768 in 1890–94 to 707 in 1895–99, but it is difficult to find long runs of public health and mortality data for the city.

55. *Izvestiia Moskovskoi gorodskoi dumy*, 1913, no. 1:27–28. Apparently residents of Solomenka could draw water from a pipe, but this involved carrying pails a considerable distance. See also *Obzor deiatel'nosti*, p. 18.

56. *Istoriia Kieva*, p. 540. See also *Kievskaia mysl'*, Jan. 9, 1913, and *Kyiv. Entsiklopedichnii dovidnik* (Kiev, 1981), p. 705. Part of Shuliavka was annexed by Kiev in 1908. The rest was administered by the district zemstvo.

57. Starozhil, pp. 42, 73, 78.

58. V. Ikonnikov, IV, pp. 41–42 and 213–16.

59. Starozhil, pp. 23–41, contains a rich discussion of Jewish life in Kiev in the 1880s.

60. *Ves' Kiev na 1902 g.*, pp. 93–94.

61. This description of Jewish traders in the Ukraine comes from the Slavophile Ivan Aksakov and is quoted in William L. Blackwell, *The Beginnings of Russian Industrialization, 1800–1860* (Princeton: Princeton University Press, 1968), p. 23.

62. Starozhil, pp. 13, 41.

63. Lybed grew from 41,968 to 107,125 people during those years, making it the most populous district in the city in 1912. The number of homes (*usad'bi*) grew by only 21 percent compared with 36 percent for Kiev as a whole for 1896–1912. See *Kievskaia mysl'*, Sept. 24, 1912.

64. Starozhil, especially pp. 29–34.

65. For one account see *Kievskaia mysl'*, June 29, 1914.

66. Pogroms had occurred in Odessa in 1820, 1859, and 1871. See Shlomo Lambroza, "The Pogrom Movement in Tsarist Russia, 1903–1906" (Ph.D. dissertation, Rutgers University, 1981), pp. 24–30. Jonathan Frankel, *Prophecy and Politics: Socialism, Nationalism, and the Russian Jews, 1862–1917* (New York: Cambridge University Press, 1981), pp. 51–52, 135, 150–51, provides bits of additional information on Kiev's pogroms.

67. For information on the "mobilization pogroms," see Lambroza, pp.

87–98. The data on the turmoil in Kiev, Odessa, and Zhitomir, and the information on the Jewish self-defense organizations, are taken from a valuable table on Russia's pogroms published by *The American Jewish Yearbook. 5667* (Philadelphia, 1906), pp. 38–65. Paustovsky, p. 111, speaks of brigades of students that were formed in 1905 to defend the Jews. The implication is that Christian students joined the ranks of these defense organizations.

68. Some information on Vasilkovskaia can be obtained from the city directories. For additional detail see *Istoriia Kieva*, pp. 356, 398, 496.

69. The reference to Kiev comes from Lambroza, p. 222, but the table mentioned in note 67 contains many references to participation in pogroms by police and other local officials.

70. Cited by Lambroza, p. 186.

71. Paustovsky, p. 216, discusses the events after Stolypin's death. For Golubev and his group, see *Kievskaia mysl'*, Feb. 28, 1914.

72. The reference to Zhitomir is from *American Jewish Yearbook* (1906), p. 45. The chilling description is from Paustovsky, pp. 622–24, and refers to a pogrom in 1919.

73. Leszek Podhorodecki, *Dzieje Kijowa* (Warsaw, 1982), p. 178.

74. Pantiukhov, p. 406, and Podhorodecki, pp. 178–79.

75. Podhorodecki, pp. 167–75, and *Istoriia Kieva*, p. 366.

76. *Stoletie Kievskago Universiteta Sv. Vladimira* (Belgrade, 1935), pp. 79–84. Some of the early faculty came from predominantly Polish institutions at Vil'na and Kremenets, including A. N. Mitskevich (Mickiewicz) who was transferred to Khar'kov University after the events of 1839. St. Vladimir was to be a Russianized substitute for universities at Warsaw and Vil'na that had been closed after the Polish Revolt of 1830.

77. Podhorodecki, p. 172. See also Ikonnikov, IV, p. 61.

78. *Kievskaia mysl'*, Mar. 25, 1914. The police census for 1910 lists 53,545 Poles in Kiev. See also Tsentral'nyi gosudarstvennyi istoricheskii arkhiv (Leningrada) (hereafter TsGIA), fond 1288, opis 25, delo 29.

79. Podhorodecki, pp. 193–95. See also *Istoriia gorodov . . . Kiev*, pp. 137, 182.

80. Paustovsky, p. 307

81. For an analysis of Minsk's elections, see *Severo-zapadnaia zhizn'* (Minsk), Mar. 17, 29–31, and Apr. 6, 1913. For Zhitomir, see *Kievskaia mysl'*, Feb. 21, 1914. In Vil'na, of all owners of income-producing property in 1913, 2,706 were Poles, 1,572 were Jews, and 733 were Russians. See TsGIA, f. 1288, op. 25, delo 8, p. 65.

82. A. Iaroshevich, "Malorossy po perepisi 1897 gg.," *Kievskaia starina*, 1905, no. 6:413–14. Of the 12 districts in Kiev Province, all were at least 78 percent Ukrainian except for Kiev District (56 percent) and the heavily Jewish Berdichev District (67 percent).

83. John-Paul Himka, "Voluntary Associations and the Ukrainian National Movement in Galicia (The 1870s)," in Andrei S. Markovits and Frank E. Sysin, eds., *Nationbuilding and the Politics of Nationalism: Essays on Austrian Galicia* (Cambridge, Mass: Harvard University Press, 1982), pp. 187–89. Ukrainians comprised about 43 percent of Galicia's population.

84. See the entry on Kiev in *Entsyklopediia Ukrainoznavstva* (Paris-New York: Molode Zhyttia, 1955) and *Kyiv. Entsyklopedychnyi dovidnyk* for Ukrainian-language summaries of Kiev's history during these years. See also *Istoriia Kieva*, pp. 356, 361–91, and 412–61.

85. Volodymyr Kubijovyc, ed., *Ukraine: A Concise Encyclopedia*, Vol. 2 (Toronto: University of Toronto Press, 1971), p. 480. From 1880 until 1906, "the

development of the Ukrainian press was exclusively confined to Western Ukraine and foreign countries" (p. 481).

86. Ibid., p. 488. See also *Istoriia gorodov . . . Kiev*, p. 196. *Kievskii telegraf* was the informal organ of Hromada between 1874 and 1876.

87. Hrushevsky, p. 505.

88. *Istoriia Kieva*, pp. 438–45, has a good discussion of Ukrainian theater.

89. Among those arrested before the celebration was Terenti Andreevich Shevchenko, grandnephew of T. G. Shevchenko. He had just returned from internal exile to his village in Kiev Province, and was arrested in Kiev for not having a permit to reside in the city. See *Kievskaia mysl'*, Feb. 25–27, 1914.

90. See the essays by Walter Hanchett and Michael F. Hamm in Hamm, ed., *The City in Russian History* (Lexington: University Press of Kentucky, 1976). *Istoriia Kieva*, p. 355, notes that 3,222 could vote in 1870, 4,157 in 1879. Voting rolls found in TsGIA, f. 1288, op. 5, delo 170 (1914), p. 135 show that 2,711 could vote in 1902, 2,907 in 1906, and 3,757 in 1910. See Michael F. Hamm, "Khar'kov's Progressive Duma, 1910–14: A Study in Russian Municipal Reform," *Slavic Review*, 40 (1981): especially 17–21 and 34–35, for a general study of municipal elections during the period.

91. The 1910 outbreak took 460 lives and afflicted at least 1,206 residents. According to V. S. Ikonnikov, Part IV, p. 531, the 1847 epidemic (1,680 cases and 990 deaths) and the 1853 epidemic (1,453 cases and 873 deaths) were among the worst in the city. Outbreaks were episodic; in 1908, for example, there were only 94 cases and 47 deaths. *Obzor deiatel'nosti*, pp. 47–48, provides some information on disease in the city for 1906–10. Plague, apparently, was not a problem after the epidemic of 1770–71.

92. *Iuzhnaia zaria* (Ekaterinoslav), Sept. 21, 1913.

93. This view is expressed in *Istoriia Kieva*. For Khar'kov see *Iuzhnyi krai* (Khar'kov), February 5 and 14, 1910, and Hamm, "Khar'kov's Progressive Duma . . ."

94. The booklet is *Obzor deiatel'nosti*. The reformist coalition called itself the "Non-Party Group," and did not formally affiliate with any political party. The 1906 council was described as half politically indifferent, one-third rightist, one-third progressive, but with no leftists or socialists (*Kievskaia mysl'*, Dec. 12, 1910). While running for reelection in 1910, they appeared not to publish a specific platform. The election turned out 59 percent of the electorate.

95. The Nationalists were supported by tsarist officials and by the local newspaper, *Kievlianin*, which on Nov. 21, 1910, stated that Kiev's council was similar in composition to the State Duma. About fifty progressive candidates were elected in 1910, about twenty-three "Black Hundreds"; thirty-seven were holdovers from the 1906 council. See also I. Zubarev in *Gorodskoe delo*, 1911, no. 1:87. For Odessa's negative image, see *Obzor deiatel'nosti*, p. 5; *Gorodskoe delo*, 1911, no. 2:202–203, and the article on "Odessa morals" in Khar'kov in *Rech'* (St. Petersburg), January 28, 1910, which was published after rightist thugs severely beat and nearly blinded correspondent Iu. Volin of Khar'kov's *Iuzhnyi krai*.

96. *Kievskaia mysl'*, Nov. 11 and Dec. 3, 1910. Data on the cancellation of sessions are from *Kievskaia mysl'*, Jan. 11, 1914. The term Kadet probably referred to all progressive activists on the council whether or not they were affiliated with the Kadet Party.

97. D'iakov even got a street named after him. See *Gorodskoe delo*, 1911, no. 6, pp. 565–66.

98. Starozhil, pp. 70–72.

99. *Kievskaia mysl'*, June 14, 1914. According to the contract, about 75

percent of the electric company's profits should have gone to the city.

100. These figures are taken from *Goroda Rossii v 1904* and *Goroda Rossii v 1910* (St. Petersburg, 1914) passim.

101. Before 1870 Kiev's income was derived largely from sales of vodka and wine. Income fluctuated, but in 1842 and 1846, for example, was about the same (75,000 rubles) as it had been in 1806. See N. Molchanskii, "Biudzhety g. Kieva v sredine XVIII v.," *Kievskaia starina*, 1898, no. 1:67–71. For later years, see *Istoriia Kieva*, p. 355, and *Goroda Rossii v 1904*, v, p. 156. Riga's German-dominated council was frequently cited for its efficiency and accomplishments. See Michael F. Hamm, "Riga's 1913 City Election: A Study in Baltic Urban Politics," *The Russian Review* 39 (1980):442–61.

102. Kiev's 1909 per capita assessment was 1.36 rubles, Khar'kov's 1.98, Odessa's 2.25, St. Petersburg's 3.51, Riga's 4.4, and Moscow's 5.86. Warsaw, which benefited more substantially from state tax revenue, assessed at 3.75. Zemstvo taxes on city property were said to be unfair because cities got few services from the zemstvos. On the other hand, city assessments were almost always well below bank assessments. In Kiev "patriots" were sometimes given lower rates than Jews. See *Gorodskoe delo*, 1913, no. 3:152, and *Obzor deiatel'nosti*, p. 74.

103. "Kievskoe gorodskoe khoziaistvo," in *Gorodskoe delo*, 1913, no. 3:152–53, and V. Rudin in *Kievskaia mysl'*, May 24, 1912. Habsburg Lvov, in the Western Ukraine, also earned one-third of its revenue from enterprises.

104. "Kievskoe gorodskoe khoziaistvo," p. 154. Only 27,514 rubles of this sum came from city funds. The rest was from private endowments.

105. See I. Zubarev in *Gorodskoe delo*, 1910, no. 18:1280.

106. See Starozhil, pp. 174–190, for a discussion of the philanthropic habits of Kiev's well-to-do. Popov's clinic was only for Orthodox Christians. Tereshchenko and Brodskii had come to Kiev from Glukhov and Zlatopol respectively. Israel Brodskii was especially interested in helping *edinovertsy* (Uniates). Data on hospital beds can also be gleaned from *Ves' Kiev*. See also *Kievskaia mysl'*, Jan. 1, 1911, and *Istoriia gorodov . . . Kiev*, p. 159.

107. The youth club was to be the first of its kind in Russia. See *Kievskaia mysl'*, Feb. 7, 1914, and *Izvestiia Moskovskoi gorodskoi dumy*, 1914, no. 6–7:33. For a survey of night shelters, often run by monasteries and charities, see *Kievskaia mysl'*, June 21, 1914. The survey covered 117 shelters and dormitories, none of which met basic hygienic standards. See also the editorial in *Kievskaia mysl'*, Feb. 9, 1915.

108. Around 1910 the tsarist government did begin to encourage city governments to borrow greater amounts of money. See *Izvestiia Khar'kovskoi gorodskoi dumy*, 1914, no. 1:315–16, and Hamm, "Khar'kov's Progressive Duma."

109. *Istoriia gorodov . . . Kiev*, pp. 135, 140.

110. For the 1903 strike see Vladimir Vakar, *Nakanune 1905 goda v Kieve* (Khar'kov, 1925), passim. See also *Pod'em revoliutsionnogo dvizheniia*, vol. 1, pp. 351–63, and Vol. 2, pp. 101–107. For one view of the Bolshevik influence in the Ukraine, see *Rabochee dvizhenie na Ukraine v gody novago revoliutsionnogo pod'ema 1910–1914 gg.* (Kiev, 1959), passim.

111. Based on a report carried in *Kievskaia mysl'*, June 27, 1914. For data on bakers living at their place of work, see Iu. I. Kir'ianov, *Zhiznennyi uroven' rabochikh Rossii (konets XIX—nachalo XX v.)* (Moscow, 1979), p. 219. The statute on rest periods was passed on July 17, 1910.

112. *Pod'em revoliutsionnogo dvizheniia*, Vol. 2, pp. 18–19, 44, and 358, and Vakar, p. 70.

113. *Pod'em revoliutsionnogo dvizheniia*, Vol. 2, pp. 466–67.

114. *Pod'em revoliutsionnogo dvizheniia*, Vol. 2, pp. 466–67.

115. Paustovsky, pp. 573–75, uses the phrase "desperate outskirts" in reference to Shuliavka and Solomenka. For the South Russian Union, see E. Koval'skaia, *Iuzhno-Russkii rabochii soiuz, 1880–81* (Moscow, n.d.), pp. 27–29, 47, 60.

116. Koval'skaia, pp. 118–19.

117. Ibid., p. 20. The reference is to conditions in 1879 or 1880. For the sample see G. Naumov, *Biudzhety rabochikh gor. Kieva* (Kiev, 1914), p. 19.

118. *Pod'em revoliutsionnogo dvizheniia*, Vol. 1, p. 55.

119. D. Golin, "Kiev," *Gorodskoe delo*, 1913, no. 21:1428–29 and *Kievskaia mysl'*, Sept. 28, 1912, survey Kiev's housing picture.

120. *Kievskaia mysl'*, Sept. 28, 1912.

121. The tobacco workers of the Solomen Kogen Company, citing "extremely difficult conditions," are one example of a group of workers which petitioned the city to lease them land for better housing. See *Kievskaia mysl'*, Jan. 26, 1914.

122. Ikonnikov, IV, p. 637, notes that in 1856 there were five bookshops in Kiev, two of which sold foreign books. For data on schools see *Istoriia Kieva*, pp. 408–10, *Gorodskoe delo,* 1909, no. 14:694–95, and *Istoriia gorodov . . . Kiev,* p. 188.

123. *Kievskaia mysl'*, Feb. 24, 1915, reported on abuses of young apprentices. See also *Gorodskoe delo*, 1910, no. 21:1529.

124. See *Stoletie Kievskago universiteta*, pp. 79–81, for data on the composition of St. Vladimir before 1860. The figure for 1879 is found in *Istoriia gorodov . . . Kiev*, p. 143. The composition of the students by religion, sex, and place of secondary training may be found in *Spisok studentov Imperatorskago universiteta Sv. Vladimira za pervoe polugodie 1877–78 goda*, appended to *Universitetskie izvestiia* (Kiev, 1878), Vol. 18, no. 1, passim.

125. Ikonnikov, IV, p. 561.

126. *Stoletie Kievskago universiteta*, p. 81. St. Vladimir's students tried to imitate the behavior of the students at Derpt (Dorpat) University (now Tartu in Soviet Estonia).

127. This picture of student life from the 1850s was published in *Kievlianin* in 1876 and reprinted in *Stoletie Kievskago universiteta*, pp. 80–81.

128. See *Pod'em revoliutsionnogo dvizheniia*, Vol. 1, pp. 4–5, Vol. 2, pp. 300, 452, 461, 466–70, 630–36, and 649. See also *Istoriia gorodov . . . Kiev*, pp. 175–78; for student unrest in Moscow, see Laura Engelstein, *Moscow, 1905: Working-Class Organization and Political Conflict* (Stanford: Stanford University Press, 1982), pp. 71, 130ff.

129. Starozhil, pp. 73, 170–72, and *Istoriia gorodov . . . Kiev*, pp. 142–43. It should be noted that in general St. Vladimir's faculty had a reputation for political conservatism.

130. *Ves' Kiev na 1902 goda*, pp. 299–300, 329, 486–88, and *Istoriia gorodov . . . Kiev*, p. 143.

131. *Izvestiia Moskovskoi gorodskoi dumy*, 1914, no. 4:36–38.

132. *Kievskaia mysl'*, Jan. 30 and June 10, 1914. Tailors, clerks, and professional people were among the members of the Society.

133. The report of this study appeared in *Kievskaia mysl'*, Apr. 11, 1914. The 1897 data may be found in *Pervaia vseobshchaia perepis'*, pp. 14–15.

134. By contrast, Moscow had thirteen newspapers and sixty-nine journals, Odessa twenty-two combined, Khar'kov fifteen combined, according to *Goroda Rossii v 1904*, passim. On printing presses, see Charles A. Ruud, "The Printing Press as an Agent of Political Change in Early Twentieth-Century Russia," *The Russian Review*, 40 (1981):379. Moscow had fifty-three rotary presses by 1907.

135. *Kievskaia mysl'*, May 19, 1914. The activities of this Committee increased after preliminary censorship was abolished in 1906–1907. The data

include publications from the region surrounding Kiev and the city itself.

136. For *Znamia* see "Istekshii god," *Novyi voskhod* (St. Petersburg), 1 (1915):3. A. A. Gol'denveizer, "Iz Kievskikh vospominanii," *Arkhiv russkoi revoliutsii* (Berlin, 1922), Vol. 6, pp. 267–69, is particularly critical of Shul'gin as a source encouraging violence against Jews in Kiev.

137. *Pod'em revoliutsionnogo dvizheniia*, Vol. 1, pp. 360–61.

138. James C. McClelland, *Autocrats and Academics. Education, Culture, and Society in Tsarist Russia* (Chicago, University of Chicago Press, 1979), pp. 50–51.

139. Assessment rates were always low in Russian cities, partly because they did not take into account the market value of property. In Kiev, some owners were granted tax relief because of periodic problems with flooding, and many no doubt used personal influence to evade taxation. Still, the low number of taxpayers relative to the size of the city indicates that many an entrepreneur in Kiev earned a very small income. Saratov had 11,869 taxpayers, Khar'kov (pop. 240,000) had 9,180, Samara (135,000) 8,192, and Kishinev (125,000) 7,450. See the property rolls in TsGIA, f. 1288. op. 5, d. 170, p. 130 for Kiev. For the other cities, see f. 1288, op. 25, d. 77, p. 71 (Khar'kov), d. 57, p. 40 (Saratov), d. 56, p. 46 (Samara), and d. 7, p. 49 (Kishinev).

140. *Gorodskoe delo*, 1915, no. 13–14:729–30.

141. Kiev did open a bakery and purchased firewood to help residents through the winter of 1915–16, but its efforts to contain price increases and provide for its populace equitably were judged inadequate by a series of critics. See *Gorodskoe delo*, 1915, no. 8:404; 1915, no. 18:945; and 1916, no. 8:404. For the successes of other cities such as Odessa and Budapest in regulating bread prices, see *Izvestiia Kievskoi gorodskoi dumy* (Kiev), 1915, no. 1:65–67.

142. The first view of Russian urban life was published in *Vestnik Omskago gorodskago obshchestvennago upravleniia* (Omsk), 1913, no. 7–8:7. Starozhil's remarks are from p. 128.

143. *Kievskaia mysl'*, April 5 and June 22, 1914. There had been 6,000 union members in 1907 (*Istoriia Kieva*, p. 544). As of early 1915 Kiev had only five consumer cooperatives, one run by the Vegetarian Society, and only one (run by the Southwestern Railway for its employees) with a large membership. See *Kievskaia mysl'*, January 20, 1915.

144. Starozhil, pp. 14–15.

145. Ibid., p. 10.

146. Ivan Turgenev, *Fathers and Sons*, trans. George Reavy (New York: Signet Classic, n.d.), p. 47.

BIBLIOGRAPHICAL NOTE

While local newspapers usually relegated coverage of municipal affairs to the back pages, they are often the best sources for the study of change and conflict in the cities of late Imperial Russia. For Kiev, *Kievlianin* (1864–1918) viewed municipal affairs from the viewpoint of the Russian Nationalist Party. The most comprehensive source is the moderate-leftist *Kievskaia mysl'* (1906–18), however, which combined a penchant for investigative reporting with an ongoing concern for the plight of the disadvantaged and the aspirations of various ethnic groups. *Kievskaia mysl'* captured the color of city council debates, pressed officials to provide services and amenities appropriate for a city of 600,000, and documented the lifestyles of local groups ranging from itinerant Chinese peddlers to bakers exhausted from their round-the-clock workdays. *Iuzhnyi Krai* (Khar'kov, 1880–1919), *Iuzhnaia zaria* (Ekaterinoslav, 1906–1915), and *Bessarabskaia zhizn'* (Kishinev, 1904–1916) are also valuable sources for the study of the cities of the South. Newspapers from virtually all of the Empire's larger cities can be examined at the State Lenin Library in Moscow.

Fondy 1284, 1288, and 1290 of the Central State Historical Archive in Leningrad contain reports and correspondence on municipal issues and conflicts written by local and state officials. *Fond* 1288 includes records of city property tax assessments with convenient tables of ownership broken down by nationality. One can thus discover something of the extent of Polish real estate in Kiev, or Jewish property in Vil'na, or German in Saratov, for example. Russians, Ukrainians, and Belorussians are grouped together as "Orthodox," however.

Comparative data on budgetary expenditures, the type of material used in local housing, the number of physicians and hospitals and the like may be found for most Russian cities in *Goroda Rossii v 1904 godu* (1906) and *Goroda Rossii v 1910 godu* (1914), both compiled by the Central Statistical Committee of the Ministry of the Interior. The census of 1897 is well known to Western scholars. For Kiev, M. V. Ptukha's *Naselenie Kievskoi gubernii* (Kiev, 1926) conveniently summarizes census data, though more detailed figures can be found in the yearly police censuses published in *Kievskaia mysl'* and in *fond* 1288 of the Central State Historical Archive.

The 1963 edition of *Istoriia Kieva*, published in Russian and Ukrainian in Kiev by a group of Soviet scholars, is particularly rich in detail. Volume 1 covers the ancient era to 1917 and includes a variety of useful fold-out maps. *Istoriia gorodov i sel Ukrainskoi SSR. Kiev* (Kiev, 1979), part of a series on the cities of the Ukraine, is also useful. The volume on Kiev includes more detail than the other volumes in the series, though in general the Soviet works pay a great deal of attention to the evolution of the labor movement but say little about late Imperial national and ethnoreligious conflict. Detailed accounts of Kiev's strikes in 1903 and 1905 can be found in V. Vakar, *Nakanune 1905 goda v Kieve* (Khar'kov, 1925), and the three-volume *Pod'em revoliutsionnogo dvizheniia na Ukraine nakanune pervoi russkoi revoliutsii* (Kiev, 1955).

Of the works of the period under study, *Gorodskoe delo* (1909–1918), a journal which examined political and developmental issues in many Russian cities, is a very important source and may be found at the University of Illinois at Urbana and at the University of Chicago. *Kievskaia starina* included articles on Kiev in the eighteenth and early nineteenth centuries. For the late nineteenth century, Starozhil (Old-timer), *Kiev v vos'midesiatykh godakh* (Kiev, 1910), provides excellent color and may be used with E. Koval'skaia, *Iuzhno-russkii rabochii soiuz, 1880–81*, I. Pantiukhov, *Opyt sanitarnoi topogafii i statistika Kieva* (Kiev, 1877), and *Kiev i ego sviatyni, drevnosti, dostopamiatnosti* (Kiev, 1900). Konstantin Paustovsky's memoirs, *The Story of a Life* (New York: Pantheon Books, 1982) are available in an English translation by Joseph Barnes and offer some chilling recollections of Kiev's pogroms. The city directories, *Ves Kiev na . . .*, can be used to study the changing economic geography of the city, while *Obzor deiatel'nosti Kievskoi gorodskoi dumy za chetyrekhletie 1906–1910 gg.* (Kiev, 1910) is a useful survey of the accomplishments of the moderate majority in the city council. *Izvestiia Kievskoi gorodskoi dumy*, published monthly, contains detailed budgetary data.

There are no works in English on late Imperial Kiev; in fact, there is little in English on any Ukrainian city, ancient, tsarist, or Soviet. Volodymyr Kubijovic, ed., *Ukraine: A Concise Encyclopedia* (Toronto: University of Toronto Press 1971) contains useful information on Ukrainian organizations and personalities in the city. Ivan Rudnytsky, ed., *Rethinking Ukrainian History* (Edmonton: Canadian Institute of Ukrainian Studies, 1981), includes several general essays on Ukrainian urban development. Ukrainian readers may also consult the one-volume *Kyiv. Entsyklopedychnyi dovidnyk* (Kiev, 1981), while Polish readers may wish to examine Leszek Podhorodecki, *Dzieje Kijowa* (Warsaw, 1982), and *Pamietnik kijowski*, 3 vols. (London: Nakladem Kula Kijowian, 1959).

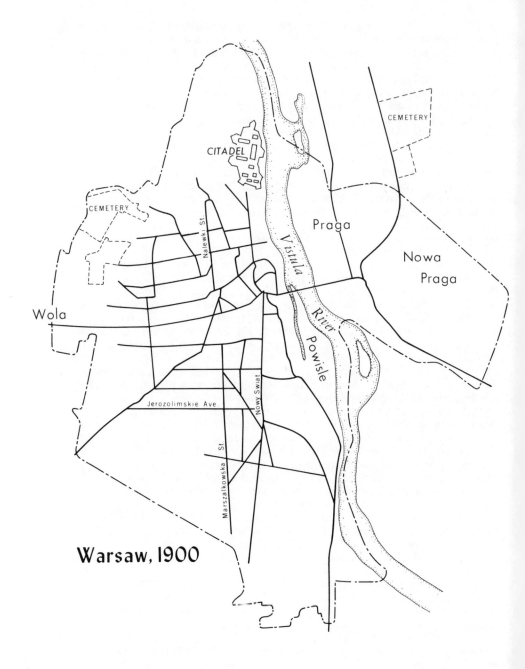

CITADEL

CEMETERY

Praga

Nowa
Praga

CEMETERY

Wola

Nalewki St.

Vistula

River

Powisle

Jerozolimskie Ave.

Marszalkowska St.

Nowy Swiat

Warsaw, 1900

5.

Warsaw

Poles and Jews in a Conquered City

STEPHEN D. CORRSIN

Warsaw—Varshava to the Russians—was the third city of the Russian Empire in the nineteenth and early twentieth centuries, trailing only St. Petersburg and Moscow in size and importance. But Warsaw was not a Russian city. Russia had gained control of it and the surrounding region after Napoleon's disastrous Russian campaign of 1812, and ruled there until the Central Powers pushed Russia out in 1915. Warsaw in this period was the chief city of the Russian Empire's Polish provinces, known variously as the Polish Kingdom, Congress Poland, or the Vistula Region.

Warsaw—Warszawa in Polish—had been the capital of the independent Polish-Lithuanian Commonwealth in the seventeenth and eighteenth centuries, until the Commonwealth was partitioned by Russia, Austria, and Prussia in the late eighteenth century. Still, Warsaw remained the greatest city of divided Poland, symbolizing the hopes of nationalistic Poles everywhere that there would someday be a reunited and independent Poland.

Warsaw was, as well, one of the greatest of Jewish cities. In the nineteenth century, and indeed until World War II, no European city could match the size and diversity of its Jewish community; only New York surpassed it in the 1880s as a result of the massive migration of the Eastern European Jews to America.

Varshava in Russian, Warszawa in Polish, and Varshe in Yiddish: all three aspects of Warsaw must be considered to produce a balanced view of the city in the nineteenth and early twentieth centuries.[1]

Warsaw was founded about 1300 in the region called Mazovia, near what was then the northeastern Polish frontier, not far from pagan Lithuania.[2] For the next three hundred years the city grew slowly. In these same centuries, Poland and Lithuania gradually became more closely associated, until in 1569 the Union of Lublin made them into two halves of a vast and united Commonwealth.

The proximity of Warsaw to Lithuania now became very important. The city took on more and more functions as the capital of the Commonwealth. Through the seventeenth and eighteenth centuries it grew significantly, although other urban centers such as Krakow, Poznan, Lviv, and Vilnius also remained important. By the 1790s, the last years of the independent but declining Commonwealth, Warsaw had over 100,000 people. But Russia, Prussia, and Austria finished dividing the Commonwealth with the partitions of 1793 and 1795 (the first had taken place in 1772). In 1795 Warsaw fell to the Prussian share. Napoleon took it from the Prussians in 1807, and it became the capital of his new satellite, the Duchy of Warsaw. The Russians took control a few years later in the wake of Napoleon's retreat westward.

During these and subsequent decades, Warsaw figured prominently in Polish rebellions against the partitioning powers: in 1794; during the Napoleonic Wars; and in the November Insurrection of 1830–31 and the January Insurrection of 1863–64 against Russia. This last revolt took the form of a widespread guerrilla war directed against the Russian authorities by a shadowy Polish government in Warsaw. It followed several years of limited but promising official liberalization; for example, in 1861–62 a city council was established in Warsaw, the Polish Jews were given almost full civil rights, and a Polish university, the Main School, was founded in the city. But the Poles responded to this liberalization first with extensive nationalist agitation and demonstrations, and then with an outright rebellion in January 1863, which reached Lithuania and Belorussia as well as all of Congress Poland. The Russians crushed the uprising with executions, reprisals, and widespread repression, withdrawing many of the earlier reforms. The next four decades brought harsh repression and political quiescence to Warsaw and Congress Poland.

THE FACE OF THE CITY

About 1910, the young Isaac Bashevis Singer came with his family from a small town to live in Warsaw.

A broad river with the sky in it stretched beneath us. Ships floated by. Over the bridge, which had intricate ironwork columns, trolleys and omnibuses raced. We came upon tall buildings, crooked roofs, iron-

work balconies. It looked as if there was always a fire raging in Warsaw,
because people were always running and shouting. It seemed like an
endless holiday. I saw a tremendous pillar, and on it a figure with a
sword in his hand. This was the monument of King Zygmunt. Beneath
him, four stone maidens drank from large beakers. . . . After passing the
better neighborhoods, we arrived at Krochmalna Street. It was evening,
and people thronged the streets. Stopping before one of the houses, the
[droshky] driver said, "This is it."[3]

Warsaw was the scene of sharp contrasts and presented many different faces to the world. Its quarters and neighborhoods varied greatly in
their socioeconomic and ethnic character. I will describe briefly several
selected areas: the wealthy city center, the impoverished river valley,
and the overwhelmingly Jewish northwest side, all on the west bank of
the Vistula; and Praga, on the river's east bank.

The city's "downtown" was centered on a series of streets running
parallel to the river: Krakowskie Przedmiescie, which led south to
Nowy Swiat; and then, as Ujazdowskie Avenue, ran southward out of
the city. Krakowskie Przedmiescie (the name, which harks back to
medieval Warsaw, means Krakow Suburb) marked the northern beginning of Warsaw's busiest and most important artery, where public and
educational institutions, the homes of the wealthy, and major churches
were concentrated.

> Krakowskie Przedmiescie, then Nowy Swiat, down to Ujazdowskie
> Avenue—this is the elegant world, the world of wealthy people. There
> are the palaces of the mighty and the homes of the rich, the seats of
> learning and art, monuments of love and praise, the temples of the
> refined world, such as the Church of the Visitation, or the Church of
> the Holy Cross with the inscription "Sursum corda!," which is con-
> stantly filled with people.[4]

Ujazdowskie Avenue, as described in an encyclopedia of the time,
was "decorated with beautiful homes and splendid villas, the favorite
place of Warsaw's residents for walking," and ran past some of the city's
loveliest parks.[5]

Directly east of these fine avenues and parks, however, in the river
valley, lay Powisle, the city's decayed and impoverished older factory
district. In his novel *The Doll*, one of the great works of nineteenth-
century Polish literature, Boleslaw Prus described this quarter.

> He [the novel's hero, Wokulski] stopped halfway along the road
> and looked at the district between Nowy Zjazd and Tamka Street,
> stretching out at his feet. . . . And he thought bitterly that this area of
> riverside earth, strewn with the refuse of the whole city, had given birth
> to nothing but two-storey houses colored chocolate and bright yellow,
> dark green and orange. To nothing but black and white fences separat-

ing empty spaces, in which a several-storey apartment house rose here and there like a pine tree spared in a forest laid waste by the axe and uneasy at its own solitude.

"Nothing, nothing . . . " he repeated, wandering through the alleys with their shacks sunk below street level, roofs overgrown with moss, buildings with shutters and doors nailed shut, with tumbledown walls, windows patched with paper or stuffed with rags. He walked along looking through dirty window-panes into dwellings, and absorbed the sight of cupboards without doors, chairs with only three legs, sofas with torn seats, clocks with one hand and cracked faces. He walked along and smiled to himself to see laborers interminably waiting for work, craftsmen employed only at mending old clothes, women whose entire property was a basket of stale cakes—and to see ragged men, starving children, and unusually dirty women.[6]

Both the wealthy city center and the impoverished lowlands were among the most heavily Polish quarters of the city. Warsaw's northwest side, however, had the largest Jewish concentration in Warsaw, and thus in all Europe. It formed the heart of what journalist Bernard Singer recalled as the "unknown Warsaw," commenting that "there still existed an invisible wall which separated the quarter from the rest of the city."[7] The development of this area as the main Jewish section began in the early nineteenth century, when a number of the city's more centrally located and desirable streets were "exempted" from Jewish residence. By the 1860s, when these restrictions were abolished, the northwest side had become the main site of Jewish residence in the city.[8]

While much of this quarter was a region of abject poverty, densely populated by petty traders, artisans, and the unemployed, it was also the home for much of the city's Jewish upper and middle classes and a major commercial and industrial area. According to one Polish writer of the time, the main north-south street of the Jewish ghetto, Nalewki Street, was the "heart of commerce in Warsaw and the Polish Kingdom."[9] Some notion of the area's diversity can be gained from Bernard Singer's recollections.

The beginning of Mila Street had a reputation for wealth. In the front rooms lived the owners of the shops on Nalewki. Its extension, called Nowomila, was an area of poverty. Artisans, tradesmen, vendors, persons of undetermined and extremely suspicious occupations, the unemployed, filled this street.

Gesia at Nalewki was a shopping street; further beyond Dzika up to Okopowa the poor found shelter. The only works of art there were the monuments done for the Jewish cemetery, [and the] free entertainment—funerals.

In the houses with low numbers on Dzielna and Pawia lived more or less respectable merchants, but further beyond "Pawiak" the streets did not differ in the least from Nowomila.[10]

When people discussed Warsaw, they were usually concerned with the areas on the west bank of the Vistula, which had the bulk of the city's population and territory. Praga, on the east bank, in many ways led a separate life. Events there rarely appeared in the newspapers, or even seemed to catch the attention of the residents of the larger city on the Vistula's west bank.

Up until the second half of the nineteenth century, Praga was little more than an overgrown country town, noted as a center for trade in agricultural products and livestock. In this period, however, Praga's population grew faster than that of any of the other major parts of the city, from 16,000 in 1882 to 90,000 by World War I.[11] A German visitor to Warsaw in the 1870s called Praga "A small hamlet, hidden among greenery, made up of wooden cottages, scattered widely across the plain."[12] Thirty years later another commentator wrote, by contrast: "In recent times Praga has changed so as to be unrecognizable. The old markets for oxen, horses, and pigs, which had been in the middle of what is now Targowa Street, have been moved beyond the city limits, and squares and tenements of the Warsaw type have been built. . . ."[13] Despite this it was also true that Praga remained a backward area in such sectors as housing, street improvements, and public works.

Major factors in Praga's development were railroad construction and the building of Warsaw's first permanent bridges over the Vistula in the 1860s and 1870s. Praga became the focal point for communications between Warsaw's factories and the huge market which the Russian Empire represented for them. Many residents of Praga found employment in the railyards or in the factories of the Nowa Praga district, which was incorporated into the city in 1887.

THE PEOPLE OF WARSAW

Warsaw's population grew rapidly, from 223,000 in 1864, to 624,000 in 1897, and, by 1914, to 885,000.[14] Only one other Polish city, Lodz, known as the "Polish Manchester" because of its textile plants, was even half Warsaw's size; in 1897 it had a little over 300,000 residents, and in 1910 more than 400,000. Other cities of the Polish lands, such as Krakow and Lviv in Austrian Galicia (southern Poland) or Poznan in Prussia (western Poland) were far smaller.[15]

Three factors cause a city's population to grow: in-migration, natural increase, and extension of boundaries. In Warsaw's case, the extension of boundaries was the least important; the city's total territory increased in this period by only one-fifth, while the population quadrupled. Natural increase was more significant. But heavy in-migration from the surrounding provinces was the most important factor of all. Warsaw became a great "human magnet," drawing in tens and hundreds of thousands of people, mostly from the impoverished Polish country-side.

In 1897, only 50 percent of the city's residents had been born in Warsaw. Another 37 percent had been born in the surrounding ten provinces that made up Congress Poland. In addition, 11 percent had been born elsewhere in the Empire (this included most of the garrison, which consisted chiefly of Russian and Ukrainian soldiers), while less than 2 percent had been born abroad, primarily in Germany or Austria-Hungary.[16]

A fairly high birth rate in the city, and the fact that most of the in-migrants were in their teens or twenties, ensured that Warsaw would have a young population. In 1897, 41 percent of the population was below the age of 20; 47 percent between 20 and 49; and only 12 percent over 49.[17]

As regards the sexual division of its population, Warsaw was quite different from most of the other major cities of the Russian Empire. In 1897, Moscow had 132 men to 100 women; St. Petersburg 121 men; and Odessa 116. Warsaw, by contrast, had 97 men to 100 women, and Lodz had 95 men. By having female majorities, Warsaw and Lodz followed the usual pattern seen in European and American cities.[18] Elsewhere in the Empire male in-migration from the countryside to the cities was heavier than female. Perhaps men from Congress Poland were more likely than others in the Empire to seek work in Germany or America, and the women to move to Warsaw or Lodz for employment.

The many thousands of people who came to Warsaw did so to improve their lot. Most of the migrants left the poverty-stricken and hopeless Polish and Jewish villages of the surrounding provinces for the same modest reasons that many others crossed the Atlantic for Amer-ica: to find a decent job, to build a better life for themselves and their children, and to escape the stultifying, locked-in worlds of the tiny villages that covered Eastern Europe.

It is impossible to say whether most, or even many, of the people who came to Warsaw bettered themselves. But at least in the vibrant commercial and industrial life of the city they perceived an opportunity to improve their lives. If they were Polish peasants, they generally became irregularly employed day laborers, or unskilled factory hands, or—chiefly girls and young women—domestic servants for the city's middle and upper class families. The Jewish new arrivals usually joined the already existing armies of street peddlers, semiskilled artisans, and the like.

But some came to Warsaw with more ambitious dreams. Among them were the offspring of Polish gentry families, many of which had been ruined in the wake of the January Insurrection. The young men and women who left, or who were expelled from their ancestral homes by the Russians, had been "thrown out of the saddle," as the saying went.

Warsaw, as the traditional capital of the region and its leading economic center, was the best place for them to try to rebuild their fortunes—or at least to earn a living.

As the chief Polish and Jewish cultural center of the region, Warsaw was also the destination for aspiring intellectuals and creative artists. The Polish historian Janusz Iwaszkiewicz no doubt spoke for many:

> Warsaw, which I had known fleetingly, since I had been there for several days in 1896, seemed to me some sort of Mecca of Polishness. I had no illusions as to the scholarly qualities of [Warsaw] University . . . but I expected that I would make up for that through contact with the Polish intellectual and scholarly elite concentrated in Warsaw. This had been my ambition for many years.[19]

If the words "Jewish" and "Jewishness" are substituted for "Polish" and "Polishness," Iwaszkiewicz's words would apply as well to many young Jewish intellectuals.

To name just a few of the outstanding Polish and Jewish artists and intellectuals who sought their fortunes in Warsaw: Helena Modrzejewska (1840–1909) was born in Krakow, gained fame as an actress in Warsaw in the 1870s, and then emigrated to the United States, where under the name Modjeska she became one of the best known actresses of the day; Isaac Loeb Peretz (1852–1915) was born in Zamosc in eastern Poland, moved to Warsaw, and eventually became one of the greatest of Yiddish writers; Boleslaw Prus (1847–1912; real name Aleksander Glowacki) was born near Lublin to the southeast and in Warsaw became one of the most popular Polish writers of the day; Nahum Sokolow (1859–1936), born in a small town near Warsaw, became an outstanding Jewish editor and publicist and, after the turn of the century, a leading figure in the European Zionist movement. Many others, of course, failed in their ambitions, ending as clerks, petty bureaucrats, or minor journalists. But those who succeeded in their careers, such as the few listed above, left marks on Polish and Jewish culture that are still visible today.

Warsaw was an ethnically divided city, with the great majority of its population made up of two groups—the Poles and the Jews. This ethnic division was one of the most significant factors in Warsaw's life and development. Religion was the primary marker of the Polish-Jewish ethnic boundary in Warsaw and in all the Polish lands. Thus the Poles were chiefly Catholics, and most Catholics were Poles. Most Jews were Jewish in both a religious and an ethnic sense of the term.[20] Table 5.1 provides data on the religious composition of the population in this period.

Assimilationist Jews, who saw themselves as Jews by descent and at least nominally by faith but as Poles by cultural, political, and ethnic identity, were the chief exceptions to the equation of religion with

TABLE 5.1

Religious Groups in Warsaw, 1864–1914

Year	Catholics		Jews		Others		Total Population
	N	%	N	%	N	%	
1864	131,808	59.1	72,776	32.6	18,322	8.2	222,906
1882	223,127	58.1	127,917	33.4	31,920	8.3	392,964
1897	347,565	55.7	210,526	33.7	66,088	10.6	624,189
1914	487,950	55.2	337,024	38.1	58,775	6.7	883,749

SOURCE: 1864—A. Zaleski et al., "Warszawa," *Slownik geograficzny Krolestwa Pol-skiego i innych krajow slowianskich*, XIII (1893), 24; 1882—*Rezul'taty odnodnevnoi perepisi naseleniia goroda Varshavy v 1882 godu*, I (Warsaw: 1883), table 10; 1897—Tsentral'nyi statisticheskii komitet, ministerstvo vnutrennykh del, *Pervaia vseob-shchaia perepis' naseleniia Rossiiskoi Imperii 1897 goda*, LI (St. Petersburg: 1904), table 1; 1910—Halina Kiepurska and Zbigniew Pustula, eds., *Raporty warszawskich oberpolicma-jstrow (1892–1913)* (Wroclaw: 1971), 123.

ethnic identity. Such individuals identified themselves as Jewish Poles (*Zydzi-Polacy* in Polish) and Poles of Mosaic faith or descent (*Polacy mojzeszowego wyznania, pochodzenia*). They were a small group but included some wealthy and influential families, of which the large and active Natanson clan was the outstanding example. One measure of assimilation was that in 1897, 13.7 percent of Warsaw's Jews claimed Polish as their native language, compared to 83.7 percent claiming Yiddish (the rest were chiefly Russian or German speakers). In all, 61.2 percent of the city's population in that year stated that its native language was Polish, 28.3 percent Yiddish, and 6.8 percent Russian.[21]

A small number of Jews, perhaps a few hundred families, converted to Christianity in Warsaw in this period. They did so either because of strong self-identification with Polish culture and identity, or from hopes of advancement and a better life for themselves and their children.[22]

Most Poles and Jews were intensely religious. Their respective neighborhoods closed down for major holidays, such as Easter and Corpus Christi for the Catholics, and Passover and the High Holy Days for the Jews. Centuries of faith were at the basis of each ethnic group's identity. To some extent the hold of traditional religion weakened in this period, and strong anticlerical elements developed among both Poles and Jews, chiefly among the secular intelligentsia and radical groups.

The Catholic hierarchy stayed out of politics. After the January Insurrection, the Russian government closed most monasteries and convents in Congress Poland and exiled both Archbishop Felinski and Bishop Rzewuski. A new archbishop, Popiel, was appointed only in

1883 after negotiations between the Vatican and the government. Popiel was a conservative who never challenged the Russians, and he stayed in office until his death in 1912. Under his rule organized Catholicism suffered relatively little from government attacks, but his caution frustrated many people and led to the formation of militant and secret, or at least unsanctioned, church groups. A Catholic press appeared as well, generally leaning toward the right and anti-Semitism. It was represented in Warsaw particularly by *Dziennik Powszechny* (Universal Daily) of Father Hipolit Skimborowicz and the aptly named *Polak Katolik* (Polish Catholic).

Judaism in Poland had no hierarchy. The post of chief rabbi of Warsaw, abolished in the 1870s, was never influential. The majority of the city's Jewish population consisted of members of ultra-orthodox Hasidic groups—it was estimated that two-thirds of Warsaw's officially registered Jewish prayer houses in 1880 were Hasidic—and most of the remainder were non-Hasidic orthodox. The city's Hasidim were intensely loyal to local or regional rabbinical dynasties. The great synagogue on Tlomacka Street, with prayers in Polish, was for the assimilationists.

Many Jews, especially younger and politically active men and women after the turn of the century, moved away from the faith of their ancestors. Deep splits in families developed. In Isaac Bashevis Singer's family, the older son, Israel Joshua, who later became a leading Yiddish novelist in Poland and America, scoffed at traditional Judaism. This infuriated their father, a Hasidic rabbi. I. J. Singer, thus, "because of his emancipated views, found it difficult to speak to [our] father, whose only response was, 'Unbeliever! Enemy of Judaism!'"[23]

Besides the Poles and the Jews, the most noteworthy ethnic group in Warsaw was the Russians. The Russians in Warsaw, who in these decades made up less than 7 percent of the population, came chiefly for governmental or military service. They formed a privileged, well-paid, and closed colony within the larger city, reading their own newspapers, going to their own Eastern Orthodox churches, and sending their children to separate schools. They were contemptuous of the local population and were despised in turn. After 1905, when it became possible to form political parties, the strongest political element among them was the Union of the Russian People, the anti-Semitic and anti-Polish "True Russians."[24]

The data in Table 5.1 show no radical changes in the composition of Warsaw's population between 1864 and 1914. There was, however, a slight downward trend for the Catholic percentage, and an upward movement for the Jewish. Because of the unreliability of data on births and deaths in Warsaw, it is impossible to be sure exactly why the Jewish share rose and the Catholic declined. Indirect and fragmentary evidence, however, indicates that Jewish fertility may have been a little higher than Catholic in Warsaw; Jewish infant and child mortality was lower, and Jews were more likely to migrate to Warsaw as families and Catholics as individual adults.[25]

All these factors reinforced one another. In particular, a family was more likely to be successful than a single parent—or an orphanage—at keeping children alive in the poverty in which most people lived. One important factor was that Catholic women were far more likely than Jews to give birth to illegitimate children, and illegitimate children were much less likely to survive than ones born to families. In 1882, 21 percent of all reported Catholic births were illegitimate, compared to less than 1 percent of the Jewish births. In that same year, the reported death rate among illegitimate infants was 44 per hundred, compared to 29 per hundred among legitimate ones.[26]

THE CITY'S ECONOMY

Warsaw was a major industrial city. But it was neither a factory town, like Lodz, nor a leader in technological innovation or the manufacturing of new products, like Riga. Instead, Warsaw was a large, multifunctional city, with a broad range of economic activities, ranging from manufacturing to trade to transport to virtually anything else that city people might try in order to earn a living.

Manufacturing was an important sector. The number of factory workers rose from 14,000 in 1879, to 38,000 in 1900, and to 80,000 in 1914. The value of factory production increased from 27 million to 193 million rubles in these decades. The most important areas were metalworking, chemicals, textiles, comestibles, and clothing, with metalworking as the leading sector. By 1913 the metalworking factories of Warsaw, led by three giant firms—Rudzki; Borman and Szwede; and Lilpop, Rau, and Loewenstein—employed 31,000 people and produced goods with a value of 58 million rubles.[27] These large firms made iron and steel products for the Russian market, especially rails, bridge materials, railroad wagons, industrial and farm machinery, and goods for the Russian military. Many smaller plants concentrated on supplying local needs, including machinery for the larger companies.

Small-scale craft industry remained a major employment sector as well. Its size cannot be figured accurately, because records after the mid–1890s were not consistent with earlier ones. In 1866, however, according to official statistics, 11,000 artisans produced 6 million rubles' worth of goods; in 1894 there were 62,000 artisans producing 57 million rubles' worth.[28]

In the next two decades the number of artisans increased, thanks in part to the heavy Jewish influx to the city; craft industry was an area in which the Polish Jews were heavily concentrated. Warsaw's artisans worked in a great range of circumstances, from cramped apartments to sizable workshops, but most were quite poor. They produced an enormous variety of goods, although such areas as clothing, comestibles, and construction were the most important.

Warsaw's west side, out beyond the Warsaw-Vienna railway station at the intersection of Jerozolimskie Avenue and Marszalkowska Street, became its most important industrial district. The western suburbs, especially Wola, also became the site for many factories. The older factory district, Powisle, declined. Meanwhile, the Jewish quarter on the northwest side was important for both craft and factory industry.

Trade, like industry, assumed many forms in Warsaw. The fancier shops, whether owned by Jews, Poles, Germans, or Russians, were near the city center, along Nowy Swiat and Marszalkowska Street; the latter became the city's main commercial thoroughfare by the turn of the century.[29] The city swarmed with peddlers and hawkers. There were tiny shops of all kinds. Since small-scale trade was a major source of livelihood for the Polish Jews, such shops proliferated on the northwest side. Bernard Singer recalled: "Nalewki [Street] sold lace, haberdasher's goods, and hosiery. Gesia traded in products from Moscow and Lodz. Franciszkanska had hides from Radom. Grzybow [Square] traded in iron."[30]

The censuses taken in the city in 1882 and 1897 show that manufacturing of all sorts was Warsaw's largest employer. In 1882 33.3 percent of the population was supported by manufacturing; 17 percent by trade; 13.3 percent by domestic and personal service; 11.7 percent by government service and the free professions; 9.3 percent by day labor; and 4.5 percent by transport and communications. (These figures refer to the employed plus their dependents, which is the way this census presented its data.)[31] In 1897 the picture was similar. Of the total population, 36 percent was supported by manufacturing; 20.8 percent by domestic and personal service combined with day labor; 19.4 percent by trade; 7.1 percent by government service and the professions (this drop relative to 1882 was largely caused by the fact that a large group of white collar workers was counted in 1897 under the heading of "personal service"); and 6.5 percent by transport and communications.[32]

Certain employment sectors were chiefly Polish, and others largely Jewish. In particular, the Jews were concentrated in two areas, manufacturing and trade. In 1882 fully 67.9 percent of the Jews were employed in these areas. Jews made up 79.3 percent of all persons in the trade category. They numerically dominated a few branches of manufacturing, specifically clothing, textiles, and tobacco products, in which they made up 60–80 percent of the total.[33]

In the Russian Empire, as Ezra Mendelsohn has pointed out, the larger and more modernized a factory was, the fewer Jewish workers it employed.[34] Several reasons were commonly cited. One was the refusal of religious Jews to work on Saturdays. Also, assimilationist Jewish businessmen, who were more likely to own larger and more modern plants than their orthodox coreligionists, were often sensitive to charges that the Jewish role in the local economy was too strong, and therefore did not hire many Jewish workers. Christian factory owners rarely hired Jews. Occasionally Polish workers drove Jewish workers out of the factories, as happened in shoemaking plants in 1911.[35]

Poles were more widely dispersed through the city's employment structure. In 1882, 36.5 percent of Warsaw's Catholics were supported by manufacturing, 18.2 percent by domestic and personal service, and 11.1 percent by day labor. They made up almost two-thirds of the total in industry and four-fifths in service, but only one out of six in the trade category. Major branches of manufacturing which they dominated numerically were metalworking, woodworking, shoemaking, and construction; they were weakest in textiles and clothing. Thus, the Polish and Jewish employment structures, by a combination of tradition and design, were in many ways complementary to one another.[36]

The stereotype of the impoverished Warsaw Jew included tailors, cigar-rollers, other artisans, and the great army of street peddlers. The image of the wealthy Jew was that of the great entrepreneurial families, many of them assimilationist, such as the Natansons, or even eventual converts to Christianity, such as the Kronenbergs. Some of these families built their fortunes in banking and commerce in the early nineteenth century, and then branched out into industry and the free professions.

The Polish lower classes included factory workers, day laborers, and female domestic servants. The latter two groups consisted chiefly of recent arrivals from the countryside. The city's Polish (or Polonized) upper classes included the surviving Polish aristocracy, plus many families of recent Jewish or German origin, reflecting the role these latter groups played in developing trade and industry in the city.

One particularly important group in both Polish and Jewish cultural and political history was the intelligentsia. This was, indeed, the period in which this term came into general use in Poland. It usually covered members of the free professions, such as writers, journalists, doctors, lawyers, scholars, and engineers. There was a strong connotation of independent work in the term, and of some degree of opposition to the existing social and political system. Both the Polish and the Jewish intelligentsias in Warsaw grew to be more or less self-proclaimed leading classes for their peoples, trumpeting their ideals in novels, the press, and underground publications, and forming at first clandestine and later, after the 1905 Revolution, open political movements.[37]

Government service was largely closed to Polish and Jewish intellectuals. Russians dominated the upper and middle levels of administrative service and the educational system; Poles were mostly restricted to the lower ranks, and Jews were kept out almost entirely.

LOCAL GOVERNMENT AND THE ISSUES
OF DAILY LIFE

The population of Warsaw and of all of Congress Poland had no voice in local government. Concessions were made by the Russian authorities in the early 1860s to local self-government in Warsaw, including an elected city council, but the January Insurrection of 1863–64 convinced the Russians that they could not allow the Poles any political room to maneuver. Henceforth Russia made no bones about the fact that it was in Poland as a conqueror. The short-lived city council was swept away; local self-government bodies that were subsequently established elsewhere in the Empire, including both city councils and the rural zemstvos, were never introduced in Congress Poland. Many of the trappings of former Polish independence which had survived into the 1860s were abolished. For example, the name "Polish Kingdom" (Tsarstvo Polskie, in Russian) disappeared from official use, and was replaced by "Vistula Region" (Privislinskii Krai).

Warsaw remained the Russian administrative and military capital of Congress Poland. It was the home of the last man to hold the title of Viceroy of Congress Poland, General Fedor Berg, and, after his death in 1874, of the governors-general of the region. Berg from the time of the January Insurrection followed a policy of harsh repression. His successors, among whom General Gurko served the longest (1883–94), ruled in quieter times, except for General Skalon (1905–14), who faced the 1905 Revolution and its aftermath.[38]

Congress Poland was an occupied land. At the turn of the century there were 200,000 Russian soldier among the 9 million people of the country. Of these soldiers, 40,000 were stationed in and around Warsaw. Cossack patrols were regular sights on the city's streets. The ring of fortifications surrounding the city was ostensibly directed against Germany, but there could be no doubt that the bleak and enormous citadel on Warsaw's northern edge existed solely to intimidate the local population.

After the governor-general, the city president was in title the next most important official, but he actually had little power. Sokrates Starynkevich (president, 1875–92) was the city president best and most kindly remembered by Polish historians (indeed, he was the only Russian official for whom they consistently had kind words). Starynkevich, in contrast to many of his colleagues, was not an extreme Russian chauvinist, was favorably inclined toward the Poles, and was involved in such city projects as the construction of water and sewer lines, transportation improvements, and the extension of the city's boundaries into its rapidly growing suburbs, especially Nowa Praga.

More powerful than the city president was the chief of police (*oberpolitseimeister,* in Russian), who reported directly to St. Petersburg. His duties went far beyond criminal matters, including also censorship, the supervision of organizations and institutions, the fire department, and internal passports. The city government was subordinated to the governor-general and the Ministry of Internal Affairs in St. Petersburg. City outlays of over 5,000 rubles had to be approved by the governor-general, while those over 30,000 rubles needed permission from St. Petersburg.[39]

All of the most important official posts in Warsaw and Congress Poland were held by Russians, often men who had reputations as extreme Russian chauvinists. Thousands of Russian bureaucrats were brought in to fill the upper and middle ranks of the administration. They received special pay and privileges.

Local publicists expressed considerable dissatisfaction with the city administration in many areas: education, housing, and extensive police' corruption, for example. But in the context of the Russian Empire, Warsaw did fairly well. From 1865 to 1914, the city budget grew almost tenfold, from 1,650,000 to 16 million rubles, while the population quadrupled. It was calculated that by the war the city had a per capita income of 18 rubles. This figure compared well to other parts of the Empire, but concerned citizens of Warsaw were more interested in the fact that it was only about half the per capita income of Berlin or Vienna.[40] Table 5.2 shows the distribution of governmental expenditures in the city.[41]

Housing was inadequate. Warsaw was overcrowded, four times more densely populated than St. Petersburg and three times more densely populated than Moscow, according to a 1913 report. The basic reason for this crowding was the belt of fortifications that surrounded the city. Until the last years before World War I the government allowed no building in or near this belt, so the rapidly growing population crammed itself ever more tightly into the narrow city boundaries and inner suburbs.[42]

TABLE 5.2

Distribution of Warsaw Governmental Expenditures, 1883 and 1914 (in percentages)

	1883	1914
Administration, courts, police	33.5	14
Streets (construction and maintenance)	20.8	24.2
Water and sewers	20.5	7.7
Charity and hospitals	3.2	16.6
Education	3	5.9
Debt service	4.6	22.3
Other	14.4	9.3

SOURCE: Kieniewicz, *Warszawa w latach 1795–1914*, 194.

Nonetheless, much building went on. By 1914 about 80 percent of Warsaw's housing stock was less than fifty years old. The obvious response to the inability to expand was to build taller buildings. In 1868, 46 percent of the residential buildings had just one floor, 47 percent had two or three, and 7 percent four or more. In 1914 these figures were 13 percent, 27 percent, and 60 percent. But Warsaw was certainly not a city of skyscrapers; the tallest apartment buildings of the early twentieth century had only nine floors.[43] Most buildings in Warsaw were made of stone or brick, over 80 percent by 1910.[44]

The larger tenements provided housing for a large portion of the population. In 1910 Warsaw averaged 116 people per residential building, compared to just 40 in nearby Lodz, 52 in St. Petersburg, and 38 in Moscow.[45] Isaac Bashevis Singer recalled moving to a tenement on the city's west side just before the war:

> No. 12 [Krochmalna Street] was like a city. The dark entrance always smelled of freshly baked bread, rolls and bagels, caraway seed and smoke. Koppel the baker's yeasty breads were always outside, rising on boards. In No. 12 there were also two Hasidic study houses, the Radzymin and Minsk, as well as a synagogue for those who opposed Hasidism. There was also a stall where cows were kept chained to the wall year round. In some cellars, fruit had been stored by dealers from Mirowski Place; in others, eggs were preserved in lime. Wagons arrived there from the provinces. No. 12 swarmed with Torah, prayer, commerce, and toil.[46]

For the upper classes, apartments with central locations became fashionable, and the older, more spacious villas lost popularity. The city's leading Polish newspaper, *Kurjer Warszawski* (Warsaw Courier), reported in 1911 that, "While it is easy to rent luxurious five room apartments, there are great difficulties in getting two or three rooms."[47] The latter, of course, was exactly the type of apartment that the middle classes were trying desperately to find.

Housing for the poor, whether in the form of enormous tenements, workers' barracks in the factory districts, or wooden shacks in the suburbs or Powisle, was dreadful. A few charitable attempts were made to improve the situation, but these only amounted to an additional several hundred small apartments with reduced rents. The main such attempt was the Wawelberg homes, founded in 1897 by Hipolit Wawelberg, a Jewish-born businessman and philanthropist who had converted to Christianity. One of his hopeful beliefs was that ethnically mixed housing for the poor would help to eliminate bigotry. For the destitute of the city, meanwhile, there were cheap night shelters and public kitchens.

At the time of the 1882 census 39 percent of the population lived in a single room, 22 percent in a single room with a kitchen, 13 percent had three- or four-room dwellings, and 25 percent had more. In 1900 only one in seven residences had a bathroom. Most of Warsaw's residents got by with occasional use of the public baths.[48]

Public services impoved a great deal between the 1870s and World War I, although all observers would have agreed that there was still a long way to go. Improvements normally came to wealthy, centrally located neighborhoods well before they reached poor or suburban sections. Services, including telephones, sewers, gas, and electric tram lines, were usually entrusted to foreign firms.

Cleanliness of the city was a major problem. Boleslaw Prus wrote in 1877: "Warsaw stands on garbage, its residents eat, drink, and breathe garbage, and when one of them dies, he rests among garbage for all eternity."[49] (But a Russian recalling the Warsaw of the early twentieth century mentioned the city's "irreproachable cleanliness."[50] Either the situation had improved drastically or Polish and Russian conceptions of urban cleanliness were markedly different.)

As late as the 1880s, Warsaw's water supply, despite the city's location on the Vistula River, was poor in quality, unreliable, and unfiltered. There were only thirty-one kilometers of water mains in the city. Outdoor privies were the rule for most of the population. Warsaw was not a healthy place to live. In the early 1880s, the city turned for both water mains and sewage disposal to an English firm, Lindley. The improvements that followed were significant but uneven. By the war there were 320 kilometers of water mains, reaching 93 percent of the buildings on the Vistula's west bank, and 66 percent in Praga (in many buildings, however, the running water did not come to individual apartments, but simply to a single place in the building). Sewer lines were less comprehensive, covering 82 percent of the west bank properties and 28 percent in Praga. Sewage was pumped far down the Vistula.[51]

These improvements probably helped the public health situation in the city. Registration of births and deaths, as noted, was very unreliable in Warsaw. Nonetheless, the general course of change in the officially registered birth and death rates probably reflects the reality of sharply declining death rates and more slowly falling birth rates.

In 1882, the officially registered birth rate was 38.7 per thousand; in 1890 (in the middle of a brief upswing) 45.1; in 1900, 34.7; and by 1913 it had fallen to 26.4. Death rates in these four years were 32.1, 24.7, 21.4 and 17.3. Thus, between 1882 and 1913 the birth rate dropped by less than one-third and the death rate by almost one-half. Warsaw was following trends seen in most of Europe and North America. Despite the general decline in death rates, however, child mortality remained distressingly high. Infants and small children faced greater risk of death than any other group younger than octogenarians.[52]

In terms of fuel, gas was used extensively—and expensively—for heating, light, and cooking. The poor often relied on kerosene. Electric lighting began to appear in the 1870s, but it only came into use on a large scale after a French company was given the concession early in the new century. As late as 1914, however, 58 percent of Warsaw's residences had neither electricity nor gas.[53]

The telephone arrived in Warsaw in 1877. It only came into wide use after 1908, when a Swedish firm got the concession. There were in 1910 in Warsaw 37 residents per telephone, compared to 54 in Moscow, 60 in St. Petersburg, and a staggering 238 in industrial Lodz.[54]

Horses remained until the eve of World War I the city's main means of transport. They pulled carts, cabs, and buses and trams as well. Public transport was not cheap, and the city's poor usually walked. First class on the horse trams cost seven kopeks, and second class cost five. In 1908 an electric tram system opened with great ceremony, and soon there were thirty-three kilometers of electric tram lines operating. At the same time, the first automobiles appeared on Warsaw's streets, but the horse remained much in evidence.[55]

Historians rarely mention Warsaw's underworld, but it flourished in this period. Its mainstay was prostitution. In 1883 Prus wrote, "There seems to be nowhere in Europe a city as dissolute as Warsaw."[56] Prostitution ranged from streetwalkers to luxurious, officially tolerated brothels. In addition, the city's industrial west side, a high crime area, by the turn of the century had two major criminal gangs, one Polish and one Jewish, whose livelihoods came from controlling prostitution.

Isaac Bashevis Singer lived near "ill-famed Krochmalna Square, where pickpockets and hoodlums loitered and dealers in stolen goods carried on with their trade. The houses facing the square also harbored a number of brothels."[57] Along the city's western border was the impoverished Wola area, "Bloody Wola . . . known . . . for its cutthroats, audacious murders, bold robberies, and daily crimes."[58]

By the turn of the century the press was expressing concern over a wave of robberies at knifepoint, and bands of youthful thieves could be found in many parts of the city. The political unrest of the 1905 Revolution also gave rise to a great deal of criminal lawlessness; it was hard to tell just where politics ended and ordinary crime began, as bombings, shootings, robberies, and official retaliations proliferated.

It is interesting to speculate about the extent to which many immigrant gangsters in American cities in the first part of this century picked up their training in the slums of the cities of the Russian Empire. Odessa's underworld is well known today because of the writings of Isaac Babel, but Warsaw's, which never found a chronicler, should not be overlooked.

CONFLICT AND COMMUNITY

These decades saw the rise of local politics in the Empire's cities. Blocs of progressives, Russian nationalists, and other coalitions and parties met in city councils and argued about sewers, trams, public buildings, and the like. This did not, however, happen in Warsaw. People were certainly interested in such issues, but since there was no city council or any other local governmental body in which the people had a voice, there was little that they could do except try to influence the Russian authorities.[59]

Politics in Warsaw tended to focus on larger issues of the Polish and Jewish national destinies: how could Poles survive under Russian rule; how should they regard the strong Jewish presence; should socialist parties be based on single ethnic groups, or should they be international in scope; to what extent should Jews participate in the politics of Poland and the Empire; should Palestine be the Jewish homeland? The only elections which took place in Warsaw were those for the Russian State Duma, the Empire's quasi-parliament, between 1906 and 1912. The issues debated in the campaigns were national, not local, but nonetheless they were of great importance for Polish-Jewish relations in the city.

The four decades following the January Insurrection of 1863–64 were, as noted, a time of harsh official repression and political quiescence in Warsaw. On the surface, the most influential political orientation was "Warsaw positivism," but this was more a *Weltanschauung* than a political movement. Its leaders, such as radical journalist Aleksander Swietochowski (editor of the weekly *Prawda*—The Truth) and novelist Eliza Orzeszkowa, praised education, secularism, economic growth, and Jewish assimilation, while opposing the romantic, revolutionary tradition that had heretofore prevailed in Polish political thought. In the long run, however, the positivists were more articulate than influential, and proved unable to create a viable liberal movement.[60]

In 1881 a major pogrom took place in Warsaw. The rioting began on Christmas day, in Powisle, and then spread throughout the city in the next two days. It began with a sudden, unexplained panic during services in a church; about thirty people were killed in the panic, someone shouted that a Jewish thief had started it, and that evening the pogrom began. About twenty Jews were killed and there was over a million rubles' worth of property damage; the Nalewki Street area organized self-defense groups, but the police and the army stood aside and let the pogrom run its course. To many, Poles and Jews alike, in the city this was a particularly shaking event. The other pogroms which swept the Empire in 1881 took place in smaller cities, and the people of Warsaw prided themselves on being more civilized than their eastern neighbors.[61]

Despite positivism and the pogrom, the actual main political outlook in late nineteenth century Warsaw was to avoid trouble. In the 1890s, however, underground political groups began to form.[62] Most important were the Polish Socialist Party, which tried to combine nationalism with class struggle; the Jewish Bund, which attempted to do more or less the same for the Jews; the Zionists, who strongly appealed to many Jews, but who remained equivocal about what should be done while the Jews were still "in exile"; the Social Democrats, who had close ties with Russian Social Democracy, included Poles, Jews, and Russians among their members, and opposed all nationalisms; and the Polish National League, the forerunner of the National Democratic Party.

This last group, led by Roman Dmowski, was the Polish version of the integral nationalist movements of twentieth century Europe. It held that nationality was the absolute factor in political life, eclipsing all others such as class. It claimed to represent all ethnic Poles, and worked hard to develop student, worker, and peasant-affiliated groups. The Party saw enemies everywhere: the socialists; Germany, which it viewed as the main threat to Polish ethnic survival, far more dangerous than backward Russia; and the Jews, whom it regarded as the main internal enemy of the Poles. Despite its claims National Democracy did not have a monopoly on Polish nationalism. Still, it was far better organized than less extreme Polish nationalist elements. Less nationalistic liberal and conservative parties, of which the strongest became the Progressive Democratic Union and the Party of Realistic Politics, found little support in Warsaw's Polish community.

The various socialist groups reached their peak at the time of the 1905 Revolution, when their combined membership in Warsaw soared into the tens of thousands and they for a time seemed to control the industrial districts. Socialism had a strong appeal to Warsaw's Poles and Jews alike, and some of the parties tried to draw members from both peoples; the Polish Socialist Party even had a Jewish Section for a time, which was, however, much weaker than the socialist Jewish Bund.

At the end of the nineteenth and the start of the twentieth centuries, political nationalism began to take hold among Jews all over the Empire for the first time. Jewish movements, based on the idea that the Jews were and must remain a separate nation, developed rapidly.[63] Emancipation and equal rights, the demands of politically concerned Jews for generations, were for many no longer sufficient goals. In Warsaw as elsewhere in the Empire, the Zionists and the socialist Bund emerged as the strongest Jewish political groups. While they had significant local leadership—men born in central Poland such as Zionist leaders Nahum Sokolow and Isaac Gruenbaum—they were part of larger movements in the Empire, not independent parties based in Poland. Jews from the east, derisively called "Litvaks" in Warsaw slang, played very important roles in local Jewish politics. This was a sore point to many Poles and also to Jewish assimilationists, who saw Jewish nationalist and socialist groups as Russian imports.

All of these Polish and Jewish political groups, and many weaker ones, formed open and organized political movements during the 1905 Revolution.[64] This upsurge of political action and violence actually lasted in Warsaw and Congress Poland from late 1904 to 1908. These years saw politics combined with desperate violence. Actions ranged from mass demonstrations to acts of terror—murder and robbery—by radical "fighting squads." In all, 100 policemen were killed and 243 wounded in the city,[65] and there were more than 360 executions of radicals in the citadel on the city's northern edge.[66] Hundreds more participants in demonstrations, innocent bystanders, soldiers, and would-be terrorists were killed by gun, knife, or bomb on the city's streets as well.

The troubles began at Grzybow Square on the west side on 4 November 1904, with an armed protest against military conscription led by the Polish Socialists. On 28 January 1905, socialists organized a general strike in Warsaw which rapidly spread from the factories to schools, offices, and public transport. (The resulting boycott of Russian schools by Poles lasted for years.) Later general strikes in October and December of 1905 won less support than the first, which had lasted for a month. The year saw hundreds die in street clashes with police and soldiers, more than 1,300 strikes, and a near-mania for organization among the Polish and Jewish populations. Besides the explicitly political groups which emerged, a number of social and educational bodies with various goals and affiliations appeared as well. Examples included the Association for Scholarly Courses, which tried to provide a substitute for a private Polish university, and the Union for Equality of Polish Women, a feminist group.

Conflicts were not only between the population and the government. Near–civil war developed in both Warsaw and Lodz between the National Democrats and the socialist groups. Both sides formed armed units; the socialists to battle the government and the right, the National Democrats to combat the left. In addition, the National Democrats tried to work with the government in suppressing the left.

In 1906 there were fewer strikes and demonstrations than in 1905, but instead there was an upsurge of terror. In all, 85 policemen, gendarmes, and soldiers were killed. August was a particularly bloody month; on 15 August, "Bloody Wednesday," a wave of bombings and shootings by the Polish Socialist Party's "Fighting Organization" took place. It led to about 160 people killed and wounded in Warsaw, 38 of them policemen or soldiers.[67] Three days later, Governor-General Skalon was wounded in a bombing; nine days after that, his temporary replacement, General Vonliarliarskii, was killed.

But the government proved it could outlast the revolutionaries, and in the end socialist losses were very heavy; there were more than 300 executions in 1907 and 1908 in the citadel alone. All the major leftist groups moved back underground, and entered a period marked by exile and factionalism. The National Democrats, even though their policies of conciliation with the government cost them much popular support (especially after 1908), emerged as the strongest organized political party in Warsaw and the region. The 1905 Revolution did, of course, bring real victories for the people of Warsaw: some degree of political freedom; a freer press; greater opportunities to form nonpolitical organizations. But the price that had been paid was very high, and in the end the hold of the Russian authorities seemed nearly as firm as before.

One of the major concessions by the government had been the establishment of the Russian State Duma. The elections to the State Duma between 1906 and 1912 aroused considerable interest in Warsaw. The issues aired were broad questions of the destiny of Poland. The "Jewish question"—essentially, the problem of how the Poles should deal with the Jewish presence, and what the Jews themselves should strive toward—ranked high among these issues.[68]

In the first elections, in 1906 and 1907, the National Democrats made skillful use of the "Jewish question" to rally Polish support and defeat Polish liberal–Jewish alliances. The National Democrats, led by Dmowski, quickly learned that "WARSAW IS IN DANGER!" (that is, from the Jews) was an effective campaign slogan, and that intimidation and acts of violence directed against Jewish voters and Polish liberal leaders were also useful. The National Democrats won these elections handily.

The fourth and last election, in 1912, was more complex. The National Democrats faced both an alliance of anti-Dmowski Polish nationalists and a Jewish nationalist coalition. The two Polish slates split the Polish vote, and the Jews won a majority in the local electoral college. Deciding that sending a Jew to the State Duma would be too provocative, the Jewish coalition elected a member of the Polish Socialist Party, a worker and political nonentity named Eugeniusz Jagiello. He was the only Polish candidate who said he would support at least the goal of Jewish equal rights.

The chief result was an economic and social boycott against the Jews led by the National Democrats. The boycott campaign, with its slogan *"swoj do swego po swoje"* (essentially "stick to your own") won wide support and left deep scars in local society. The chief of police shortly afterwards reported to St. Petersburg that there had been a "significant worsening of Polish-Jewish relations, not only in Warsaw, but in the whole region," and that the boycott "continues to gain strength and will not soon die out."[69]

Polish historians have blamed the Russian authorities for encouraging the rising tensions and conflicts between Poles and Jews in Warsaw from the 1880s on, sometimes suggesting, for example, that the pogrom was instigated by the Russians, or that "Litvaks" were deliberately sent to Poland. However, no substantial evidence has ever been brought forward to support these notions. In a broad sense, the generally repressive and specifically anti-Polish and anti-Jewish atmosphere and policies of the Russian Empire exacerbated ethnic separatism and conflict. But the Russian authorities were usually more concerned with keeping a lid on things than with actively stirring up trouble.

One of the key factors in local politics from 1905 to the war was the rise of the first effective means of mass communications—the low-cost, high-circulation periodical press.[70] Warsaw's newspaper tradition reached back to the eighteenth century, but it was only in the last quarter of the nineteenth that it became a major element in the life of the city.

Up to 1905 the harsh Russian system of prepublication censorship ensured that the political voice of the press was muted. But the events of 1905 changed the situation. Not only was the population mobilized to unprecedented levels of political concern and activity, but censorship became far less restrictive. It became easier to establish a periodical, and political reporting and commentary was much more open. Henceforth the press both reflected major political events and was a major factor in them. Every significant political group tried to publish its own periodicals or at least to influence existing ones.

Warsaw's ethnic complexion was reflected in the press. Two separate press systems developed, one Polish, the other Jewish. By its very structure, the press was thus integrative within each ethnic group, as newspapers tried to reach and to speak for as many of "their own" people as they could; but at the same time it was divisive between ethnic groups, in that all but a very few titles aimed just at the Poles, or at the Jews.[71] Also, in content most of the successful newspapers increasingly emphasized ethnic division and conflict; tension and alarm, after all, sold newspapers. Polish dailies raged against the "Jewish danger" in 1906 and 1912, and called for boycotts. Yiddish-language newspapers attacked Polish nationalists, and made their fortunes from the 1913 Mendel Beilis ritual murder trial in Kiev.

The Polish press was large and varied, and prospered from the mid–nineteenth century on. Even though newspapers in Austrian and German Poland operated under fewer governmental constraints, Warsaw's titles were the most widely read in the Polish lands. The most popular were the daily *Kurjer Warszawski*, and *Tygodnik Illustrowany* (Illustrated Weekly). Leading cultural and political figures, such as novelists Prus and Henryk Sienkiewicz, and Dmowski and Swietochowski, all were active in the press.

After 1905 the daily press became thoroughly political. The National Democrats were especially successful at developing a range of well-edited titles aimed at all sorts of readers, from the intelligentsia to semiliterate workers and peasants. *Kurjer Warszawski*, meanwhile, espoused a cautious nationalism; the conservative *Slowo* (Word) looked to some sort of conciliation with Russia; the liberal *Nowa Gazeta* (New Gazette) tried to improve relations between the Polish and Jewish communities, only to find itself regarded as a traitor by both sides; and socialist papers were quickly suppressed.[72]

In 1864 there were in Warsaw five Polish dailies and fourteen weeklies; in 1914 there were fourteen dailies and sixty-one weeklies. In 1870 the five leading Polish dailies had, in a city of about 250,000 people, a combined circulation of 13,600. In 1909, when the city had approximately 750,000 residents, the five leading Polish dailies printed each day 123,000 copies. Thus, while the population trebled, circulation of these dailies rose ninefold.[73]

The Jewish press developed more slowly at first.[74] In the late nineteenth century it consisted mostly of two periodicals, one in Hebrew, *Ha-Zefirah* (usually translated The Dawn), and the other an assimilationist title in Polish, *Izraelita* (The Israelite). (For several years Nahum Sokolow edited both papers; this was the only time *Izraelita* had anything good to say about Zionism.) Since the first language of most of Warsaw's Jews was Yiddish, neither of these reached many readers.

But in 1905 the government finally began to allow the printing of Yiddish newspapers, and the Yiddish-language press blossomed spectacularly. By 1914 Warsaw had the highest circulation Yiddish newspapers in Europe. Readership came to be concentrated in two dailies, both of which lasted, competing furiously with each other, until September, 1939. These were *Haynt* (Today, founded 1908), and *Der Moment* (1910). These and other Yiddish titles presented a mixture of Jewish nationalism, sensational crime stories and scandals, prizes, and high quality writing by leading authors such as Isaac Loeb Peretz and Sholom Aleichem. The editor of *Haynt* thus explained his journalistic philosophy: "A reader, like a pig, eats everything, and likes the taste of s——."[75]

Real boons for the Yiddish press included the Beilis trial, and also the serialization of popular and sometimes erotic novels. I. B. Singer remembered that his older siblings "read the daily papers, including the serialized novels. I heard them talking about veiled ladies, horrible secrets, and fatal passions."[76]

CONCLUSION

Warszawa, Varshe, Varshava: the historic Polish capital; the greatest Jewish center in Europe; the third city of the Russian Empire. Warsaw was all of these.

A question that has been debated for many years—perhaps pointlessly—is the extent to which Russia is European, or Asian, or some unique combination thereof. If such a question had been applied to them, there is no doubt that most of Warsaw's residents would have replied that they were Europeans and Westerners, and, in any case, certainly not Russians.

This can be seen in the comparisons they made when discussing their city's problems. Statistical and descriptive data show that Warsaw's population characteristics were in many ways more like those of European than Russian cities (for example, in the ratio of men to women); and that the city was generally more advanced in social services (consider, for instance, that among the Empire's largest cities Warsaw had by 1910 the highest per capita numbers of doctors and telephones, the highest percentage of brick and stone buildings, and the second-highest percentage of paved streets). Despite this, the citizens were dissatisfied. They compared their lives and their city to Krakow, to Vienna, and to Berlin, and found their own wanting. The fact that they were, in many respects, better off than the residents of Moscow, Odessa, and St. Petersburg mattered little to them.

As a community Warsaw was deeply split along both ethnic and class lines. Lines between Poles and Jews were certainly shifting; more Jews adopted Polish language, dress, and customs, for example, but at the same time they remained consciously, ethnically Jewish. There was considerable contact between the two peoples, but little feeling of community. Poles and Jews remained as they had always been: essentially alien to and separate from one another. Residential patterns, economic activities, politics, religion, and the press all served to emphasize and exacerbate ethnic distinctiveness and conflict in Warsaw. Social interaction, and the technological revolution in transport and communications, and rapid economic change transformed the city in many ways but did not improve ethnic relations or lead to the development of a "melting pot."''' Indeed, perhaps in large part because leading political figures chose to emphasize ethnic conflict, mass political mobilization in Warsaw led to the politicization of ethnicity and the encouragement of interethnic rivalry and hostility.

Class struggle, another major source of conflict, was intertwined with ethnicity. Socialist movements, particularly the Polish Socialist Party and the Jewish Bund, both of which made use of nationalism, were strong in Warsaw. But class was also a divisive factor. National Democrats regarded all socialists as enemies, whether the latter were Poles, Jews, or Russian; and the socialists regarded the National Democrats with equal hostility. Bundists and Zionists were bitter foes of one another. Unlike in Russia proper, however, in Poland nationalism ultimately proved the strongest force. Socialism, not to mention Bolshevism, did not triumph in Warsaw or Poland as a whole at the end of World War I; and deep gulfs between the city's Polish and Jewish communities persisted in independent Poland.

Many years later, Isaac Bashevis Singer recalled his departure from Warsaw in 1917, after seven years of boyhood in the city. The Germans and Austrians had occupied the city for two years; famine and disease were decimating the population; to the east, the Tsar had been overthrown. Thirteen-year-old Isaac and his mother were going to stay with relatives in Austrian Galicia.

> With a screeching of whistles, the train began to move. On the platform, my brother Joshua seemed to grow smaller.
> Buildings, benches, and people moved backwards. It was thrilling to watch the world glide away, houses, trees, wagons, entire streets revolving and drifting apart as if the earth were a huge carousel. Buildings vibrated, chimneys rose out of the earth, wearing smoky bonnets. The towers of the Sobor, the famous Russian church, loomed over everything, its crosses glittering like gold in the sun. Flocks of pigeons, alternately black and gold, soared above the spinning, whirling city. Like a king or a great wizard, I rode through the world, no longer fearing every soldier, policeman, Gentile boy, or bum. What I had dreamed of for years was coming true.[78]

NOTES

1. On the history of Poland in the "partitions era" (1795–1918) see Piotr Wandycz, *The Lands of Partitioned Poland, 1795–1918* (Seattle: University of Washington Press, 1974). Basic works on Warsaw from the mid-nineteenth century to World War I are: Stefan Kieniewicz, *Warszawa w latach 1795–1914* (Warsaw, 1976); Jacob Shatzky, *Geshikhte fun Yidn in Varshe*, III (New York: Yivo Institute for Jewish Research, 1953); and Stephen D. Corrsin, "Political and Social Change in Warsaw from the January 1863 Insurrection to the First World War: Polish Politics and the 'Jewish Question'" (Ph.D. dissertation, University of Michigan, 1981).

In this period, the Russian Empire was officially on the Julian calendar, while Poland, with the rest of Catholic Europe, had used the Gregorian calendar for several centuries. In the nineteenth century the Gregorian Calendar was twelve days in advance of the Julian; the difference is thirteen days in the twentieth century. In Congress Poland this created a situation in which the government used one set of dates and most of the population used another. I have used the Gregorian calendar, as is the custom in Polish historiography.

2 A capable historical survey beginning in prehistory is Marian M. Drozdowski and Andrzej Zahorski, *Historia Warszawy*, 2nd ed. (Warsaw, 1975).

3. Isaac Bashevis Singer, *In My Father's Court* (New York: Farrar, Straus, Giroux, 1966), p. 59.

4. Aleksander Janowski, "Rzut oka po kraju," in *Opis ziem zamieszkanych przez Polakow pod wzgledem geograficzynm, etnograficzynm, historycznym, artystcznym, przemyslowym, handlowym i statystycznym*, II (Warsaw, 1904), 132. All translations into English from Polish and Russian in this essay are by me, except where otherwise noted.

5. "Warszawa," *S. Orgelbranda encyklopedja powszechna z ilustracjami i mapami* (1898–1903 ed.), XV, 151.

6. Boleslaw Prus, *The Doll*, trans. David Welsh (New York: Twayne, 1972), pp. 73–74.

7. Bernard Singer, *Moje Nalewki* (Warsaw, 1959), p. 7.

8. Adam Wein, "Zydzi poza rewirem zydowskim w Warszawie (1809–1862)," *Biuletyn Zydowskiego Instytutu Historycznego*, no. 41 (1962): 45–70.

9. Janowski, "Rzut oka po kraju," p. 86.

10. B. Singer, *Moje Nalewki* p. 86.

11. See Jozef Kazimierski et al., eds., *Dzieje Pragi* (Warsaw, 1970), for a history of Praga.

12. Irena and Jan Kosim, "Fritza Wernicka opis Warszawy z 1876 roku," *Warszawa XIX wieku*, fasicle 1, Studia warszawskie, vol. 9 (Warsaw, 1970), p. 326.

13. Janowski, "Rzut oka po kraju," pp. 137–38.

14. The most thorough studies of Warsaw's population can be found in Corrsin, "Political and Social Change in Warsaw," pp. 52–106, and Maria Nietyksza, *Ludnosc Warszawy na przelomie XIX i XX wieku* (Warsaw, 1971).

15. Edward Grabowski, "Skupienia miejskie w Krolestwie Polskim," *Ekonomista*, 14, no. 1 (1914): 31.

16. Tsentral'nyi statisticheskii komitet, ministerstvo vnutrennykh del, *Pervaia vseobshchaia perepis' naseleniia Rossiiskoi Imperii 1897 goda*, LI (St. Petersburg, 1904), Table 7.

17. Ibid., Table 25.

18. Adna F. Weber, *The Growth of Cities in the Nineteenth Century: A Study in Statistics* (1899; rpt. Ithaca, N.Y.: Cornell University Press, 1963), provides invaluable comparative statistical information on European and American cities.

19. Quoted in Janina Zurawicka, *Inteligencja warszawska w koncu XIX wieku* (Warsaw, 1978), pp. 49–50.

20. For a discussion of faith, language, and ethnic identity in Warsaw, see Corrsin, "Political and Social Change in Warsaw," pp. 83–96.

21. *Pervaia vseobshchaia perepis'*, LI, Table 13.

22. Witold Pruss, "Spoleczenstwo Krolestwa Polskiego w XIX i poczatkach XX wieku," *Przeglad Historyczny*, 68 (1977):282.

23. I. B. Singer, *In My Father's Court*, p. 207.

24. For a possibly unique memoir about Russian life in Warsaw, see the Ivan Shumilin Papers, Bakhmeteff Archive, Columbia University Libraries, folder "Staraia Varshava."

25. A more detailed analysis can be found in Corrsin, "Political and Social Change in Warsaw," pp. 69–83.

26. "Warszawa," *S. Orgelbranda encyklopedja*, XV, 151

27. Kieniewicz, *Warszawa*, p. 224. Witold Pruss, *Rozwoj przemyslu warszawskiego w latach 1864–1914* (Warsaw 1977) is a detailed study of Warsaw's industry.

28. Kieniewicz, *Warszawa*, p. 232.

29. See Stanislaw Herbst, *Ulica Marszalkowska* (1949; rpt. Warsaw, 1978).

30. B. Singer, *Moje Nalewki*, p. 8.

31. For analysis of the censuses' employment data, see Corrsin, Political and Social Change in Warsaw," pp. 133–75, and Nietyksza, *Ludnosc, Warsawy*, pp. 137–93. The 1882 census results were published as: *Rezul'taty odnodnevnoi perepisi naseleniia goroda Varshavay v 1882 roku. Rezultaty spisu jednodniowego ludnosci miasta Warszawy 1882 roku*, 3 vols. (Warsaw, 1883–85).

32. *Pervaia vseobshchaia perepis'*, LI, Table 22.

33. Corrsin, Political and Social change in Warsaw," pp. 142, 150.

34. Ezra Mendelsohn, *Class Struggle in the Pale: The Formative Years of the Jewish Workers' Movement in Tsarist Russia* (Cambridge: Cambridge University Press, 1970), p. 23.

35. On the 1911 incident, see Samuel A. Portnoy's translation of Vladimir Medem's *Fun mayn leben, Vladimir Medem. The Life and Soul of a Legendary Jewish Socialist* (New York: Ktav, 1979), p. 485.

36. Corrsin, "Political and Social Change in Warsaw," pp. 141, 147, 149–50.

37. Ibid., pp. 151–62.

38. Kieniewicz, *Warszawa*, pp. 179–81. Of course, the Imperial municipal government statutes of 1870 and 1892 were never applied in Congress Poland.

39. Ibid., p. 191.

40. Ibid., p. 194.

41. Some of the striking percentual shifts in Table 2 resulted from major construction products. The sewers and water mains, for instance, were mostly built in the early 1880s.

42. The fortifications included a ring of several dozen forts surrounding the city, as well as the citadel.

43. Jerzy Cegielski, *Stosunki mieszkaniowe w Warszawie w latach 1864–1964* (Warsaw, 1968), p. 85.

44. Tsentral'nyi statisticheskii komitet, Ministerstvo vnutrennykh del, *Goroda Rossii v 1910 godu* (St. Petersburg, 1914); pp. 774–883 cover Congress Poland.

45. Ibid.

46. I. B. Singer, *In My Father's Court*, pp. 226–27.

47. *Kurjer Warszawski*, 10 March 1913.

48. Kieniewicz, *Warszawa*, p. 201.

49. Boleslaw Prus, *Kroniki*, III (Warsaw, 1954), 132–33.

50. Shumilin Papers, "Staraia Varshava," p. 22.

51. Kieniwicz, *Warszawa*, p. 220.

52. Nietyksza, *Ludnosc Warszawy*, pp. 98–120.

53. Kieniewicz, *Warszawa*, p. 219.

54. *Goroda Rossii v 1910 godu.*

55. Kieniewicz, *Warszawa*, pp. 214–16.

56. Prus, *Kroniki*, VI, 13.

57. I. B. Singer, *In My Father's Court*, p. 17.

58. *Praca Polska*, 8 March 1906.

59. A survey of Polish political history can be found in Wandycz, *Lands of Partitioned Poland*. Studies of Jewish politics in the Russian Empire, unfortunately, almost completely ignore developments among the Jews of Warsaw and Congress Poland, or dismiss them as trivial (even though Congress Poland had one-fourth of the Empire's Jews, and Warsaw had the largest Jewish urban community in Europe).

60. For a selection of Swietochowski's essays, see his *Liberum veto*, eds. Samuel Sandler and Maria Brykalska, 2 vols. (Warsaw, 1976).

61. Shatzky, *Geshikhte fun Yidn in Varshe* III, 95–110, discusses the pogrom.

62. Wandycz, *Lands of Partitioned Poland*, pp. 275–303.

63. Mendelsohn, *Class Struggle in the Pale*, p. viii.

64. The most thorough work on 1905 in Warsaw is Halina Kiepurska, *Warszawa w rewolucji 1905–1907* (Warsaw, 1974).

65. Halina Kiepurska and Zbigniew Pustula, eds., *Raporty warszawskich oberpolicmajstrow (1892–1913)* (Wroclaw, 1971), p. 89.

66. Kieniewicz, *Warszawa*, p. 301.

67. Kiepurska and Pustula, eds., *Raporty*, pp. 71, 74

68. For detailed studies of these elections, see Corrsin, "Political and Social Change in Warsaw," pp. 273–322, and idem, "Polish Political Strategies and the 'Jewish Question' during the Elections in Warsaw to the Russian State Duma, 1906–1912" (paper delivered at conference entitled "Poles and Jews: Myth and Reality in the Historical Context," at Columbia University, March 1983).

69. Kiepurska and Pustula, eds., *Raporty*, p. 119.

70. On the press, see Corrsin, "Political and Social Change in Warsaw," pp. 226–72; Jerzy Lojek, ed., *Prasa polska w latach 1864–1918* (Warsaw, 1976); Marian Fuks, *Prasa zydowska w Warszawie, 1823–1939* (Warsaw, 1979); and idem, *Fun noentn ovar*, 2 vols. (New York, 1956–57).

71. Many Jews read Polish newspapers, and a few Jewish newspapers were printed in Polish, such as the assimilationist *Izraelita* and the Zionist *Glos Zydowski*. But the essential point—separate publications aimed at separate audiences—is nonetheless valid.

72. Zenon Kmiecik, *Prasa warzawska w latach 1908–1918* (Warsaw, 1980) covers this period in great detail for the Polish press.

73. Corrsin, "Political and Social Change in Warsaw," 235–36.

74. Shatzky, *Geshikhte fun Yidn in Varshe*, III, 307: "Warsaw had until 1905 no Jewish press in the modern sense of the term."

75. B. Singer, *Moje Nalewki*, p. 161.

76. I. B. Singer, *In My Father's Court*, p. 73.

77. Corrsin, "Political and Social Change in Warsaw," pp. 9, 26, elaborates on this point.

78. I. B. Singer, *In My Father's Court*, pp. 267–68.

BIBLIOGRAPHICAL NOTE

Archival materials for the study of the history of Warsaw were largely destroyed during World War II. The most valuable surviving primary source consists of the periodical press. Particularly important (and available in this country, chiefly at the New York Public Library) titles include: *Kurjer Warszawski* (1821–1939), *Prawda* (1881–1915), *Tygodnik Illustrowany* (1859–1939), *Izraelita* (1866–1913), *Haynt* (1908–1939), and *Moment* (1910–1939). For the study of the city's population, the two censuses which were taken in Warsaw in 1882 and 1897 are quite valuable: *Rezul'taty odnodnevnoi perepisi naseleniia goroda Varshavy v 1882 roku. Rezultaty spisu jednodniowego ludnosci miasta Warszawy 1882 roku*, 3 vols. (Warsaw: 1883–85); *Pervaia vseobshchaia perepis' naseleniia Rossiiskoi Imperii 1897 goda*, LI (St. Petersburg 1904). The 1897 Imperial Russian census is available in microfiche in many American libraries; the 1882 locally organized Warsaw count is, to the best of my knowledge, available outside of Poland only as a microfilm at the University of Michigan Graduate Library. My dissertation, "Political and Social Change in Warsaw from the January 1863 Insurrection to the First World War: Polish Politics and the 'Jewish Question,'" is the most thorough study in English of Warsaw in the half-century before World War I. In it can be found detailed analyses of the sources, in particular the censuses.

There is an enormous literature in Polish on the history of Warsaw. Much of it has appeared in recent years. The serials *Rocznik Warszawski* and *Kronika Warszawy* publish information on "Varsaviana" studies. An important essay which appeared in the former's first (1960) issue is Stanislaw Herbst, "Historia Warszawy: Stan i potrzeby badan." Juliusz W. Gomulicki discusses three centuries of Polish writing about the city in his "Trzysta lat ksiazki o Warszawie (1643–1944)," in Stanislaw Tazbir, ed., *Z dziejow ksiazki i bibliotek w Warszawie* (Warsaw: 1961). The bibliography in Marian M. Drozdowski's and Andrzej Zahorski's *Historia Warszawy*, 2nd ed. (Warsaw: 1975), lists major works on the city, as does the introductory discussion of sources in Stefan Kieniewicz's very thorough compilation, *Warszawa w latach 1795–1914 (Warsaw: 1976).* The multivolume series *Studia warszawskie*, which appeared in twenty-five volumes in 1968–79, is a mine of valuable articles.

There is much less secondary material on the Jews. Polish sources are usually of little help; Polish writers have generally lacked the linguistic expertise, or simply the interest, to study Jewish Warsaw. A standard source is Jacob Shatzky's three-volume *Geshikhte fun Yidn in Varshe* (New York: Yivo Institute for Jewish Research, 1947–53); the third volume covers from the 1860s to the 1890s. The Yivo Institute in New York has research materials prepared by Shatzky, as well as a large collection of relevant books and periodicals. The demographics of the Jewish population can be studied adequately through the censuses, but a great deal of work remains to be done on the culture and politics of Jewish Warsaw.

Tverskaia ulitsa—now Gorky Street—in Moscow, circa 1900. *Russland* (Munich, 1916), p. 39.

Sukharev Square and market at the turn of the century. In the
background is the Sukharev water tower, one of Moscow's land-
marks until razed in the 1930s, when the square was renamed
Kolkhoznaia. This and the following Moscow photos are from
the Museum of the History and Reconstruction of Moscow.

A second view of Sukharev Square, Moscow.

A shoemaker working at one of Moscow's
open-air markets at the turn of the century.

Moscow's City Council building on Voskresenskaia Square, built
by the architect D. I. Chichagov in 1890–92. The building now
houses the Lenin Museum.

The Riabushinskii mansion, also on Malaia Gruzinskaia Street. It was built in the art nouveau style by F. O. Shekhtel', president of the Moscow Society of Architects.

The Shchukin mansion in Moscow on Malaia Gruzinskaia Street, built at the end of the nineteenth century in the "Russian style" by the architects Erickson and Freidenberg.

Barges on the Fontanka, St. Petersburg, about 1900. *Russland*, p. 6.

View of St. Isaac's Cathedral, St. Petersburg. From a photograph in the Victoria and Albert Museum, London.

С. Петербургъ
St.-Pétersbourg

Петропавловская Крѣпость.
Forteresse de St. Pierre et St. Paul.

View of SS. Peter and Paul Fortress, St. Petersburg—note the factory chimneys in the background. From a picture postcard in the National Museum of Finland, Helsinki.

Kiev: the Contract Hall on the Podol, completed in 1819 and rebuilt in 1878, in a late nineteenth-century photo. *Istoriia Kieva* (Kiev, 1963), p. 256.

Kiev's Main Street, the Kreshchatik, in the late nineteenth century. Russia's first electric steetcars were introduced in Kiev in the 1890s. *Istoriia Kieva*, p. 481.

Home and shed on Vasil'kovskaia Street. Kiev's outlying neighborhoods such as this one in Lybed District contained many small wooden houses and much open land. *Istoriia Kieva*, p. 497.

On the Podol in Kiev—the Samson Fountain and a turn-of-the-century market. *Istoriia Kieva*, p. 475.

View of the Podol with the Bratskii Monastery in the center, about 1900. Titus D. Hewryk, *The Lost Architecture of Kiev* (New York: The Ukrainian Museum, 1982), p. 21.

The Arsenal. This armaments plant was one of Kiev's largest factories. *Istoriia Kieva*, p. 468.

A turn-of-the-century People's Reading Hall and the site of Kiev's first Ukrainian Theatre. *Istoriia Kieva*, p. 442.

St. Sophia Church (1037) and Belltower (1746); at right is the monument to Bogdan Khmelnitsky (1888) in Sofiiskaia Square, Kiev, circa 1900. Z. Shamurina, *Kiev'* (Moscow, 1912), p. 1.

Entrance to Monastery of the Caves, Kiev. *Russland*, p. 81.

Turn-of-the-century Warsaw. *Russland.*

Riga: view of the city from the harbor. *Russland*, p. 91.

Herder Square, Old Town Riga, in the 1870s. N. Asmuss, *Album von Riga* (Riga, 1871).

St. Peter's Lutheran Church, a center of German and Latvian religious life and an Old Town landmark since the mid-fifteenth century. Asmuss, *Album von Riga.*

Jewish chicken seller, Odessa. *Russland.*

Deribasovskaia Street at corner of Rishel'evskaia Street. From a centennial volume produced by the Odessa city administration, *Odessa, 1794–1894* (Odessa: Tipografiia A. Shul'tse, 1895), opposite p. 40.

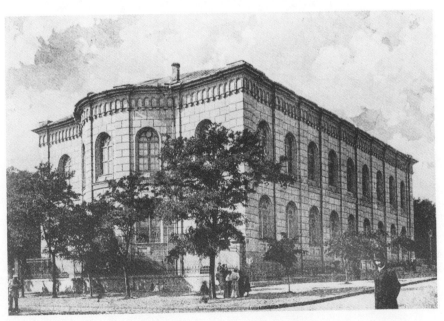

Odessa's main synagogue, corner of Rishel'evskaia and Evreiskaia Streets. *Odessa, 1794–1894*, p. 403.

Odessa: flea market on Prokhorovskaia Square. *Odessa, 1794–1894,* p. 357.

Selling rugs on the Maidan—"the Persian Square"—Tiflis's oldest quarter. This and other Tiflis photos are from the Tbilisi City Museum.

A pottery shop on the Maidan.

Fishmongers on Maidan Square, Tiflis.

A late nineteenth-century view from the Maidan of a Georgian Church and the Nariqala fortress.

The Maidan, Tiflis—from an early nineteenth-century painting by Gagarin.

Dezertirskii Bazaar, Tiflis.

A view of old Tiflis in the nineteenth century. At the upper left, Metekhi church and prison; at upper right the fortress of Nariqala.

Tiflis: watermills on the Kura.

Baku's waterfront, circa 1900. All Baku photographs are from a private collection.

View of Baku's Inner City (*Krepost'* in Russian); fifteenth-century wall in foreground; in back, on higher ground, palace complex of Shirvanshahs.

Zoroastrian temple in the oil district Surakhany just outside Baku. First erected in the eighth century, antedating the spread of Islam to the area, it was rebuilt in the nineteenth century by Zoroastrians who had returned after over a thousand years of self-imposed exile in India.

View of Baku's bay from the Inner City; the Maiden Tower is on the right.

View of the southwest wall of Baku's Inner City; in the foreground the Governor's Park and enclosing fence. From this vantage point, the bay is to the right.

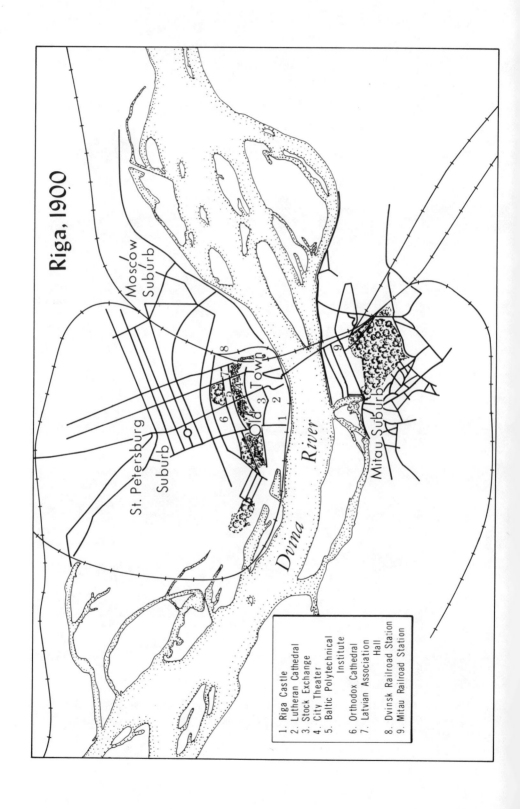

Riga, 1900

Moscow Suburb

St. Petersburg Suburb

Old Town

Mitau Suburb

Dvina River

1. Riga Castle
2. Lutheran Cathedral
3. Stock Exchange
4. City Theater
5. Baltic Polytechnical
   Institute
6. Orthodox Cathedral
7. Latvian Association
   Hall
8. Dvinsk Railroad Station
9. Mitau Railroad Station

6.

Riga

Growth, Conflict, and the Limitations of Good Government, 1850–1914

ANDERS HENRIKSSON

The Baltic port of Riga was commonly described as the most "European" of Imperial Russia's great cities. Historically it has been a German town. Founded at the dawn of the thirteenth century by Bishop Albert of Buxtehude, it began as an outpost on the eastern frontier of medieval Latin Christendom. As headquarters of the crusading Teutonic Order, the city lay at the center of the Catholic drive to conquer and convert the peoples of the eastern Baltic littoral. Most of medieval Riga's inhabitants were colonists lured eastward from Lübeck, Bremen, and other north German towns by the prospect of commercial gain. The Dvina river reached deep into Russia, making the city at its mouth a transshipment point where fortunes could be amassed from the lucrative trade in timber, herring, furs, and hides.

The sixteenth century brought the Lutheran Reformation. With it arrived the end of ecclesiastical rule and the inception of a period of shifting political allegiances. From 1522 to 1581 Riga was a sovereign political entity. Independence was followed first by Polish and then by Swedish rule. Incorporation into the Russian Empire did not come until 1710, when the city was conquered from the Swedes by the armies of Peter the Great.

Russian rule neither severed Riga's ties to the West nor substantially altered its German character. Until the middle of the nineteenth century immigration from Germany continued to rebuild a population which had been decimated by siege and starvation during the Great Northern

War. Although St. Petersburg emerged as a major rival, Riga played an important role in Russia's commercial relations with Europe. Cultural and intellectual life remained thoroughly German.

An important legacy of Riga's checkered political history was a tradition of self-government by privileged estates. For centuries prior to the Russian conquest municipal government had been the preserve of three powerful corporate estates—a merchant guild, an artisan guild, and a magistracy composed of twenty merchants and lawyers. Representing the summit of affluence, power, and prestige, the estates jealously defended their authority against all challengers. Russian rule did little to change this. The capitulations of 1710, which defined the terms of Russian dominion in the Baltic provinces, simply reconfirmed the power of the estates. Save for a brief interlude at the close of the reign of Catherine the Great,[1] the estates were left largely to their own devices until 1877, when the Russian municipal reform of 1870 was implemented in Riga and other Baltic towns. Although estates rule was a relic of the past when the changes of the late Imperial era unfolded, estates tradition continued to influence the attitudes and behavior of the propertied elite who controlled city government. Hence municipal politics after 1877 were characterized by local assertiveness against Imperial authority, an equation of civic responsibility with social prestige, and a firm resolve on the part of the governing elite not to share power with a wider spectrum of the urban community.

While Germans historically played the leading role in local life, Riga's population had always been a colorful blend of different national and religious communities. Migrant Latvian peasants from the surrounding countryside had comprised the bulk of the city's humbler classes since the Middle Ages. Like the Germans, the Latvians were Lutheran, a circumstance which favored the intermarriage between the two groups as well as the Germanization of upwardly mobile Latvians. The first Russians to settle in substantial numbers were Old Believers fleeing Tsarist persecution in the seventeenth century. They were joined a century later by a growing colony of Orthodox Russian merchants and by peasant migrants from neighboring Russian provinces. Other groups included Yiddish-speaking Jews, who began arriving from the Pale of Settlement during the nineteenth century, and immigrants from England and Scandinavia, many of whom Germanized after two or three generations' residence.[2] National and religious diversity was to lend both flavor and friction to life in late Imperial Riga.

THE EMERGENCE OF A BALTIC METROPOLIS

Mid–nineteenth century Riga numbered among the more significant Russian provincial cities. As the third busiest port after St. Petersburg and Odessa, it was an important international commercial center. It was also the hub of Baltic regional government. Riga castle, once the bastion of the Teutonic Knights and still fronted by a monumental statue of the Order's Grand Master Wolter von Plettenberg, a German hero who saved the Baltic from Muscovite conquest in 1502, was the residence of the Baltic governor-general. As capital of Livland, Riga was also home to a provincial governor and a diet which represented the corporate interests of the province's landed German aristocracy.

Riga's population of approximately one hundred thousand, fifth largest in the empire, typified the multinational character of Russia's western borderlands. An 1867 census showed that, judged on the basis of "everyday language," the city was 42.8 percent German, 25.1 percent Russian, 23.5 percent Latvian, and 5.1 percent Jewish.[3] The German community represented not only the largest group, but also the socially and politically dominant one. After a century and a half of Russian rule, Riga's German heritage remained very much intact. The language of municipal, provincial, and, until 1867, even crown authority was German,[4] as was the language of business, finance, and cultural life. The uppermost layer of society was formed by a merchant patriciate which owned the great trading houses and dominated municipal politics. Aside from a handful of Russians, this affluent, powerful group was exclusively German. Many more Russians, as well as Jews and Latvians, could be found among the humbler practitioners of trade, but Germans still constituted a solid majority among shopkeepers and other petty tradesmen.[5] German preeminence was even more marked in the free professions and the civil service. According to the 1867 census, 74.5 percent of professionals and 78.8 percent of government workers were German. Without exception the skilled master craftsmen whose prosperous shops lined the twisting thoroughfares of the central business district were German. While Russians, Latvians, and Jews comprised a substantial minority among artisans, most of them were semiskilled workers, repairmen, and odd-jobbers who earned a precarious living in the poorer reaches of the suburbs.[6] The unskilled laborers, servants, factory hands, and others who made up the lower strata of society were chiefly Latvian and Russian.

The primary motive force in Riga's economy was trade. Mechanized factory industry was still in its infancy. Riga's small industrial complex consisted of a porcelain factory, a pair of steam sawmills, a cotton spinnery, a handful of tobacco processing plants, two flax mills, two woolen mills, and a scattering of small food and beverage processing enterprises. In 1864 Riga could boast only twenty factories that employed fifty or more workers. The very largest, a British-owned sawmill, had a labor force of 570.[7]

At the close of the 1860s, Riga stood on the brink of profound change. The last decades of empire were to be a period of rapid growth and modernization. The value of commercial traffic through the port of Riga rose eightfold between 1870 and 1913.[8] Industrial development was even more striking. By the end of the Imperial era Riga ranked as one of Russia's greatest industrial centers.

Several factors underlay this sweeping transformation. Riga entered the railroad age in 1861, when a line connecting the city to Warsaw and St. Petersburg began operation. A decade later Riga had rail access to the black soil region of the south and by the early 1900s to the Pacific Ocean and the Far East. The railroad was a powerful stimulus to economic growth, opening vast new markets and previously untapped reserves of commercial commodities and raw materials for industry. Like many other Russian cities, Riga also benefited from state-sponsored efforts to encourage industrial development. The raising of tariffs on imported manufactured goods, the availability of low-cost state loans, and the awarding of lucrative government contracts to local manufacturers all contributed significantly to industrial growth. Foreign investment provided an additional impetus. Many of the largest industrial concerns were at least partly foreign owned. Finally, the role of local entrepreneurs, financiers, and technocracts should not be overlooked. Much of Riga's industry was locally owned and managed.[9]

The pace of industrial development, however intense at times, was uneven. The 1870s and 1880s saw gradual but substantial progress which laid the foundations for later expansion. Many of Riga's leading machinery and heavy equipment manufacturers, including the huge railroad car producer Russo-Baltic Wagon, traced their origins to this period. Riga participated fully in the general Russian industrial boom of the 1890s. Machine-building and metalworking, together with light industries like wood finishing and textiles, grew dramatically. By the end of the decade Riga had also emerged as an important center for the production of rubberware and chemicals. Between 1890 and 1900 the labor force in Riga's factories tripled; and twenty-seven major industrial corporations were chartered during the period 1894–1899 alone.[10] The depression which afflicted Russian industry during the early years of the twentieth century did not spare Riga, where its effects contributed to the bloody and tumultuous events of 1905. Recovery from the slump and the revolutionary turmoil which it inspired arrived in 1907, ushering in a fresh burst of growth which lasted until the outbreak of war in 1914. Renewed prosperity brought both diversification and expansion to local industry, as the value of goods produced in the city's 205 largest factories increased by 177.1 percent between 1908 and 1913.[11]

The eve of World War I saw Riga's industry at the zenith of its prerevolutionary development. Like that of neighboring St. Petersburg, it was highly diversified and based on import and export processing. Pride of place went to machine-building and metalworking. Ten huge plants produced machinery for industrial and military use, while nine others manufactured tools, wire, and machine components. Two great shipyards built marine equipment and ships, including many naval vessels. The presence of the Russo-Baltic and Phoenix corporations made Riga a leading center for the manufacture of railroad cars. After 1907 Russo-Baltic Wagon expanded into new areas, emerging as a manufacturer of automobiles, agricultural machinery, and airplanes. Other branches of industry also flourished. The giant Provodnik Corporation, founded with French capital in 1888, had become by 1914 the largest rubberware producer in Russia and the second leading manufacturer of automobile tires in the world. Its Riga plant employed 14,000 workers.[12] The chemical industry produced cellulose, paint, dyes, varnish, perfume, soap, fertilizers, and industrial chemicals. Riga's textile industry included cotton, woolen, flax, and jute mills. Other significant industries were boot manufacturing, wood finishing, glass making, and tobacco processing.

Economic development was accompanied by dramatic population growth and by fundamental shifts in the city's national and social composition. Between 1867 and 1913 the population grew by nearly 500 percent to 481,000 as the burgeoning economy attracted tens of thousands of migrants. Riga had always been a magnet to Latvian peasants fleeing rural poverty and oppression at the hands of aristocratic landlords. For many the city presented the only escape from a life of drudgery and hopelessness—in the words of a Latvian folk saying, "Great roads, small roads, all lead to Riga (Lieli celi, mazi celi, vis uz Rigu aizteceja)." Until the very end of the nineteenth century the overwhelming majority of newcomers were Latvian. At the turn of the century the pattern began to shift. Latvians continued to arrive in Riga, but the development of the Russian railroad network and the expansion of Riga's economic hinterland brought ever greater numbers of peasant migrants, chiefly Russians, Poles, and Lithuanians, from more distant points. In 1867 a 64.3 percent majority of Riga's inhabitants had been born in the city, 21.8 percent elsewhere in the Baltic, and only 8 percent in other parts of Russia. By 1913 the percentage of native born had plummeted to 35.3, while migrants from the Baltic comprised 33 percent and those from other provinces 29.9 percent.[13]

The shifting national composition of the population is reflected in the censuses of 1867, 1881, 1897, and 1913. The once preponderant German element declined steadily until it represented less than a sixth of the total. In contrast the Latvians increased their relative share dramatically, emerging as the numerically dominant nationality. Russians, Poles, Jews, and Lithuanians also registered substantial gains.[14]

The social structure of the city as a whole and of the various national communities within it also underwent profound change. The Germans, despite their relative numerical decline, managed to defend their social and economic position rather well. Other groups nonetheless made substantial inroads. This was particularly true for the Latvians. In the past upwardly mobile Latvians had Germanized as a matter

TABLE 6.1

Riga's Shifting National Composition, 1867–1913
(in percentages)

	1867	1881 (nation- ality)	1881 (everyday language)	1897	1913
Latvians	23.5	32.8	29.5	41.6	38.8
Germans	42.8	31.0	39.4	25.5	16.4
Russians	25.1	19.7	19.6	16.9	22.4
Jews	5.1	12.2	8.7	6.5	4.5
Poles	—	3.0	1.9	5.0	7.4
Lithuanians	—	—	—	2.3	5.3
Others	3.3	1.3	0.9	2.1	5.2

SOURCE: *Die Resultäte der am 3. März in den Städten Livlands ausgeführten Volkszählung* (Riga, 1871); *Ergebnisse der baltischen Volkszählung vom 29. Dezember 1881* (Riga, 1883–1885); *Pervaia vseobshchaia perepis' naseleniia Rossiiskoi imperii 1897 goda*, XXI (St. Petersburg, 1905); *Perepis' naseleniia v g. Rige i Rizhskom patrimonial'nom okruge ot 5 dekabria 1913 g.* (Riga, 1914).

of course.[15] Hence there had been no Latvian upper and middle classes; to be Latvian was to be lower class. The growth of Latvian national consciousness, the sheer size of the Riga Latvian community and the increased opportunities for upward mobility created by industrialization, however, all worked against Germanization. Fewer and fewer Latvians were assimilated into the German community after the 1860s, and by the 1880s Riga had a small but growing Latvian bourgeoisie.

International commerce continued to be a German preserve, a fact sourly noted in 1902 by a Russian journalist who described the Riga Exchange as a "German citadel."[16] Finance and banking were also dominated by Germans. Both the Latvians and the Russians developed systems of credit unions free of German control, but the principal investment institutions, the Riga Commerce Bank, the Municipal Discount Bank, and the Exchange Bank, were all in German hands. Industrialization opened new avenues to riches for those endowed with capital, entrepreneurial skill, and good fortune, but many of those who benefited from these opportunities were German. Some were merchants who invested commercial capital in industry. Others were engineers or machinists able to capitalize on their technical expertise. By the turn of the century local Germans owned or controlled nearly a hundred industrial firms, including the bulk of the machine-building, metalworking, wood-finishing, chemical, tobacco, and food-processing industries. Russian industrialists owned a half dozen establishments, including the Kuznetsov porcelain factory, which was one of the largest of its kind in the Russian Empire. Jews figured prominently in the wood-finishing industry, owning five of the city's largest mechanized sawmills. Latvians controlled a major brewery, a small iron foundry, a sawmill, and a dye factory.[17]

Greater change was evident in the middle layers of society. Russification measures implemented by the Imperial authorities during the 1880s broke the German hold on the civil service.[18] German predominance in the free professions also eroded substantially. By 1897 Germans accounted for only 47 percent of the professionals, while the Russian share had risen to 19.2 percent and the Latvian to 18.6 percent. Latvians and Jews registered striking gains in local trade, thanks largely to the increasing availability of credit and the expansion of the local market as the city population grew. In 1897 the once dominant Germans comprised only 31.2 percent of tradesmen, while Latvians accounted for 28.4 percent, Jews 18.4 percent, and Russians 17.1 percent. Data on the national composition of occupational categories for the 1913 census have never been published; but some indication of the national structure of the middle and upper strata of society at the end of the imperial era can be gleaned from the results of a 1912 survey which categorized property owners by nationality.[19] The survey reflects trends which had been evident since the 1880s. Germans were still disproportionately represented among the more affluent elements of society, especially at the very summit. In Russian eyes Riga was still a "city of the Germans" on the eve of the First World War.[20] Yet other groups, especially the Latvians, made steady progress.

The most sweeping transformation took place at the lower end of the social spectrum, among the men and women who toiled in the mills, factories, dockyards, and workshops of the growing city. The fate of those who engaged in craft production is difficult to gauge with precision. Different trades met with different fates. Many artisans, especially

TABLE 6.2

Property Ownership in Riga by Nationality, 1912

Value of property in rubles	Total properties	Properties owned by:				
		Germans	Latvians	Russians	Jews	Others
Up to 500	389	54	263	24	6	42
500–2,000	918	188	547	84	22	79
2,000–5,000	804	234	371	114	31	54
5,000–10,000	645	197	269	82	48	49
Over 10,000	2,829	1,089	1,045	279	294	122

SOURCE: J. Krastins, ed., *Riga, 1860–1917* (Riga, 1978), pp. 182–83.

in the textile and metalworking trades, were ruined by factory competition. Others prospered. Plumbers, carpenters, and masons, for example,
benefited from the building boom that accompanied urban growth.
Moreover, the old German artisan elite was able to weather the changes
relatively well by producing hand-crafted luxury goods for the wealthy
or by taking employment as skilled hands or foremen in industry. Some
artisanal skills were rewarded well in the factory. One master cabinet
maker complained in 1895 that he and other shopowners could not
compete successfully for skilled hands with the railroad car industry,
which hired cabinet makers to finish passenger car interiors.[21] The
demand for construction workers, on the other hand, opened opportunities for newcomers. By the late 1890s German masters regularly took on
Latvian apprentices; by the turn of the century Latvians dominated the
construction trades.[22] Many more migrants found work as factory laborers. In 1890 Riga already had a factory proletariat of more than 16,000.
Ten years later this figure had mushroomed to 47,500, and by 1913 it
stood at 76,280, fourth largest in Russia.[23] The working class was predominantly Latvian, but included substantial numbers of Russians,
Jews, Lithuanians, and Poles.[24]

AN EXEMPLARY CITY?

In 1910 a correspondent for the liberal Russian journal *Gorodskoe
delo* (Urban Affairs) praised Riga as an "exemplary" city favored with
modern amenities, an honest and capable municipal administration,
good transportation facilities, a high standard of public health, and an
abundance of well-groomed parks.[25] In no small part this glowing assessment was accurate, but in other ways it was superficial. Serious urban
ills lurked beneath Riga's tidy, bustling surface.

The quality of life undeniably improved during the late Imperial
period, although the more affluent strata of society drew disproportionate benefit from most of the improvements. Among the most striking
changes were those in the physical substance and outward appearance
of the city. Mid–nineteenth century Riga still had the look of a medieval
German stronghold. The central Old Town was girded by a massive
stone wall a meter thick and nearly ten meters high. Behind the grim
presence of the wall lay a warren of serpentine streets which wound
their way through a jumble of densely packed stone buildings. A visitor
once remarked that "The whole appears a huge mass of rock, bored
through with holes for houses . . . its streets like so many shafts and
strata in a mine."[26] Dark, cold, and fetid with the stench of the stagnant
moat that lay outside the wall, the Old Town was nonetheless the hub
of government, trade, and industry. Here the bulk of the merchant

patriciate and the German artisan elite lived in cramped flats above their shops. Three suburbs comprised the remainder of the city. In appearance, in stark contrast to the city center, they resembled a typical Russian provincial town. Broad, straight streets lined with pillared wooden buildings lent the suburbs an air of spaciousness. Yet the three suburbs differed substantially from one another. The St. Petersburg suburb, in the northeast, was comparatively affluent. East of the city lay the shabby, sprawling Moscow suburb, at once the most populous and the poorest district. Across the Dvina from the Old Town the Mitau suburb housed most of the city's harbor workers.

Mid-nineteenth century Riga offered few modern amenities. The city water system, a relic of the seventeenth century, supplied pumps in the Old Town with water drawn from the river at a point downstream from the city, where its quality was very poor. Sewage disposal was primitive. The Old Town was served by plank-covered trenches leading to the moat and the river. In the suburbs waste was either deposited in open pits or simply thrown into the street. The combination of polluted drinking water and inadequate sewage disposal led to recurrent epidemics of cholera and typhus. On a more positive note, Riga provided its citizens with an excellent municipal school system. Financed and administered by the estates, it included two secondary, one middle, and fourteen elementary schools. Tuition rates were modest, but all instruction was in German.

The most striking physical change of the late Imperial era came in 1857 with the demolition of the city wall, which was deemed no longer capable of withstanding bombardment. Freed from the stony embrace of its ancient fortifications, the Old Town was opened to fresh air and sunlight. Removal of the wall initiated a sweeping redevelopment of the city center. The area once occupied by the battlements, the moat, and an open field separating the fortified Old Town from its suburbs was gradually transformed into Riga's most fashionable and attractive district. The moat was converted into a flowing, fresh-water canal lined with trees and flower beds. The once barren ground beyond the canal grew into a pleasant neighborhood of parks, gardens, and broad boulevards where elegant residences were interspersed with schools, public buildings, museums, and shops. Here, in multistoried brick apartment blocks replete with modern luxuries like elevators and steam radiators, lived Riga's prosperous bourgeoisie.

The population explosion of the late nineteenth and early twentieth centuries had by far its greatest impact on the suburbs, where construction proceeded at a furious pace.[27] Although wood remained the most common suburban construction material the number of sturdier structures grew steadily. Half of the residential buildings erected between 1910 and 1913 were brick. A trend toward multistoried apartment buildings also took hold shortly before World War I. Roughly two-thirds of the brick residential buildings completed during the period 1907–1913 had five or more stories.[28]

The St. Petersburg suburb remained the wealthiest, its innermost districts merging imperceptibly with the elegant outer circumference of the city core. In the main, however, the suburbs were the preserve of the lower classes, especially factory workers, 96.9 percent of whom lived there in 1900.[29] Life in the suburbs bore little resemblance to that in the city center. Housing was crowded and poor in quality. Basic amenities were often unavailable. In general, conditions became progressively worse as one journeyed outward from the center toward the ring of mills and factories which encircled the city.

The provision of basic services improved during the late Imperial era, but residents of the city center were usually the first and sometimes the only ones to benefit from them. The first attempt to improve the water supply came in 1863, when the estates built a waterworks equipped with a steam pump capable of delivering river water directly to private residences and public pumps; but the new system did not extend beyond the inner reaches of the St. Petersburg and Moscow suburbs. The Mitau suburb was not connected at all. Worse still, the water was unfiltered and, although drawn from upstream of the city, still polluted. Small fish and other aquatic creatures commonly made their way to home faucets.[30] The city government expanded the system deeper into the suburbs during the 1880s and 1890s, but, thanks to the dumping of industrial effluvients into the Dvina, the pollution problem grew more severe. Even the conservative *Düna-Zeitung* (Dvina News) complained in 1897 that "The question of the water supply has become a burning one . . . and has assumed the proportions of a calamity of the most serious kind."[31] Under pressure from the press and from public opinion, the city government finally acted in 1899, commencing construction of a new water system that tapped a source of unpolluted ground water northeast of the city. The new system was put into service in 1903, providing parts of the city with good drinking water for the first time, but serious problems persisted. The outer reaches of the suburbs were never connected to the system and no water mains bridged the Dvina to the Mitau suburb until 1910.[32] The city was almost equally tardy in seeking a remedy to the problem of sewage disposal. The estates considered a sewer construction project as early as 1875, but no concrete steps were taken by the municipal authorities until 1894, when construction of a modern underground sewer system began. Characteristically, only the central third of the city was supplied with sewer mains by the end of the Imperial era.[33]

Polluted drinking water and the lack of sewers caused serious public health problems. Cholera and typhus continued to present grave hazards. Predictably, the worst effects of pestilence were visited upon the poor, who could ill afford to purchase bottled water and who normally lived beyond the reach of the city water and sewer systems.[34] The severity of the situation is reflected in the death rate. While the annual incidence of death per thousand fell from nearly thirty in the 1870s to about twenty in the early 1890s, it began to rise slightly, chiefly as a result of overcrowding, as the century drew to a close.[35] The municipal authorities nonetheless did take steps to improve public health. By the beginning of the twentieth century, the city possessed a smallpox vaccination center, four emergency first aid stations, an 800-bed hospital, a leprosarium, a sanitorium for tuberculosis victims, a mental asylum, and a disinfection institute whose task was to combat cholera and typhus. A second city hospital was built in 1910. Another important advance in the struggle against disease was made in 1897 with the opening of a municipal slaughterhouse, where meat was prepared in hygienic conditions. Public health standards in Riga did not, moreover, compare unfavorably with those in other large Russian cities. One Russian observer, marveling that sanitation officials had prevented contamination of the water supply during an outbreak of cholera in 1909, went so far as to label the municipal public health system "outstanding."[36]

The first gas streetlights were introduced by the estates in 1862. The network of gas lines was gradually expanded by the city government, but many suburban streets, especially on the outskirts, remained either unlit or illuminated only by dim and inefficient kerosene lanterns.[37] Interior gas lighting became available in the 1870s, and the first electric lights in Riga were installed in the City Theater in 1887. Eighteen years later the city began operating a central electrical generating station which served public buildings and private residences in the city center. Although the station's output rose tenfold between 1906 and 1914, interior lighting remained a luxury available only to the comparatively wealthy.[38]

Major strides were made in public transit. Horse-drawn trolleys were introduced in 1882; in 1901 the trolleys, although privately owned, were electrified on the initiative of the city government. Electrification was accompanied by an extension of the trolley system to the suburbs. Between 1900 and 1914 the length of track quintupled, and the introduction of cheap rush-hour fares in 1911 enabled many workers to commute to the factories on the city's outer rim.[39] Passenger transportation across the Dvina was provided by a municipally owned fleet of sixteen steam ferries.[40] City streets, which remained the most important traffic conduits, were well maintained. Those in the city center had been paved long before the mid-nineteenth century; and as the city grew more and more suburban streets were paved, although many smaller lanes and byways were simply strewn with gravel. Major arteries received a three-to-six-meter brick center lane designed for faster traffic.[41]

Recreational and cultural facilities improved considerably. Many of the parks and gardens that graced the fashionable districts of the city center were laid out by the city government, which also planted trees, shrubs, and flowers along the major suburban boulevards. East of the canal a park donated to the city in 1817 by the patrician Wöhrmann family boasted gaslit concert and dining pavilions. After 1900 the city made a concerted effort to establish small parks and green areas in the suburbs, where they helped to relieve the bleak tedium of neighborhoods dominated by hastily constructed, architecturally unimaginative apartment blocks.[42] In 1901 the city also created a cottage community in a wooded area five kilometers northeast of the St. Petersburg suburb. Reachable by trolley and zoned exclusively for residential use, it became a popular summer haven for the middle class. The municipal authorities also actively supported cultural life. The estates constructed a German-language theater in 1863; and municipal subsidization of Latvian and Russian performing arts commenced in 1886. A Russian theater was built at city expense in 1902 and a Latvian one in 1908. The city had possessed a public library since the beginning of the nineteenth century. Library branches were opened in each of the suburbs between 1906 and 1914. In 1901 the city government donated land for a Latvian ethnographical museum and in 1905 it established a municipal art gallery.

The history of education in late Imperial Riga is marked both by progress and setbacks. The period opened on an auspicious note when in 1861 the estates, in cooperation with the Baltic aristocracy, established the Baltic Polytechnical Institute. A university-level German institution offering degrees in engineering, mechanics, commerce, architecture, and agronomy, it produced graduates destined to play a major role in Riga's economic growth. The city also founded twenty-one elementary schools, some of which used Latvian or Russian as the medium of instruction, during the 1870s and 1880s. The forcible Russification of the Baltic educational system which began in the 1880s, however, cast a pall over Riga's schools. The city simply lost interest in expanding or improving a school system over which it exercised little control and in which Russian was the only permissible language of instruction. The school system consequently failed to keep pace with the growth of the city, and increasing numbers of parents were unable to secure a place in school for their children. Not until 1906, when Russification was partially relaxed, permitting the use of other languages in elementary schools, did the city embark on a major new program of school construction, and even then a shortage of classroom space persisted. In 1914 one in five school age children did not attend class. Russification notwithstanding, the school shortage affected the Germans less severely than other national groups. Although Jews and Latvians made substantial gains in the school population, Germans were proportionately overrepresented, especially in the secondary schools, where in the 1906/1907 school year they comprised 34.5 percent of the student body.[43] Ironically, Russification failed to increase significantly the relative numbers of Russians in the schools.

Municipal government was a force for change and progress in Riga. Whatever its shortcomings, the municipal government was distinguished by a strong sense of civic duty, honesty, and a reasonably high standard of competence. *Gorodskoe delo* described Riga as a "well administered German city" whose officials were renowned for their "integrity, energy and conscientiousness." In the eyes of correspondent D. Protopopov, Mayor George Armitstead and his colleagues were diligent, skilled administrators who more closely resembled the directors of a successful business enterprise than typical representatives of local Russian government.[44]

Throughout the period 1877–1914, the reins of power remained firmly in the grasp of the traditional German ruling elite. The base of urban self-government was, to be sure, broadened in 1877 with the implementation of the 1870 Russian municipal reform. The estates had restricted the franchise to a privileged oligarchy of about 1,500 merchants, professionals, and artisan masters. In contrast, the 72-member town council created by the reform was elected by more than 5,200 taxpayers.[45] Yet the franchise was still narrow enough to ensure minimal change in the social and national composition of city government. Members of the estates comprised 79.2 percent of the town council elected in 1877.[46] Robert Büngner, the first mayor, was a senior magistracy official. The 1892 municipal counterreform further consolidated the position of the German elite, whose dominance is reflected in the succession of mayors who followed Büngner. August von Oettingen (1886–1889), one of the few Baltic aristocrats to participate in Riga politics, had once been governor of Livland. Ludwig Kerkovius (1890–1901) typified the Riga patrician who adapted to changing times by investing in industry. George Armitstead (1901–1912), Germanized grandson of a British immigrant, was an engineer and industrial entrepreneur. Educated at Oxford, Zürich, and the Baltic Polytechnical Institute, he owned a chemical plant and sat on the board of the Baltic Cellulose Corporation. Wilhelm von Bulmerincq, elected in 1913 as Imperial Riga's last mayor, was the scion of a prominent patrician family. Like Büngner, he was a lawyer, and had served as a city official for more than two decades prior to his election. The dominion of the German elite is also apparent from the national composition of the town council. Germans retained a majority of seats until 1913, when their share was reduced to half.

Attitudes and behavior associated with the estates system carried over to the new institutions. In no small part the lessons and experience of the past lay at the root of the well-developed sense of civic duty and

TABLE 6.3

National Composition of the Riga Town Council
(Number of Seats)

	1877	1882	1886	1890	1893	1897	1901	1905	1909	1913
Germans	65	61	61	57	70	71	61	56	43	40
Russians	4	5	5	6	4	3	10	12	10	15
Latvians	2	4	5	6	2	3	8	12	26	23
Others/										
Unknown	1	2	1	3	4	3	1	—	1	2
Total	72	72	72	72	80	80	80	80	80	80

SOURCE: *Rigasches Adress-Buch 1885* (Riga, 1885); *Rigasches Adress-Buch 1901* (Riga, 1901); *Rigascher Almanach*, 1880–1914; and election coverage in the Riga daily press, 1877–1913.

the administrative competence exhibited by Riga's elected officials. The men who served on the town council viewed themselves as inheritors of a proud, centuries-old tradition of urban self-government. In his 1878 inaugural speech Mayor Büngner laid particular stress on the need to preserve the spirit and values of the estates within the new institutions.[47] This belief in the virtue of continuity shaped the attitude of Riga's elite toward municipal administration throughout the late Imperial period.

The estates system had placed high value on civic patriotism and on involvement in city politics. The collective identity of the German elite was in a real sense defined by participation in estates self-government and by a sense of loyalty to the urban community. Riga's elite was consequently well versed in the art of self-government. Although the Imperial government wielded final authority over the estates, they had generally been left to their own devices. Estates self-government had, after all, functioned rather well, maintaining public order and meeting its fiscal and administrative obligations without the need for frequent state intervention. The estates tradition gave Riga an advantage which few Russian cities outside the Baltic provinces enjoyed. Smugly aware of this, Riga's officials were prone to view the weaknesses displayed by other city governments with ill-concealed condescension. When, for example, the 1892 counterreform became law, City Secretary Nicolai Carlberg commented: "The Russian municipal statute of 1870 had, on the whole, not proven successful. This was not, however, the fault of the statute, but rather of those for whom it was designed." Only the Baltic cities, he continued, prized the freedom afforded by self-government and understood its responsibilities.[48]

Interest in city politics was not, moreover, limited to a narrow circle. It extended to the voting public as a whole. A Russian observer found that the city administration was constantly under the watchful eye of an informed public.[49] Voter turnout for city elections was very high. During the 1870s and 1880s it hovered between 65 and 80 percent. Participation declined in the wake of the 1892 counterreform, possibly because many Latvians saw no reason to vote without hope of victory. As the economic strength of the Latvian bourgeoisie grew, however, interest revived. The 1901 election saw a 61-percent turnout; and in 1913 a striking 87 percent cast ballots in the most hotly contested election of the period.[50]

Another factor affecting the character of municipal administration was the relative diversity that prevailed within the town council. The German elite was uniform neither in occupation nor even in social class. Merchants, traditionally a leading force in city politics, normally comprised at least a third of the council. As the economy changed, industrialists, bankers, and technocrats figured more and more prominently in municipal administration. Members of the free professions, who had played an important role in the estates system, also continued to be active, usually occupying between a quarter and a half of the council seats. Artisan masters managed to preserve their voice as well. Masons, smiths, coopers, bakers, and others usually accounted for about a tenth of the council. While the elite character of city government often prejudiced it in favor of the more established and affluent elements of the population, its social and occupational diversity ensured that it did not become the patron of one narrowly defined clique. The clash of interests within the council could, on occasion, be sharp. Artisan councilmen fought a protracted, if ultimately losing, battle against construction of the municipal slaughterhouse, which they saw as a threat to the city's private butcher shops. Similarly, the 1890s witnessed a struggle between merchants and industrialists over the construction of a permanent bridge for vehicular traffic over the Dvina. The industrialists wanted the bridge as a link between southside factories and the city's harbor facilities on the north bank, while the merchants, whose warehouses stood on the north bank, successfully opposed construction.

Other features of government by the German elite were less positive. Despite protestations to the contrary, the city authorities clearly catered to the interests of the upper and middle classes. To expect a government elected by the wealthiest property owners to behave otherwise would perhaps be unrealistic. In a sense there were two late Imperial Rigas. The comfortable, bourgeois Riga that comprised the city center and the southwestern districts of the St. Petersburg suburb might fairly be called "exemplary." Residents enjoyed modern amenities, efficient civic services, pleasant parks and gardens, a vibrant cultural life, and good housing. The other Riga, consisting of the grimy working class districts that ringed the sparkling center, was hardly a model urban

community. Housing conditions ranged from barely adequate to abys-
mal, and pressing needs for basic amenities like drinking water, sewers,
and streetlights were often unanswered. Part of the blame for this rests
with the inadequate revenue base of the city government, but the
priorities of the ruling elite were also a factor. City officials saw no
pressing need to allocate public resources to improve the lot of the lower
classes. A municipal survey of housing conditions undertaken in the
1880s, for example, found conditions in the poorer districts "horrifying," but concluded that nothing could be done about it. It had always
been the lot of the poor to live in squalor.[51] Even Mayor Armitstead, a
dedicated public servant who strove to improve and broaden civic services, was careful to disclaim municipal responsibility in the case of
those for whom "no place is set at the table of nature."[52]

City officials also consumed much time and energy defending the
interests of the local elite against perceived threats from the Imperial
government. Riga's elite had initially been unhappy with the 1877
reform. They considered its extension of the franchise to lesser property
owners too liberal and feared that its implementation would lead to
increased state intervention in local affairs. Worse still, the reform did
not abolish the estates. The magistracy continued to function as municipal judicial authority until 1889, while the guilds clung to vestiges of
their former power until 1917. This made it possible for the elite to fight
a stubborn battle against the gradual transfer of municipal property and
authority from the old institutions to the new. Oddly, many of the
leaders in this struggle, including Mayor Büngner, held both estate and
municipal office. The city authorities finally made peace with the
Imperial government in the 1890s, when the futility of opposition to the
autocracy had finally become manifest and the 1892 counterreform
assuaged fears that the traditional ruling classes would fall victim to
some form of "democratization." The long conflict nonetheless
absorbed much of the city government's energy for nearly fifteen years,
distracting its attention from other issues.

Not all of the counterproductive friction that marred relations
between city and state, however, was caused by the former. The Imperial authorities, disinclined to trust any elected officials, were especially
wary of Riga's German administration. Alexander III and his chief
advisors subscribed to a form of Russian nationalism which encouraged
them to view German minorities as potential subversives. This belief,
however ill-founded, was shared by the Tsar's principal lieutenant in
Riga, Livland governor Mikhail Zinoviev, who once described the local
Germans as "foreigners."[53] These suspicions had a significant destructive effect on politics in Riga, leading the state repeatedly to intervene
peremptorily in municipal affairs and to Russify city schools, courts,
and administrative institutions. The city government resisted bitterly,
declaring Russificatory acts illegal and appealing them to the Senate,

but defiance brought only the dismissal of mayors Büngner and von Oettingen for insubordination. Cooler heads prevailed on both sides by the mid-1890s, but the effects of Russification were almost wholly negative. The city's vain attempts to prevent it, like the attempts to defend estates rights, consumed time and energy that might more profitably have been spent in other ways; in the end, the city administration was compelled to operate in an unfamiliar language.

The city government was also inhibited by legal limitations on its sources of revenue. Income from a real estate tax, the principal levy allowed to the city, never netted more than a quarter of the funds required by the annual city budget.[54] What is more, the city was obliged to subsidize local crown institutions, including the police and the military garrison. The municipal authorities responded to the financial challenge in several ways. On several occasions they unsuccessfully petitioned the Imperial government for assistance in funding the police force. Equally futile were efforts to obtain permission to institute a graduated municipal income tax, the first of which was made in 1863 by the estates and the last by the town council in 1906. The city was more successful in finding sources of revenue other than taxes in order to support a budget which nearly tripled between 1877 and 1914. The major public works projects of the 1890s and 1900s were financed by loans taken from Riga banks.[55] Still more significant was income from municipal enterprises, including the river ferries, the slaughterhouse, a grain elevator in the harbor, the municipal bank, the gas and water works, and the electrical station. By the mid-1900s income from these and other municipal enterprises constituted the most important single source of revenue.[56] The city government was able to pay the interest on its debt and to embark upon several ambitious public works projects; but the strictures imposed by the 1870 and 1892 municipal statutes on the city's right to levy taxes, not to mention the burden imposed by fiscal obligations to the crown, undeniably impaired the municipal administration's ability to provide its constituents with amenities and services.

CONFLICT AND COMMUNITY

Differences among the various national, religious, and social groups who comprised Riga's polyglot population were a frequent source of conflict. Cultural and social life were fragmented to a considerable extent along national lines. Each of the principal nationalities possessed its own network of cultural institutions, clubs, charities, political organizations, credit unions, and insurance societies. More seriously, Riga became the scene of bitter national strife between rival Latvians, Russians, and Germans.

A child of the 1860s, Latvian nationalism appealed chiefly to the emerging Latvian bourgeoisie and intelligentsia. It provided upwardly mobile Latvians with a sound sense of collective identity and group solidarity which helped them to assert their independence and to succeed in a society dominated by an entrenched German establishment. Not surprisingly, Latvian nationalism was often assertively anti-German. As Fricis Veinbergs, editor of the nationalist Rīgas avīze (Riga News), noted in 1902, the goal of Latvian nationalism was, after all, "to establish the independence of Latvian society from German society."[57] One of the guiding principles of Latvian nationalism, moreover, was the conviction that Riga was rightfully a Latvian city where the Germans represented an alien element. The principal nationalist organization was the Riga Latvian Association, established in 1868. Although its membership was never large,[58] it was the chief spokesman for Latvian national interests in the city, coordinating Latvian participation in municipal politics, subsidizing cultural undertakings, offering scholarships, and administering a variety of institutions which provided credit and other forms of assistance to Latvian business.

Russian merchants and officials found it peculiarly galling to be all but excluded from the ruling circles in one of their own country's great cities. Many of them found solace in a form of nationalism which viewed the German establishment as an unreliable foreign element and which exhorted Russians to consider it their patriotic duty to wrest control of city government from German hands. The Russificatory policies of Alexander III were greeted warmly by many local Russians, not least because they brought state subsidy for nationalist political and cultural activity within Riga.[59] If the anti-German tenor of Russian nationalism was relatively constant, Russian attitudes toward Latvians were more complicated. The Russians initially supported and encouraged Latvian national assertiveness, perceiving it as a force which could weaken the German establishment. The Russians did not, however, want the Latvians to succeed in replacing the Germans as the leading element in the city. For Russian nationalists the notion of Latvian nationhood was merely a "fantasy image" which hindered the inevitable assimilation of the Latvian people into the Russian mainstream.[60] Such views left little room for compromise, and over the long run Russian-Latvian relations deteriorated. By the turn of the century the two had even ceased to collaborate against the Germans. The Russians had no central organization comparable to the Latvian Association; but a variety of institutions, including a social club (the "Bee"), two daily newspapers, a credit union, a literary society, a mutual aid society for salesclerks, a church-sponsored school league, and several charities, catered specifically to the Russian community.

Until the outbreak of revolution in 1905, nationalism held little attraction for the Germans, whose collective identity still focused on social class. To the Germans language was a subsidiary function of class; and in Riga the upper classes spoke German and the lower classes Latvian. To be Latvian, therefore, was to be lower class, and nationalists who claimed to represent Latvian interests were in reality nothing more than radical demagogues who sought to encourage pretensions and incite unrest among the rabble. At the same time, the Germans dismissed local Russian nationalists as agents in the service of a meddlesome Imperial bureaucracy. The violence visited upon the Germans as a national group in 1905 finally convinced many of them that the wisest course lay in national solidarity. The principal manifestation of the new German national consciousness was the establishment in 1906 of the German National Union. A province-wide organization whose Riga chapter boasted more than 15,000 members by 1908, the National Union dedicated itself to "the unification, maintenance and strengthening of the entire German population in cultural, spiritual and economic affairs."[61] To this end it established a system of private German-language schools, subsidized German cultural life, and provided assistance to German businesses. The rise of German nationalism poured fuel on the fires of national rivalry in Riga, but its strength and drawing power should not be overestimated. It represented a radical departure from tradition, and many Germans found it unbecoming to loyal Russian subjects and beneath the dignity of an established ruling class. In one celebrated incident the director of the Municipal Discount Bank, a German patrician named Wannag, physically assaulted a colleague who had dared to sport a National Union badge in the halls of the stock exchange.[62]

National rivalry was intertwined with class conflict between the established elite and the *nouveaux riches* who comprised the non-German bourgeoisie. The German patriciate not only dominated politics, trade, and industry, but also dwelt in a rarified social milieu. It was a closely knit group, bound together by family relationships, business ties, and membership in selective clubs and fraternities.[63] The power and exclusiveness of the German establishment were a constant source of frustration for successful and ambitious outsiders.

Nowhere did class and national conflicts manifest themselves more strikingly than in municipal elections. The German elite blithely assumed that control of the city government was theirs by hereditary right. Stressing the virtues of experience and "continuity," resting on the laurels of their not inconsiderable achievements in city government and, at least until after 1905, eschewing any national motive, German election committees sponsored slates of candidates which won every contest from 1877 to 1913. The Germans owed their electoral triumphs chiefly to their numerical strength among property owners, but various forms of intimidation and chicanery, especially after the turn of the century, also contributed.[64] For rival committees backed by the Latvian

Association, the paramount issue was greater representation in city
government for the Latvians as a national group. At the heart of Latvian
politics lay anger at the town council's failure to reflect either the
changing national composition of the population or the growing economic clout of the Latvian bourgeoisie. The Latvians normally approached the elections with a set of specific national demands. Typical
of these would be a call for more city patronage jobs for Latvians or, at
least until the Russification of the educational system, for more Latvian
schools. The elections also had important symbolic value for Latvian
nationalists. Riga was Latvia's greatest city[65] and it was a point of pride
for nationalists to seek a larger role in its government. The program of
the 1882 Latvian committee characteristically complained that "The
Latvian in Riga, in the heart of his native land, remains a foreigner."[66]
Twenty years later the nationalist daily *Baltijas vēstnesis* (Baltic Herald)
stressed the value of a Latvian electoral victory as an expression of
Latvian achievement, declaring it the patriotic duty of every Latvian to
vote against the German administration even if he had no quarrel with
its actual policies.[67]

An element of opposition to the elitism and conservatism of the
city government also normally surfaced in the Latvian electoral platform. Calling themselves "liberal" or "progressive," the Latvian committees regularly attacked the German administration for insufficient
attention to the needs of the poor and to the suburban districts as well as
for inadequate provision of schools, medical facilities and social services. Yet progressivism was clearly secondary to nationalism for the
Latvian committees, which never formulated a coherent reform program. Greater national representation on the town council remained
the paramount issue throughout the period 1877–1913. The Latvian
nationalists were, after all, a relatively affluent, propertied group who
did not stand to benefit from any major diversion of city funds to
improve social services for the poor. In any case, given the limited
resources available to the city and the already ambitious programs run
by the German administration, there was probably little that the Latvians could have done to broaden the scope of the city government's
activity even if they had found themselves in power. Single-minded
concentration on the national issue did not, however, appeal to all
Latvian voters. A minority opposed it, charging that the nationalist
leaders represented only the wealthiest strata of Latvian society and
that they consequently ignored the plight of the humbler classes. In
1909 the leftist *Juanā dienas lapa* (New Daily News) went so far as to
declare that "progressive" Latvians had nothing to gain from supporting
the nationalist election committee, because the election should be
viewed as a struggle of the people against the entrenched establishment
instead of a nationality contest.[68] The upshot of this challenge was the
formation of a rival "progressive" Latvian committee for that year's

election. Unable, however, to attract much support from the propertied voting public, the leftists fared poorly and never again organized as a separate bloc.

From 1877 to 1897 the Latvians entered the electoral fray in alliance with Russian electoral committees. Each time the two committees nominated a joint slate. Like the Latvians, the Russians viewed the elections chiefly as a nationality contest. True to their nationalist ideology, the Russians stressed the patriotic merit of voting against the "separatist German clique" who used municipal government as a forum for acts of defiance against the Imperial authorities.[69] In 1901, however, the Russians employed a radically new tactic, abandoning their erstwhile Latvian partners in favor of an alliance with the Germans, an arrangement which endured through the election of 1913. Several factors lay behind the Russian shift. The incompatibility between Russian and Latvian nationalist ideology had imposed mounting strains on the Russo-Latvian entente. The Russian leadership, moreover, came from the uppermost crust of the Russian merchantry, a group which was more at ease dealing with the German patriciate than with the newly emergent Latvian business and professional classes. A strong element of pragmatism also figured into Russian calculations. Alliance with the Latvians had led only to repeated defeat. Cooperation with the Germans, on the other hand, ensured the Russians a set number of places on the German election committee slate.

Relations between the German patriciate and the non-German bourgeoisie were colored by animosity and mistrust, but the broader social conflict between haves and have-nots, especially factory workers, was more bitter and violent. Working class life in late Imperial Riga was not easy. Wages were low, especially for the women and girls who comprised more than a quarter of the factory labor force, work hours were long and tedious, the absence of safety precautions rendered many workplaces physically hazardous, and in many factories foremen used fines and threats of dismissal to establish a reign of terror over their unfortunate subordinates. Outside the factory, the most serious problem for workers was housing. Construction of apartment blocks with roomy flats and high rents more than kept pace with the requirements of the middle and upper classes, but Riga had a perpetual shortage of humbler accommodations. In 1913 only 60 percent of the city's apartments were small enough (one to two rooms) to suit the budgets of working class families. Worse still, rising property values caused rents to soar, doubling during the 1890s and leaping a further 37.4 percent between 1900 and 1914.[70] Thousands dwelt in overcrowded, dilapidated tenements, while others, still less fortunate, had no homes and slept in public doss-houses maintained by charities. Perhaps the most miserable conditions, however, were found in the city's many basement apartments, which had often been originally designed as root cellars or storage rooms. Ill-ventilated, badly lit, and subject to flooding during the spring, these subterranean dwellings were a menace to the health of their occupants.

Working class discontent, expressed in the form of strikes, riots, and individual acts of violence, began to flare with growing frequency in the 1890s, culminating in the bloody "Riga Riots" of May 1899. Sparked by a clash between police and jute mill workers striking for better wages and shorter hours, the 1899 disturbances involved more than 12,000 workers from twenty-eight factories.[71] Labor turbulence was a pronounced feature of the 1905 Revolution in Riga. Over 80,000 workers took part in an eight-day general strike in January, 1905. Sporadic riots, demonstrations, and strikes continued through the spring and summer; and in mid-October striking workers revolted and seized control of the city for several weeks. Violence marred the entire revolutionary period, causing 169 deaths and an estimated 500 serious injuries. Most of the casualties were workers killed or wounded by the police and military, but more than a score of factory supervisory personnel were among the dead.[72]

The 1905 Revolution saw the first manifestation of widespread working class political activism in Riga. Worker demands during the 1899 riots had been purely economic, but in 1905 strikers and demonstrators began to call for a constitution, guarantees of free speech, "four-tail" suffrage for a national legislature, and other political reforms. Although the Imperial government was the most common target of worker criticism, the Riga city authorities also came under frequent attack. Demands for a democratically elected town council which would pay attention to the plight of the poor surfaced repeatedly at working class political meetings and demonstrations.[73] The evidence indicates that the Riga labor movement remained politicized long after the suppression of the revolutionary disturbances in December 1905. More than 20,000 workers laid down their tools on May Day, 1908, in a symbolic gesture of class solidarity and support for political democratization; and during the period 1910–1912 Riga was swept by a wave of strikes whose goals were often political. The largest of these, involving 25,000 workers, began as a protest against the 1912 Lena Goldfield massacre and, more broadly, against the brutality visited by tsarist authorities upon their opponents throughout the Empire.[74]

The impact of socialism on working class politics is unmistakable. Marxist theories began to gain currency among younger members of the Latvian, Russian, and Jewish intelligentsia during the early 1890s. The principal disseminator of the new ideas, which were first introduced in social democratic literature brought from Germany, was the Latvian newspaper Dienas lapa (Daily News). Edited by the youthful Jānis Pliek-šāns, who was a gifted literary figure as well as a political polemicist, Dienas lapa was left alone by the censors, who were more concerned with Latvian nationalism as a threat to public order, until 1895. Before the end of the decade young socialists, among them the staff of *Dienas lapa*,[75] had forged links to the city's factory workers, participating in clandestine "political evenings" and circulating literature, a task facilitated by the high literacy rate prevalent among Latvian workers.[76] Student radicals helped workers to organize strikes and formulate demands during the 1899 riots; and by the outbreak of revolution in 1905 a Latvian Social Democratic Workers Party had established underground cells in the city's major industries. The Latvian socialists, moreover, did not stand alone. Both the Russian Social Democrats and the Jewish Bund maintained an organized presence in Riga's schools and factories. All three parties figured prominently in the events of 1905, providing workers with organizational support and weapons while helping them to channel and articulate their grievances. Socialist influence on the labor movement reached its zenith in autumn, when a federated Latvian-Russian-Jewish socialist committee functioned as an *ad hoc* city government, enacting laws, regulating prices and rents, and using its militia as a police force. Local membership in the Latvian party alone reached nearly 8,500 during the revolution;[77] and, although arrests and suppression caused membership to decline after 1906, Marxist socialism seems to have retained a strong appeal to the working class. The Latvian Social Democrats organized the 1908 May Day demonstration and exerted no small influence on the strike movement of 1910–1912. The clearest indication of socialist strength is the result of the 1907 State Duma election, in which the Social Democrats outpolled their rivals in every Riga district save the city center, where the Baltic Constitutional Party, a moderately conservative German force, attracted the most support.[78]

Riga's upper and middle classes, who tended to view with fear and contempt the crowds of shabby, unkempt laborers who thronged the streets, fully reciprocated worker animosity. The conservative *Rigasche Rundschau* (Riga Observer), for example, attributed a rise in crime, prostitution, and beggary to the growth of the lower classes, whose presence gave the city "a stamp of boundless dissipation."[79] Worker truculence and political activism were sources of grave concern to the more affluent segment of society; and diatribes warning of the perils presented by democracy, socialism, and mob rule were commonly featured in the conservative press. The comfortable bourgeoisie certainly viewed working class morality with a jaundiced eye, but their fear of crime and violence was based on more than mere prejudice. Riga did have a serious crime problem. In 1907, for example, there were sixty-two murders, thirty-four attempted murders, and hundreds of recorded burglaries, muggings, and armed assaults.[80] Politically motivated violence, moreover, did not come to a complete halt after the 1905 Revolution. In one case, police investigating the murder of a foreman at the

Aetna nail factory in December 1906 were set upon by an armed party of Latvian workers. Two policemen were killed in the ensuing shootout. In the end, police discovered a cache of weapons, ammunition, and explosives hidden in a worker dormitory and arrested ten workers who later admitted to being part of a socialist "battle organization."[81]

Although class and national strife was endemic in late Imperial Riga, the urban environment also played a constructive, transformative role. Life in the teeming city opened new opportunities, broadened horizons, encouraged a wider sense of community, and provided schooling in the art of politics. Civic pride and community spirit (Gemeinsinn) had historically been most pronounced among the German elite, but was never theirs alone. An important traditional expression of community life was the celebration of two city festivals—the Hunger Sorrow, commemorating the city's survival of a long and terrible medieval siege, and the Flower Festival, which blended the annual celebration of an ancient Latvian nature deity with the observance of St. John's Day. Both celebrations brought the urban community together in a variety of activities which included parades, public banquets, dances, and musical performances. Significantly, the civic festivals continued to flourish as the city grew. The 1908 Flower Festival attracted more than 60,000 participants from all nationalities and walks of life.[82]

Municipal politics also served as a focus of community interest after 1877. Although only a propertied minority could vote, the quadrenniel city elections, and to a lesser extent the daily activity of the town council, were followed by a far wider audience. On a smaller scale, the emergence of scores of clubs, charities, cultural societies, credit unions, consumer associations, temperance unions, and other private organizations gave thousands of people an opportunity to interact in an environment which reached beyond the narrow compass of the family, the neighborhood, and the workplace. Involvement in these organizations provided training of sorts in basic political and administrative skills. Some private institutions had an important influence on the life of the community as a whole. This was particularly true for the leading charities, which often received financial support from the city government and which helped to forge links among various groups and classes in their effort to improve the quality of urban life. Principal among them were the Literary Practical Citizens' Association, a long-established philanthropic organiztion (founded in 1801) which administered several schools, an orphanage, a relief fund for widows, a society designed to help artisans cope with the changing economic climate, and three public kitchens; the Anti-Beggary League, which provided food and shelter to the homeless; the Medical Aid Society, which offered first aid and an ambulance service to accident victims; and the Association for the Furtherance of the Public Welfare, which lobbied the city government for the establishment of public parks and gardens in working class areas, opened several tearooms in an effort to combat alcoholism, and published pamphlets on family medical care and hygiene in five languages. Another private organization noteworthy for its political influence, if not for the size of its membership, was the Society for Urban Social Policy. Established in 1907 by Mayor Armitstead and Secretary Carlberg, it devoted itself to the study of municipal government as an agent for the improvement of the public well being.

In another sense the city environment provided the essential backdrop for the emergence of Latvian national consciousness. The city provided Latvians with increasing opportunities for advancement through education, business success, and professional development; and it was only in the city that the Latvian population was sufficiently concentrated to establish a network of national organizations and to maintain a viable, independent cultural life. Late nineteenth century Riga was the crucible of Latvian literary culture. Before the 1870s Latvian national culture centered on the folkways of the rural village. By the close of the century, however, Riga had four Latvian daily newspapers and several Latvian literary and political magazines which expressed views on a wide range of topics. At the same time, Latvian writers, many of them based in Riga and drawing inspiration from the life of their conationals in the urban environment, created a sophisticated Latvian-language literature. Riga was also the undisputed center of Latvian political activity. Municipal elections provided the Latvian bourgeoisie with its first opportunity to participate in the political process; and both nationalism and socialism, which were the principal currents in Latvian politics, developed in the city and appealed primarily to urban constituencies.

The urban environment had a profound transformative effect upon the peasant migrants who entered the factory labor force. The assimilation of these people into their new surroundings was rendered easier and more complete by the structure of agrarian relationships in the Baltic provinces. The Latvian peasantry had been emancipated shortly after the Napoleonic Wars, and, unlike their Russian counterparts, were not tied to repartitional communes. Moreover, a series of mid-century agrarian reforms enabled peasants to purchase their holdings from their aristocratic landlords. These circumstances abetted the bifurcation of the peasantry into a minority of prosperous landowners and substantial tenants on the one hand and a mass of impoverished minor tenants and landless agricultural laborers on the other. Most of the migrants came from the latter group. Once in the city their ties to the land became tenuous. Although some worked in the city to pay off rural debts, their situation bore little resemblance to that of Russian workers, who maintained obligations to their rural communes. Very few Latvians, moreover, were seasonal workers. Their settlement in the city was permanent. The rapidity and thoroughness with which Latvian migrants adopted urban patterns of behavior and dress led the *Rigasche Rund-schau* to note the striking difference between Riga, where, to the editor's chagrin, it was difficult to distinguish between former peasants and members of "good society," and other Russian cities, whose streets seemed so crowded with people readily identifiable as transplanted rural folk.[83]

City life and factory work provided an environment conducive to social organization and political activism among the lower classes. This was especially true for the Latvians. As early as the 1860s, Latvian workers and masters in the larger factories had begun to establish mutual aid societies which helped members in time of need, administered schools, maintained libraries, and held evening sessions devoted to lectures and discussions. Many of the societies secretly kept illegal strike funds. Interaction with radical elements of the urban intelligentsia also had an impact on working class political consciousness and articulateness; and during the final two decades of the Imperial period the city's workers, often in league with leftist intellectuals, repeatedly demonstrated their ability to mobilize in support of specific political and economic goals. Riga's many large industrial plants, where sizable and multifaceted labor forces were closely concentrated, served as incubators of labor unrest. Although artisans and other groups ranging from gravediggers to washerwomen managed to formulate demands and engage in protest activity during the 1905 Revolution, workers from Russo-Baltic Wagon, the Aetna Wire Corporaton, Provodnik, and other major factories consistently took the lead in the labor movement. Labor activism did, however, span the national divisions in the city's working class. Although Germans, whom the workers perceived as representatives of the monied classes, were the most frequent targets of labor violence,[84] the working class seems in the main to have eschewed the nationalism so readily adopted by large elements of the urban bourgeoisie. Russian, Latvian, and Jewish socialists cooperated relatively well during the 1905 Revolution, and the only "national" demand which emerged with any frequency from workers was for an end to the linguistic Russification of local schools, courts, and administrative institutions.

Few if any periods in Riga's long history saw changes comparable in magnitude and depth to those which unfolded during the last half-century of Imperial Russian rule. It was a period of progress and achievement. Riga's elected municipal government performed creditably despite interference by meddlesome bureaucrats, the shortcomings of the municipal statutes, and the limited vision of the propertied elite who controlled it. Its dedication, skill, and success in improving the quality of life in the city were truly exemplary. Riga was probably the best-governed large city in late Imperial Russia. In another sense the urban environment was the crucible in which both Latvian nationalism and one of Russia's most aggressive and best organized labor movements were forged.

There was, however, a dark side to Riga's success story. The social, economic, and ethnic transformation of the city produced bitter conflict among nations and social classes. It also exacted a heavy toll in human misery. Poverty, overcrowding, disease, and urban blight were a steady accompaniment to life in Riga. Riga's experience demonstrates the failure of Russian social and political institutions, even when guided by skillful hands, to cope adequately with the pressures of industrialization and urbanization.

NOTES

1. In 1786 Catherine dissolved the estates in favor of the institutions provided by the 1785 Municipal Charter. The estates were restored and Catherine's innovations abolished, however, by Tsar Paul in 1797.

2. The English community had become especially prominent by the mid–nineteenth century. Led by seventy or eighty merchants, it boasted an Anglican church and its own private club. Wilhelm Lenz, *Die Entwicklung Rigas zur Grosstadt* (Kitzingen am Main, 1954), p. 6.

3. Census data for 1867 are based on *Die Resultäte der am 3. März in den Städten Livlands ausgeführten Volkszählung* (Riga, 1871).

4. An imperial decree of 1867 replaced German with Russian as the language of crown offices in the three Baltic provinces.

5. In 1867, 53.6 percent of those engaged in trade were German, 29.3 percent were Russian, 8 percent were Jewish, and 5.7 percent were Latvian.

6. According to the 1867 census, 64.6 percent of artisans were German, 16.8 percent Russian, 9.7 percent Jewish, and 7.1 percent Latvian.

7. H. von Stein, *Der Rigaschen Börsen-Comite in den Jahren 1816 bis 1866* (Riga, 1866), pp. 196–200.

8. V. K. Iatsunskii, "Znachenie ekonomicheskikh sviazei s Rossiei dlia khoziaistvennogo razvitiia gorodov Pribaltiki v epokhu kapitalizma," *Istoricheskie zapiski* (1954), p. 114.

9. For further detail on local entrepreneurship see Anders Henriksson, *The Tsar's Loyal Germans. The Riga German Community: Social Change and the Nationality Question, 1855–1905* (Boulder, Colo., 1983), pp. 74–80.

10. Lenz, p. 38; I. Skolis, *Riga: Ocherki po istorii goroda* (Riga, 1967), pp. 121, 143.

11. *Ocherki ekonomicheskoi istorii Latvii, 1900–1917* (Riga, 1968), p. 92.

12. Ibid., p. 96.

13. For a more detailed examination of migration patterns see Stephen Corrsin, "The Changing Composition of the City of Riga, 1867–1913," *Journal of Baltic Studies*, 13 (1982):27–32.

14. Data for 1881, 1897, and 1913 are based on *Ergebnisse der baltischen Volkszählung vom 29, Dezember 1881* (Riga, 1883–1885), *Pervaia vseobshchaia perepis' naseleniia Rossiskoi imperii 1897 goda*, XXI (St. Petersburg, 1905) and *Perepis' naseleniia v g. Rige i Rizhskom patrimonial'nom okruge ot 5 dekabria 1913 g.* (Riga, 1914). Evaluation of Riga's changing national composition is

complicated by the fact that each of the four censuses taken during the period measured nationality by different criteria. The 1867 census inquired after "everyday language," while the 1881 census measured both "everyday language" and "nationality," the 1897 census "native language," and the 1913 census the language of daily use in the family. Moreover, all of the census data on language seriously underestimate the size of the Riga Jewish population, much of which spoke German or Russian in preference to Yiddish. Measured by religious affiliation, Riga was 5.1 percent Jewish in 1867, 11.9 percent in 1881, 8.5 percent in 1897, and 7 percent in 1913. See Corrsin, pp. 22–26.

15. See Wilhelm Lenz, "Volkstumswechsel in den baltischen Ländern," *Ostdeutsche Wissenschaft*, III–IV (1956–1957):181–200, and Andrejs Plakans, "The Latvians," in *Russification in the Baltic Provinces and Finland, 1855–1914*, ed. Edward Thaden (Princeton, 1981), pp. 231–33.

16. Cited in the *Rigaer Tageblatt*, 20 November 1902.

17. See Henriksson, pp. 117–42.

18. In 1897 only 18.8 percent of government workers were German, while 35 percent were Russian, 20.8 percent Polish, 12.5 percent Latvian and 11 percent Lithuanian.

19. The survey also shows a pattern of distribution by value which contrasts strikingly with some other Russian cities, where the great majority of real estate owners were small holders. The predominance of large, valuable holdings in Riga reflects the high cost of real estate there. Middle and lower middle class families who could afford to purchase real estate in other cities had no choice but to rent their dwellings in Riga. The skewed value distribution may also indicate that the traditional social elite retained large tracts of urban real estate until the end of the Imperial era.

20. D. Protopopov, "Po okrainam," *Gorodskoe delo*, 1910, no.18:1222.

21. *Düna-Zeitung*, 9 August 1895.

22. Latvians accounted for 51.8 percent of all construction workers in 1897.

23. Only Moscow, St. Petersburg, and Lodz had larger working class populations than Riga. Skolis, p. 143; Michael F. Hamm, "Riga's 1913 City Election: A Study in Baltic Urban Politics," *Russian Review*, 39 (1980):443; B. Ia. Vilks, *Formirovanie promyshlennogo proletariata v Latvii vo vtoroi polovine XIX veka* (Riga, 1957), p. 109.

24. Latvians were especially numerous in the machine-building, metalworking, and chemical industries, while in 1897 Russians, most of them female, comprised almost three-quarters of the tobacco processing labor force.

25. "Primer kul'turnago goroda," *Gorodskoe delo*, 1910, no. 11–12:761–65. See also Protopopov, passim.

26. J. G. Kohl, *Russia* (London, 1844), p. 236.

27. In 1880 there were 268 construction starts in Riga. The period 1895–1899 averaged 964 per year, and in 1911 there were 1,500. Skolis, p. 127; *Rigasche Stadtblätter* 9 (1896):271.

28. J. Krastins, ed. *Riga, 1860–1917* (Riga, 1978), p. 197.

29. Ibid., pp. 52–53.

30. Louise Pantenius, *Jugenderinnerungen aus dem alten Riga* (Hannover, 1959), p. 10.

31. *Düna-Zeitung*, 19 July 1897.

32. By 1914 only 39 percent of the city area was served by the water system. *Ocherki ekonomicheskoi istorii Latvii, 1900–1917*, p. 153.

33. Protopopov, p. 1223.

34. During the period 1880–1900, for example, nearly two-thirds of all

typhus cases occurred in the Moscow suburb. *Ocherki ekonomicheskoi istorii Latvii, 1860–1900* (Riga, 1972), p. 467.

35. Burchard von Schrenck, *Beiträge zur Statistik der Stadt Riga und ihrer Verwaltung, 1881–1911*, 2 vols. (Riga, 1909 and 1913), I, 334.

36. "Primer kul'turnago goroda," p. 763.

37. In 1899 the Moscow suburb had only 1 streetlamp per 630 inhabitants, while the city center enjoyed a rate of 1 per 187. D. K. Ozolin, "O kommunal-'nom khoziaistve Rigi v 90-kh godov XIX v.," *Problemy istorii*, 6 (1962):152. See also Nicolai Carlberg, *Die Stadt Riga: Verwaltung und Haushalt in den Jahren 1878–1900* (Riga, 1901), pp. 190–191.

38. In 1913 only 16.5 percent of private residences had gas or electric lights. Krastins, p. 206, *Ocherki ekonomicheskoi istorii Latvii, 1900–1917*, p. 152.

39. In 1914 more than 52 million passengers, many of them commuting workers, rode the trolleys. Lenz, p. 85.

40. By 1914 the ferries carried an average of 30,000 passengers daily. *Ocherki ekonomicheskoi istorii Latvii, 1900–1917*, p. 149.

41. The city devoted particular attention to street improvement after the turn of the century, increasing the total paved surface by a third during the period 1900–1913. Ibid.; Protopopov, p. 1222.

42. Lenz. p. 82.

43. Ibid., p. 85. During the period 1889–1907 Russian representation in the elementary school population increased only marginally, rising from 12.1 percent to 13.1 percent. Schrenck, pp. 279–303.

44. Protopopov, pp. 1222–25.

45. In Riga and the other Baltic towns a special provision in the city statute permitted members of the free professions who did not own property to vote upon payment of a special tax.

46. *Rigasche Stadtblätter*, 1878, no. 4:44; no. 8:86–87; no. 10:104.

47. Eduard Hollander, "Riga unter der neuen Städteordnung, 1878–1882," *Baltische Monatschrift*, 29 (1882):463.

48. Nicolai Carlberg, "Städtische Selbstverwaltung in den Ostseeprovin-zen," in *Baltische Bürgerkunde* (Riga, 1908), pp. 204–205.

49. B. Borisovich, "Gorodskoe samoupravlenie i obshchestvennaia samodeiatel'nost' v. gor. Rige," *Gorodskoe delo*, 1910, no. 21:1485.

50. For a more complete treatment of the 1913 election see Hamm, passim.

51. Lenz, p. 59.

52. Nicolai Carlberg, "George Armistead als Sozialpolitiker," *Hefte der Gesellschaft für Kommunale Sozialpolitik in Riga*, 6 (1913):39.

53. *Rigaer Tageblatt*, 15 February 1887.

54. Carlberg, *Die Stadt Riga*, pp. 2ff.; idem, "Städtische Selbstverwaltung," pp. 214–15.

55. The city debt grew from 3.28 million rubles in 1899 to 29 million in 1914. Loan repayment accounted for 5 percent of city expenditure in 1890, 6.6 percent in 1899, and 14.9 percent in 1907; Carlberg, "Städtische Selbstverwal-tung," pp. 214–15; Lenz, p. 54; *Ocherki ekonomicheskoi istorii Latvii, 1900–1917*, p. 145.

56. Carlberg, "Städtische Selbstverwaltung," pp. 214–15.

57. "Baltische Chronik," supplement to *Baltische Monatschrift*, 54 (1903):147–48.

58. Latvian Association membership hovered between 800 and 1,000 dur-ing the late Imperial era. Its members came almost exclusively from the intel-ligentsia and the bourgeoisie. Lenz, pp. 20, 75; *Livländischer Kalender auf das Jahr 1906* (Riga, 1907), p. 108; *Rigasche Stadtblätter*, 1895, no. 22:176.

59. The *Rizhskii vestnik*, a Russian-language daily newspaper founded in 1867 by local nationalists, began, for example, to receive state subsidy during the early 1880s.

60. *Rigaer Tageblatt*, 14 March 1887.

61. *Erster Jahresbericht über die Tätigkeit des Deutschen Vereins in Livland* (Riga, 1907), p. 1.

62. *St. Petersburger Zeitung*, 10 July 1907.

63. Principal among these were the Leisure Club, whose members were wealthy merchants; the Blackhead fraternity, established in 1232 as a merchant militia but transformed by the nineteenth century into an exclusive club for patrician bachelors; and the Fraternitas Rigensis, a Dorpat University fraternity whose alumni organization embraced the great majority of German professional people in Riga. As the merchant guild began to shed its public responsibilities during the late nineteenth century, it too began to take on the appearance of a select private club for the German elite.

64. Chicanery and intimidation took a variety of forms. German-controlled electoral commissions regularly failed to include significant numbers of qualified Latvians on voter lists; wealthy Germans fictitiously transferred property titles to conationals who would otherwise be disenfranchised; and the absence of a secret ballot made it possible to intimidate voters at the polling stations. See Hamm, p. 455; G. I. Vigrabs, *Pribaltiiskie nemtsy* (Iuriev, 1916), pp. 113–14; and Margarethe Lindemuth, *Das Deutsch-lettische Verhältnis vor dem Weltkrieg auf Grund der lettischen Presse* (Heidelberg, 1939), pp. 45–46.

65. There was, properly speaking, no Latvia before 1918. Latvians inhabited Kurland, southern Livland, and parts of Vitebsk province. Creation of an autonomous Latvia from these disparate jurisdictions figured prominently, however, among Latvian nationalist goals.

66. *Rigasche Zeitung*, 10 November 1882.

67. Cited in the *Rigaer Tageblatt*, 14 February 1902.

68. *St. Petersburger Zeitung*, 28 January 1909.

69. See Düna-Zeitung editorials of January–February 1899 and a *Rizhskii vestnik* article reprinted in the *St. Petersburger Zeitung*, 6 April 1889.

70. *Ocherki ekonomicheskoi istorii Latvii, 1860–1900*, p. 466; *Ocherki ekonomicheskoi istorii Latvii, 1900–1917*, p. 147; Ozolina, p. 163.

71. Skolis, p. 149; *Ocherki ekonomicheskoi istorii Latvii, 1860–1900*, p. 147; *Rigasche Rundschau*, 5–6 July 1899.

72. Andrew Ezergailis, *The 1917 Revolution in Latvia* (Boulder, 1974), pp. 5–7; *St. Petersburger Zeitung*, 29 May 1909.

73. "Baltische Revolutionschronik," supplement to *Baltische Monatschrift*, LVII (1906):137ff.

74. Skolis, p. 162; *St. Petersburger Zeitung*, 22 May 1908.

75. Plakans, p. 258.

76. Thanks to a network of village schools maintained by the Lutheran Church, the Baltic aristocracy and the peasant communities themselves, the great majority of peasant migrants to Riga brought with them the ability to read and write.

77. Bruno Kalnins, "The Social Democratic Movement in Latvia," in *Revolution and Politics in Russia*, eds. A. Rabinowitch and J. Rabinowitch (Bloomington, Ind., 1972), p. 144.

78. *St. Petersburger Zeitung*, 15 February 1907.

79. *Rigasche Rundschau*, 5 September 1898.

80. *St. Petersburger Zeitung*, 18 January 1908.

81. Ibid., 17 December 1906, 28 May 1907.
82. Ibid., 25 June 1908.
83. *Rigasche Rundschau*, 5 September 1898. See also *Ocherki ekonomicheskoi istorii Latvii, 1860–1900*, pp. 204–205; Vilks, p. 90.
84. There was also an outbreak of violence against Jews in an Old Believer neighborhood of the Moscow suburb. On the whole, however, relations between Jews and other groups, especially the Latvians and Germans, were good.

BIBLIOGRAPHICAL NOTE

Among the best sources of general information on late Imperial Riga are the city's many newspapers and periodicals. The most useful dailies are the *Rigaer Tageblatt* (1882–1914), the *Zietung für Stadt und Land/Rigasche Rundschau* (1867–1914), the *Rizhskii vestnik* (1867–1916), and the *Baltijas vestnesis* (1868–1916). The *Rigasche Stadtblätter*, a weekly publication which appeared from 1817 to 1914, contains a wealth of diverse information, including summaries of city council debates for some years. The *Rigaer Handels-Archiv* (1874–1914), organ of the Riga Exchange, is rich in information on economic development and trade; and the *Baltische Monatschrift*, a journal published in Riga and Reval from 1859 to 1914, frequently carried articles on city politics and urban life.

A variety of city publications provide information on municipal government, schools, public works, living conditions, trade, industry, and other topics. Principal among them are Eugen Blumenbach, *Die Gemeinde der Stadt Riga in 700 Jahren, 1201–1901* (Riga, 1901); Nicolai Carlberg, *Die Stadt Riga: Verwaltung und Haushalt in den Jahren 1878–1900* (Riga, 1901); Burchard von Schrenck, *Beiträge zur Statistik der Stadt Riga und ihrer Verwaltung, 1881–1911*, 2 vols. (Riga, 1909 and 1913); Alexander Tobien, *Statistisches Jahrbuch der Stadt Riga*, 2 vols. (Riga, 1891–1892); idem, *Das Armenwesen der Stadt Riga* (Riga, 1895); and the annual *Berichte über die Verwaltung und Haushalt der Stadt Riga*.

The censuses of 1867, 1881, 1897, and 1913 constitute a vital source of information on demographic, social, and ethnic change. The first three have been published in full: *Die Resultäte der am 3. März in den Städten Livlands ausgeführten Volkszählung* (Riga, 1871), *Ergebnisse der baltischen Volkszählung vom 29. Dezember 1881* (Riga, 1883–1885), and *Pervaia vseobshchaia perepis' naseleniia Rossisskoi imperii 1897 goda*, XXI (St. Petersburg, 1905). The results of the 1913 census, unfortunately, have appeared only in partial form: *Perepis' naseleniia v g. Rige i Rizhskom patrimonial'nom okruge ot 5 dekabria 1913 g.* (Riga, 1914).

Both the Riga City Archive and the Livland Provincial Archives are part of the Central State Historical Archive of the Latvian S.S.R. The best starting point for an investigation into these holdings is Patricia K. Grimsted, *Archives and Manuscript Repositories in the USSR: Estonia, Latvia, Lithuania, Belorussia* (Princeton, 1981). Microfilm copies of some provincial and city archives are also available at the Johann Gottfried Herder-Institut in Marburg, West Germany. The filmed collection, which comprises chiefly Riga estates records and the archives of the provincial chancellery, is described in Kurt Dulfer, "Die baltische Archivfilme," *Baltische Geschichtsforschung* (1953) no. 3/4; (1954) no. 1; (1956) no. 2.

A rich and varied memoir literature, most of it German, provides close, if often biased, insight into life in late Imperial Riga. Among the best memoirs are Gustav Hernmarck, *Erinnerungen aus dem öffentlichen Leben eines Rigaschen Kaufmanns, 1849–1869* (Berlin, 1889); Bernhard Hollander, "Erinnerungen an die Jahren 1902–1905," *Baltische Blätter für allgemein-kulturelle Fragen*, II (1924), pp. 111–25; Louise Pantenius, *Jugenderinnerungen aus der alten Riga* (Hannover, 1959); and Wolfgang Wachtsmuth, *Wege, Umwege, Weggenossen* (Munich, 1954).

The secondary literature is copious but uneven in quality. Good surveys include Wilhelm Lenz, *Die Entwicklung Rigas zur Grosstadt* (Kitzingen am Main, 1954); Bernhard Hollander, *Riga im 19. Jahrhundert* (Riga, 1926); J. Krastins, ed., *Rīga, 1860–1917* (Riga, 1978); and I. Skolis, *Riga: Ocherki po istorii goroda* (Riga, 1967). Two Soviet economic surveys, *Ocherki ekonomicheskoi istorii Latvii, 1860–1900* (Riga, 1972) and its companion volume *Ocherki ekonomicheskoi istorii Latvii, 1900–1917* (Riga, 1968), are indispensable for research on trade and industry. Other major contributions on Riga's social and economic development include Dz. Ozolina, "Par Latvijas pilsetu burzuazijas nacionalo grupu ekonomiskam pozicijam pirma pasaules kara prieksvakara," *Latvijas PSR zinatnu akademija vestis* (1971), no. 12, 51–69; *Beiträge zur Geschichte der Industrie Rigas*, 3 vols. (Riga, 1910–1912); and B. Ia. Vilks, *Formirovanie promyshlennogo proletariata v Latvii vo vtoroi polovine XIX veka* (Riga, 1957). On municipal politics see Dz. Ozolina, "O kommunal'nom khoziaistve Rigi v 90-kh godov XIX v.," *Problemy istorii*, 6 (1962):137–64; Nicolai Carlberg, "Städtische Selbstverwaltung in den Osteeprovinze," *Baltische Bürgerkunde* (Riga, 1908), pp. 196–226; Margarethe Lindemuth, *Das deutsch-lettische Verhältnis vor dem Weltkrieg auf Grund der lettischen Presse* (Heidelberg, 1939); Gerhard Masing, *Der Kampf um die Reform der Rigaer Stadtverfassung, 1860–1870* (Riga, 1936); Dz. Ozolina, *Rigas pilsetas tevi un vinu komunala politika, 1877–1913* (Riga, 1976); and Reinhard Wittram, *Liberalismus baltischer Literaten* (Riga, 1931).

7.

Odessa and the Problem of Urban Modernization

FREDERICK W. SKINNER

No city better illustrates the pattern and progress of urban modernization in late Imperial Russia than the Black Sea port of Odessa. Founded in 1794 in the wake of the Second Russo-Turkish War (1787–92), Odessa displayed one of the most dynamic growth rates of any Russian city and emerged in a matter of decades as the major commercial center of the south and one of the leading cities of the Empire. By 1863 it had become the fourth most populous city after St. Petersburg, Moscow, and Warsaw; the second most active port after St. Petersburg; the rival of Kiev as the main center of culture and learning in the southern provinces; and without doubt one of the most carefully planned and beautifully designed cities in the entire country. However one measures the development of this remarkable city, it affords an outstanding example of the quickening pace of Russian urbanization in the late Imperial period. It offers an excellent vantage point from which to view a number of far-reaching changes affecting Russian society during the last half century of tsarist rule.[1]

PEOPLES AND WORKPLACES

Odessa's rate of growth to 1914 was nothing short of phenomenal. In the period 1800–92 alone, the population increased by an astonishing 3,677 percent compared to rates of 220 percent for Moscow, 323 percent for St.

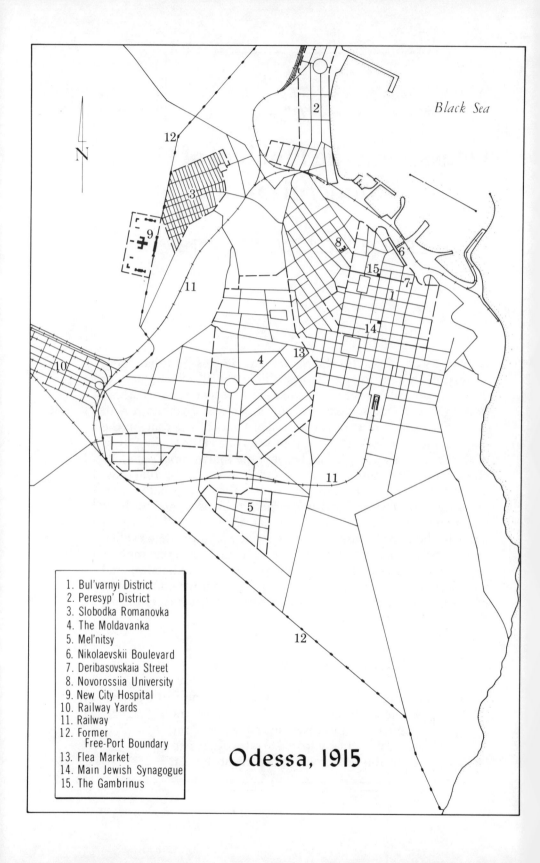

Black Sea

1. Bul'varnyi District
2. Peresyp' District
3. Slobodka Romanovka
4. The Moldavanka
5. Mel'nitsy
6. Nikolaevskii Boulevard
7. Deribasovskaia Street
8. Novorossiia University
9. New City Hospital
10. Railway Yards
11. Railway
12. Former
     Free-Port Boundary
13. Flea Market
14. Main Jewish Synagogue
15. The Gambrinus

Odessa, 1915

Petersburg, 417 percent for Warsaw, and 525 percent for Riga.[2] Even allowing for the minuscule base from which the Odessa percentile is projected, the figure testifies to extraordinary dynamism in the city's growth pattern. As Odessites liked to say, evidently with some pride, such rates of growth were only encountered in America.

During the first half century of its existence, Odessa's population grew in absolute terms from 2,349 persons in 1795 to some 8,000 in 1802; 32,995 in 1826; and 96,444 in 1852.[3] Even more spectacular was its rate of growth in the second half of the century: 118,970 in 1863; 193,513 in 1873; 238,689 in 1884; 340,526 in 1892; and 403,815 in 1897.[4] By 1914 the population had swelled to 655,246.[5] In-migration served as the primary source of growth—in 1892 only 45.2 percent of the population had been born in Odessa, in 1897 43.6 percent.[6] Even so, the population displayed more permanency than those of other leading cities. In Moscow only 27.4 percent of the inhabitants had been born in the city in 1902; in St. Petersburg the indigenous population stood at 31.7 percent in 1900, 32.0 percent in 1910; in Baku the corresponding figure for 1913 is 35.5 percent.[7]

The evolution of Odessa's class (estate) structure from the era of the Great Reforms to the outbreak of World War I is reflected in Table 7.1. The table indicates that the traditional and upper classes (nobility, clergy, honorary citizens, and military) comprised a small percentage of the population, averaging an even 13.0 percent over the period. Surprisingly, the merchant class formed an even smaller percentage, ranging from a high of 5.3 percent in 1863 to a low of 1.2 percent in 1897 (national urban figure in 1897: 1.3 percent).[8] One would expect the number to be higher in a city oriented almost exclusively toward trade, but the figures indicate that the bulk of commerce in Odessa, as in the other cities of Russia, was controlled by a relatively small number of individuals.[9] By far the largest estate comprised the *meshchane* who accounted for an average of 58.3 percent of the population during the period (national urban figure in 1897: 44.3 percent).[10] Many of these people stood at or near the lower end of the social scale and differed little from the urban poor below them except for their separate legal status. Of the 196,775 *meshchane* counted in the census of 1892, for example, 1.7 percent were employed in laundry and bathing establishments, 2.6 percent in taverns and inns, 2.6 percent in the building trades, 3.9 percent in food processing, 5.3 percent in transport, 6.3 percent in agriculture, and 7.2 percent in industry. Another 6.6 percent worked as domestics and 10.4 percent earned their livelihood as seamstresses or shoemakers; 391 of the 607 prostitutes listed in the census (64.4 percent) classified themselves as *meshchane*. On the other hand, 24.1 percent were engaged in commercial pursuits, 4.8 percent were trained professionals, and 2.1 percent derived their income from returns on capital investment and ownership of immovable property.[11] The *mesh-*

TABLE 7.1

Population of Odessa by Estate, 1858–1914

	1858		1863		1873		1892		1897		1914	
	N	%	N	%	N	%	N	%	N	%	N	%
Nobility	3,147	3.0	7,821	6.6	12,409	6.4	17,144	5.0	22,308	5.5	12,512	1.9
Clergy	598	0.6	662	0.5	1,279	0.7	167	0.1	1,814	0.5	1,003	0.1
Honorary citizens	160	0.1	339	0.3	991	0.5	6,982	2.0	4,513	1.1	17,794	2.7
Merchants	4,872	4.7	6,296	5.3	9,124	4.7	4,704	1.4	4,965	1.2	9,064	1.4
Meshchane	72,675	69.8	75,772	63.7	95,495	49.3	196,775	57.8	232,561	57.6	339,629	51.8
Foreigners	4,365	4.2	6,267	5.3	17,428	9.0	21,697	6.4	19,422	4.8	8,420	1.3
Peasants	3,925	3.8	4,978	4.2	23,118	11.9	83,153	24.4	109,553	27.1	200,177	30.5
Military & families	6,748	6.5	11,295	9.5	25,831	13.3	6,738	2.0	—	—	59,556	9.1
Other	8,003	7.3	5,540	4.6	7,838	4.2	3,166	0.9	8,679	2.2	8,091	1.2
Total	104,493	100.0	118,970	100.0	193,513	100.0	340,526	100.0	403,815	100.0	655,246	100.0

SOURCE: A. Skal'kovskii, *Zapiski o torgovykh i promyshlennykh silakh Odessy* (St. Petersburg, 1865), 12–13 (for 1858); Ibid., 155–56 (for 1863); *Perepis' naseleniia g. Odessy, proizvedennaia 5-go sentiabria 1873 goda* (Odessa, 1875), 4–5 (for 1873); *Rezul'taty odnodnevnoi perepisi g. Odessy i dekabria 1892 goda* (Odessa, 1894), pt. I, sec. I, table 7 (for 1892); *Pervaia vseobshchaia perepis' naseleniia Rossiiskoi imperii 1897 g.*, XLVII (St. Petersburg, 1904), viii (for 1897); *Obzor Odesskogo gradonachal'stva za 1914* (Odessa, 1916), 37 (for 1914).

chane thus ranged across the broad middle spectrum of the social order, bridging wealth and poverty, connecting "bourgeois to underworld."[12] In terms of numbers and presence, they were the most distinctive and productive element in Odessa's economy; by their signs of at least partial upward mobility and attendant economic success, they formed the ranks, along with the merchantry, of a nascent bourgeoisie.

Two of the other classes deserve brief mention. It is apparent that the peasantry was underrepresented in Odessa, constituting at most (1914) only 30.5 percent of the population. In Moscow peasants comprised 43.2 percent of the citizenry in 1871, 49.2 percent in 1882, and a full 67.2 percent in 1902; the figures for St. Petersburg are comparable.[13] This testifies to the less industrialized nature of Odessa's economy compared to that of the city's peers to the north, although the rather substantial increase in the peasant population after 1873 suggests that Odessites were succeeding to some extent in developing the industrial sector of their economy. The other class comprises the foreign nationals who, by virtue of their extensive trading operations in the city, were more numerous in Odessa than in the two capitals. Thus foreign subjects formed on average 5.2 percent of the population (1858–1914) as compared to averages of 1.3 percent in Moscow (1871–1902) and 2.2 percent in St. Petersburg (1869–1910).[14] The foreign element, though numerically small in comparison to the Russian segments of the population, exercised a powerful influence in shaping the cosmopolitan character of the city that remains perhaps Odessa's most outstanding characteristic.

The latter point introduces the other major key to understanding Odessa's personality—the complex ethnic mix of the home population. As a result of tsarist colonization policies, which offered various financial inducements to emigration from abroad, non-Russian peoples early on were attracted to Odessa and quickly became a fixture in the town's social order. Charles Sicard, an immigrant from Marseilles who came to the city in the first quarter of the century, commented in his memoirs: "I went there for several months and ended up staying forever. Such was the case with practically all of the foreigners who are living in Odessa today."[15] Along with the French came Italians, Greeks, Albanians, and Bulgarians in much larger numbers, the former two peoples settling in Odessa itself and the latter forming several colonies on the outskirts of the city. Germans arrived in New Russia by the tens of thousands; those who found their way to Odessa settled partly in the environs, where they formed the colonies of Bol'shoi Libental, Malyi Libental, and Liustdorf and engaged in agriculture, and partly in the city proper, where they practiced their trades as handicraftsmen and imparted a permanent name to one of the thoroughfares—Remeslennaia (Artisan) Street. There were as well English, Spanish, Jewish, Czech, Polish, Rumanian, Slovenian, Serbian, Armenian, Georgian, Tatar, and Turkic immigrants and even some from Egypt and Persia. Surprisingly, given Odessa's

location in the Ukraine, relatively few Ukrainians joined in this stream
of migration—in 1897 only 9.4 percent of the population was classified
as Ukrainian by language, although this figure does not take into
account those Ukrainians who had been Russified and thus considered
Russian to be their native language. Yet in 1897 the Russian-speaking
contingent itself comprised only 49.3 percent of the population; another
166,657 persons (Ukrainians excluded), or 41.3 percent of the population, were speaking an amazing forty-nine different languages.[16] Above
all, it was this cosmopolitan character that lent Odessa its distinctiveness and accounted for much of its charm. At the same time, such
heterogeneous ethnicity could not help but raise the eyebrows of Russians of "solid" stock, particularly those from the heartland of the
country, who debated among themselves whether this polyglot be-
hemoth of the south was in fact a "Russian" city.[17]

Unhappily for Odessites of the Jewish faith, the city was to prove in
time a very Russian place. Table 7.2 shows the breakdown of the
population by religion for the period 1858–1914 and testifies to the
increasing strength of the Jewish community—from 13.5 percent of the
population in 1858 to 33.5 percent in 1914. Also noteworthy is the fact
that, notwithstanding the horror of the pogroms that drove many Jewish
families into emigration around the turn of the century, the community
as a whole managed to hold its own at a full one-third of the population
while the Orthodox population continued a slow but steady decline. For
the most part, relations between the Russian and Jewish elements were
amicable in the first half of the century; indeed local administrators,
recognizing the importance of the Jews to the economic success of the
community, rose to their defense on more than one occasion in the face
of efforts by central authorities to place ever further restrictions on their
activities.[18] But in time, as their numbers continued to grow and their
more industrious members began to gain a hold over the economy,
relations deteriorated seriously. From the Russian perspective, there
certainly was cause for alarm: by 1910 the Jews controlled 61 percent of
the 4,897 handicraft shops, 64 percent of the 376 industrial enterprises,
69 percent of the 2,513 trade and commercial establishments, 83 percent of the membership in the first two merchant guilds, and 88 percent
of the grain trade.[19] In the face of this virtual monopolization of the
leading sectors of the economy, local officials began calling for the
adoption of new measures designed to reduce the influence of the Jews
in the community and they stood aside as inflamed mobs engaged in the
most terrible of pogroms.[20] In the end, as detailed later, Odessa found
itself torn apart by violent racial conflict between those very elements
that had been most responsible for the earlier prosperity of the city.

What lured the Jews and so many others to Odessa was the opportunity for gainful employment on the docks and handsome turnover of
profit in the houses of trade. There was, to be sure, a great deal of money

TABLE 7.2

Population of Odessa by Religion, 1858–1914

	1858		1863		1873		1892		1897		1914	
	N	%	N	%	N	%	N	%	N	%	N	%
Orthodox	81,317	77.8	79,034	66.4	125,349	64.8	195,679	57.5	225,869	55.9	341,808	52.2
Jewish	14,100	13.5	30,283	25.5	51,377	26.6	112,235	33.0	138,935	34.4	219,423	33.5
Catholic	4,400	4.2	4,133	3.5	8,616	4.5	19,862	5.8	24,261	6.0	57,832	8.8
Protestant	3,150	3.0	3,356	2.8	4,726	2.4	7,921	2.3	9,571	2.4	19,865	3.0
Armenian	624	0.6	633	0.5	888	0.4	1,214	0.4	1,520	0.4	9,287	1.4
Old Believer	371	0.3	825	0.7	1,231	0.6	934	0.3	1,365	0.3	2,753	0.4
Other	531	0.6	706	0.6	1,326	0.7	2,681	0.8	2,294	0.6	4,278	0.7
Total	104,493	100.0	118,970	100.0	193,513	100.0	340,526	100.0	403,815	100.0	655;246	100.0

SOURCE: A. Skal'kovskii, Zapiski o torgovykh i promyshlennykh silakh Odessy (St. Petersburg, 1865), 12 (for 1858); Ibid., 156 (for 1863); Perepis' naseleniia g. Odessy, proizvedennaia 5-go sentiabria 1873 goda (Odessa, 1875), 6–7 (for 1873); Rezul'taty odnodnevnoi perepisi g. Odessy I dekabria 1892 goda (Odessa, 1894), pt. I, sec. 1, table 2, (for 1892); Pervaia vseobshchaia perepis' naseleniia Rossiiskoi imperii 1897 g., XLVII (St. Petersburg, 1904), vii (for 1897); Obzor Odesskogo gradonachal'stva za 1914 (Odessa, 1916), 37 (for 1914).

to be made in the city. If the value of all exports and imports clearing
Odessa's harbor averaged 16,737,000 gold rubles annually in 1831–55,
the average in 1856–60 amounted to 34,572,000, in 1876–80 to
65,016,000, in 1896–1900 to 93,492,000, and in 1911–13 to
103,271,000.[21] The inauguration of railway service in 1865 (Odessa-
Balta line), coupled with increased tillage of land in southern Russia and
the opening up of several new shipping lanes between Odessa and other
Black Sea and Mediterranean ports, contributed to this commercial
boom; the introduction of telegraphic (1855) and international tele-
phonic (1895) service and the establishment of new credit societies,
banking facilities, insurance companies, and trading houses in Odessa
itself helped rationalize the process.[22] But speculation in commerce,
particularly in the grain export business, could prove a risky venture as
well. A string of bad harvests in the late sixties and early seventies,
compounded by the deleterious effects of the Russo-Turkish War of
1877–78, led to a fall in exports that forced a number of companies into
bankruptcy. Others found their profit margins shrinking as superior and
cheaper American, Canadian, and Australian grain entered the market,
while the famine of 1891 and the depression of 1896–1901 adversely
affected one and all. The war with Japan in 1904 and the revolutionary
events of 1905 had a disastrous effect on trading activities—grain exports alone plummeted from 147,000,000 pood in 1903 to 95,518,000 in
1906 and 45,534,000 in 1908.[23] As a result of this economic slowdown,
along with a bureaucratic logjam impeding modernization of the port
facilities and continuing unrest among the dockworkers, many wealthy
merchants began vacating the city (membership in the first two merchant guilds declined from 956 in 1906 to 639 in 1909) to relocate their
operations elsewhere, particularly in the ports of Kherson and Nikolaev,
which offered cheaper labor and insignificant worker unrest.[24]

In the face of these mounting difficulties, local officials increased
their efforts to diversify the city's economy. Great hopes were placed in
foreigners, especially Belgians, who, it was noted in 1896, were bringing
in large amounts of capital to set up factories.[25] But whatever the expectations may have been for rapid industrial development, the results
proved disappointing. In 1901 only 20,629 persons, or 4.3 percent of the
population (total: 471,793), were employed in the 477 "industrial"
enterprises listed in that year.[26] By 1914 the number of workers had
increased to some 30,000 (4.5 percent of the population), but the number
of factories and mills had declined to 418.[27] Moreover, of those enterprises staying in business, a full 70 percent engaged in the food-
processing sector and thus were heavily dependent on the health of
trade.[28] All in all, while some diversification had taken place, Odessa's
economic well-being continued to rest on success in the marketing of
grain and other key export commodities.[29]

Of course there were other ways of making money in Odessa, both via the pay envelope and, to adopt the jargon of the underworld, *pod stolom* (under the table). The 1897 census indicated that 102,338 persons (50.1 percent of total employed) worked in trades or professions other than manufacturing, mining, transport, and trade.[30] The large number of retail establishments provided employment for thousands of persons, as did the construction industry during the heyday of Odessa's public and private building program in the mid to late nineteenth century. With the development of the lucrative health spas on the outskirts of the city, tourism became a major business and supported a variety of subsidiary services (bathing establishments alone employed 4,059 persons in 1897).[31] By the turn of the century thousands of small shops offered employment to an estimated 25,000 artisans.[32] Domestic servants were also in high demand among the bourgeoisie and entitled elite—a total of 28,807 persons (14.1 percent of the work force) found employment in this line of work in 1897.[33] Altogether, 204,639 persons (just over half the population) managed to find gainful employment in Odessa in 1897.

Then there were the peddlers, vice artists, prostitutes, and smugglers who plied their separate trades in the back streets of this sprawling maritime town. As early as 1873 the city prefect complained about the "various kinds of speculators and adventurists" who were flocking to Odessa, as well as the "dens of thieves, drinking parlors, and houses of prostitution" that were keeping his understaffed (always understaffed!) police force on constant patrol.[34] (In fact there were other problems with the police force—it was reported in 1882 that the lower ranks were on the take from tavern and pub owners who were in violation of city sanitation codes.)[35]

Prostitution was big-time business in Odessa, as it is in any port city. There were three types of houses available to the customer, depending upon his preferences and ability to pay: 30 kopeks brought entrance to the first type, 50 kopeks to the second, and 1 ruble to the third. Contingent on the degree to which the madame looked after her girls (monthly salaries ranged from 7 to 15 rubles) and the client was generous with his tips, a prostitute could earn anywhere from 20 to 50 rubles per month—not a bad wage when one considers that most dockworkers averaged 6 rubles per month. But the girls had to work hard for their money. Most began at six or seven in the evening and did not quit work until five or six in the morning (on Sundays and major holidays the working "day" extended from noon until morning), during which time they entertained from five to twenty or more guests.[36]

Traffic in contraband was big business as well. The contrabandist, captured so perfectly by Isaac Babel in the character of Benya Krik, became a permanent feature in Odessa society and built the city's

reputation for gangsterism that agitated so many Russians in the north.
And in fact Odessa became known not only as a free port, a status it
enjoyed from 1819 to 1857, but as a source of "free" goods for the rest of
the country. But this is not all of the story. As devotees of such luxury
items as foreign perfumes, wines, liqueurs, herbs, porcelain, linen, and
silk began to search out more prosaic articles as well, the contrabandist
readily rose to the task: he found it a simple matter to transfer his skills
to the smuggling of revolvers, sticks of dynamite, and the latest number
of *Iskra* and other underground literature arriving in Odessa from centers abroad.[37]

This, then, was late Imperial Odessa. It presented a rough and at the
same time cultivated face, reminiscent of Seattle or San Francisco in the
earlier days. What made it different was its bondage to higher authority.
Despite the sense of a free-spirited ambience one gains from reading its
social history, the city in the end represented but a cog in the machinery
of state. Its success ultimately depended upon the extent to which the
governing authorities could provide it with direction and the means for
proper development.

THE URBAN ENVIRONMENT

On the eve of the Great Reforms, all was not right in Odessa. The
population, to be sure, had passed the 100,000 mark, total turnover of
trade was averaging better than 30 million rubles per year, a university
was in the process of being founded, many graceful buildings in the
neoclassical style dotted the landscape, and a magnificent stone staircase, lying in wait for the artistry of Eisenstein, connected the city with
the port in a rhythmic cascade of steps and landings. But at the base of
that staircase sprawled a most miserable sight: a sad-looking port consisting of two small harbors, their wharves rotting away and their
bottoms rapidly filling with silt, lacking in any slips, dockyards, workshops, breakwaters, or even a suitable admiralty, and offering only the
most primitive of methods for the loading and unloading of goods.[38] In
the city proper, the droshky provided the only means of public transportation, the streets were unpaved and lit at night by feeble alcohol
lamps, the citizens drew their water from inadequate cisterns and wells,
there was no sewerage system apart from open ditches along the sides of
the streets, and the population on the average was dying at an annual
rate of one out of every twenty-three persons (1851–60) compared to
rates of one out of thirty-one for Brussels (1850–56), one out of forty-one
for London (1850–59), and one out of forty-five for Stuttgart (1850–59).[39]
Could this really be Russia's "southern beauty," as the guidebooks so
eloquently proclaimed? Not to one foreign visitor, who wrote that there
was "nothing to render [the city] agreeable to the traveller"; another

noted the city's "appearance of antiquity" due to the disrepair of its buildings and observed that Odessa "labors under many disadvantages."[40]

What had gone wrong? The building of Odessa had gotten off to a successful start in the first quarter of the century, due in large measure to the special interest taken in the project by Alexander I. Through the emperor's willingness to provide the necessary funds, material, and manpower, Odessa by 1825 had grown into a major commercial center of some 30,000 persons that, for its day, equaled in comfort and conveniences the average preindustrial city of the West. During this period the central core of the city, laid out in the form of two gridirons set at a 45-degree angle to one another, came fully into view, as did the port, which by the end of Alexander's reign attained the configuration still present at mid-century. Due to the scarcity of wood in the region, the city was built almost entirely of stone that was quarried in the outlying areas as well as beneath the city itelf.[41] By 1814 some 2,600 houses had been constructed; those located away from the city center were of one or two stories and stood adjacent to one another, while those in the central district were several stories high, separated by courts or gardens, and contained commercial establishments on their ground floor.[42] The most respectable shops and homes, the city theater, and the main municipal and state-run buildings were to be found in the latter area, which included the fashionable Bul'varnyi District.

The problem of Odessa's development in the pre-reform era lay, rather, in the ensuing thirty-year reign of Nicholas I. Not only did Nicholas show less interest in the project, perhaps in part because he considered Odessa only a "nest of conspirators,"[43] but he displayed little imagination in responding to the developmental needs of a rapidly growing community and refused to ease the bureaucratic and financial strictures that were, in effect, strangling the city. Odessa underwent substantial expansion during this period, the city boundaries coming by mid-century to embrace the suburbs of Peresyp' to the north, Moldavanka and the future site of Slobodka Romanovka to the west, and Mel'nitsy to the south. It was also at this time that Nikolaevskii (now called Primorskii) Boulevard, the city's main architectural landmark with its ensemble of neoclassical buildings and elegant staircase, was laid out at the edge of the plateau overlooking the sea (1826–41). But the quality of life for those who inhabited the city did not show signs of similar improvement. The streets remained choked in two to three inches of dust during the dry months and became a "slough of despond" during the wet season, the water continued brackish and unclean, the sewage still followed its open course to the sea, infectious diseases persisted in their virulent killing. The plague, which first struck Odessa in 1813, returned with a vengeance in 1829 and threatened again in 1837–38; cholera made its first appearance in 1830 and attacked with increasing fury in the succeeding decades; all of the lesser maladies against which modern man is protected were regular visitors and contributed to abnormally high morbidity.[44] By the 1850s the average annual death rate stood at 45.5 per 1,000.[45] The greater part of this mortality stemmed directly from the city's lack of public services and amenities. Until this problem could be corrected, Odessa would remain not only a dusty place but a guarantor of disease and premature death.

By mid-century it became increasingly apparent to municipal authorities that traditional approaches toward urban development, above all the overweening role of the central government in the planning process, could no longer satisfy the needs of a city undergoing an extremely rapid rate of expansion. The "main deficiency," the city prefect observed in 1858, lay in the "absence of active participation in [municipal affairs] by the citizens of the city."[46] Alexander II agreed. Persuaded by his advisers that the stagnation of the previous era had resulted in large measure from the heavy-handed interference of the state in local affairs, the emperor in 1863 refashioned the statutes regulating municipal government, administration, and finance in such a way as to extend primary responsibility for urban development to the city itself. The progress registered over the next thirty years testified to the wisdom of this action: operating with expanded powers of initiative and having access to increased sources of revenue, city planners in Odessa achieved their greatest successes of the prerevolutionary era.[47]

Odessa immediately felt the change. Whereas the pre-reform city council had rarely met, and then only to rubber-stamp directives sent down from higher officials, the new council held a total of 178 sessions during its first three-year term alone (1864–66) and debated and acted upon a wide range of issues, not the least of which concerned progress in urban development.[48] The municipal budget felt the change as well. Altogether, income increased four times in the reform era (from 825,256 rubles in 1864 to 3,294,985 in 1892), while expenditures rose five times (from 751,439 to 3,804,768).[49] The growth of income resulted in part from the addition of a number of new items to the budget, the most important being a tax of one-half kopek levied on each pood of grain exported from the harbor, but it derived primarily from the increased returns on existing items in conjunction with the rapid growth of the city. The rise in expenditures proceeded naturally as the municipal government channeled these funds into programs of benefit to the community. More than half of total spending (58.3 percent) supported the three vital programs of education (5.9 percent); welfare (16.1 percent); and urban development, comprising lighting, sanitation, construction, and maintenance of the streets and city property (36.3 percent). An additional 12.2 percent provided funding for support of the municipal government and other city-based institutions. All told, a full

70.5 percent of the money spent by Odessa during this period served the needs and purposes of the community.[50]

Odessa did not expand substantially beyond the old free-port boundaries during the reform era, testifying to intensive rather than extensive development. The most significant new influence in the shaping of the city came with the inauguration of railway service in 1865. Huge marshalling yards, covering more than a half square mile in area, housing up to a hundred railway cars at a time, and employing as many as a thousand workers, were laid out to the west of the Moldavanka.[51] Other innovations in city planning included use of the circle rather than the square, as evidenced in the Moldavanka and Peresyp' districts, and the laying out in the same areas of large blocks without regard to a uniform street plan—the flour mills and granaries of the Moldavanka and the factories of Peresyp' required larger and more irregular spaces than the original gridiron pattern could accommodate. On the other hand, the planning of Slobodka Romanovka reintroduced the original gridiron design but for nonaesthetic and purely speculative purposes; built in the 1850s and 1860s by private entrepreneurs, the suburb provided tract-type housing for working class families and was to become in time one of the most disadvantaged areas of the city in terms of its public services.

But if Odessa did not grow substantially from without, it underwent rapid internal change. A correspondent for a local newspaper noted in 1870: "In walking about the city, what struck me most was that so many buildings are rising like mushrooms everywhere. I saw new structures on practically every street."[52] The introduction of the railroad, the availability of easier credit with the formation of the Odessa Municipal Credit Society (1871), the rising wealth and confidence of the entrepreneurial classes, and the new assertiveness of the municipal government all contributed to the building boom of the 1870s, 1880s, and 1890s. Next to commerce, building activity became the most important source of employment. By the 1880s thousands of persons were being hired annually to cut and transport stone and work on construction projects. Massive structures were raised in as little time as one or two years at a cost of hundreds of thousands of rubles to private investors, institutions, the city, and the state. By the turn of the century, on average, 1,000 buildings were being constructed annually. Such intensive development had the effect of increasing population density from 31,500 persons per square mile in 1863 to 90,000 per square mile in 1892, although densities were greater in the central quarters of the city than in the outlying districts.[53]

Unquestionably of greatest significance, however, in this era of rapid urban development was the modernization of the port and the introduction within the city of a full range of public services and amenities.[54] The port underwent substantial improvement, the state spending upwards of 12 million rubles of its own money to advance the project. The existing harbors were deepened and two new ones were built; a large outer breakwater (1 1/2 miles in length) was constructed; new piers were added and the famed Odessa lighthouse was moved to its present location at the end of the longest one; electric lighting was installed and the streets leading into and servicing the area were paved; rail lines were extended along the length of the waterfront and overhead carriers and conveyer systems were introduced to expedite the transfer of grain; elevators, warehouses, dry docks, repair facilities, and the like were built. In the city, all of the streets and squares in the central district and one-half to three-quarters of those in most of the suburbs were covered with granite-block paving, and sidewalks were installed. Some 2,142 gas lamps were erected along the streets (another 16,057 were emplaced in buildings), and by 1895 electricity was illuminating the port area, city theater, and Nikolaevskii Boulevard. A closed water supply system was constructed in 1870–73 that connected the city with the Dniester River, twenty-seven miles away. Sewer pipes were laid and indoor plumbing installed in 1883–87, directing waste water away from all the central quarters and greater or lesser parts of the suburbs (most of the low-lying Peresyp' area excluded), with the effect of reducing the death rate from 35.6 per 1,000 in 1874–75 to 25.9 per 1,000 in 1885 and an average of 23.5 per 1,000 in the 1890s.[55] And the municipal transportation system was revolutionized with the introduction of the tramway, first horse-drawn, later powered by steam (electrical service came in 1910).

By all of these improvements, the municipal government succeeded at last in modernizing the various systems upon which the future of the city ultimately depended. Yet the impression should not be left that the legacy of the pre-reform era had been entirely laid to rest. There were in fact a number of defects in the building program of these years that pointed up the limits of urban modernization in the late Imperial period. The most obvious deficiency concerned the failure of municipal authorities to pursue the development of public services and amenities as evenly in the suburbs as in the central quarters of the city. In every case, the outlying districts benefited least from introduction of the new services mentioned above. The effect of this underdevelopment was most seriously felt in the area of public health. By 1900 92.1 percent of the houses in the wealthy Bul'varnyi District had been connected to the water supply system and 87.0 percent were equipped with indoor plumbing; in Slobodka Romanovka the corresponding figures were 28.1 percent and 11.1 percent in Peresyp', 29.4 percent and 3.2 percent. The death rates for these districts in the same year reveal the tragic results of this maldistribution: Bul'varnyi—13.9 per 1,000; Slobodka Romanovka—31.3 per 1,000; Peresyp'—34.0 per 1,000 (rate citywide: 23.6 per

1,000).[56] In this neglect of the less privileged districts, the city betrayed its bourgeois bias. The standard Soviet charge that in the late Imperial city a sharp division existed between the well-built, modern center of the city and the poorer suburbs is amply borne out by the example of Odessa.[57]

The other major deficiency concerned the slight amount of interest shown in improving standards of housing available to the poor. Housing constituted the one area of urban development not falling under the purview of the municipal government (sanitation inspection excepted), and there is little evidence to suggest that authorities considered this a serious flaw in the mandate under which they operated. Table 7.3 shows discrepancies in housing for the three districts examined above (data are for occupied apartments in 1892) and indicates that the poorer suburbs were again those quarters suffering the greatest neglect. Yet it was precisely in the outlying districts that the population was increasing most rapidly in conjunction with the economic development of these areas. In 1897 Bul'varnyi had grown by 7.8 persons per 100 of the 1892 population (from 44,380 to 47,858), Peresyp' by 20.6 (from 16,834 to 20,303).[58] Rent levels of course made a difference—annual rent per apartment in Bul'varnyi in 1892 averaged 269.3 rubles, in Peresyp' 44.9.[59] Desire to save on transportation costs by securing proximity of residence to workplace undoubtedly helped to shape growth patterns as well. But put most bluntly, the poor simply had nowhere else to go in their search for dwelling space. Lack of adequate housing prompted one local newspaper to suggest in 1891 that the most appropriate way to celebrate the city's forthcoming centennial would be for the municipal government to erect low-cost public housing for the poor, but the call fell on deaf ears.[60] Even a warning by the city prefect that the "densely packed quarters" of the working class posed a serious threat to the safety of the "social system" brought no response.[61] The poor thus had to await the arrival of a new type of municipal authority before the imbalance in housing patterns could be eradicated.

Still, despite these serious shortcomings, it must be concluded that

TABLE 7.3

Discrepancies in Housing in Odessa, 1892

District	Persons per Room	Persons per Window	Persons per Stove
Bul'varnyi	1.8	1.0	3.1
Slobodka Romanovka	3.2	1.3	4.4
Peresyp'	3.2	1.6	6.7

SOURCE: *Rezul'taty odnodnevnoi perepisi g. Odessy 1 dekabria 1892 goda* (Odessa, 1894), pt. II, sec. 1, table 2.

the city planners of Odessa carried out a program of considerable distinction during the era of municipal reform. When one takes into account the magnitude of the problems facing the community in practically all aspects of its life in the early 1860s, the amount of progress registered during the following thirty years can only be described as a remarkable achievement. It redounded to the credit of the municipal government that Odessa could enter the year of its centennial on a note of such success in its physical development.

Unfortunately for the city and at least most of its inhabitants, the reform era had just drawn to a close. Perhaps it can be said that the beginning of the end came one day in 1891 when the city prefect sat down in his office at Deribasovskaia 2 and penned the following to the tsar: "In my judgment it would be most sound to provide for the right of broad intervention in municipal affairs [by higher administrative officials] so as to do away with the irresponsible independence of city councils, thereby ensuring united action of the organs of municipal self-government with the intentions of the state."[62] The prefect, along with his cohorts across the land who were in the process of transmitting similar recommendations, found a ready ear in the person of Alexander III, who on June 11, 1892, issued a revised municipal statute that severely restricted the competence of local officials everywhere. By this act the emperor ushered in the era of "counterreform" that was to carry through the reign of Nicholas II and prove of such decisive consequence in the final years of Odessa's prerevolutionary historical development.

Perhaps most illustrative of the change in direction resulting from promulgation of the new statute was the diminution in the size of the electorate.[63] If the earlier statute had, through high property qualifications, restricted the electorate to but a fraction of the total population— in 1863 only 2,657 persons or 2.2 percent of Odessa's population (total: 118,977) were declared eligible to vote, in 1889 only 5,913 or 2.0 percent (total: 301,039)—the new statute raised the qualifications to such heights as to render the electoral process practically meaningless.[64] The 1892 list for elections to the city council contained the names of 1,824 persons and institutions; the mathematics works out to just 0.5 percent of the population (total: 340,526).[65] Moreover the Jews, now a full third of the citizenry, were completely barred from either participating in elections or holding public office.[66]

As a result of this narrowing of the franchise to the monied elite, the post–1892 city councils turned sharply to the right in their political complexion, a development greeted with applause by the city prefect and viewed with increasing alarm by correspondents for *Gorodskoe delo*, the leading urban journal of the time.[67] The height of the reaction took place between 1907 and 1912 when General Ivan Tolmachev, a member of the Union of Russian People and an anti-Semite almost by profession, held sway over the city in his capacity as prefect. He indicated in 1907 that he was doing all in his power to "strengthen" the right and "paralyze" the left; by 1909 he was able to report that "not a single candidate of the left" had been elected to the city council in voting held earlier that year.[68] He neglected to mention that the opposition had been denied access to the local press and public informational meetings and that, on the day of the election, scores of "volunteers" from the Black Hundreds organization circulated within the voting hall and engaged in open agitation.[69] Such tactics continued under the regime of Mayor Pelikan, whose thugs stuffed ballot boxes and intimidated voters to ensure the victory of the "right" people.[70]

Such a system of government, which after 1905 became ever more preoccupied with the problem of order, could not help but exert a negative influence on Odessa's urban modernization program. The sorry state of finances with which it operated served only to compound the issue. Odessa's financial picture in the period 1895—1914 is shown in Table 7.4. While the table indicates that both income and expenditures grew at a respectable rate, testifying to what would appear to be a sound fiscal condition, the last column points in the other direction by detailing the extent to which the city engaged in deficit spending of immense proportions in order to meet its financial obligations. A combination of factors accounted for such serious discrepancy in the annual budgetary schedules. On the income side of the ledger, the shortfall derived in large measure from a decline in customs receipts as the slowdown in trade set in, the loss of substantial tax revenue as wealthy merchants and others began to quit the city, and the reversion to the state beginning in 1903 of proceeds from the 1/2-kopek tax, which had proved one of the most lucrative sources of income during the reform era.[71] On the side of expenditures, the city was forced to increase its spending in the social sector to meet the needs of a rapidly growing population (funding for health, education, and welfare, for example, more than doubled, rising from 1,105,389 rubles in 1895 to 2,812,727

TABLE 7.4

Odessa's Municipal Budget, 1895–1914
(in rubles)

Period	Receipts	Outlays	Deficit
1895–1899	20,951,562	22,020,413	1,068,851
1900–1904	28,942,991	30,606,882	1,663,891
1905–1909	33,466,095	36,117,403	2,651,308
1910–1914	43,828,526	47,642,473	3,813,947
Total	127,189,174	136,387,171	9,197,997

SOURCE: Annual budgetary schedules in *Obzor Odesskogo gradonachal'stva za 1895–1914* (Odessa, 1896–1916).

rubles in 1914), and it found itself ever more burdened by the large annual payments it was required to make to the state (quartering of troops alone cost the city 9,045,179 rubles during the period, while support of the local branches of state institutions consumed another 3,715,649 rubles).[72] Moreover, the central government began investing less heavily in the city's developmental program as it encountered growing demands on its own budgetary resources and Odessa was left to pick up the slack to the best of its diminishing abilities. All of this combined to produce the largest deficits in the city's financial history— even the negotiation of loans totaling 21 million rubles could not stem the hemorrhage of red ink.[73] But in this regard Odessa did not stand alone. Moscow's budget experienced a deficit of 2 million rubles in 1912 and 3 1/2 million in 1913; Kiev's fell short by over one million in 1913, Nizhnii Novgorod's by 2 million in 1912, and Baku's by 600,000 in the same year.[74] Clearly the cities of Russia were in the throes of a deep financial crisis as the country approached the year that would test it in war.

And so, as a correspondent for *Gorodskoe delo* put it, "rich and happy Odessa" had been transformed into "ravaged and hapless Odessa."[75] Perhaps "demodernization" is the best term to use in describing the city's building program in these final years. Progress did not cease altogether—the tramway system was upgraded, the city took over the waterworks and expanded its network, a large community hospital was erected at a cost of some 2 million rubles—but the overarching reality was one of decline in the pace of development relative to the progress that had been achieved in the reform era. The port again lapsed into lassitude as proposals for its further modernization inched their way through the corridors of power, the suburbs continued to suffer neglect in the improvement of their services, facilities at the health resorts (a major source of revenue for the city) were allowed to fall into ugly disrepair, the huge tenement buildings housing the poor became ever more congested, and private construction starts ground to a halt.[76] The observations of a visitor from St. Petersburg encapsulate the demise of a once proud city:

> In admiring Odessa—its straight, rationally planned streets and wide sidewalks lined with trees, its old buildings, its parks, and the boundless dark blue sea, I thought to myself how perfectly the city had been conceived and brought into being . . . , how many generations had labored over its development, and in what clumsy hands it finds itself at present. The old timers in Odessa, who are in love with their "Little Paris," point with sadness to the noticeable signs of decay in the outward appearance of the city that has taken place of late, beginning with the progressive deterioration of the streets and ending with the discolored, shabby appearance of the town hall, which stands out like a dirty blotch against the blue of the sea.[77]

Of course there was no money, or at least not enough of it, to fund urban development programs as lavishly as before. But that was only a part of the problem. More to the point was the serious social discord that had begun to divide the city.

CONFLICT AND COMMUNITY

The Gambrinus, described by the writer Alexander Kuprin, was known in every port around the Black Sea and as far away as New York, Sydney, and the isle of Ceylon.[78] When calling at Odessa, every sailor was sure to visit this tavern dedicated to the King of Beer, even though it meant "picking one's way, under the cover of darkness, to the very center of the city." Inside the subterranean, dimly lit hall on a platform off to one side sat a Jew, the club entertainer—"a meek, droll, tipsy, baldheaded fellow, with the appearance of a moth-eaten ape of indeterminate years"—and sitting on his lap was his little white dog, affectionately called Belinka. This was Sashka, whose violin could instantly respond to the most varied of requests, from a Russian folk melody to a Viennese waltz to the "capricious guttural sounds" of an African chant. The patrons responded wildly to his playing and rewarded him with ruble notes and more mugs of beer than he should have accepted, given the generally inebriated state of his existence. He ruled over an international community of drinkers and could stop a quarrel in a moment with "meek and fun-provoking mirth gaily beaming from his eyes hidden under the sloping skull." For a few hours each night in Odessa, differences were forgotten or quickly put aside in the company of Sashka and his "doggie Belinka."

The Gambrinus was the most famous bar in Odessa but only one of many that provided a place for social commingling. There was the Fankoni, for example, frequented by merchants who came to hear "all the news of the day," or the Bavariia, patronized by the "curious," including many students who called the place their "mortuary" for the headaches suffered the next morning. Restaurants, buffets, tea houses, and coffee shops served a similar purpose; so did the churches and synagogues, charitable associations, reading rooms, bazaars, and baths; so did the clubs that catered to such interests as painting, horticulture, drama, yachting, horse-breeding, cycling, and aviation.[79] Through all of these outlets the public found means for coming together—but did these islands of community tie the city together or serve only to fracture it into more disparate subgroups?

Certainly from the perspective of those who devoted their lives to the maintenance of order, Odessa did not project an image of social tranquility.[80] The annual reports of the city prefect, for example, called attention to the large number of street children, products of a high rate of illegitimacy, who roamed the city as a "corrupt proletariat" that was destined in a short while to become the "dangerous contingent" in the adult population. They also complained of the 20,000 homeless dock-workers and the 30,000 factory and railway workers who constituted the "most restive element in the life of the community" because of the spell cast over them by "propaganda from ringleaders of the anti-government movement." Then there were the university students, too many of whom were "aliens—Jews, Armenians, Georgians, and the like—that is, those who are most inclined toward disturbing the peace." Finally, always and everywhere, there were the Jews who, in addition to the long list of lamentable practices for which they were known, stood at the head of the revolutionary movement as part of their "destructive work to maintain an oppositional attitude among the populace at large." The root cause of all of this disorder, according to city officials, stemmed from a fundamental flaw in the makeup of society: Odessites were lacking in "normal civic consciousness" because all they cared about was how to make a "quick profit" before the next person in line.

This characterization of Odessa as a kind of all-city counting house accorded with a popularly held view that should not be dismissed out of hand.[81] But surely more lay behind this perceived lack of community spirit than a preoccupation with making money. Could the Jews, for example, take much pride in place under the increasingly more straitened terms of their existence? Could the unemployed workers, living three to a room in the disease-ridden suburbs? Could members of the intelligentsia, denied the opportunity to vote for progressive munic-ipal leadership? Could the professionals, finding their expertise no lon-ger of service to the city? In fact, all of the problems discussed up to this point contributed in one way or another to the growth of community disorder. It is left to examine how these circumstances affected key segments of the population and how they reacted to a world changing rapidly about them.

The Jews

The Jews of Odessa formed the second largest Judaic community in Russia after Warsaw and were universally held to be the least traditional of any inhabiting the Pale. Their low level of knowledge of the Torah and general lack of interest in the teachings of the faith, together with the tendency of their elite to accept linguistic and cultural assimilation with Russia, prompted the coining of one of the most popular Jewish sayings of the day: "The fire of Hell burns around Odessa up to a distance of ten parasangs."[82] In a socioeconomic sense, however, the Jews were but a microcosm of Odessa society. Almost all were *mesh-chane* (95.5 percent in 1897) and were to be found for the most part in the service trades and the small retail and handicraft shops that formed the backbone of the urban economy. In 1897 almost three-quarters of those employed (72.1 percent) worked either as domestics (10.7 percent), petty manufacturers (13.2 percent), clothiers (15.3 percent), or tradesmen (32.8 percent), while others joined the ranks of the proletariat as day laborers, factory workers, and apprentices in workshops.[83] Many were abjectly poor—in 1900 63 percent of all Jewish dead had to be buried at public expense; in 1903 one-third of the community was required to accept Passover charities.[84] Yet some Jews accumulated great wealth in the entrepreneurial, banking, and industrial establishments and played a role in the economy far out of proportion to their numbers. In 1897 only 1.2 percent of the Jews were merchants, yet they comprised 31.2 percent of the merchant class.[85] By 1910 Jews controlled 50 percent of the wholesale trading houses, 64 percent of the industrial enterprises, 70 percent of the banks, and 88 percent of the grain exporting companies. Jews also distinguished themselves in the professions, accounting in 1910 for 27 percent of the technicians, 56 percent of the lawyers, and 70 percent of the physicians. There was as well a large number of Jewish students at the university (a maximum of 746 in 1906 out of a total enrollment of some 3,000) and many Jewish intellectuals enriched the cultural life of the community.[86] Altogether, the Jews were broadly based in the economy and prominent throughout society.

From the vantage point of the Russians, Ukrainians, Greeks, and others trying to make a living in Odessa, the main problem with the Jews was not that they observed the Sabbath on Saturday or even, contrary to the complaints of authorities, that their children occupied too many seats in the classroom, but that their leading members were engaging in unfair business competition through their near total monopoly of the grain trade. The Jews had only arrived gradually at this position. In the first half of the nineteenth century, Greek, Italian, and French firms controlled the export market and the Jews had been relegated to the position of middlemen, buying from producers and selling to the large exporting houses. In the latter half of the century, however, as foreign merchants either quit the city or were bought out by Jewish interests, the Jews did begin to take over the market and then to capture it almost entirely. Such a dominant position in this key sector of the economy, rendered all the more visible by the downturn in trade that hurt the smaller commercial houses most severely, made the Jews likely targets for those harboring a grudge or suffering economic dislocation. The city prefect reported in 1899 that the Jewish monopoly was causing "justifiable grumbling and deserved indignation, especially among the lower classes."[87] In time-honored fashion, the disadvantaged, abetted by the authorities, had begun searching for scapegoats.

On October 17, 1905, a passerby stopped a Jewish friend on a sidestreet in Odessa and whispered in his ear, "Very soon they will kill you—many will be slaughtered." The Jew laconically replied, "We've heard that tune since the age of Gabriel."[88] But this time the warning had the ring of immediacy, for the next day Odessa exploded in violent civil conflict. Attacks on Jewish life and property had taken place in 1820, 1859, 1871, 1881, and 1900, but nothing could match the fury of the pogrom that convulsed all of Odessa from October 18 to October 21, 1905.[89] The troubles began when reactionary elements organized a large street demonstration to counter a parade being staged by workers and students to celebrate the news of the October Manifesto. It was only a matter of time before clashes broke out between the two groups of demonstrators; by nightfall, as Jewish homes and businesses began coming under attack, it became increasingly apparent that a political demonstration had degenerated into an ugly racial war. For the next three days, as the authorities practiced "neutrality" and the police and regiments of Cossacks joined the side of the rioters, mobs roamed the Moldavanka and other Jewish quarters, ransacking property and torturing and killing Jews. The Jews organized self-defense squads (many consisting of university students) but, while checking the attack in isolated instances, could not stave off a city gone mad. When the pogrom at last came to an end, some five hundred persons had been killed and several thousand others injured, while damage totaling more than 3 million rubles had been inflicted on over 1,600 pieces of property. In the perpetration of this violence, Odessa justifiably earned its reputation as the "modern home of the pogrom."[90]

The bloodshed of 1905 marked a watershed in the history of the Jewish community. In response to the horror of those four days in October, attitudes hardened, outlooks changed, and the bonds with the larger community were all but shattered. Many of the Jews now entered full force into the work of the Jewish self-defense movement so as to be prepared in the event of a renewed outburst of violence.[91] Others simply gave up on Russia and passed into emigration via the very city that had once been their home and now was called the "Gate to Zion."[92] And some, having already been shown the way by the young Lev Bronstein (Leon Trotsky), joined the ranks of the revolutionaries to bring the whole rotten edifice down to the ground.

The Workers

Maxim Gorky, who worked on the Odessa docks in the early 1890s, must surely have had his own experiences in mind when he penned the following lines:

> Pitifully comic were the long lines of stevedores shouldering tons of grain into the iron bellies of the ships in order to earn for themselves a few pounds of that very bread, to be consumed by their own stomachs.

> The ragged, sweating men, stupified by exhaustion, noise, and heat,
> and the mighty machines these men had created, now glittering cor-
> pulently in the sun . . . —this was contradiction containing a whole
> cruelly ironic poem.[93]

No one in Odessa worked harder for less money under more trying
conditions than those who labored on the docks. And the irony was
apparent for, though earning the most meager of wages, the dockworkers by their sweat generated most of the wealth that fattened the
city.

Who were these people and how did they live? A study published in
1904, based upon a sampling of 269 persons, provides the following
profile.[94] A full 58.0 percent were peasants who had fled the impoverished countryside, another 36.4 percent came from the ranks of the
meshchanstvo, and 5.6 percent, incredibly, were noblemen or honorary
citizens; almost all (85.6 percent) were in-migrants who had come to
Odessa in search of employment. The majority queued up at three in the
morning to obtain work for the day and labored from 5:00 A.M. to 6:00
P.M. during the summer, from 7:00 A.M. to 4:30 P.M. during the winter.
Of the dockworkers, 43.8 percent earned 3 to 5 rubles per month; 33.7
percent, 5 to 10 rubles; 19.1 percent, 10 to 15 rubles; and 3.4 percent, 15
to 30 rubles. Most spent a minimum of 18 kopeks per day on food and
lodging (3 kopeks for bread and tea in the morning, 11 kopeks for dinner,
and 4 kopeks for lodging), or 5.40 rubles per month; 94.4 percent did not
have their own dwelling space and slept either in doss-houses (80.7
percent) or on the streets (19.3 percent).

But these are cold statistics. The voice of one of these workers helps
bring them to life:

> We are dirty and tattered, but we do have a heart and are able to feel and
> think. We read newspapers and know that workers in other countries
> live better than we do. How desperately we want to live as others do! At
> night we steal our way up to the city to look at the lighted streets and
> the smartly clad, cleanly dressed people. We hide in the corner of a
> tavern just to sit at a table and be with people—as everyone does![95]

There had long been a tradition in Odessa of harboring people
opposed to the status quo. The Hetaireia society, which guided the
Greek independence movement, set up its headquarters in Odessa in
1821, and Bulgarian and Polish nationalists operated from the city as
well. A few of the Decembrists came from Odessa, it was from here that
agents for Alexander Herzen spirited the *Kolokol* into Russia, Populists
operated extensively in the city in the seventies and eighties, and
Marxist organizations began making their appearance in the early
nineties.[96] In 1895 the city prefect called Odessa "the main hotbed of
sedition" in the country and from 1900 the city became a leading center

in the burgeoning strike movement.[97] Clearly there were revolutionary groups to which the worker quoted above could turn in his search for a better life.

Russia's first labor organization, the South Russian Workers Union, was founded in Odessa in the summer of 1875 and, though broken up by the police in December of the same year, served as the progenitor of a host of circles and groups that sprang into existence in the 1880s and 1890s to organize the labor movement in Odessa.[98] The Odessa Committee of the Russian Social Democratic Workers Party, established in the city at the beginning of 1900, unquestionably acquired the greatest significance. Controlled initially by the Economist wing of the party, the committee began to swing over to the Leninist (Bolshevik) faction following the Second London Congress of 1903; by March 29, 1905, when the committee elected Lenin himself as its delegate to the Third Party Congress, the local branch of Russian Social Democracy had gone over fully to the camp of the extremists.[99] University students, many of them Jewish, played a large role in the party's organizational activities.[100] Some effort was made to mobilize the thousands of petty craftsmen operating in the city but much more interest was shown in the dockworkers, always a volatile group and easily provoked, and factory workers employed in the larger industrial establishments, such as the workshops of the Main Odessa Railway, repair facilities of the Russian Society of Shipping & Trade, and the Gul'e-Blanshard, Gen, and Bellino-Fenderikh metallurgical plants. Student cafeterias and working class bars (the Kommercheskii, Makedoniia, and Yalta, among others) provided a ready-made forum for agitation, though one easily penetrated by the police, while the Brodskii commercial house and Leifer mercantile establishment served as convenient fronts for the receipt of Bolshevik literature dispatched from abroad.[101] Although data are lacking on the overall strength of the organization, it is evident that members of the Odessa Committee operated extensively throughout the city and enjoyed widespread support among the laboring population.[102]

The first manifestation of labor unrest in Odessa came in July and August 1871 when workers at the Fadeev sheepskin factory went out on strike over wages. From 1871 to 1894 more than twenty additional strikes took place, affecting such disparate groups as railway workers (1873), machinists and printers (1875), and tobacco workers and dock-hands (1886–94).[103] But it was not until 1900, when students and workers joined forces in mounting a large street demonstration on May Day, that the labor movement assumed a mass character and became an integral part of the revolutionary struggle. Now a pattern was set that, with certain interruptions, continued on down to the collapse of the regime.[104] In 1901 there was steady agitation among university students, and strikes were staged in May, July, and October by railway, dock, and tobacco workers. In 1903 there were further disorders at the university and strikes broke out in May and June affecting some 3,500 workers, while a general strike in July, in which over 30,000 persons participated, shut down the entire city for three days. In 1904 worker unrest continued in both industrial and handicraft enterprises and agitation at the university forced cancellation of classes at the end of the year. In 1905 all of Odessa found itself caught up in the national upheaval that continued on into 1906 (361 enterprises were struck in 1905; 158, affecting 16,612 workers, in 1906). Only with the arrival of General Tolmachev in 1907 did the situation begin to turn. The university was purged of "leftist elements" (students and faculty alike) and monarchical societies were organized to put an end to agitation; similar societies, in the form of artels, were set up in the port area as part of a general crackdown on labor unrest.[105] Yet in 1910 the strike movement came back to life in the workshops of the Russian Society of Shipping & Trade and the Gen metallurgical factory, while the university was closed at the end of the year due to renewed agitation among the student body. In 1911, eleven major strikes broke out in the city; in the first three months of 1912 alone, the number increased to eighteen. The process had begun to repeat itself and, though stayed momentarily by the sudden outburst of patriotism attending Russia's entry into World War I, built logically and quickly to a second denouement.[106]

The city prefect, attempting to explain to the tsar how he could have lost control of the city for three days during the general strike of July 1903, took pains to note the degree to which the railway and factory workers had been politicized by socialist propaganda, about which he had already had occasion to report in 1899 and 1901.[107] Certainly the work of political activists, seizing upon the economic grievances of a disgruntled population, played a paramount role in the revolutionary events of these years. But also of importance was the deteriorating condition of the urban environment that directly affected the well-being of those very same people who took to the streets in the name of socialism. This can be seen, for example, in the demands for improved sanitary conditions and better health care programs contained in the lists of grievances drawn up by striking workers.[108] The city prefect noted the connection as well when he observed in 1900 that, in light of "increasing public ferment," the city could no longer ignore the "congested disposition" of housing in the lower-class neighborhoods and that only by improving public welfare could authorities hope to "paralyze to at least a certain extent criminal propaganda among the workers."[109] It was not that the city had completely turned its back on the poor—welfare institutions continued to receive funding (an average of 5.3 percent of annual municipal spending for the period 1895–1914); cafeterias, tea houses, and recreation halls were opened and operated at public expense; makeshift work was provided during times of high unemployment; private citizens maintained the tradition of donating generously to charity.[110] Nonetheless one gains the impression that the city viewed the plight of the poor more as a necessary evil to be kept at bay through palliative measures than as a fundamental problem requiring immediate corrective action. Certainly nothing was done to right the imbalance in developmental patterns that rendered the working-class suburbs a lesson in civic neglect. The outbreak of cholera epidemics in the port area and less affluent neighborhoods in 1900, 1908, and 1910 served only to drive home the point that those who inhabited these spaces were not quite as equal as the rest of the citizenry.[111] So too, in its own way, did a petition from wealthy *dacha* owners that the tramway company add one or two separate cars for "the common people and servants" so that they "would not mix with the clean and cultivated passengers."[112]

There is, to be sure, a great deal of distance between inadequate plumbing and the toppling of a dynasty; yet the physical circumstances of life in Odessa must surely have contributed to the general problem of revolutionary unrest. At the very least, it is not unreasonable to assume that the poor living and working conditions foisted upon the lower members of the population confirmed their belief that the ruling elements did not have their best interests at heart, and that this in turn helped shape their attitudes in the larger political struggle. It was assuredly in this manner that a pamphleteer retrospectively viewed the problem in an appeal to workers following the collapse of the regime in 1917:

> Why is it that the central parts of the city are so well appointed at the same time that the outskirts are neglected and abandoned? Why is it that magnificent theaters adorn the city at the same time that the schools are in such wretched condition? Why is it that the housing question is so caught up in the interests of homeowners that the poor are all but left out in the cold? Why is it that the cost of living continues to mount to a point where life is next to impossible? Such examples could be cited many times over and they all speak to one and the same issue—the base manner in which the tsarist authority treated the mass of the urban population and the shamelessness with which the wealthy profited by their privileged position.[113]

But now all of this could be laid to rest. If the workers actively participated in the forthcoming elections to the city council, they could "take all power in the city into their own hands and conduct municipal affairs in the interests of everyone, not just the well-to-do."[114]

The Modernizers

And what of the trained professionals—the urban planners, engineers, architects, sanitation experts, and the like—who had been most responsible for the great strides made in the era of municipal reform and who continued to take an interest in the progress of Odessa? To what extent did the breakdown in urban modernization affect this key group in society? Here the evidence is far less plentiful and one can only draw tentative conclusions. Still there is room to believe that the professionals were undergoing similar disaffection; some, it is clear, had gone over to the side of the revolution.

There is no question but that those whose work brought them into daily contact with the poor, such as the physicians, social workers, hygienists, and others holding membership in the Odessa Branch of the Russian Society for Safeguarding Public Health, expressed growing concern and at times open anger over the failure of municipal authorities to resolve outstanding problems relating to sanitation, housing, and health.[115] There is evidence as well that members of the "third element" of the local zemstvo board, especially statisticians, were engaging in illegal political activities.[116] Then there are the isolated individuals who had clearly turned their backs on the existing order: L. A. Tarasevich (1868–1927), *privat-dotsent* at Novorossiia University and pathologist at the Odessa Bacteriological Station, who began providing large subsidies to the Social Democrats after the 1905 Revolution and went on to enjoy a distinguished career in the Soviet medical establishment; Konstantin Levitskii, civil servant in the local administration and candidate of law, who came under police surveillance in 1904 in connection with his clandestine political activities on behalf of the Odessa Social Democratic Committee; the dentist Gershanskii, whose intercepted mail (1905) yielded several numbers of the Leninist organ *Vpered* posted from Geneva; the physician Bogolomets, who electrified an Odessa audience of some 1,500 persons on November 18, 1904, by calling for the overthrow of the tsarist regime as a means of eradicating the "social disease" afflicting the working class.[117] Other prominent Odessa professionals, while not formally joining the ranks of the revolutionaries, became increasingly convinced of the bankruptcy of tsarism and offered their services to the new Soviet government immediately following the October (Bolshevik) Revolution. These included N. F. Gamaleia (1859–1949), the noted microbiologist, who had founded both the Odessa Bacteriological Station (with I. I. Mechnikov in 1886) and the Odessa Bacteriological & Physiological Institute (1899); and P. N. Diatroptov (1859–1934), a well-known Soviet hygienist, who had directed the Odessa Bacteriological Station from 1892 to 1907 and later taught courses in hygiene at Moscow University.[118]

Finally, there is this small, seemingly innocuous item appearing in the proceedings of the Odessa Branch of the Imperial Russian Technical Society for 1904: "A highly grievous phenomenon has been observed of late in the life of our society . . . —a noticeable slackening of activities and apparent decline of interest in the work and well-being of the organization on the part of the membership."[119] Observing that membership exceeded 400 persons, the item went on to lament the fact that very few had even taken the time to tour a new school built by the society and that meetings were held more and more infrequently due to lack of interest in delivering papers. In an effort to revivify the society, the authors proposed organizing a large industrial-trade fair, which, despite all manner of obstacles placed in its way by government officials, did indeed take place in 1910.[120]

The local branch of the Imperial Russian Technical Society had received its charter in 1871 and stood at the forefront of Odessa's modernization drive in the mid to late nineteenth century.[121] What, then, is one to make of this sudden loss of interest in its activities? It could very well be that the membership considered it pointless to deliver reports on technical matters when the city no longer had as much use for them. Undoubtedly this was a part of the problem. But could it not also have been the case that the members were directing their energies elsewhere, for example in furthering the work of those clandestine political parties advocating the return to a rapid modernization program in which the skills of the professional could once again be utilized? The pattern of behavior exhibited by the other professional groups would seem to point in such a direction. While the available evidence does not permit a definitive response to this question, it appears quite likely that the members of the society, geared toward serving the public interest and conditioned by training and experience to support liberal causes, had not simply opted out of the political process.

The overall picture that emerges from this discussion is of a regime losing the support of its professional class. Unquestionably this was the most ominous sign of all. Everything hung on the loyalty of the experts, above all the regime's credibility as a modernizing agent. If the professionals had begun going elsewhere in their search for employment, the staying power of tsarism could be considered all but exhausted.

From its position as vanguard in the national urban modernization campaign, Odessa thus fell victim to the forces of social upheaval. The municipal government represented the one intracity institution with the capability of maintaining the bonds of community but in fact became the principal cause of community disorder. Rather than serving as a vehicle through which the creative energies of society could be channeled into productive labor of benefit to the city as a whole, as had been the case during the reform era, the local governing bodies after 1892 served only to fragment society and cause the city to lose its sense of direction. As a result, civic energies sought other outlets, community spirit took flight, and Odessa broke apart in ugly disarray. From being an instrument of modernization, the municipal government became an agent of destruction and urban decay.

Yet there was still that archipelago of community wherein people could congregate, share their experiences, and forge alliances in pursuit of a better tomorrow. One such island remained the Gambrinus.[122] Sashka had come within a hair's breadth of losing his life in the pogrom of 1905—a stonemason's chisel was already headed downward when someone grabbed the hand from behind and shouted, "Stop, you devil— why, it's Sashka!" The assailant froze dead in his tracks and peered at Sashka with dumb disbelief; then, spying Belinka trembling nervously nearby, he swept the poor dog up by the hind legs, raised it high in the air, and dashed in its skull on the sidewalk before him. Sashka withdrew into his grief, then turned defiant, and finally could contain his anger no longer: when at the tavern a beefy undercover agent importunately demanded the playing of the national anthem "in honor of our beloved monarch," he jumped up in a rage, shouting obscenities, and brought his violin crashing against the head of this despicable hireling. Since this was a "political matter," they took him to the Boulevard station. When he returned to the Gambrinus after the police were done, his left arm showed the signs of tsarist revenge—the limb hung lifeless and was crumpled beyond belief, the elbow drawn in toward the waist and the hand curled up about the chin. But when a patron sorrowfully inquired if this was the end to the music, Sashka drew an ocarina out of his pocket with his good hand, placed the stem to his mouth, and, swaying to the beat as much as his broken body would let him, began piping the "deafeningly-mirthful *Chaban.*" "Man may be crippled," the playing proclaimed, "but art will endure all things, and will all things conquer."

CONCLUSION

One can sympathize in a way with those nineteenth-century traditionalists who argued over the degree to which Odessa could be considered a generic product of the "Russian" urban experience. On the face of it, there was a great deal about the city that made it seem to stand alone. It had been founded at the end of the eighteenth century on the very southern fringe of the Empire in an area known as New Russia. Its population was composed to a large extent of Jews from the western borderlands and of immigrants from the Balkan and Mediterranean region whose linguistic, cultural, and religious diversity imparted a uniquely cosmopolitan air to the city. Its unnaturally rapid rate of growth accorded more with American than Russian standards of urban development, prompting Odessites to dub their city the Chicago of Russia. It did not even bear a Russian name. A foreigner aptly remarked in 1855 that Odessa had a little of everything, including "Italian houses, Russian officials, French ships, and German artisans."[123] It was not merely for effect that contemporaries referred to the city as Russia's "southern window" on Europe.[124]

There were other differences as well which, if not quite as singular as those cited above, seemed to confirm Odessa's aberrant urban status. One thinks especially of the preponderance of the *meshchane* in the socioeconomic life of the community, the all-pervading nexus of market, bourse, and exchange, the petty crime and notorious thievery, the early attachment to the underground, the virulent anti-Semitism, the disreputable *Tolmachevshchina*. Yet, as important as these attributes are in sorting out the traits of Odessa's own personality, they are only marginally useful in determining the significance of the city in the overall scope of Russian urban history. This is where the heartland critics missed the mark in their efforts to decipher Odessa. The point to be stressed is that it was not Italian houses or German artisans that really mattered in the end, as fascinating as such exotica might be, but the much more fundamental reality of the Russian autocracy and the subordinate status of Odessa in the hierarchy of power. From this perspective, there was very little about Odessa that could be considered truly unique. All the cities of the Empire, despite regional differences and separate historical records that set them apart as well, operated within a generally uniform framework of relations between state and society that tended to standardize their larger experiences. The key question to ask, then, is how policies of state affected the course of Odessa's development and how the latter in turn reflected changes occurring throughout the society. The ways in which Odessa differed from Moscow or St. Petersburg or Warsaw, while important for purposes of comparison, are only incidentally germane to the main sociodrama.[125]

What, then, can one conclude from this study of Odessa? Three general observations come readily to mind. First, the record of Odessa's development in the late Imperial era serves to confirm the proposition advanced by William Blackwell that the decade of the 1860s be selected as the "turning point between the premodern and modernizing Russian city." It was in this decade, as Blackwell observes, that "the two capital cities of Russia began to grow rapidly, a number of new industrial and commercial cities appeared, a railroad network connecting cities and markets was built, and the first comprehensive urban administrative reform was promulgated (1870)."[126] This periodization accurately describes the situation in Odessa. It was precisely in the decade of the 1860s, beginning with the reform of the city's municipal government charter in 1863, that Odessa set out on a rapid modernization program. The progress registered over the following three decades far surpassed that of the previous seventy years, indicating that the reforms of the 1860s were as instrumental in the development of Russia's cities as they were in the socioeconomic improvement of the country as a whole. Urban modernization therefore represents another dimension of the reform program inaugurated in the wake of Russia's defeat in the Crimean War.

Second, the particular path of development pursued by Odessa in the late Imperial era underscores yet again the dominant position of the state in Russian society; it points up as well the importance to urban modernization of the governmental statutes regulating municipal government, finance, and city planning. When the state, through these statutes, granted primary responsibility for urban development to the local institutions of government and provided them with the requisite amount of financial support, as it did during the reform era, the city enjoyed considerable success; when it withdrew these prerogatives, the pace of development that had been enjoyed fell off precipitously.[127] It is highly debatable whether Odessa could have received the start it did had the state not stepped in with massive funding and technical assistance. But the course of the city's subsequent development strongly suggests that urban modernization proceeded most successfully when the central governmental apparatus interfered the least. The record of the reform era testifies to the amount of progress that could be achieved when primary authority was extended to the local level. The degree of state control over the planning process must therefore be taken into account in evaluating the uneven pace of urban modernization in late Imperial Russia.

Finally, the breakdown of modernization in Odessa in the two and a half decades preceding the revolution suggests still another factor in the decline and eventual collapse of the old regime. By all accounts, Russia could survive in the world at large only to the extent that it mounted and maintained a thoroughgoing modernization program. This was the lesson of the defeat in the Crimean War. Alexander II took the lesson to heart and promulgated the series of reforms that enabled Russia to develop rapidly over the next thirty years. The modernization of Russia's leading cities formed an integral part of this national effort. But in the 1890s urban modernization began to stall and by the early years of the new century a serious decline had set in. Because of the importance of the city to the success of modernization in the country as a whole, this breakdown boded ill for the continued stability of the tsarist regime and perhaps for the very survival of the Empire. It was not simply a question of the disaffection of urban society, though that became an issue; it was a question of the integrity of Russia as a nation. Yet no one in a position of authority made a serious effort to remedy this deteriorating and potentially damaging situation. Only the modernizers and a few radical politicians understood the significance of this dilemma.

NOTES

I would like to acknowledge the support of the International Research and Exchanges Board, which made much of the research for this essay possible. I would also like to thank the University of Montana for its support and financial assistance.

1. For a general discussion of modernization theory, see Cyril E. Black, *The Dynamics of Modernization: A Study in Comparative History* (New York, 1966). For a discussion of modernization in the context of Russian urban history, see William L. Blackwell, "Modernization and Urbanization in Russia: A Comparative View," in Michael F. Hamm, ed., *The City in Russian History* (Lexington, Ky., 1976), pp. 291–330.

2. *Stoletie Odessy, 22 avgusta 1894 goda* (Odessa, 1894), p. 62.

3. Data from the following: A. Skal'kovskii, *Pervoe tridtsatiletie istorii goroda Odessy, 1793–1823 (Odessa, 1837),* p. 48 (for 1795); *Odessa, 1794–1894. Izdanie gorodskogo obshchestvennogo upravleniia k stoletiiu goroda* (Odessa, 1894), p. 103 (for 1802); *Odesskii vestnik,* 1828, No. 77, p. 333 (for 1826); A. S. Borinevich, "Perepis' Odessy 1 dekabria 1892 g.," *Izvestiia Moskovskoi gorodskoi dumy,* May 1893, no. 1, sec. 2:14 (for 1852).

4. Data from the following: A. Skal'kovskii, *Zapiski o torgovykh i promyshlennykh silakh Odessy* (St. Petersburg, 1865), p. 153 (for 1863); *Perepis' naseleniia g. Odessy, proizvedennaia 5-go sentiabria 1873 goda* (Odessa, 1875), p. 5 (for 1873); *Obzor Odesskogo gradonachal'stva za 1884* (Odessa, 1885), appendix 4 (for 1884); *Rezul'taty odnodnevnoi perepisi g. Odessy l dekabria 1892 goda* (Odessa, 1894), Pt. I, Sec. 1, Table 1, p. 2 (for 1892); *Pervaia vseobshchaia perepis' naseleniia Rossiiskoi imperii 1897 g.,* XLVII (St. Petersburg, 1904), p. iv (for 1897).

5. *Obzor Odesskogo gradonachal'stva za 1914* (Odessa, 1916), p. 37. By 1917 the population had increased to some 800,000 but much of this increase resulted from the large influx of war refugees. Figure from S. S. Zak, *Rabochii klass i gorodskie vybory* (Odessa, 1917), p. 4.

6. *Pervaia vseobshchaia perepis',* XLVII, p. ix.

7. A. G. Rashin, *Naselenie Rossii za 100 let (1811–1913 g.g.): statisticheskie ocherki* (Moscow, 1956), pp. 138, 144, 146.

8. Ibid., p. 122.

9. In 1854, for example, only 8,529 persons received permission to engage in trade in all of southern and southeastern Russia. P. G. Ryndziunskii, *Gorodskoe grazhdanstvo doreformennoi Rossii* (Moscow, 1958), p. 350.

10. Rashin, p. 122.

11. *Rezul'taty odnodnevnoi perepisi . . . 1892 goda,* Pt. I, Sec. 2, Table 17, pp. 178–81.

12. William L. Blackwell, *The Beginnings of Russian Industrialization, 1800–1860* (Princeton, 1968), p. 104. See Ibid., pp. 100–10 for a good discussion of the structure of urban society as a whole.

13. Specific figures for St. Petersburg: 42.0 percent in 1881, 63.3 percent in 1900, 68.7 percent in 1910. Rashin, pp. 125, 129.

14. Ibid., pp. 125, 129.

15. Charles Sicard, "Notice sur onze années de la vie du duc de Richelieu à Odessa pour servir a l'histoire de sa vie," *Sbornik Imperatorskogo Russkogo istoricheskogo obshchestva,* LIV (St. Petersburg, 1886), p. 72.

16. *Pervaia vseobshchaia perepis',* XLVII, Table 24, pp. 152–53. For an excellent discussion of all of Odessa's main ethnic groups, see Patricia Herlihy, "The Ethnic Composition of the City of Odessa in the Nineteenth Century," *Harvard Ukrainian Studies,* I, 1 (March 1977):53–77.

17. S. N. Iuzhakov, "Iubilei Odessy," *Russkoe bogatstvo*, 1894, no. 9:122, 144, and passim.

18. See Shlomo Lambroza, "The Pogrom Movement in Tsarist Russia, 1903–1906" (Ph.D. dissertation, Rutgers University, 1981), p. 267. Apparently there were some Jews living in Odessa (called Khadzhibei until 1794) at the time of its capture from Turkish forces in 1789 and they quickly assumed a prominent position in the life of the fledgling community. Herlihy, "Ethnic Composition," p. 65. By 1826 the Jewish population already numbered 4,226 persons and comprised 12.8 percent of the total population (32,995). "Narodonaselenie Odessy," *Odesskii vestnik*, 1828, no. 77:332–33; no. 78:337–38.

19. Tsentral'nyi gosudarstvennyi istoricheskii arkhiv Leningrada, f. 1284, op. 194, d. 74 (1911), ll. 3–5—hereafter cited as TsGIA. See also *Pervaia vseobshchaia perepis'*, XLVII, Table 22, p. 137, and *Encyclopedia Judaica* (New York, 1971), XII, pp. 1320–21.

20. In 1884, the city prefect called for the institution of a quota system in the local secondary school and university system so as to restrict the number of Jewish students, a proposal that caught the attention of Alexander III ("This is a question that would be good to resolve once and for all") and was passed into law in 1887. The law stipulated that no more than 10 percent of the student body could consist of Jews. TsGIA, f. 1284, op. 223, d. 15 (1885), ll. 58–60; f. 1284, op. 223, d. 120 (1888), l. 40. In 1904, the prefect again went on the attack, proposing this time that Russian be substituted for Yiddish in the lower Jewish schools, a matter that the Education Minister agreed to take under advisement. TsGIA, f. 1284, op. 194, d. 53 (1905), l. 4.

21. M. L. Harvey, "The Development of Russian Commerce on the Black Sea and Its Significance" (Ph.D. dissertation, University of California at Berkeley, 1938), p. 159.

22. Ibid., p. 158. On the telegraph and telephone, see A. Skal'kovskii, "Pochty i telegrafy v Odesse, 1808–1869 g.," *Trudy Odesskogo statisticheskogo komiteta*, IV (Odessa, 1870), pp. 185–92, and "Telefony v Rossii," *Izvestiia Moskovskoi gorodskoi dumy*, Sept. 1897, No. 1, Sec. 2:44–59. On credit and banking operations, see N. S. Petlin, *Opyt opisaniia gubernii i oblastei Rossii v statisticheskom i ekonomicheskom otnosheniiakh, v sviazi s deiatel'nost'iu v nikh Gosudarstvennogo Banka i chastnykh kreditnykh uchrezhdenii*, II (St. Petersburg, 1893), pp. 306–24. For the growth of trading firms, see S. I. Plaksin, *Kommerchesko-promyshlennaia Odessa i ee predstaviteli v kontse XIX stoletiia i istoriia razvitiia torgovykh firm* (Odessa, 1901).

23. L. A. Velikhov, "Moia poezdka v Odessu," *Gorodskoe delo*, 1910, no. 6:375. One pood equals 36.11 pounds.

24. Ibid., p. 375. For other discussion, see Harvey, pp. 198–203. For official discussion of the problem at the local level, see TsGIA, f. 1284, op. 69, d. 174 (1876), ll. 4–5; f. 1284, op. 69, d. 341 (1878), ll. 9–10; f. 1284, op. 70, d. 492 (1881), ll. 2–8, 35; f. 1284, op. 223, d. 218 (1890), ll. 2–5; f. 1284, op. 223, d. 180 (1892), ll. 2–3; f. 1282, op. 3, d. 390 (1900), l. 7; f. 1284, op. 194, d. 53 (1905), l. 2; f. 1284, op. 194, d. 53 (1908), l. 2; f. 1284, op. 194, d. 86 (1909), l. 2; f. 1284, op. 194, d. 88 (1910), l. 2.

25. TsGIA, f. 1284, op. 223, d. 42-B (1897), l. 3.

26. *Otchet Odesskogo komiteta torgovli i manufaktur za 1901* (Odessa, 1902), appendices 2, 3(a).

27. *Obzor Odesskogo gradonachal'stva za 1914*, pp. 3, 36. A total of 403 industrial enterprises was listed for 1913, indicating that the decrease in 1914 from the 1901 level did not result from Russia's entry into World War I. *Obzor Odesskogo gradonachal'stva za 1913* (Odessa, 1914), p. 34.

28. *Obzor Odesskogo gradonachal'stva za 1914*, p. 3. The main metal-

working enterprises were those manufacturing agricultural equipment, iron products, tinplate, wire, and bolts.

29. For a discussion and analysis of the problems associated with developing a diversified economy, see Patricia Herlihy, "Odessa: Staple Trade and Urbanization in New Russia," *Jahrbücher für Geschichte Osteuropas*, XXI, 2 (1973):184–95. See also Jeremiah Schneiderman, *Sergei Zubatov and Revolutionary Marxism: The Struggle for the Working Class in Tsarist Russia* (Ithaca, 1976), p. 287.

30. *Pervaia vseobshchaia perepis'*, XLVII, p. xvi.

31. Ibid., p. xvii.

32. S. M. Kovbasiuk, ed., *Odessa: Ocherk istorii goroda-geroia* (Odessa, 1957), pp. 79–80.

33. *Pervaia vseobshchaia perepis'*, XLVII, p. xvii.

34. TsGIA, f. 1284, op. 69, d. 150 (1874), ll. 10–11.

35. TsGIA, f. 1284, op. 223, d. 113 (1883), ll. 12–14.

36. Data are based on an analysis of 100 questionnaires filled out by prostitutes who had entered the city hospital for treatment of venereal disease. M. S. Onchukovaia, "O polozhenii prostitutok v Odesse," *Trudy Odesskogo otdela Russkogo obshchestva okhraneniia narodnogo zdraviia*, 1904, no. 4:51–52. Average dockworker salary from V. K. Vasil'evskii, "Polozhenie portovykh rabochikh v Odesse," Ibid., p. 44.

37. Kovbasiuk, p. 82; *Istoriia gorodov i sel Ukrainskoi SSR. Odessa* (Kiev, 1979), p. 108; *Revoliutsiia 1905–07 g.g. na Ukraine: sbornik dokumentov i materialov* (Kiev, 1955), I, pp. 273–74.

38. P. Beliavskii, "Odesskii port," *Trudy Odesskogo statisticheskogo komiteta*, I (Odessa, 1865), pp. 265–90.

39. M. I. Finkel', "Issledovanie o smertnosti v Odesse v desiatiletnii period s 1851 goda po 1860 god vkliuchitel'no," Ibid., p. 158.

40. J. Murray, *Handbook for Northern Europe*, II (London, 1849), p. 609; Capt. Spencer, *Turkey, Russia, the Black Sea, and Circassia* (London, 1854), pp. 241–42.

41. The stone is soft shell limestone which, while offering the advantage of being easy to cut into uniform building blocks with a minimum of skill, is highly susceptible to weathering by wind and rain—thus the "appearance of antiquity" observed by Spencer. In time, huge catacombs were dug out beneath the city that have played an important role in Odessa's history. This was where the contrabandists hid their goods, as well as the revolutionary literature arriving from abroad, and it was here that the partisans set up their headquarters during the German and Rumanian occupation in World War II.

42. Skal'kovskii, *Pervoe tridtsatiletie istorii goroda Odessy*, pp. 134, 223.

43. Cited in *Istoriia gorodov i sel . . . Odessa*, p. 103.

44. Patricia Herlihy, "Death in Odessa: A Case Study of Population Movements in a Nineteenth-Century City," *Journal of Urban History*, IV, 4 (1978):424–27. "Slough of despond" from Ibid., p. 420. A total of 2,632 persons died from the plague in 1812; 2,458 in 1829. Ibid., p. 426.

45. Finkel', p. 158.

46. TsGIA, f. 1281, op. 6, d. 88 (1859), ll. 36–37.

47. For the provisions of the new statute, see TsGIA, f. 1287, op. 37, d. 2082, ll. 17–22, 46–161, 313–20; f. 1341, op. 110, d. 22, ll. 2–6; and in published form in *Novyi poriadok gorodskogo obshchestvennogo upravleniia v. Odesse* (St. Petersburg, 1863). The statute was superseded by the general statute of 1870 in mid-1873.

48. *Odessa, 1794–1894*, p. 93.

49. Ibid., pp. 794, 797.

50. Percentile figures derived from budgetary data in Ibid., pp. 794–97.

51. David J. Fox, "Odessa," *Scottish Geographical Magazine*, LXXIX, 1 (1963):10–11; *Nedelia stroitelia*, 1885, No. 30, p. 4. For the introduction of the railroad, see A. Skal'kovskii, "Biografiia Odesskoi zheleznoi dorogi," *Trudy Odesskogo statisticheskogo komiteta*, I (Odessa, 1865), pp. 291–310; "Odesskie zheleznye dorogi," *Pamiatnaia knizhka Odesskogo gradonachal'stva za 1870 g.*, I (Odessa, 1870), pp. 100–101.

52. *Odesskii vestnik*, 1870 No. 1, p. 2.

53. *Nedelia stroitelia*, 1900, No. 8, p. 111.

54. For an extended discussion of the following, see Frederick W. Skinner, "Trends in Planning Practices: The Building of Odessa, 1794–1917," in Hamm, ed., *The City in Russian History*, pp. 139–59.

55. G. Pozniakov, "Dannye o smertnosti v Odesse," *Izvestiia Moskovskoi gorodskoi dumy*, 1889, No. 3, Sec. 4:8 (for 1874–75); "O dolgoletnei zhizni v Odesse," *Vedomosti Odesskogo gradonachal'stva*, 1891, No. 279, p. 3 (for 1885); *Otchet sanitarnogo biuro Odesskogo gorodskogo obshchestvennogo upravleniia za 1900 god* (Odessa, 1902), p. 5 (for 1891–1900). Urban rate nationwide in 1907: 26.8 per 1,000. "Narodnoe zdrav'e v gorodakh Rossii po poslednim offitsial'nym dannym," *Gorodskoe delo*, 1910, no. 5:276.

56. *Otchet sanitarnogo biuro . . . za 1900*, pp. 2, 5, 7.

57. See, e.g., V. Shkvarikov, *Ocherk istorii planirovki i zastroiki Russkikh gorodov* (Moscow, 1954), pp. 5–20 passim; A. V. Bunin, *Istoriia gradostroitel'nogo iskusstva* (Moscow, 1953), pp. 477–86 passim; Kovbasiuk, pp. 61–62; *Istoriia gorodov i sel . . . Odessa*, p. 103.

58. *Pervaia vseobshchaia perepis'*, XLVII, p. iv.

59. *Rezul'taty odnodnevnoi perepisi . . . 1892 goda*, Pt. II, Sec. 1, Table 2, pp. 10, 14.

60. *Odesskii listok*, 1891, month and day not noted.

61. TsGIA, f. 1284, op. 3, d. 489 (1901), l. 12.

62. TsGIA, f. 1284, op. 223, d. 171 (1891), l. 37.

63. For the statute in published form, see *Gorodovoe polozhenie ll-go iiunia 1892 goda (s dopolneniiami po prodolzheniiu 1895 goda)* (Moscow, 1901). For commentary on its provisions, see Walter Hanchett, "Tsarist Statutory Regulation of Municipal Government in the Nineteenth Century," in Hamm, ed., *The City in Russian History*, pp. 107–13.

64. Suffrage figure for 1863 from *Odessa, 1794–1894*, p. 89; population figure from Table 7.1. Suffrage figure for 1889 from the list published in *Vedomosti Odesskogo gorodskogo obshchestvennogo upravleniia*, 1889, no. 46:1–16; population figure from *Izvestiia Moskovskoi gorodskoi dumy*, May 1893, no. 1, sec. 2:15.

65. Suffrage figure from the list published in *Vedomosti Odesskogo gorodskogo obshchestvennogo upravleniia*, 1892, No. 93, Addendum, pp. 1–7; population figure from Table 7.1. In 1913 the number of eligible voters was 2,400 or 0.4 percent of the population (total: 648,472). Suffrage figure from Kovbasiuk, p. 106; population figure from *Obzor Odesskogo gradonachal'stva za 1913*, p. 35. The pattern was the same elsewhere. In Moscow, for example, about 6,000 persons (0.7 percent) were declared eligible to vote in 1893 out of a total population of some 900,000. Hanchett, "Tsarist Statutory Regulation," p. 111.

66. *Gorodovoe polozhenie ll-go iiunia 1892 goda*, Article 24, Note 3. In 1909 a Jew, one Aaron Brodskii, ran under an assumed Christian name and won election to the State Duma; however, his real identity was discovered and in 1910 the Senate disbarred him from office. TsGIA, f. 1284, op. 194, d. 88 (1910),

l. 2; f. 1284, op. 194, d. 74 (1911), l. 3. The 1870 Statute had stipulated that no more than one-third of the membership of the city council and the city executive board could consist of "non-Christians," and it specifically barred Jews from the mayoralty. There were no restrictions, however, on Jews exercising the electoral privilege as long as they met property qualifications. *Gorodovoe polozhenie s raz"iasneniiami i dopolneniiami po pozdneishim uzakoneniiam i rasporizheniiam pravitel'stva* (St. Petersburg, 1873), Articles 54, 88.

67. TsGIA, f. 1284, op. 223, d. 198 (1894), ll. 2–3; f. 1284, op. 194, d. 86 (1909), l. 3. See *Gorodskoe delo* (1909–18) for incisive commentary on the political situation in Odessa.

68. TsGIA, f. 1284, op. 194, d. 53 (1908), l. 2; f. 1284, op. 194, d. 88 (1910), l. 3.

69. *Gorodskoe delo*, 1909 no. 8:403–404. See also Kovbasiuk, p. 106.

70. *Kievskaia mysl'*, May 19, 1914; Kovbasiuk, pp. 107–108.

71. The ½-kopek tax had been authorized by Imperial decree on June 26, 1861. In the period from 1864 to 1892, the tax brought a total of 8,457,313 rubles into the municipal treasury; most of the revenue was used to finance streetpaving but the funds supported other urban development projects as well. *Odessa, 1794–1894*, pp. 794–97. In 1903 the city prefect specifically cited loss of the proceeds as the reason for the city's deficit in that year. TsGIA, f. 1284, op. 194, d. 69 (1904), l. 5. A dispute between the city and the state over ownership of the port (and thus over the question of which entity should receive the tax revenue) had broken out as early as 1890. For details, see TsGIA, f. 1284, op. 223, d. 171 (1891), ll. 19–28.

72. Data from annual budgetary schedules in *Obzor Odesskogo gradonachal'stva za 1895–1914* (Odessa, 1896–1916).

73. *Gorodskoe delo*, 1909, no. 4:163.

74. Ibid., 1913, no. 2:90–95.

75. Ibid., 1909, no. 11:563.

76. No new buildings were constructed in 1907 and only two were built in 1908. Velikhov, "Moia poezdka v Odessu," p. 375.

77. Ibid., p. 376.

78. The following characterization of the Gambrinus, a bar that still exists in Odessa (although rebuilt after its destruction in World War II), is taken from Alexander Kuprin's story "Gambrinus," as found in Alexandre Kuprin, *Gambrinus and Other Stories*, trans. Bernard Guilbert Guerney (New York, 1925), pp. 11–69. Quotations respectively from pp. 21, 14, 32, 42. Sashka was an actual historical figure (real name Aaron Moiseevich Goldstein). For a moving account of his funeral in Odessa in 1920, see Konstantin Paustovsky, *Years of Hope*, trans. Manya Harari and Andrew Thomson (New York, 1968), pp. 184–87.

79. Grigorii Moskvich, *Illiustrirovannyi i prakticheskii putevoditel' po Odesse* (Odessa, 1904), pp. 18–21, 59–64 passim. On the aviation club, the first to be organized in Russia (1908), see Kovbasiuk, p. 116; *Istoriia gorodov i sel ... Odessa*, pp. 112–13.

80. The following characterization is drawn from the annual reports of the city prefect. Quotations respectively from TsGIA, f. 1284, op. 223, d. 198 (1894), ll. 5–8; f. 1284, op. 194, d. 69 (1904), l. 3; f. 1284, op. 194, d. 86 (1909), l. 4; f. 1284, op. 194, d. 88 (1910), l. 2; "Vsepoddanneishii otchet Odesskogo Gradonachal'-nika na 1895 god," bound with *Prilozheniia ko vsepoddanneishim otchetam Odesskogo Gradonachal'nika za 1891–1897 g.g.* (Odessa, 1892–98), l. 2.

81. See, e.g., A. Kirpichnikov, "Stoletie Odessy (22 avgusta 1794 g.—22 avgusta 1894 g.)," *Istoricheskii vestnik*, LVII (Aug. 1894):389–411 passim.

82. Cited in *Encyclopedia Judaica*, XII, p. 1322.

83. *Pervaia vseobshchaia perepis'*, XLVII, Table 22, pp. 136–37; Table 24, pp. 152–61.

84. Lambroza, pp. 45, 271.

85. *Pervaia vseobshchaia perepis'*, XLVII, Table 24, pp. 152–61.

86. TsGIA, f. 1284, op. 194, d. 74 (1911), l. 4; *Encyclopedia Judaica*, XII, pp. 1320–21; Lambroza, pp. 269–71. Total university enrollment figure is an estimate based upon a figure of 3,071 for 1908. Kovbasiuk, p. 113. In 1897, 2,677 persons had been enrolled in the university and other institutions of higher learning. *Pervaia vseobshchaia perepis'*, XLVII, p. xvi.

87. TsGIA, f. 1282, op. 3, d. 390 (1900), l. 7.

88. Cited in *Odesskii pogrom i samooborona* (Paris, 1906), pp. 13–14.

89. Lambroza, pp. 273–75; Schneiderman, pp. 288–89; *Encyclopedia Judaica*, XII, p. 1323. For official commentary on the 1871 pogrom, see TsGIA, f. 1284, op. 67, d. 180 (1872), ll. 6–9.

90. Schneiderman, p. 288. The number killed has been variously set at from 300 to 800 persons but the figure most commentators settle on is 500, of whom 300 to 400 were Jews. By far the most thorough study in English is Lambroza, pp. 278–94. For other accounts, see *Encyclopedia Judaica*, XII, p. 1323; *Odesskii pogrom i samooborona*, pp. 13–18, 63; *American Jewish Yearbook*, 1906, pp. 50–51; Louis Greenberg, *The Jews in Russia*, II (New Haven, 1951), pp. 76–81; Sidney Harcave, *The Russian Revolution of 1905* (London, 1964), p. 204; Howard D. Mehlinger and John M. Thompson, *Count Witte and the Tsarist Government in the 1905 Revolution* (Bloomington, Ind., 1972), pp. 57–65.

91. See Lambroza, pp. 229–62; *Odesskii pogrom i samooborona*, pp. 77–94; *Encyclopedia Judaica*, XII, pp. 1323–24.

92. *Encyclopedia Judaica*, XII, p. 1324. See Lambroza, pp. 38–39 for official emigration policies.

93. Maxim Gorky, "Chelkash," in *A Sky-Blue Life and Selected Stories*, trans. George Reavy (New York, 1961), p. 43.

94. "Polozhenie portovykh rabochikh v Odesse," pp. 36–49 passim. Data are based on registration forms filled out in 1900 by 260 dockworkers who took their dinners at a cafeteria run by a local temperance society. Length of the working day from L. O. Narkhevich, "K voprosu o polozhenii bezdomnykh rabochikh v Odesskom porte," *Trudy Odesskogo otdela Russkogo obshchestva okhraneniia narodnogo zdraviia*, 1904, no. 4:111. For a general discussion of labor conditions in Odessa at the turn of the century, see Schneiderman, pp. 289–91.

95. Cited in "Polozhenie portovykh rabochikh v Odesse," p. 48.

96. *Istoriia gorodov i sel . . . Odessa*, pp. 103, 106–108; Kovbasiuk, pp. 70–78; Herlihy, "Ethnic Composition," pp. 58–59; Schneiderman, p. 291; V. V. Straten, "Iuzhno-Russkii Rabochii Soiuz v Odesse: Sotsial-demokraticheskoe dvizhenie v Odesse do 1896 goda," *Letopis' revoliutsii*, 1924, no. 2:192.

97. "Vsepoddanneishii otchet Odesskogo Gradonachal'nika za 1895 god," l. 2.

98. *Istoriia gorodov i sel . . . Odessa*, pp. 107–108.

99. Ibid., pp. 108–109; Kovbasiuk, pp. 79–83, 87–90.

100. Lambroza, pp. 275–76; Kovbasiuk, pp. 86–87; *Revoliutsiia 1905–07 g.g. na Ukraine*, I, pp. 227–30, 247–52, 261–63, 550; II, Pt. 1, pp. 414–15, 557.

101. *Revoliutsiia 1905–07 g.g. na Ukraine*, I, pp. 300, 628; II, Pt. 1, p. 221.

102. Ibid., I, pp. 609–12, 626–29, 639.

103. *Istoriia gorodov i sel . . . Odessa*, p. 107.

104. TsGIA, f. 1284, op. 3, d. 489 (1901), ll. 12–13. The following account is drawn from Kovbasiuk, pp. 83–103; *Istoriia gorodov i sel . . . Odessa*, pp. 108–11;

Revoliutsiia 1905–07 g.g. na Ukraine, I–II passim. Strike data for 1905–06 from Ibid., II, Pt. 2 pp. 49, 75. For official commentary on these events, see TsGIA, f. 1284, op. 194, d. 68 (1902), ll. 4–5; f. 1284, op. 194, d. 69 (1904), ll. 2–3; f. 1284, op. 194, d. 53 (1905), ll. 2, 4; f. 1284, op. 194, d. 74 (1911), l. 2.

105. TsGIA, f. 1284, op. 194, d. 53 (1908), l. 2; f. 1284, op. 194, d. 86 (1909), ll. 2–4; f. 1284, op. 194, d. 88 (1910), ll. 2–3. The number of students at the university dropped from 3,071 in 1908 to 2,058 in 1912. Kovbasiuk, p. 113.

106. In July 1914 some twenty factories were shut down by strikes; in 1916 there were sixteen strikes in the course of the year. Kovbasiuk, pp. 110–18 passim.

107. TsGIA, f. 1284, op. 194, d. 69 (1904), ll. 3–4. For the earlier references, see Ibid., f. 1282, op. 3, d. 390 (1900), l. 6; f. 1284, op. 194, d. 68 (1902), l. 4.

108. *Revoliutsiia 1905–07 g.g. na Ukraine,* II, Pt. 1, pp. 73, 209; Pt. 2, pp. 83–84.

109. TsGIA, f. 1282, op. 3, d. 489 (1901), ll. 12–13.

110. TsGIA, f. 1284, op. 223, d. 180 (1892), ll. 5–8; f. 1282, op. 3, d. 283 (1899), ll. 3–4; f. 1282, op. 3, d. 489 (1901), l. 11; f. 1284, op. 194, d. 53 (1905), l. 4; f. 1284, op. 194, d. 86 (1909), l. 4; f. 1284, op. 194, d. 88 (1910), l. 3; f. 1284, op. 194, d. 74 (1911), l. 3. Figure on municipal spending for welfare from annual budgetary schedules in *Obzor Odesskogo gradonachal'stva za 1895–1914* (Odessa, 1896–1916).

111. TsGIA, f. 1284, op. 3, d. 489 (1901), ll. 12–13; f. 1284, op. 194, d. 86 (1909), l. 4; f. 1284, op. 194, d. 74 (1911), l. 3. The epidemic of 1910 affected 1,220 persons, of whom 341 died.

112. *Vedomosti Odesskogo gradonachal'stva,* 1894, no. 207:2.

113. Zak, "Rabochii klass i gorodskie vybory," p. 2.

114. Ibid., p. 3.

115. See, e.g., *Trudy Odesskogo otdela Russkogo obshchestva okhraneniia narodnogo zdraviia,* 1901, no. 3:5–29; 1904, no. 4:22–131.

116. The city prefect noted in his report for 1886, e.g., that many of the persons under both open surveillance and secret observation were statisticians attached to the zemstvo *uprava.* TsGIA, f. 1284, op. 223, d. 47 (1887), 10–11.

117. On Tarasevich, see P. Diatroptov, "L. A. Tarasevich," in *Bor'ba za nauky v tsarskoi Rossii* (Moscow-Leningrad, 1931), pp. 43–45, and *Bol'shaia sovetskaia entsiklopediia* (2nd ed.), XL, pp. 615–16; on Levitskii, *Revoliutsiia 1905–07 g.g. na Ukraine,* I, p. 648; on Gershanskii, Ibid., II, Pt. 1, pp. 71–72; on Bogolomets, Ibid., I, pp. 471–75, and Kovbasiuk, p. 92.

118. I am indebted to Professor John F. Hutchinson of the University of Toronto for calling my attention to Tarasevich, Gamaleia, and Diatroptov. On Gamaleia, see *Bol'shaia sovetskaia entsiklopediia* (2nd ed.), X, pp. 182–83; on Diatroptov, Ibid., XIV, p. 311.

119. "Zaiavlenie," *Zapiski Odesskogo otdeleniia Imperatorskogo Russkogo tekhnicheskogo obshchestva,* 1904, no. 7–8:69.

120. On the exhibition and the problems it encountered, see *Gorodskoe delo,* 1910, no. 8:540–42; no. 10:681–85; no. 11–12:802–807; no. 13–14:951–54.

121. See "Otchet o deiatel'nosti Odesskogo otdeleniia Imperatorskogo Russkogo tekhnicheskogo obshchestva za pervoe 25-ie ego sushchestvovaniia (1871–1896 g.g.)," *Zapiski Odesskogo otdeleniia Imperatorskogo Russkogo tekhnicheskogo obshchestva,* 1897, No. 2–3, pp. 39–101.

122. Kuprin, *Gambrinus,* quotations respectively from pp. 63, 67, 69, 73.

123. C. Koch, *The Crimea: With a Visit to Odessa* (London, 1855), p. 135, as cited in Fox, "Odessa," p. 9.

124. Iuzhakov, "Iubilei Odessy," p. 121.

125. For similar discussion regarding the drawing of generalizations in Russian urban history, see J. Michael Hittle, *The Service City: State and Townsmen in Russia, 1600–1800* (Cambridge, 1979), pp. 16–17.

126. Blackwell, "Modernization and Urbanization in Russia," pp. 294–95.

127. As detailed throughout this study, there were of course many different factors contributing to the breakdown of urban modernization in the post–1892 period. Yet promulgation of the revised municipal statute in 1892 stands out as the single most critical factor, which impacted directly or indirectly on the others. For similar discussion and analysis, see Michael F. Hamm, "The Breakdown of Urban Modernization: A Prelude to the Revolutions of 1917," in Hamm, ed., *The City in Russian History*, pp. 183–88.

BIBLIOGRAPHICAL NOTE

Of the wealth of archival material pertaining to Odessa's development in the late Imperial era, the most valuable by far are the annual reports of the Odessa city prefect (*gradonachal'nik*), which not only provide important data on key events of the reporting year but offer insight into high official thinking regarding the city and its residents. The reports in their original form are located in Tsentral'nyi gosudarstvennyi istoricheskii arkhiv Leningrada (Central State Historical Archive of Leningrad), f. 1263 (Committee of Ministers) for the period prior to 1905, f. 1275 (Council of Ministers) for the period from 1905; for the entire period, a copy of each report, together with a lengthy *Survey* (*Obzor*) containing data on population movement, economic activity, health, crime, education, building programs, and the like, is to be found in f. 1284 (Department of General Affairs). Much of the information in the *Obzor* is also available in published form in the annual *Obzor Odesskogo gradonachal'stva*. Other key archival material is located in f. 1287 (Economics Department/Ministry of Internal Affairs), f. 1288 (Main Administration for Local Economy/Ministry of Internal Affairs), f. 1290 (Central Statistical Committee/Ministry of Internal Affairs), and f. 1293 (Technical-Building Committee/Ministry of Internal Affairs).

Official publications of the Odessa municipal government represent another key resource. The reports of the administrative board (*uprava*) are contained in the annual *Otchet Odesskoi gorodskoi upravy*, while the proceedings of the city council (*duma*) are found in *Vedomosti Odesskogo gorodskogo obshchestvennogo upravleniia* (1864–78, 1880–94) and *Izvestiia Odesskoi gorodskoi dumy* (1894–1917). For rich data on all aspects of Odessa's historical development, see *Odessa, 1794–1894: izdanie gorodskogo obshchestvennogo upravleniia k stoletiiu goroda*, 2 vol. (Odessa, 1894). For annual budgetary schedules, see the latter, Vol. 2, for 1864–92 and the annual *Otchet Odesskoi gorodskoi upravy po ispolneniiu smety dokhodov i raskhodov goroda Odessy* for 1893–1914; budgetary data are also available in the annual *Obzor Odesskogo gradonachal'stva*. For census data, see the latter and the following: *Perepis' naseleniia g. Odessy, proizvedennaia 5-go sentiabria 1873 goda* (Odessa, 1875); *Rezul'taty odnodnevnoi perepisi g. Odessy 1 dekabria 1892 goda* (Odessa, 1894); *Pervaia vseobshchaia perepis' naseleniia Rossiiskoi imperii 1897 g.*, XLVII, *g. Odessa* (St. Petersburg, 1904). On sanitation and health, see the annual *Otchet sanitarnogo biuro Odesskogo gorodskogo obshchestvennogo upravleniia*; on economic matters, the annual *Otchet Odesskogo komiteta torgovli i manufak-*

tur. Again, such data can be found in the annual *Obzor Odesskogo gradonachal'stva*, though in abbreviated form.

Journals and newspapers of particular value for their broad coverage of Odessa include *Gorodskoe delo* (1909–18), *Izvestiia Moskovskoi gorodskoi dumy* (1877–1916), *Trudy Odesskogo statisticheskogo komiteta* (1865–70), and *Vedomosti Odesskogo gradonachal'stva* (1869–1916). On sanitation and health, see the *Trudy Odesskogo otdela Russkogo obshchestva okhraneniia narodnogo zdraviia* (1900–1904). On urban development, see *Nedelia stroitelia* (1881–83, 1885–1901), *Stroitel'* (1895–1905), *Zapiski Odesskogo otdeleniia Imperatorskogo Russkogo tekhnicheskogo obshchestva* (1885–1916), and *Zodchii* (1901–16).

Of the large amount of secondary literature, the following books and articles are particularly useful: Gabriel de Castelnau, *Essai sur l'histoire ancienne et moderne de la Nouvelle Russie*, III (Paris, 1820); Alexander de Ribas, *Staraia Odessa: istoricheskie ocherki i vospominaniia* (Odessa, 1913); S. N. Iuzhakov, "Iubilei Odessy," *Russkoe bogatstvo*, 1894, No. 9, pp. 120–44; *Istoriia gorodov i sel Ukrainskoi SSR. Odessa* (Kiev, 1979); A. Kirpichnikov, "Stoletie Odessy (22 avgusta 1794 g.–22 avgusta 1894 g.)," *Istoricheskii vestnik*, Aug. 1894, pp. 389–411; S. M. Kovbasiuk, ed., *Odessa: ocherk istorii goroda-geroia* (Odessa, 1957); V. K. Nadler, *Odessa v pervye epokhi ee sushchestvovaniia* (Odessa, 1893); K. L. Olenin, *"Vek": Odesskii istoricheskii al'bom, 1794–1894* (Odessa, 1894); A. Orlov, *Istoricheskii ocherk Odessy s 1794 po 1803 god* (Odessa, 1885); *Revoliutsiia 1905–07 g.g. na Ukraine*, 2 vol. (Kiev, 1955); A. Skal'kovskii, *Pervoe tridtsatiletie istorii goroda Odessy, 1793–1823* (Odessa, 1837); Ibid., *Zapiski o torgovykh i promyshlennykh silakh Odessy* (St. Petersburg, 1865); K. Smol'ianinov, *Istoriia Odessy* (Odessa, 1853); *Sbornik Imperatorskogo Russkogo istoricheskogo obshchestva*, LIV (St. Petersburg, 1886); V. Zagoruiko, *Po stranitsam istorii Odessy i Odesshchiny*, 2 vol. (Odessa, 1957–60).

8.

Tiflis

Crucible of Ethnic Politics, 1860–1905

RONALD GRIGOR SUNY

To Georgians the "mother of cities" (*dedakalaki*) has always been their traditional political center, Tiflis. Yet the present-day capital of Soviet Georgia became primarily Georgian in population only in 1970. For most of its modern history, Tiflis has been a cosmopolitan town of mixed nationality, with the dominant demographic position held by Armenians. The phenomenon of urban centers being populated primarily by members of one nationality while the surrounding countryside is peopled by another ethnic group is familiar to students of Eastern Europe and the Caucasus. In the Baltic littoral, Germans lived in towns while Latvians and Estonians worked the land; in Lithuania, the Lithuanians occupied the countryside and traveled to Vilna or other market towns where they came into contact with the local Poles and Jews. Most of the major cities of the Ukraine were, in fact, inhabited by Russians, Poles, and Jews, while Ukrainians lived in the villages. Likewise in Transcaucasia, the urban population, already distinct from the country people by occupation, social status, and political leverage, differed most immediately from the rural population in language, national past, and ethnic consciousness.

Since the early middle ages, Tiflis (Tbilisi in Georgian) had been the historic capital of Georgia, the seat of the court of the kings of Kartli. However, as a trading center frequented by caravans from Persia and the Middle East, Tiflis had attracted merchants who were predominantly Armenian. By the time Russia summarily annexed the Kingdom

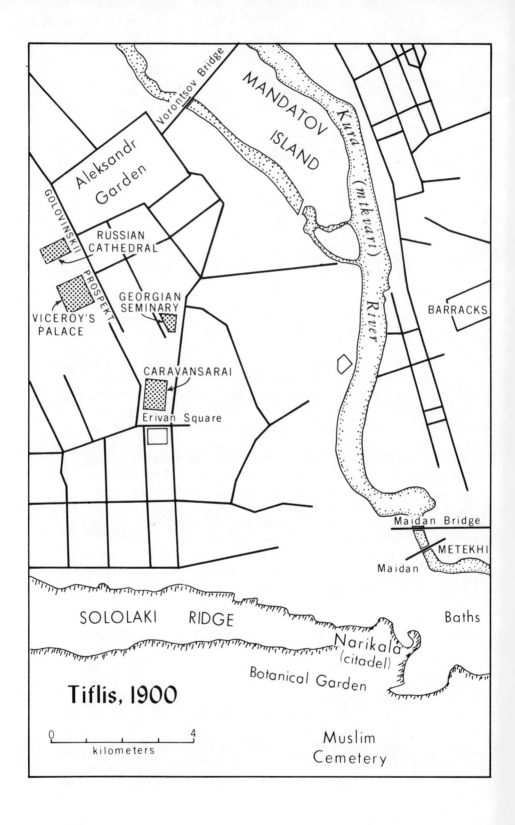

Vorontsov Bridge

MANDATOV ISLAND

Kura ('mtkvari) River

Aleksandr Garden

GOLOVINSKII PROSPEKT

RUSSIAN CATHEDRAL

GEORGIAN SEMINARY

VICEROY'S PALACE

CARAVANSARAI

Erivan Square

BARRACKS

Maidan Bridge

METEKHI

Maidan

SOLOLAKI RIDGE

Baths

Narikala (citadel)

Botanical Garden

Tiflis, 1900

0   4
kilometers

Muslim Cemetery

of Kartli-Kakheti (eastern Georgia) in 1801, nearly three-quarters of the twenty thousand inhabitants of Tiflis were Armenian (74.3 percent in 1803) and less than a quarter Georgian (21.5 percent).[1] The peasantry in the countryside around Tiflis was largely Georgian as was the nobility both in the countryside and the town. Within the city the hired workers, who were the lowest class, and some artisans were Georgian, but most of the artisans, the merchants, and the wealthier people of property were Armenian. Thus, the two Christian peoples of Transcaucasia were divided along lines of ethnicity, geography, and social class. In Transcaucasia, as elsewhere in the Russian Empire, nationality tended to reinforce lines of class identification.

While Tiflis's role as a Georgian political and cultural center has been well appreciated, the city's importance as an intellectual and political center for the Caucasian Armenians and, to a lesser extent, the Azerbaijanis, has receivedmuch less attention. As a result of Tbilisi's designation as the capital of the Soviet Republic of Georgia in 1921 and the subsequent emigration of thousands of Armenians south to their own republic, Georgian and Armenian scholars study the complex development of ethnic politics in Caucasia separately and in isolation from each other. Thus, Georgians underplay the significance of the Armenian contribution to the growth of their capital as well as the anti-Armenian sources of their own nationalism. Soviet Armenians emphasize the history of their own capital, Erevan, and the present territory of the Armenian republic without full investigation of the cosmopolitan past of their people, the centrality of the Tiflis Armenians in the history of Armenian nationalism, and their own condescension toward their Georgian neighbors. When both Armenian and Georgian, as well as Russian and Azerbaijani, developments are seen as a whole in nineteenth and early twentieth century Caucasian history, the interrelation of all these nationalities in the rise of their respective national ideologies becomes apparent, and Tiflis takes on a new aspect as the crucible of both Georgian and Armenian nationalism and socialism, as well as the scene of an intense ethnic and class struggle between these two nationalities.

DEMOGRAPHIC CHANGE AND THE ETHNIC EQUATION

Surrounded by mountains and lying along the banks of the Kura, the city of Tiflis took its name from the Georgian word *tbili* (warm), a reference to the mild climate and hot springs which attracted settlers to the site as early as the last centuries before Christ. Written sources indicate that a fortress had been built at Tiflis by the fourth century A.D. The Iranian *pitiakhsh* (governor) resided there, and by the sixth century the town had replaced Mtskheta as the major political center in Georgia. Georgian sources credit their king Vakhtang Gorgasali (452–502) with the construction of Tiflis and its establishment as the capital of Kartli (eastern Georgia).[2] Besides the Persians, the Arabs, Seljuks, Mongols, and Ottoman Turks at one time or another laid siege to and captured the town before its annexation by the Russian Empire in 1801.[3] Travelers over the centuries repeatedly spoke of the town's beauty and charm, but when some enthusiasts went so far as to call it "the Paris of the Caucasus," a local wag returned the compliment sardonically, referring to Paris as "the Tiflis of France." Two American missionaries passed through in 1830 and were impressed by the ethnic diversity and liveliness of the place:

> Tiflis has the appearance of an excessively busy and populous place. Its streets present not only a crowded, but, unlike many oriental cities, a lively scene. Every person seems hurried by business. Nor is the variety of costumes, representing different nations and tongues, many of which are curious and strange, the least noticeable feature of the scene. The Russian soldier stands sentry at the corners of streets, in a coarse great-coat concealing the want of a better uniform and even of decent clothing. The Russian subaltern jostles carelessly along in a little cloth cap, narrow-skirted coat and tight pantaloons, with epaulettes dangling in front of naturally round shoulders. In perfect contrast to him stands the stately Turk, if not in person, yet represented by some emigrant Armenian, with turbanned head and bagging *shalwar* [pants]. The Georgian priest appears, cane in hand, with a green gown, long hair and broad brimmed hat; while black flowing robes, and a cylindrical lamb-skin cap, mark his clerical brother of the Armenian church. The dark Lesgy, with the two-edged *kama* (short sword), the most deadly of all instruments of death, dangling at his side, seems prowling for his victim as an avenger of blood. The city-bred Armenian merchant waits upon his customers, snugly dressed in an embroidered frock-coat, gay calico frock, red silk shirt, and ample green trousers also of silk. The tall lank Georgian peasant, with an upright conical sheepskin cap, and scantily clothed, looks as independent in his *yapanjy* (cloak of felt), as Diogenes in his tub. His old oppressor, the Persian, is known by more flowing robes, smoothly combed beard and nicely dinted cap. In the midst of his swine appears the half-clad Mingrelian, with a bonnet like a tortoise shell tied loosely upon his head. And in a drove of spirited horses, is a hard mountaineer, whose round cap with a shaggy flounce of sheepskin dangling over his eyes, and the breast of his coat wrought into a cartridge box, show him to be a Circassian.[4]

With the establishment of Russian hegemony over Transcaucasia (by 1828), the Georgians and Armenians experienced, for the first time in a century, a relatively long period of peaceful development, protected by the tsarist army from raids by Caucasian mountaineers and periodic incursions by their Muslim neighbors. Gradually urban life revived, and the opportunities presented by Russian rule for economic advancement, European education, and careers in government and military attracted the more ambitious among the local peoples. Both the Georgians and the Armenians began to experience significant social changes as they left isolated villages and ventured into the growing towns. Through the nineteenth century the weight of the urban population in Transcaucasia increased and the percentage of people living in the countryside slowly dropped. In 1866, 82 percent of Georgia's population lived in the countryside while only 18 percent lived in towns or cities; thirty-one years later the first all-Russian census showed that the rural population had dropped slightly, to 79 percent, and the urban had risen to 21 percent.[5] Precisely in this contact with their countrymen and foreigners in the towns, the peoples of Caucasia underwent a process of national formation, of growing awareness of their connections with their ethnic brothers and their separation from those who could not understand their language and customs.

Closely connected to the developing sense of nationality and distance from other ethnic groups was the social distance, the growing economic and political gap, which separated the upper and lower strata in Tiflis, a distance at once greater than had been experienced in the village and at the same time colored by ethnic differences unknown outside of town. It was not long after a Georgian *glekhi* (peasant) migrated to Tiflis that he discovered that his fellow workers (*musha*) were much like him in background, but that the bosses, the rich merchants and industrialists of the city, the famed *mokalake*, spoke another language (Armenian), lived in a different part of town (Sololaki), and enjoyed rights and privileges that identified them with the Russian authorities.

According to the census of 1897, the city of Tiflis had a population of 159,590. It was the provincial capital of the province of the same name, as well as the seat of the highest tsarist official in Caucasia, the viceroy or governor-general. Tiflis Province was only 21.4 percent urban, and Tiflis was the only city of any size (the second largest city was Akhaltsikhe with 15,357 inhabitants). It is no wonder, then, that to Georgians Tbilisi was known simply as *kalaki* (the city). Life in Tiflis was distinct and different from life in rural Georgia. Here the direct presence of the Russian state could be felt, for the palace of the viceroys dominated the main thoroughfare, Golovinskii Prospekt. Next to it was the imposing Russian Orthodox cathedral, and across the avenue stood the memorial to Russian war dead. To the east of the palace was Erivan Square, the major crossroads of the city, with its caravansarais and trading houses. At one side of the square was the imposing city government building, designed in Moorish style. Above the square the streets ascended the mountain, Mtatsminda, which loomed over the city. Here was Sololaki, the neighborhood of the wealthy Armenian bourgeoisie. If one moved down toward the Kura River and eastward, one entered the oldest parts of the city, the narrow, winding streets of the Persian town with its mosques and hot springs baths. Across the Kura was the old district of Havlabar, largely Armenian, but far from wealthy. Here was the monastery of Khojevank, which served as a pantheon for Armenian writers, and the large hospital built by the wealthy merchant Aramiants.

Even as it grew in size, expanded to the west, and acquired European-style architecture, Tiflis remained poised between the cultures and customs of the Middle East and the western influences of its Russian governors. Both the Persian *maidan* (square) at the eastern end of the city and the institution of the bazaar and its guilds, which acted as a powerful social group within municipal politics, were reminiscent of the Iranian world. The more recently built railroad districts and workers' quarters at the western edge of the city reminded one of any industrializing city in Europe. The new "proletariat" moved into Didube and Nadzaladevi. The latter district was known locally as Nakhalovka (from the Russian word *nakhal*, impudent person) because workers built their own small homes there against the wishes of the authorities. No services were provided here by the city—no water, no sewers, sidewalks, or streetlights. This physical segregation of the workers in a district far from the more affluent sections of the city was a palpable analogue to the social distance between the peasant-workers and the people of property.

In Georgia the household and the family unit were still the principal forms of social and economic organization. Outside of towns more than 90 percent of the population of Tiflis province lived in such household units. But in the towns the percentage of individuals living alone rose to 14.1. For every 1,000 men in Tiflis there were but 675 women. These men without families were the poorest workers who had migrated from villages, either too young to have families or too poor to bring their wives and children with them into the city. In general households were smaller in the towns. Whereas over 46 percent of households in the province had six or more persons, in towns that figure was only 28.6 percent, and the majority of households had four members or less.

Like many cities of the Russian Empire at the end of the nineteenth century, Tiflis had a large immigrant population. In 1897, 43.7 percent of its citizens were native to the city or the district; 17.2 percent were migrants from other districts of Tiflis province; 33.9 percent had come from other provinces (almost half of them from Kutaisi province); and 5.2 percent were foreigners. A significant number of the immigrants and foreigners were Armenians. Though a precise figure cannot be determined, a reasonable estimate based on place of origin is that 20,000 of the 60,000 immigrants and foreigners were Armenians, 20,000 were Georgians, and the rest were Muslims and Europeans. One-third of all urban dwellers in Tiflis province were Armenians, while only 14.8 percent of rural dwellers were. Georgians made up 44.3 percent of the population of the province, but only 26.3 percent of the city, while Russians were only 7.5 percent of the provincial population and 24.7 percent of the city's.[6]

The major demographic trend in Tiflis in the nineteenth century was the steady decline of the Armenian proportion of the population and the rise of the Georgian and Russian components. As Tiflis grew from a town of 20,000 in 1801 to a city of 159,000 in 1897, the percentage of Armenians dropped from 74 to 38, largely as a result of the influx of poor Georgian villagers reluctantly leaving the densely populated, land-poor countryside. In absolute terms all three nationalities were increasing their numbers in the city, but the rate of growth was highest for Russians and lowest for Armenians.[7] Between 1865 and 1897 the number of Russians grew by 190 percent (from 12,462 to 36,357), while the Armenians increased by only 88 percent (from 28,488 to 55,553).[8] Thus, by the latter half of the nineteenth century the Armenians no longer had a majority in the city, merely a plurality, and the percentages of each nationality in the urban population were moving toward equality. The influx of Russian officials, army officers, and craftsmen, as well as Georgian peasants, was not only changing the ethnic composition of the town, but creating an ever-larger working class made up largely of Georgians. What distinguished these Georgians most significantly from the Armenians and the Russians in Tiflis was their almost complete isolation from positions of political and economic power.

THE ECONOMY AND SOCIAL STRATIFICATIONS

This demographic shift, while increasing the weight of non-Armenians in the urban population, did not diminish the Armenians' social, political, and economic preponderance. Descendents of Georgia's medieval tradesmen and merchants, the Tiflis Armenians had by the time of the Russian annexation become completely entrenched both in local crafts and in the lucrative trade with Persia, Europe, and Russia proper. Attempts in the first half of the century by Muscovite merchants to displace the Armenians had failed, and the Armenian-dominated guilds (*amkari*) maintained control over commerce and manufacture in Tiflis.[9] By mid-century some observers argued that the development of Tiflis's economy was being hindered by the ancient restrictions on growth, innovation, and foreign craftsmen imposed by the guilds, but not until 1867 did the state feel confident enough to dissolve the merchant guilds. The craft guilds remained intact, and prior possession, traditions of enterprise, and accumulated wealth helped keep the Armenians in a dominant economic position.[10]

The Soviet historian of Tbilisi Sh. Chkhetia paints a detailed picture of Armenian control in mid-century Tiflis:

> In the second half of the 1860s in Tbilisi there were about 3,000 shops and commercial enterprises, among them: 17 caravansarais, 5 hotels, 9 confectioners, 4 saloons, 441 *dukhani* [cafes] 96 *kharchevan'* [eateries], 71 wine cellars and warehouses, etc. Most of these commercial enterprises belonged to Armenians, in whose hands was held almost all trade; thus, of the 17 caravansarais, 14 belonged to: Begbutiants, Artsruni, Ananiants, Kherodianants, Korkhmaziants, Shnoiants, Shainiants, Movsesiants and Co., Sarkisiants, Vardants, Khalatiants, Tamamshiants, and other Armenian capitalists, who were the spiders of Tbilisi commercial-industrial capital of that time. Armenians also owned most of the hotels, wine cellars, *dukhani*, etc. Approximately two-thirds of the commercial industrial class was made up of Armenians.[11]

As this description makes clear, the economy of Tiflis in the 1860s was still preindustrial. Enterprises were quite small, except for some of the larger caravansarais which carried on foreign trade. These were almost entirely held by Armenians, though a few Russians and foreign merchants owned "trade houses and stores."[12] Tiflis was the portal through which raw silk and silk goods passed from Persia and eastern Transcaucasia to Russia and Europe. Transit trade rather than local production accounted for most of the goods sold by Tiflis merchants. Indeed, much more was imported into Transcaucasia in the 1860s than was exported.[13] Between 1821 and 1831, in 1846 and in 1864, low tariffs encouraged transit trade from Europe and Persia to cross Russian Transcaucasia rather than go through Turkish Trebizond. The great bulk of this trade went through Armenian hands, and Russians often referred to the goods from Persia as *armianskie tovary* (Armenian goods).

Besides being an important trading center, Tiflis was also the most important "industrial" city in the Caucasus in the period before the oil boom of the 1880s raised the Caspian port of Baku to predominance. Right to the end of the nineteenth century, manufacture in Georgia was carried out in the more than four thousand artisanal workshops found in cities and towns or in individual village households where women used time free from field and housework to craft the necessities of life. Figures from 1888 show that 78 percent of workshops in Georgia were either operated by a single craftsman or run with one assistant.[14] While the size of workshops grew somewhat toward the end of the century, the dominant position in local industry was held by this small-scale hand work well into the twentieth century.[15]

Though no rapid program of industrialization transformed the urban economy of Tiflis from the basically small-scale production which had characterized it for centuries, a steady increment of new industrial enterprises appeared in fields where there had either been no craftsmen (such as soapmaking, until now a home endeavor) or in areas where the small workshops simply could not keep up with demand, such as brickmaking.[16] As fashions changed, certain craftsmen—like those who made oriental slippers (*koshi*)—suffered, while others—like those who made European shoes—thrived, even when faced by new competition from mechanized production. Other traditional products, such as the *burka* (felt cloak) were taken over by manufacturers, in this case by G. Adelkhanov, who turned out 100,000 a year, mostly for the Caucasian cossack troops.[17] A few large factories appeared to produce textiles, tobacco products, and leather goods, but the number of artisans continued to grow and reached 12,650 in Tiflis by 1903.[18] Artisans remained at 5–7 percent of the city's population until well into the twentieth century, though the new factory production reduced their importance somewhat.[19]

The traditional artisanal economy was itself changing rapidly in the last decades of the nineteenth century. A tendency to hire workers, rather than rely solely on the old apprentice system, was already noticeable in the 1840s, but by the late 1880s nearly a quarter of the workshops in Georgia had more than one hired worker. Cheap peasant labor brought in by the railroads and the new machine production challenged the withering monopolies of the old craft guilds over employment opportunities and the size of the labor force. In the 1870s the *kharazi* (cobblers), the *choni* (hat makers), and the *dertsik* (tailors) had been among the most important guilds of Tiflis; by 1910 they had either disappeared or faced ruin.[20] Among the crafts which managed to maintain themselves, the old system of training apprentices and journeymen to become full masters was steadily replaced by harsher and more distant treatment of employees. Apprentices were often kept for years as domestic servants, and journeymen were ruthlessly exploited by the masters or by middlemen who supplied materials and then sold the finished product. A study of Tiflis artisans in 1903 revealed that

> the great majority of journeymen receiving payment for piecework . . . work in their own apartments, obtaining orders and materials from the masters. The journeymen receiving fixed money wages spend all day in the shops, usually living in the same buildings in which they work, damp, cold, and completely unsanitary, huddling together at night on the floor, on tables and counters.[21]

The gradual and steady transformation of the traditional artisanal economy into a capitalist industrial one affected even the most fiercely individualistic small tradesman, the legendary *kinto*, who was fast disappearing into the class of wage laborers.

Though transit trade and small craft production remained important in the economy of Tiflis, new, larger-scale industrial production provided opportunities for enterprising people to build their fortunes. Some capital investment came from eager Russian merchants and even from foreigners, but most of the new workshops and factories were built with local Armenian capital. The extension of railroads to Transcaucasia—the line between Tiflis and Poti on the Black Sea was opened in 1872 and between Tiflis and Baku in 1883—linked isolated areas of Transcaucasia together and created a larger, more accessible market for the products of Tiflis and other cities. In 1870 the Russian tariff was introduced in the Caucasus, replacing the lower duties imposed six years earlier and creating a protected area in which infant industries could grow without serious competition from cheaper European goods. Industry was now considered more important in the development of Transcaucasia than the transit trade, and the Armenians rapidly entered the world of manufacturing.

By the end of the nineteenth century, the position of Armenian merchants and industrialists in the economy of Tiflis and western Transcaucasia was unassailable. Of the 9,725 merchants in the city in 1897, 43.4 percent were Armenian (4,727), 26.1 percent were Georgian (2,619), and 6 percent Russian.[22] More impressively, of the 150 largest "industrial" establishments in Georgia in 1900, 44 percent belonged to Armenians, about the same amount belonged to Russians and foreign capitalists, and only 10 percent was owned by Georgians and 2 percent by Azerbaijanis.[23] When one considers only the city of Tiflis, the Armenian presence is even more striking; about one-half of large enterprises and most of the largest enterprises were Armenian.[24] The wealthiest Armenians—the Arzumanovs, Avetisians, and Mantashevs in the oil industry; the Adelkhanovs in leather goods; the Tumaniants, Kevorkovs, Avetisovs, and Pitoevs in commerce; the Egiazarovs, Ter-Asaturovs, Bozarjiants, and Enfianjiants in tobacco—made up a fraternity of entrepreneurs who worked together in a variety of joint-stock companies, pooling their capital to maintain the primacy of the local bourgeoisie in the face of Russian and foreign competition.[25]

While the Armenians occupied the middle levels of Tiflis social life, the Georgians held the lowest and highest positions. At the top, Georgian nobles sat close to the Russian viceroy, in his advisory council and administration, and had already proven themselves in the Caucasian and Crimean wars to be able and loyal officers. Such fidelity was rewarded by the tsarist government through the terms of the peasant emancipation which gave the Georgian nobility the most favorable land and monetary settlement of any gentry group in the empire.[26] Yet this estate which had so successfully adapted itself to Russian rule in the first half of the century failed to make the adjustment to the post-emancipation economic order. Georgian nobles were unable to break their dependence on their serfs ("the peasants have always fed us," one noble petition pleaded), develop the necessary entrepreneurial "spirit," and find the necessary capital resources to build an agriculture based on free, hired labor to compete effectively with the wealthy Armenians. Their history in the second half of the century was one of economic decline, political displacement by the Armenians, and a turn toward a nostalgic but quite impractical nationalism. As the role of Tiflis in the economic and political life of both Georgians and Armenians grew, the largely rural nobility found adjustment to the dynamics of urban life difficult. The image of the Georgian *tavadi* (prince) or *aznauri* (noble) in this period is of a splendidly dressed aristocrat idly ambling up and down the fashionable Golovinskii Prospekt.

At the bottom of both urban and rural society were the Georgian peasants, more and more of them migrating to the new factories and large workshops of Tiflis, Batumi, and Kutaisi. A contemporary description by the liberal publicist Niko Nikoladze gives a sense of the first generation of Georgian workers in the mid–1860s:

> The urban population of Georgia is not numerous. It is concentrated in Tiflis and two or three insignificant cities such as Kutaisi, Gori, etc. In all these places it has up until now been sharply demarcated into two classes: *mokalake [meshchane]* [townsman] and *musha* (worker) . . . . The *musha* in Georgia has no civil rights. He is not even a city dweller and not even temporarily emancipated. He is simply a runaway. Imeretian, Gurian, Mingrelian, and Rachian peasants who cannot bear the landlords' power and "tolerate the lord's whip" run away to Tiflis and, on the other hand, Kartlian and Kakhetian peasants (from Tiflis Province) save themselves in Imereti, Guria, etc . . . . The break with family and home saves the peasant from the landlords' power but makes him dependent on the bourgeoisie and bureaucracy, as a slave to a piece of bread. The work of the vast majority consists of carrying stones, sand, and lime for construction, sacks and heavy goods for merchants, water and firewood to inhabitants, and for such work they rarely receive two or three *abaza* (40, 60 kop.). The European proletariat has a family—true, aggravating him, but for all that, sweetening often the bitterness of his life; the Georgian *musha* also has a wife and children but "over the mountains, across the plains."[27]

Whereas earlier in the century artisanal production of household goods and clothing had been almost entirely in the hands of Armenian craftsmen, the influx of Georgian peasants both increased the number of workers in the city and changed the ethnic and economic makeup of the producing class. Instead of setting up their own workshops, which would have required skills and capital which the peasant-workers did not possess, these new migrants either became day laborers, petty tradesmen (*kinto*), or apprenticed themselves to existing masters. The actual number of artisanal workshops in Tiflis fell over time (from 2,175 in 1888 to 2,000 in 1893), while at the same time those with five or more workers increased in number (from 23 to 54).[28] Some of the larger workshops were called "factories," but before 1870 they usually employed only three to six persons.[29] The largest number of workers in such factories were in the tobacco plants. Machines were rarely used, most work was done by hand, and the workday was twelve or thirteen hours long. One observer in the 1880s wrote of the hardships faced by these workers:

> No less well-based are the complaints of workers about their bosses, who here often exploit the labor of the unenlightened people. The Asian worker, unfamiliar with the state language and Russian jurisprudence, often undeservedly suffers from the factory owners; he does not know *artel* organization, and each worker defends his own interest separately. Neither in case of sickness nor accident does he have help from the boss, who calmly replaces him with someone else, forcing the suffering one on the mercy of public charity. . . . Because of the complete absence of correct supervision of their work by the police, it is possible to meet many 8–9 year old children working 12–13 hours a day in the most unhygienic conditions.[30]

Factory production, if it can be called that, was almost entirely linked to agricultural production in some way. Flour mills along the Kura were driven by the water of the river. Breweries, grape and fruit beverage plants, leather and soap mills, operated along with the tobacco, textile, lumber, and brick plants. Once the railroad came to Tiflis, the city became the center of transportation in Transcaucasia, and the Main Railroad Workshops developed as the largest body of workers, indeed the very backbone of a proletariat in Georgia. The railroad workers were newly recruited from villages; almost three-quarters of them had worked in the yards there less than five years in 1895. And they were mixed by nationality; in 1900 more than 50 percent were Russian, Ukrainian, or Polish; 43.8 percent were Georgian; and 6.2 percent were Armenian.[31] The Georgian contingent in the working class was probably disproportionately represented among the poorest paid and least skilled workers, though evidence for this is hard to come by. The skilled workers in the railroad yards were usually Russian, and the larger factories owned by Armenians, such as Adelkhanov's shoe factory, usually hired Armenians. One Soviet scholar estimates that at the turn of the century the working class of Georgia was roughly 45–50 percent Georgian by nationality, 30–35 percent Armenian, 10–15 percent Russian, and 5–10 percent Azerbaijani and others.[32]

GUILDS AND GOVERNANCE

The rural background and agrarian orientation of most Georgians, whether noble or recently proletarianized peasant, contrasted sharply with the urban and bourgeois character of the prominent Tiflis Armenians. In time, stereotyped attitudes about the inherent or racial character of these two nationalities developed on the basis of their historic position in the economy and society of the country. A Russian observer, S. Maksimov, early in the 1870s echoed many other travelers to the Caucasus:

> Trade in the Caucasus is entirely in the hands of clever and calculating Armenians. Armenians are higher than Georgians in intelligence and in love for work, and for that reason there is nothing surprising in the fact that Georgian properties are rapidly falling into Armenian hands. Georgians are dependent on them just as the Poles are on the Jews and similarly feel toward them the same contempt and hatred (if not more than the Poles feel toward the Jews). The commercial Armenians reveal much cleverness, wilyness, are always ready with flattery; their thirst for profit leads them to cheating and swindling.[33]

The Russian ethnographer P. I. Kovalevskii spoke of the Georgians as "merry [and] sociable," but also as noted for their "laziness, insufficient energy and enterprise, instability, lack of self-restraint, little ability in work, light-minded and superficial attitude toward business and matters at hand."[34] The British Georgianist and diplomat Oliver Wardrop wrote in the 1880s of his perceptions of relations between Armenians and Georgians:

> A local proverb says "a Greek will cheat three Jews, but an Armenian will cheat three Greeks," and the Georgian, straightforward, honest fellow, is but too often cruelly swindled by the artful children of Haik. When the fraud is very apparent, the Armenian often pays for his greed with all the blood that can be extracted from his jugular vein.[35]

However doubtful the accuracy of such national stereotypes described by numerous visitors to Transcaucasia, it might be noted that they reflect characteristics which have more to do with the class position of the most visible representatives of either ethnic group than with inherent or genetic features of a whole people. Not only were there successful Georgian entrepreneurs equipped with the necessary business acumen, there were also Armenian peasants, both in Transcaucasia and Anatolia, who were not known for their "cleverness, wilyness, or flattery," but who displayed attitudes and patterns of life and work much closer to their Georgian counterparts. Ethnic stereotypes contributed to perceptions and misperceptions of these two peoples, but they were much more indicative of the positions that Armenians and Georgians held in Caucasian society and the roles they played in the economy and political life of the cities than they were of "race." Also the dominant elites of each people, that group to which social inferiors might look up to for guidance and leadership, were quite different and molded national culture along different lines. The Armenians had long ago lost their nobility, the *nakharars* of the medieval kingdoms, and were socially and politically dominated by the urban bourgeoisie in cities like Constantinople, Smyrna, and Tiflis, while the Georgians had few native examples of bourgeois leadership and instead had as models a traditional landed nobility then in its final decline. The Armenian businessman was simultaneously a model and a target of hostility—even for fellow Armenians.

Armenian economic dominance provoked keen resentment among the Georgians that their increasing presence in the city was not reflected in the distribution of material rewards. The Georgians also resented the Armenians' nearly absolute control over municipal government. While final authority in Transcaucasia always rested with the Russian military-bureaucratic administration, local government was delegated to the wealthy men of property in Tiflis. Given the ethnic mix of Tiflis's population, the tsarist administration was hard put to implement a system of municipal government of which both the Georgian nobility and the Armenian businessmen would approve. The tsarist government had eagerly recruited the Georgian nobles, particularly in the first two-thirds of the century, as officers and governors, while the Russians relied upon the Armenians to help develop the Transcaucasian economy and the Middle Eastern trade.

With the abolition of the Georgian kingdom in 1801, real control of the city of Tiflis shifted from the Georgian noble *mouravi*, under whom an Armenian *melik* had supervised commerce and industry, to the Russian governor and the Armenian guildmasters, the *amkarbashis*. In 1840 the influence of the guilds was officially recognized in a municipal statute that created a city board on which sat representatives of property owners, merchants, and craftsmen.[36] The *mokalakebi*, the great merchants and master artisans of Tiflis who half a century earlier had been serfs of the Georgian king, were integrated into the Russian social hierarchy when Viceroy Vorontsov in 1854 declared them to be *pochetnye grazhdane* (hereditary eminent citizens) and thus free from military recruitment, the soul tax, and corporal punishment.[37] In this way the Armenian businessmen, who had begun the century as bound servants of the Georgian kings and nobles, developed with Russian patronage into full-fledged burghers, at least within the limits of bureaucratic absolutism.

Only a few of the Great Reforms were extended to Transcaucasia in the 1860s, and as Soviet historian of emancipation P. S. Zaionchkovksii notes, "in Georgia feudal-serf-owning remnants were preserved to a greater degree than in the central regions of Russia."[38] In 1866 the judicial reform of 1864 was extended to Caucasia, thus eliminating the local courts and laws and integrating the region into the Imperial system. The Transcaucasian administration was revamped the following year, consolidating various departments and abolishing the viceroy's diplomatic chancellory.[39] Yet no zemstvos (local land assemblies) were established in Transcaucasia, which meant that the Georgian nobility did not enjoy the local political influence that their Russian counterparts exercised. Taken together, these reforms had a contradictory effect in Transcaucasia. They introduced judicial and administrative norms congenial to the local merchants and industrialists, while at the same time preserving to the greatest extent possible the seigneurial order in the countryside and the ultimate authority of the tsarist bureaucracy.

In the first half of the 1860s, the Russian government began tentatively to reform the municipal administration in the Empire and to introduce elected institutions. The need for such a reform in Tiflis became suddenly apparent to officials when a popular revolt revealed the potential threat to Russian authority from the traditional guilds. When in June 1865 the mayor of Tiflis and the tsarist treasury imposed a new tax on the populace without its prior consent, the guilds decided to shut down all businesses in the city. The acting governor, Grigol Orbeliani, ordered the strike to end, but the guild masters (*ustabashis*) were unable to convince the guild members and their allies to return to work. On June 27 approximately ten thousand artisans, shopkeepers, merchants, and simple workers marched through the streets holding meetings and protesting the new taxes. They plundered the house of the mayor, Shermazan Vartanov, and stoned and killed the tax collector, Bazhbeuk Melikov. Only on the fourth day, and after the appointment of a new mayor and the revoking of the tax, was order restored.

What was most remarkable about the June Days in Tiflis was the joint activity of the Armenian craftsmen and shopkeepers with the poorer Georgian workmen, or as Niko Nikoladze put it in Herzen's *Kolokol*, the *musha* shook hands with the *mokalake*, "forgetting that yesterday the *mokalake* cheated his ally of today, the *musha*, and that tomorrow the same story will be repeated."[40] In the heat of the protest over taxes and the arbitrary treatment of the townspeople by the government, the Georgian wood and stone haulers joined the Armenian artisans and merchants in a common action against the police regime. Relations between workers and masters in the mid–1860s were still close in this paternalistic preindustrial society; only at the turn of the century would such relations be strained, and only in late 1905 would they be severed.

On the advice of local officials the government in Petersburg reacted quickly to the events of June 1865 and issued a new plan for the municipal government of Tiflis, one which shifted the balance of local power away from the traditional guilds. Based on similar charters granted to Saint Petersburg (1846), Moscow (1862), and Odessa (1863), the law of August 11, 1866, divided the population of Tiflis into four estates for purposes of choosing the city's government. Each estate—the hereditary nobility, the personal nobility and eminent citizens, the simple citizens who owned property or were engaged in business, and those who owned no real estate but paid city taxes—elected one hundred electors who then chose twenty-five delegates to the city assembly. A mayor was chosen by electors from all estates but had to be a person of substantial wealth, owning property worth at least ten thousand silver rubles. This electoral system brought the nobles into urban government for the first time under Russian rule. Along with the eminent citizens, they made up less than ten percent of the city's population, yet they now became the de facto rulers of Tiflis.[41] The so-called simple citizens made up about 16 percent of the population, but neither they nor the property-less who made up 40–45 percent had much influence in the assembly. One-half of the assembly thus was elected by and made up of the top ten percent of the city's inhabitants.

Most affected by these reforms were the guilds which lost their former prominence after 1866. The very next year, the state reduced the powers of the craft guilds, abolished the merchant guilds altogether, and subordinated the remaining guilds to the city administration. Of approximately one hundred guilds, only seventeen remained after 1867.[42] The lesson of 1865 as learned by the tsarist bureaucracy was well expressed by Baron Nikolai: "The disorders which occurred in Tiflis in 1865 revealed that corporations united thus, without any ties to government, could be harmful to the public tranquility."[43]

The law of 1866 represented the nadir of Armenian power in Tiflis in the nineteenth century and the most concerted attempt to shift municipal power from the Armenian merchants to the Georgian nobility. As destructive as the reform was for the traditional guilds and their influence in government, the law proved to be only a temporary encumbrance to the reassertion of bourgeois power in the town. The integration of Tiflis into the urban administrative system of the Russian Empire was completed in 1874, when the Municipal Statute of 1870 was extended to certain cities in the Caucasus.[44] By this law a city council (duma) was to be elected by adult males who owned real estate or paid taxes in the city. Three curias were established based on the amount of tax paid, and each curia elected one-third of the council's deputies. In practice this meant that a handful of the wealthiest men in the city elected the first third of the council, the next wealthiest elected a second third, and hundreds of propertied people elected the last third. The city council then would elect an uprava (board) and a mayor. What was novel about this system was that it dispensed with the division of the population by estates (*soslovie*) and instead distinguished members of the population by wealth and property. The *tsenz* or property qualification which gave a man the right to vote established a new principle for political participation and power, one quite familiar to bourgeois Europe but new to tsarist Russia. The preponderance of power in the new city council lay with the wealthiest third of the population, the few rich businessmen who chose one-third of the assembly and from whose number the mayor was likely to emerge. Thanks to this law, the Armenian bourgeoisie reemerged as the leading political force in Tiflis. During the next five decades, until the revolution of 1917, all but two of the eleven mayors of Tiflis would be Armenians.

The "bourgeois" principle of representation based on one's economic status rather than on birth and *soslovie* helped the Armenian *mokalake* to maintain his paramount place in the city even as demographic movements were reducing his relative weight in the population. As the Georgian nobility failed to adjust to the spreading market economy and lost its ancient lands to middle class creditors or land-hungry peasants, it was pushed aside politically. In the last quarter of the nineteenth century social and intellectual tensions developed between the old noble elite and the Armenian bourgeoisie, tensions which provided the basis for ethnic attacks in the press and the council and a rise of political nationalism.

POLITICAL NATIONALISM AND COUNCIL POLITICS

Whatever religious or ethnic prejudices existed among the peoples of Tiflis toward their neighbors, a full sense of nationality was only beginning to develop among Armenians and Georgians in the first half of the century. The awareness of nationality, and its political expression in nationalism, was in Transcaucasia related to the urban experience. Caucasian villages had traditionally been inhabited by one ethnic group, and the relative autarchy and isolation of the villages precluded intense competition and hostility from developing once Russian arms had established peace in the region. But with the growth of Tiflis into a trading and artisanal center and with the consequent migration of peasants into the city, each ethnic group came up against the other in a context of material scarcity and competition for limited resources. Whereas in the village almost all one's neighbors had spoken the same language and attended the same church, in town the contrast between linguistic and religious compatriots and foreigners was much more stark. The relative ease with which a Georgian peasant-worker could speak to and understand another Georgian, even one of another social class, created a bond of communication with that fellow Georgian and a distance from those who could understand him less well. This "social communication" extended beyond language into the areas of religion, traditions, customary preferences, modes of bringing up children, ideas of honor and trust. Social differences reinforced ethnic distinctions, and both became intermixed into a complex amalgam of images and expectations. Urban life intensified the antagonisms that may have existed more mutely in the countryside, and nationality became the basis for rewarding some people and excluding others. In one sense, then, nationalism was an argument for differential treatment, for privileges to be dispensed within a closed ethnic circle.

Ethnic rivalry did not erupt into political conflict until the last decade of the century. When elections were held in 1875 for the first Tiflis duma and mayoralty, the largely Armenian city council elected Prince Ia. D. Tumanov, a Georgian, mayor. He was succeeded the next year by the noted activist and spokesman for the Georgian nobility, Dmitri Kipiani. Political and intellectual discussions in the press, such as they were in the twilight of the Great Reforms, were colored much more by references to the penetration of industry and capitalism, by concern over the future of the noble estate, and the all-national liberal and revolutionary opposition to autocracy than by ethnic hostilities.

Within Tiflis itself three major political tendencies began to take shape in the late 1870s and 1880s—a cosmopolitan liberalism closely associated with Armenians but also favored by leading Georgian intellectuals and journalists; a multinational revolutionary populism influenced by Russian *narodnichestvo*; and a new and virulent nationalism, among representatives of both the Georgian gentry and the Armenian intelligentsia. The Georgian variant of nationalism tended to be conservative and nostalgic, while the Armenian form was revolutionary and messianic. Among the Armenian bourgeoisie the traditional conservatism of a religiously centered community was challenged by a vigorous liberalism expressed in the pages of Grigor Artsruni's newspaper *Mshak* (Cultivator), founded in Tiflis in 1872. While accepting Russian authority as the "lesser evil," Artsruni and his supporters hoped to convince the tsarist government to alleviate the oppressive situation of the Armenians in Turkey. Within the city council liberal reformers, led by A. S. Matinov, P. A. Izmailov, and A. A. Tamamshev, introduced a program of municipal improvement. These young professionals turned to an Armenian businessman, I. E. Pitoev, in order to gain access to the merchants who dominated the assembly. Pitoev organized a "party" which met periodically in his apartment to discuss plans for Tiflis. His influence was paramount, and, as one contemporary put it, the statement "Isai wants it" had a "magic effect" on the others in the group.[45] Such private meetings of duma deputies were unheard of in the Russia of Alexander II, and according to the memoirist Tumanov, "thanks to the circle of Is. Eg. Pitoev, private conferences of deputies received the right of citizenship here twenty years earlier than in other cities of Russia."[46]

At the end of 1878, the Pitoev-Izmailov party won the elections to the city council, and when the deputies met to choose their mayor, bitter differences divided the new members from older members. While the new deputies voted for the Armenian Bebutov, older deputies split their votes between the incumbent mayor, the Georgian noble Dmitri Kipiani, and the Armenian M. E. Alikhanov. After much maneuvering an Armenian businessman, A. Korganov, was chosen, but he declined to serve and A. S. Matinov (1843–1909) was elected as a compromise choice.[47] The victory of the Pitoev-Izmailov party brought ethnic considerations into council politics for the first time, though they were still muted. Though Matinov served as mayor of Tiflis until 1890, the most influential of the council members was P. A. Izmailov, the vigorous spokesman for a new water system, bridges, a city hall, and other renovations for the city. This party was responsible for turning Tiflis, or at least part of it, into a modern European city, but its critics condemned the reformers for "the one-sided bourgeois direction of this party." Like the council which it led, the reform party was largely representative of the rich Armenian community.

Among the Georgians, the liberal tendency was advocated by the former radical Niko Nikoladze (1834–1928), a member of the first Russian-educated generation of the Georgian intelligentsia. At first Nikoladze was associated with Prince Bebutov's newspaper, *Tiflisskii vestnik* (Tiflis Bulletin) (1873–1882), the first privately owned Russian language newspaper in the Caucasus; but in 1878, he founded his own paper, *Obzor* (Survey) (1878–1880), which soon came into a fatal conflict with the censor. Convinced that "progress . . . depends solely on the steady growth of the power and consciousness of the people," Nikoladze urged young activists to turn away from the revolutionary movement and to enter zemstvos, municipal governments, and business, where they could most effectively influence the people.[48] Close to Nikoladze and the orthodox liberals was the so-called second generation (*meore dasi*) of the Georgian intelligentsia, men like Giorgi Tsereteli and Sergei Meskhi, who collaborated on the newspaper *droeba* (Times) (1866–1885). The antinationalist flavor of Caucasian liberalism was most clearly felt in the Russian daily, *Novoe obozrenie* (New Review) (1884–1905), founded by the wealthy A. V. Stepanov (1844–1887) and edited by the Tumanov brothers. Yet for many Georgians the Tumanovs and Tseretelis were suspect because of their closeness to the enterprising Armenians.

The second political tendency in the 1870s and 1880s, revolutionary populism, emerged in the last decade of the reign of Alexander II as the reforming impulses of the emperor were quenched and the questions raised in the reform period about the future role of Russia in the modern world were left unanswered. Small groups of Georgians and Armenians who had studied at Russian universities confronted the strategic question of working together with the oppositional movements among Russians or developing an exclusively national movement.[49] The revolutionary populism of the 1870s marked the high point of cooperation and joint activity by young Georgians, Armenians, and Russians, but populist efforts suffered from the arrests of 1876–1877 and the mass trials of the late 1870s. Yet the activists who remained in Georgia were able to rally in the early 1880s and establish a journal in Tiflis, *imedi* (Hope) (1881–1883), and a newspaper in Kutaisi, *shroma* (Labor) (1881–1883). The populist press strongly attacked the nationalist views of the Georgian gentry for their neglect of the peasant question and their exclusive chauvinism. For the gentry the agrarian problem was a technical matter requiring the import of new technology; for the populists there was no solution without the confiscation of the land from the nobility. When the populist papers were closed by the government, the editors of *droeba* opened their pages to the populists, but the repression of revolutionary and reform movements under the new emperor, Alexander III (1881–1894), and the end of the relative tolerance of nationalist expression had the effect in Transcaucasia of discouraging local activists from participating in broad political movements aimed directly at the autocracy and encouraged a turn toward ethnic politics and local solutions. In 1882 the Armenian populists left the Tiflis committee of *Narodnaya volia* (The People's Will) in which they had worked with Georgian populists and formed an exclusively Armenian revolutionary circle concerned with the plight of Turkish Armenians.

The growth and success of nationalist movements in Eastern Europe, particularly in the Balkans, in the late nineteenth century had a galvanizing effect on the peoples of the Russian Empire. The Russian victory over the Turks in 1877–1878 briefly raised hopes that the Armenian peasants of Anatolia would be brought under Russian protection, but the Treaty of Berlin imposed on Russia prevented any meaningful reforms from being enacted. The so-called Armenian Question agitated diplomats and intellectuals and placed the Armenians in the Caucasus before a stark political choice: should they work toward improving the situation in Turkey through revolutionary means or should they engage in reformist activity within Russia and place their hopes on Great Power diplomacy? In Tiflis Artsruni and the liberals tended to favor the more moderate proposal, but young radicals, many of them former populists, began in the 1880s to organize secret circles for the liberation of Turkish Armenia. While moderates established national welfare societies—like the Society for Publishing Books in Armenian (1880) and the Society for Armenian Welfare (1881)—young people were reading the novels of the romantic nationalist Raffi which presented images of revolutionary heroes ready to sacrifice themselves for the Armenian cause.

The tsarist government stimulated the turn to nationalism when in 1885 it summarily ordered the elimination of education in the Armenian language above the first two grades. The young radicals organized a campaign against the new law and founded illegal schools for Armenian instruction. Within a year the schools were reopened, though with stricter surveillance by government appointees and the notable absence of teachers considered unreliable by the state. The attack on the language was a major factor which led to the foundation of the first Armenian revolutionary parties, *Hnchak* (Bell), founded in Geneva in 1886 by Caucasian Armenians, and the Armenian Revolutionary Federation (*Dashnaktsutiun*), established in Tiflis in 1890.

The same combination of tsarist repression and growing interest in specifically national concerns affected the Georgians in the 1880s. The Society for the Spread of Literacy among Georgians, founded in Tiflis in 1879, was responsible for sponsoring the publication of textbooks and grammars. In 1885 the first chorus for Georgian folk songs was founded, and the following year its first concert was given under the direction of the Czech musician Joseph Ratili. Ethnographers, both Russian and Georgian, turned their attention to the riches of Georgian life and traditions. Georgians themselves began to sense the value inherent in things long taken for granted. The neoromanticism in the poems and stories of Kazbeki and Vazha-Pshavela was founded on an appreciation of the oldest still-preserved forms of Georgian life, those of the peoples of the mountains, the exalted free spirits uncompromised by the exactions of urban life, bureaucratic or foreign rule. Even as this Georgian consciousness was growing, particularly in the urban population, the Russian state attempted to implement a program of Russification. In 1882 the word *Gruziia* (Russian for Georgia) was prescribed in published works. The local representative of the Ministry of Education, Ianovskii, tried to eliminate Georgian from the schools. As with the Armenians, so with the Georgians, resistance to the threat of Russification took on extra-legal, revolutionary dimensions.

In May 1886, an eighteen-year-old former student of the Tiflis Seminary named Laghiashvili stabbed the hated Russian rector of the seminary. Almost immediately the assassin became a hero to many of his fellow students, sixty of whom were expelled. Pavel, Exarch of Georgia and an official representative of the tsarist government, anathematized Georgia for the murder. The Georgian patriot Dmitri Kipiani, a former mayor of Tiflis, wrote angrily to the Exarch and demanded that he leave Georgia. Retired from government service, Kipiani had become a vocal advocate of Georgian national rights before the tsarist authorities, and in the early 1880s he had written a strong letter to Ianovskii protesting the elimination of Georgian in the schools. For this action he had been censured by the emperor but applauded by his fellow gentrymen, who elected him Marshall of the Kutaisi Nobility. For his letter to Exarch Pavel, Kipiani was exiled to Stavropol, and there, mysteriously, he was murdered the following year. His funeral in Tiflis became a massive demonstration against the tsarist regime which was suspected of being the instigator of Kipiani's murder.

Less radical but more influential among Georgians than either liberalism, populism, or the confrontational nationalism of the seminary students were the views of the noble writer Ilia Chavchavadze (1837–1907), who in 1877 founded his own Georgian-language newspaper, *iveria* (1877–1906), to rival *droeba*. As the voice of a conservative nationalism opposed to the cosmopolitan liberalism of his former friends, Chavchavadze editorialized against the rise of capitalism and a proletariat in Georgia. Instead he called for the preservation of a natural economy, the paternalistic ties between nobles and peasants, and the organic unity of the whole Georgian people in an essentially agrarian society. For Chavchavadze there was no need for class warfare in Georgia, for historically harmony had reigned between the *aznaureba* (nobility) and its peasantry. Like many of his fellow gentrymen Chavchavadze was deeply concerned about the erosion of the noble estate's economic and social position and sought to prevent its further decline. Accepting the proposal of the liberal Nikoladze, Chavchavdze agreed to serve as the president of the Georgian Nobles' Bank and use the money which nobles had received after emancipation for the improvement of their agriculture. Through the bank which he headed for forty years, Chavchavadze encouraged not only the development of the gentry economy but also the establishment of schools and cultural institutions which aided the revival of Georgian national consciousness. Prince Chavchavadze was known at the time as the Georgian Gambetta and the public meetings of the bank's shareholders were referred to as the *gruzinskii parlament* (the Georgian parliament).[50]

The growing concern with the future of Georgians and Armenians in a Russifying, modernizing autocratic Empire found its way into the politics of the Tiflis city council. In the elections of 1883 and 1887 there had been no intense battles along ethnic or party lines, but in November 1890 an opposition formed to the ruling party. The opposition was most influential among the electors of the first curia, i.e., the richest men in the city. The ruling party was most completely supported in the third curia, and the second curia was divided between the two parties. Before the election a group led by K. M. Alikhanov and M. I. Tamashev organized a meeting in the so-called furnished palace rooms to draw up a list of deputies for the council. This oppositional list was given the name "palace rooms" by the public and greatly displeased the members of the city board, which drew up its own list. The chief complaint seemed to be that the opposition had included too many newcomers to city politics, particularly Georgians and Karabagh Armenians, on their list. When the elections were held for the first curia on November 4, many of the people on the opposition's list were elected. The city board then joined with its former enemies, the supporters of the Armenian newspaper *Ardzagank* (Echo), the Georgian A. A. Ioannisiani, and Prince Bebutov, in the elections of the second curia, and together they elected the candidates on the list of the board. When the third curia met, the lines had already been drawn on ethnic lines, and non-Armenians, angry at being excluded in the elections to the second curia, voted against the candidates of the city board. At the conclusion of the elections, little had actually changed in the composition of the council. Only eight new people had been elected in the first curia and five in the second. Ideologically the opposition had never differed greatly from the ruling party. But the significance of the complicated election procedures was that resentments and ethnic slights had led to a much tenser atmosphere within the city's *pays légal*. The reelected mayor, A. S. Matinov, was forced by the opposition to step down, and Prince N. V. Argutinskii-Dolgorukov of an old Armenian noble family was chosen in his stead. Still the council remained in the hands of the Armenian bourgeoisie which held an absolute majority; of the seventy-two council deputies, forty were Armenian and only twenty Georgian.[51]

The ethnic conflicts in the council heightened in the next few years. In 1892 the municipal counterreform of Alexander III raised the property qualification for council electors and eliminated the division of the electorate into curiae. This maneuver simply strengthened the hold of the wealthiest men in the cities over the council, and in Tiflis this meant the even more complete hold of the Armenians over the council. When the city board put forth its list of seventy-seven candidates in 1893, only ten were Russian, seven Georgian, and two German; the rest were Armenian.[52] An opposition formed, and the liberal newspaper *Novoe obozrenie* supported its claims to representation, though it was critical of its use of national motifs and its disorganization. The opposition was easily beaten, and the party of Matinov and Izmailov remained dominant in the council. When Argutinskii-Dolgorukov retired as mayor in September, Izmailov himself was chosen by a vote of 62 to 8 to become the first mayor from the ranks of professional people, the "third element."[53]

Both in 1893 and 1897 almost all the Georgians elected to the Tiflis city council refused to take their seats in protest against the small representation of their community.[54] Liberals like Nikoladze proposed a system of proportional representation by ethnicity, but others like Tumanov opposed the idea of election by nationality, believing that such a system would only increase national tensions.[55] From 1893 to 1897 the city council attempted to put aside ethnic considerations in its daily practice, and concentrated on sanitation and health concerns. Municipal infirmaries were set up with doctors employed by the council. Veterinary supervision of the city slaughterhouse was improved in response to the cholera epidemic of 1892–1893. "Merchants of the old school" resisted the programs of the municipal reformers, but the young bureaucrats and professional men pushed forward. Ethnic conflict reemerged in the elections of 1897 when a Russo-Georgian slate, led by the chauvinist writer Velichko, challenged the dominant *upravtsy* (board members). By campaigning against all Armenians rather than directing its attack toward the ruling party, the opposition produced a backlash among the electors and assured its own defeat. Young, wealthy Armenians were joined by the Avlabar merchants and others who had not favored the ruling reform party and swept them back into office.[56]

By the turn of the century, the complaints by Georgian noblemen and the writings of anti-Armenian nationalists fed a growing perception by the authorities that Armenians were a subversive, revolutionary threat to Russian hegemony over Caucasia. The tsarist government began restricting Armenian cultural and political life, closing charitable organizations and schools. In May 1899 the government issued a law, applicable only to Caucasian cities, which gave the governor-general the power to remove deputies from the city council and officials from the municipal administration. With the Armenophobe Prince Golitsyn heading the Caucasian government, it was not long before the Armenian political and religious hierarchy was attacked. In 1902 the entire city council of Tiflis was arraigned for corruption and taken to court.[57] The case was dismissed, however, for lack of evidence. The next year the government seized the properties of the Armenian church, thus triggering a revolutionary campaign by the nationalistic Dashnaktsutiun directed at Russian officials. In 1904 Golitsyn himself was wounded by an Armenian assassin and soon left the Caucasus. Ethnic friction, so long dormant or contained within the confines of the city council, now exploded into the streets, just as the social conflicts between workers and bosses, intellectuals and the state, coalesced into a broad revolutionary assault on the autocracy.

CLASS AND ETHNIC CONFLICTS, 1905

Both the socioeconomic structure of Tiflis and the partiality of tsarist legislation toward the men of great property prevented Georgians from participating in the government of the city which they had conceived of as their national capital since the early Middle Ages. The revival of Georgian culture and national consciousness among the gentry and intelligentsia notwithstanding, the real economic and political weight of Georgians in their own country was steadily undermined by

Russian officialdom and the Armenian bourgeoisie. Particularly grating was the practice of wealthy Armenians of buying up the property of impoverished Georgian nobles. When the Baratovs lost their estate to the merchant Aramiants, the viceroy himself intervened to request that it be returned, but the Georgian princes were unable to come up with the necessary six hundred thousand rubles. Again, the millionaire Aleksandr Mantashev bought the exquisite home of Prince Mukhranskii in the heart of Tiflis and then rejected an offer by the Georgian Nobles' Bank to buy it back from him.[58] The Georgian elite was being undermined by the economic and social trends of the last decades of the nineteenth century and appeared powerless to reverse the process. Neither tsarist reforms, liberal politics, nor the economic support of banks and government provided avenues for the advancement of the declining nobility. The Georgian patriotic intelligentsia also found paths to its own further development blocked by the political restrictions imposed by tsarism. And Georgian peasant-workers, forced from their villages into the slums of the towns, also found limited possibilities for secure material development and a better life.

By the early 1890s Georgian society was being transformed by the new demands of a market economy and early industrialization, but none of the ideological alternatives of the 1880s—liberalism, populism, or gentry nationalism—seemed to provide the mass of Georgians with a way out of their political predicament. Georgian nationalism in its gentry variant was too narrowly concerned with the problems and aspirations of the traditional landed elite to appeal effectively to the Georgian masses. Populism, perhaps because of the absence of communal forms of ownership among Georgian peasants, had limited appeal in the villages and remained a movement attractive only to radical young intellectuals. Liberalism too had a narrow social base, primarily in the Armenian bourgeoisie and intelligentsia. As an arena of political activity, the Tiflis city council was too heavily dominated by Armenian men of property to appeal to the Georgian lower classes, and the entry of workers into politics took another direction, a more violent form of revolutionary opposition. For leadership workers turned to the embryonic socialist intelligentsia made up of déclassé Georgian noblemen and their friends.

Early in the 1890s a small group of Russian-educated intellectuals returned to Georgia from the north, bringing with them an alternative vision of Georgia's future. Noe Zhordania, Philipe Makharadze, and others had become acquainted with Russian Marxism while studying in Warsaw, and in late 1892 Zhordania organized the first conference of Georgian Marxists, soon known as the *mesame dasi* (third generation), developed an intellectual critique of the capitalist society then emerging in Georgia, and proposed a program of activity to overthrow the autocratic monarchy and permit the free development of a democratic society leading eventually to socialism. By 1895 the Marxists had taken over the illustrated journal *kvali* (Trace) and soon became the most powerful intellectual movement among Georgians. As worker organization and strike activity accelerated in the last half of the decade, the Marxists linked their ideological struggle with practical work in factories and workshops. By the early twentieth century Marxism provided an analysis and political strategy for workers in Tiflis, Batumi, Kutaisi, and elsewhere, as well as for the rebellious peasants of western Georgia. By 1905 the Marxists, now adherents of the Menshevik form of Social Democracy, were the de facto leaders of a massive national liberation movement, the dimensions of which had not been seen anywhere else in the Russian Empire.

The phenomenal success of Marxism and the failure of other political ideologies in the 1890s were closely connected to the particular way in which capitalism and political reform developed in Georgia. Georgians who tried to better their lives by moving to Tiflis remained at the bottom of the economic ladder and nearly totally outside the political arena. The traditional Georgian leaders, the gentry, failed to exercise leadership in the city by the last quarter of the century, and their form of nostalgic nationalism, which targeted Armenians as the victimizers of the Georgians, had only limited resonance among workers. The new class of Georgian workers, strategically located in the heart of economic and political power, brought together in workshops and factories by the process of industrialization, was in a position to make its weight felt much more potently than peasants scattered in isolated villages. Yet given the property qualifications for the city council and the absence of other forms of political representation, workers were excluded from the *pays légal*. The Marxists, on the other hand, provided an ideology which placed workers at the center of the historical moment, an ideology which recognized the advent of capitalism and rejected nostalgia about the agrarian past, but one which, unlike liberalism, did not stop with a celebration of market society or a rationalization of the power of propertied men, but rather proposed that the contradictory nature of bourgeois society contained the potential for its eventual overthrow. In Marxism Georgians had a nonnationalist doctrine which at one and the same time was a weapon against their ethnic enemies, against Russian autocracy and the Armenian bourgeoisie.

The multinational working class of Tiflis had not been particularly active in the 1890s, except for a few "advanced workers" who studied with Social Democrats in clandestine circles. As the new century opened, workers launched a series of strikes and participated in demonstrations. Whereas in the three decades between 1870 and 1900 only nineteen strikes were recorded in Tiflis, in the year 1900 alone there were seventeen strikes at fifteen enterprises. The most impressive action was taken by railroad workers in August 1900, and in the following year economic strikes were accompanied by a more overtly political attack on autocracy. Three thousand people marched through the streets of Tiflis to mark May Day, 1901, and they unfurled red banners, defying and clashing with the police. Transcaucasia soon earned a nationwide reputation as an area of vigorous resistance to tsarist authority. Armenian terrorists carried out a number of political assassinations, while workers in Tiflis, Batumi, and Baku escalated their strike movement. Peasants in western Georgia, inspired and led by Social Democrats, refused to pay taxes and boycotted Russian officials. By early 1905 the grievances of workers were taken up by the Tiflis city council and reformist members of the Caucasian administration. The council voted unanimously in early February to petition the government to grant workers the right of assembly, free expression of their demands, and freedom for unions.[59]

The tsarist government had lost its grip over much of the population of Caucasia by 1905, and Tiflis was so completely dominated by the opposition that the newly appointed viceroy, County Vorontsov-Dashkov, felt obliged to turn to the Social Democrats to keep order in the town. When rumors of a possible Armeno-Azerbaijani clash, such as had just occurred in Baku, reached the palace, the viceroy agreed to arm six hundred workers to patrol the streets. Other political concessions were made by the conciliatory viceroy to breach the gap between the state and the bulk of society. Promises of a new judiciary system, of zemstvos for Caucasia, and the restoration of Armenian church properties were made. But with the Social Democrats heading the lower class opposition and calling for a truly representative assembly for the nation, and the propertied men of the city council negotiating for civil rights and an end to military intervention in social life, the government found itself almost completely isolated and without support from any significant group in society. Its ultimate option continued to be the army, and when workers and city employees were joined by many shopkeepers in a general strike on June 20, martial law was declared and all public meetings prohibited.

The first half of 1905 was marked by unity among the various social groups and nationalities in Tiflis, as workers and city council deputies, Georgian intellectuals and Armenian businessmen, all acted in concert to force political reforms from the tsarist bureaucracy. But the gap between state and society was matched in the second half of the revolutionary year by fragmentation of the opposition. As the socialist-led lower classes of the town openly challenged the more moderate politicians in the city council, the middle class began to pull back from its confrontational posture of a few months earlier. The mayor of Tiflis, the Armenian liberal Khristofor Vermishev, hoped to avoid a clash with the government by prohibiting the public from attending the session of the city council scheduled to discuss the zemstvo question. But on

August 25, two thousand people crowded into the crescent-shaped council chamber in the city hall. The deputies left the hall, and the crowd, led by Social Democrats, held their own meeting. Similar gatherings were held on the 26th and 27th in defiance of the government, but when the crowd broke into city hall on the 29th, Cossacks stormed the building, indiscriminately firing into those assembled. Though reports differ, at least sixty people were killed and possibly two hundred wounded. Tiflis now had its own "Bloody Sunday," and a general outrage followed. Sixty-two members of the council resigned; Mayor Vermishev was dismissed; and a one-day general strike protesting the bloodshed shut down the city.[60]

The social divisions between the propertied middle class and the lower classes, intensified in Tiflis by ethnic divisions, continued to grow in the last months of 1905. The October Manifesto of Nicholas II granted a representative assembly and certain fundamental rights to his subjects, but different social groups received it differently. Crowds surged into the streets overjoyed at the victory of society over the government, and the city council immediately adopted the program of the liberal Constitutional Democratic Party (Kadets). But both wings of Social Democracy, Menshevik and Bolshevik, called for continuation of the struggle for full democracy. On the right a new and open enthusiasm for the tsar was manifested in several patriotic demonstrations. Twenty thousand people, among them many Russian railroad workers, marched in Tiflis singing "God Save the Tsar." The parade was guarded by soldiers, but as it moved through the city, bombs were thrown and shots rang out. The soldiers fired into buildings from which they thought the first shots had come. Forty-one people were killed, sixty-six wounded. Sadly for the revolutionary opposition, the events of August and October revealed that the all-nation, united struggle against autocracy which had been so evident in the first half of 1905 had not survived the summer. In the coming months the broad oppositional front was steadily shredded, as more moderate social groups and parties accommodated themselves to the tsar's new "constitutional" order.

Five years into the twentieth century Tiflis was a city in turmoil, riven by the rivalries and conflicting interests of Armenians and Georgians, the Russian state and Caucasian society, workers and the propertied middle class. The restoration of order by the tsarist administration, accomplished only at the cost of lives and recently won liberties, lasted precariously for more than a decade. But the problems of the city's various communities had not been solved, only postponed. The majority of Tiflis's population remained outside the legal political arena. The Armenian bourgeoisie, its city council, and an able mayor, Aleksandr Khatisov, continued to govern the town, but in uneasy relationship with bureaucratic absolutism on the one hand and the largely disenfranchised Georgians on the other. On the eve of the First World War, two British travelers noted that Tiflis, now within six days' journey of London, is "as much the capital of the Armenians as of any other race, for it has been the Armenians who have built up this modern city, and who at present have the larger share in its control and administration."[61]

Even as ethnic divisions and inequities continued, the broad-based opposition to the tsarist regime remained visible in the city—in the Social Democratic newspapers, the elections to local and state dumas, and in periodic strikes and demonstrations. Here on the common ground of political hostility to the monarchy Armenians and Georgians often found themselves on the same side. When the former deputy to the Second State Duma, Severian Jugeli, died in Metekhi prison in 1909, the Armenian mayor, Khatisov, and the Georgian deputy to the State Duma, Gegechkori, jointly organized a funeral-demonstration. Workers carried red flags through the streets of Tiflis until mounted Cossacks demanded their removal. The mayor and the deputy were briefly detained by the police, but workers surrounded both police and the arrested until the viceroy wisely decided to have them released.[62] This incident, like their successes in the elections to the State Dumas, revealed to all the latent power of the Georgian Social Democrats and their labor constituents. Georgians had a new and battle-hardened political leadership in the Mensheviks, several of whom—Zhordania, Irakli Tsereteli, Nikolai Chkheidze, and Evgenii Gegechkori—became nationally known politicians as leaders of the Social Democratic factions in the successive state dumas. At the same time, the Marxists consolidated and expanded their support among the Georgian intelligentsia, the workers, and the peasantry. When in February 1917 the old structures of tsarism collapsed, they took with them the props which had kept the Armenian bourgeoisie in power. The Marxists' argument that only political revolution could end the dual dominance of Russian autocracy and the Armenian bourgeoisie was confirmed as the Georgian Social Democrats took control of the new institutions of city government, the soviets, and began the arduous process of democratizing the antiquated administration.

NOTES

1. Sh. K. Chkhetiia, *Tbilisi v XIX stoletii (1865–1869)* (Tbilisi, 1942), p. 145.

2. S. A. Meskhia, *Goroda i gorodskoi stroi feodal' noi Gruzii xii–xiii vv.* (Tbilisi, 1959), pp. 28–29.

3. For a general history of Tiflis up to the nineteenth century, see N. I. Badriashvili, *Tiflis, I: Ot osnovaniia goroda do xix v.* (Tiflis, 1934).

4. Eli Smith, *Researches of the Rev. E. Smith and Rev. H.G.O. Wright in Armenia: Including a journey through Asia Minor, and into Georgia and Persia, with a visit to the Nestorian and Chaldean Christians of Oormiah and Salmas* (Boston, 1833), I, pp. 206–207.

5. Iu. Kacharava, A. Kikvidze, P. Ratiani, and A. Surguladze, *Istoria Gruzii*, II (Tbilisi, 1973), p. 42.

6. Filip Makharadze, *Gruziia v deviatnadtsatom stoletii. Kratkii istoricheskii ocherk* (Tiflis, 1933), p. 69. The statistical material is from *Pervaia vseobshchaia perepis' naseleniia Rossiiskoi imperii, 1897 g., LXIX, Tiflisskaia guberniia* (St. Petersburg, 1905), pp. vi–xiv.

7. A one-day census of Tiflis was held on March 25, 1876; of the 104,024 inhabitants 37,610 (36.1 percent) were Armenian; 30,813 (29.6 percent) were Russian; 22,156 (21.3 percent) were Georgian; 13,445 (12.9 percent) were Germans, Persians, Tatars, Greeks, Jews, etc. *Putevoditel' po Tiflisu* (Tiflis, 1896), p. 39.

8. Makharadze, *Gruziia*, p. 69. The first decade of the new century continued to be a period of growth for the city. In 1904, 196,935 people were recorded as living in Tiflis; by 1910 that figure had risen to 303,150, i.e., by 54 percent in six years. *Goroda Rossii v 1904 godu* (St. Petersburg, 1906), p. 0226; *Goroda Rossii v 1910 godu* (St. Petersburg, 1914), p. 890. But the ethnic balance began to shift in favor of the Armenians. By 1910 the percentage of Russians in the city (21.5 percent) had declined from the 1904 level (28.8 percent), while the Armenians had increased from 29.5 percent in 1904 to 41.2 percent in 1910. *Goroda Rossii v 1904 godu*, p. 0236; *Goroda Rossii v 1910 godu*, pp. 914–915. Though figures for Georgians are not given in the sources with any precision, it can be estimated that they were about 25 percent in 1904 and slightly less in 1910. This rise in the weight of the Armenians is not easy to explain. In part it can be explained by migration of Armenians from Turkey in the turbulent period from the mid–1850s through 1909; in part it resulted from difficult years of revolution and economic depression which hit the Georgian working class hardest and stimulated many of them to migrate back to their villages. But these are guesses to be examined later when other evidence comes to light.

9. For more on the Tiflis Armenians in the first half of the nineteenth century, see my paper: "Russian Rule and Caucasian Society, 1801–1856: The Georgian Nobility and the Armenian Bourgeoisie," *Nationalities Papers*, VII, 1 (1979):53–78.

10. Though one must be wary of the biases of foreign travelers and the tendency to stereotype Caucasian nationalities, the observations of Reverend Eli Smith made in 1830 provide information on the degree of control of the Armenians over commerce in Tiflis in the early nineteenth century:

> With the exception of one Georgian, two or three Greeks, and a Swiss firm that commenced business while we were there, every merchant in Tiflis is Armenian, and nearly the same is true of the mechanics. In this fact is exhibited the natural disposition of the nation. ... For if there is one trait more prominent than any other, and common to the whole nation from Constantinople to Tebriz, it is love of money.... When the bad passions of an Armenian are fully awake, no deed is too base or too dark for him to do. The merchants of Tiflis are said to be very clannish in their trade; ready, by every means, to injure a foreigner who may attempt to establish himself among them. An instance was mentioned to us of a European's being ruined and forced to leave the place, by their combining to undersell him in the articles with which he commenced business. (Smith, *Researches*, I, pp. 212–14)

11. Chkhetiia, *Tbilisi*, pp. 208–209.

12. Ibid., p. 209.

13. Ibid., p. 214.

14. E. V. Khoshtaria, *Ocherki sotsial'no-ekonomicheskoi istorii Gruzii. Promyshlennost', goroda, rabochii klass* (XIX v.–nachalo XX v.) (Tbilisi, 1974), p. 100. Those with 2–4 workers made up 21 percent, and those with 5–8 workers made up 0.3 percent.

15. The Central Statistical Committee of the Ministry of Internal Affairs gave the following figures on factories and artisanal workshops:

Year	Factories	Workers (N)	Workshops	Artisans (N)
1904	206	4,431	932	2,010
1910	99	3,874	1,002	1,165

SOURCE: *Goroda Rossii v 1904 godu*, p. 0278; *Goroda Rossii v 1910 godu*, p. 977.

16. Khoshtaria, *Ocherki*, p. 80.

17. Ibid., pp. 46–47.

18. P. V. Gugushvili, *Karl Marks v gruzinskoi publitsistike i obshchestvennosti do 1898 goda* (Tbilisi, 1963), p. 38.

19. For a treatment of artisans in central Russia at the turn of the century, see Victoria E. Bonnell, "The Roots of Rebellion in Urban Working Class Life: A Study of Artisanal Trades in St. Petersburg and Moscow on the Eve of 1905," paper read at the American Association for the Advancement of Slavic Studies annual meeting, New Haven, Conn., October 1979.

20. S. T. Arkomed [Gevork Gharajian], *Rabochee dvizhenie i sotsialdemokratiia na Kavkaze (s 80-kh godov po 1903 g.)* (Moscow-Petrograd, 1923), pp. 35–36.

21. Gugushvili, *Karl Marks*, p. 39.

22. M. A. Adonts, *Ekonomicheskoe razvitie Vostochnoi Armenii v XIX veke* (Erevan, 1957), p. 524.

23. Khoshtaria, *Ocherki*, p. 165.

24. Ibid., pp. 165–66.

25. The principal area to which foreign capital was attracted was the extractive industries—copper, manganese, and oil in Baku, refineries in Batumi. The single area where native Georgian nobles were able to penetrate the world of capitalist production was in the manganese industry, where they outnumbered all other ethnic groups (Khoshtaria, p. 166).

26. See Ronald Grigor Suny, "'The Peasants Have Always Fed Us': The Georgian Nobility and the Peasant Emancipation, 1856–1871," *Russian Review*, 38, 1 (January 1979):27–51.

27. *Kolokol*, September 15, 1865.

28. I. G. Antelava, E. A. Ordzhonikidze, and E. V. Khoshtaria, *K voprosu o genezise i razvitii kapitalizma v sel'skom khoziaistve i promyshlennosti Gruzii* (Tbilisi, 1967), pp. 77–78.

29. Chkhetiia, *Tbilisi*, p. 243.

30. S. Gulishambarov, *Obzor fabrik i zavodov Tiflisskoi gubernii* (Tiflis, 1887), p. 232.

31. Khoshtariia, *Ocherki*, pp. 188–89, 195.

32. Ibid., pp. 195–96.

33. S. Maksimov, *Russkie gory i kavkazskie gortsy* (n.p., 1873), p. 56.

34. P. I. Kovalevskii, *Kavkaz: I* (St. Petersburg, 1914), p. 234.

35. Oliver Wardrop, *The Kingdom of Georgia; notes of travel in a land of women, wine, and song; to which are appended historical, literary and political sketches, specimens of the national music, and a compendious bibliography* (London, 1888), pp. 13–14.

36. *Polnoe sobranie zakonov*, XV, no. 13:369; Chkhetiia, *Tbilisi*, pp. 259, 313–17.

37. G. V. Khachapuridze, *K istorii Gruzii pervoi poloviny XIX veka* (Tbilisi, 1950), p. 464.

38. P. A. Zaionchkovskii, *Otmena krepostnogo prava v Rossii*, 3rd ed. (Moscow, 1968), p. 333.

39. Semen Esadze, *Istoricheskaia zapiska ob upravlenii Kavkazom*, II (Tiflis, 1907), pp. 42–43.

40. *Kolokol*, no. 204, September 15, 1865.

41. Chkhetiia, *Tbilisi*, p. 327.

42. Kacharava et al., *Istoriia Gruzii*, II, p. 28.

43. Chkhetiia, *Tbilisi*, p. 277. After 1867, craft *amkaris* were united under an *uprava* (board) made up of the *ustabashis* and a chief *starshina* (elder). But the board could not call a general meeting of the *amkaris* without police permission, and individual *amkaris* lost their judicial powers, their authority over initiation of apprentices, and the ability to rid themselves of an undesired leader. All these prerogatives were given to the *uprava*. Whereas earlier an *amkari* had been able to install its own *ustabashi*, now the elected leader had to be approved by the governor (ibid., pp. 278–79).

44. Walter Hanchett, "Tsarist Statutory Regulation of Municipal Government in the Nineteenth Century," in Michael F. Hamm, ed., *The City in Russian History* (Lexington, Ky., 1976), pp. 102–107; Esadze, *Istoricheskaia zapiska* II, pp. 72–73. Baku did not receive municipal self-government until 1878. A. Sh. Mil'man, *Politicheskii stroi Azerbaidzhana v XIX–nachale XX vekov* (Baku, 1966), p. 208. Kutaisi and Batumi did not receive it until 1888, Sukhumi and Poti until 1892, and Gori, Dusheti, Akhaltsikhe, Akhalkalaki, Sighnaghi, and Telavi until 1894. Kacharave, et al., *Istoria Gruzii*, II, p. 29.

45. Prince Giorgi Mikailovich Tumanov, *Kharakteristiki i vospominaniia, zametki kavkazskago khronikera*, II (Tiflis, 1905), p. 110.

46. Ibid.

47. Ibid., pp. 91–92.; Kacharava, et al., *Istoriia Gruzii*, II, p. 29.

48. Niko Nikoladze, "Osvobozhdeniia N. G. Chernyshevskago," *Byloe* 1906, no. 9:243.

49. See Ronald Grigor Suny, "Populism, Nationalism, and Marxism: The Origins of Revolutionary Parties among the Armenians of the Caucasus," *The Armenian Review*, 32, 2–126 (1979): 134–51.

50. Wardrop, *Kingdom of Georgia*, p. 13.

51. For accounts of these elections, see *Novoe obozrenie*, November 5, 1890; November 17, 1890, February 2, 1893; February 28, 1893; March 12, 1893.

52. *Novoe obozrenie*, May 6, 1893.

53. Izmailov was politically a liberal but able to work with the bureaucracy. He was interested in developing the *samodeiatel' nost'* of urban society, its "self-activity." He was responsible in his years as a man of power and influence in Tiflis for building the theater, trolley lines, schools, hospitals, and introducing insurance programs (Tumanov, *Kharakteristiki*, I, pp. 94–95).

54. D. M. Tumanov, *Zametki o gorodskom samoupravlennii na Kavkaze* (Tiflis, 1902), p. 4.

55. Ibid., pp. 22–23.

56. Ibid., pp. 45–47.

57. Alexander Khatissian, "The Memoirs of a Mayor," *The Armenian Review*, 2 3(7) (1949):43.

58. Ibid.

59. *Revoliutsiia 1905 goda v Zakavkaz'i [Khronika sobytii, dokumenty i materialy]. Po materialam Muzeia Revoliutsii Gruzii* (Tiflis, 1926), p. 16.

60. Ibid., pp. 65, 158.
61. Noel and Harold Buxton, *Travel and Politics in Armenia* (London, 1914), p. 58.
62. Razhden Arsenidze, "Zametki. (N. Korganov, Ia byl drugom Stalina')," typescript in B. I. Nicolaevsky Collection, Hoover Institution, uncatalogued.

BIBLIOGRAPHICAL NOTE

Optimally one would begin a study of Tiflis (Tbilisi) in the prerevolutionary period with a visit to the museum of the city on Sololaki Mountain, next to the huge metal statue of *deda-kalaki* (mother of the city). Besides viewing the exhibits, one can search through files of documents and photographs, maps, and city plans. The libraries of Tbilisi hold complete runs of the major newspapers of the period, the most important of which is *Novoe obozrenie*, the liberal daily. The nationalist *iveria* and the Marxist *kvali*, much more influential in Georgian intellectual life, had relatively little news on municipal affairs. Memoirs and travelers' reports offer eye-witness accounts of the physical and political environment of the city: among the more interesting are A. E. Rozen, *Zapiski dekabrista* (St. Petersburg, 1907); Baron August von Haxthausen, *Transcaucasia. Sketches of the Nations and Races Between the Black Sea and the Caspian* (London, 1854); Alexandre Dumas, père, *Adventures in Caucasia* (Philadelphia-New York, 1962); A. Khatisian, "Kaghakapeti me hishataknere," *Hayrenik amsagir*, X, 7 (115)–XI, 5 (125) (May 1932–March 1933); also his *Munitsipal'noe khoziaistvo goroda Tiflisa* (Tiflis, 1909); and Giorgi Mihailovich Tumanov, *Kharakteristiki i vospominaniia, zametki kavkazskago khronikera* (3 volumes: Tiflis, 1900–1907).

The best histories of Tiflis are by Soviet historians. A major study was begun by N. I. Badriashvili, *Tiflis, I: ot osnovaniia goroda do XIX v.* (Tiflis, 1934). Unfortunately, the second volume was never published, and Badriashvili's later work was a small guidebook: *Tbilisi* (Tbilisi, 1957). The other important work on pre-Russian Tbilisi is: Shota Ambakovich Meshia, *Goroda i gorodskoi stroi feodal'noi Gruzii, XVII–XVIII vv.* (Tbilisi, 1956). On nineteenth-century Tiflis, see Sh. K. Chkhetia, *Tbilisi, v XIX stoletii (1865–1869)* (Tbilisi, 1942). On early twentieth-century events, see N. Badriashvili (compiler), *1905 god v Tiflise. Fakticheskie materialy po dannym muzeia i arkhiva Tiflisskogo Soveta R. K. i C. D. i gazetnykh khronik* (Tiflis, 1926).

For a sense of the city one might look at the various guidebooks and studies on municipal architecture. Guidebooks include: G. Gogia, *Tbilisi, Kratkie svedeniia dlia turista* (Tbilisi, 1962); T. Kvirkveliia, *Tbilisi* (Moscow, 1969); O. Mkeshelashvili, *Tbilisi, Kratkii spravochnik-putevoditel'* (Tbilisi, 1967); and Vakhtang Dzhaoshvili, *Tbilisi, ekonomiko—geograficheskii ocherk* (Tbilisi, 1971). On the architecture of the city, see Nodar Dzhanberidze, Meri Karbelashvili, Simon Kintsurashvili, *Arkhitektura Tbilisi, putevoditel'* (Tbilisi, 1961); Vakhtang Beridze, *tbilisi khurotmodzghvreba, 1801–1917 tslebi, II* (Tbilisi, 1963); and N. Dzhashi, *Arkhitektura sotsialisticheskogo Tbilisi* (Tbilisi, 1963).

Two special works on aspects of Tiflis's social and political life deserve to be mentioned. The first is the more conventional: *Revoliutsionnoe proshloe Tbilisi* (Tbilisi, 1964), a collection of essays on aspects of the revolutionary movement in Tiflis from 1890 to 1921. The second is an appreciation of Tiflis by the Georgian poet and scholar Iosif Grishashvili: *Literaturnaia bogema starogo Tbilisi* (Tbilisi, 1977).

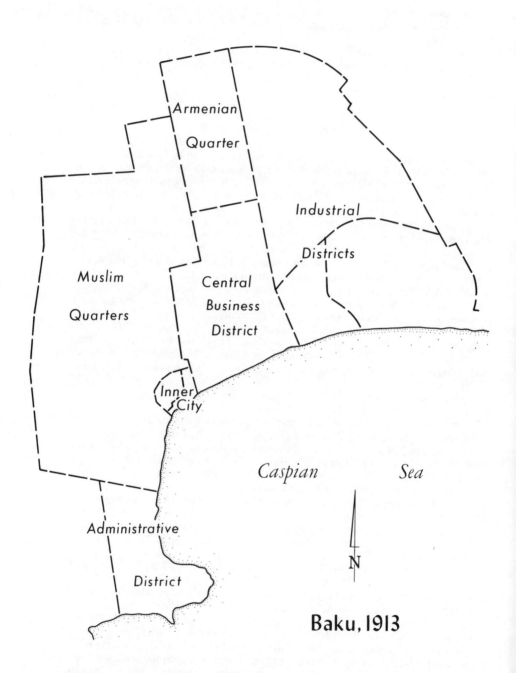

Armenian
Quarter

Industrial

Districts

Muslim

Quarters

Central
Business
District

Inner
City

Caspian   Sea

N

Administrative

District

Baku, 1913

9.

Baku

Transformation of a Muslim Town

AUDREY ALTSTADT-MIRHADI

Early in the nineteenth century, Baku was a walled Muslim town situated at the border of Christendom and the Muslim world. When Russian forces occupied it in 1806, its population of between 3,000 and 5,000 was composed predominantly of Turkic and Persian Muslims. Its exports included salt, saffron, and oil which had been dredged from shallow pits for at least nine centuries. For over ten centuries, Baku had been part of the Muslim world. During much of this time, it was the residence and for a time the capital of a seven-hundred-year-old local dynasty, the Shirvanshahs. It bore the stamp of the vast Turco-Iranian Islamic cultural belt in which it lay. Beginning in the sixteenth century, this region was brought decisively into the Persian Empire of the Safavids and therefore had Shi'ism imposed on it by Shah Ismail (1501—1524). The eventual adoption of Shi'ism not only led to the unitary cultural-spiritual development of the eastern Caucasus with Persia, but drove a wedge between the Turks of this area and other Turks who remained Sunni, including the Ottomans to the west.[1]

By the turn of the twentieth century, Baku had become an industrial and commercial city. Already in the 1890s, it was the oil-producing center of the industrializing Russian Empire. Trade in petroleum products and other commodities with Russia and Iran had grown as quickly as oil output. The oil industry and trade, like the city's social, political, and cultural life, were dominated by its three major ethnoreligious communities—Muslim Turks, Orthodox Russians, and Gregorian

Armenians.[2] The population grew and the city expanded until the old walled town was only one of more than twenty quarters (*mahalla*). Baku became a boom town; it was as if the industry of Pittsburgh and the frontier lawlessness of Dodge City had been superimposed on Baghdad. Westernized Baku was marked by gas lights, paved streets, and telephones, and by drinking, gambling, and prostitution. It held for contemporaries the same romance as did the American frontier for the eastern tenderfoot—and the same dangers:

> There used to be a proverb among the Russian businessmen: "Whoever lives a year among the oil owners of Baku can never again be civilized." Thus spoke the honorable merchants of St. Petersburg. They always made their wills when they had to go to Baku.[3]

Merchants converged on Baku to capitalize on its thriving markets. New classes—an industrial proletariat and bourgeoisie—predictably came into conflict. Villages on the city's periphery were transformed into industrial settlements. They experienced the crowding and shortages of housing and other services that plagued the city itself. Baku and its oil districts became a center of the Empire's revolutionary movement. This chapter will describe Baku's changing environment, examining the impact of Western elements and various other factors from administrative reform to industrial and commercial growth. Although Baku became an industrial town, it did not lose its Muslim character. Instead that character was fitted into a new mold by the opportunities and pressures of this changing environment.

THE FIRST DECADES OF RUSSIAN RULE

The Russian conquest immediately began to affect Baku's Islamic character. Initially, it brought peace and soldiers. With the establishment of peace in the area after the First Russo-Iranian War (1804–1813), many who had fled the area returned, and trade gradually revived. Military rule under the Russian commanders introduced the Muslim population to Russian law, and perhaps avoided wartime abuses such as the seizure of religious properties and the violation of Muslim homes.

The commanders attempted to rule by a combination of Russian civil and local customary law (*adet*). Ignorance of the latter led to the expansion of the former, threatening the power of the Muslim judges (*qadis*) and the Muslim way of life.[4] It is likely that many disputes were settled within the traditional framework, however, and that the penetration of Russian law was initially superficial.

By the 1830s Russians began to invest in the Caucasus, setting up joint-stock companies in Baku and other towns. This influx of capital, coupled with the beginning of steamship cartage on the Caspian Sea, stimulated Baku's commercial life. The expanded market began slowly to draw regional merchants. In the 1840s administrative reform created the viceroyalty of Transcaucasia, bringing these provinces into the Imperial system and supplanting direct military rule. Russian civil law advanced further against Muslim religious and customary law. But the major turning point for Baku came in 1859 when an earthquake leveled the provincial capital, Shemakha, and Baku became the new capital of the province. In the same year, two local Russian investors, V. A. Kokorev and P. I. Gubonin, established the first oil refinery and the shipping firm Caucasus and Mercury. In the oil industry, they later offered stiff competition to Armenian interests. Caucasus and Mercury became Baku's major shipping firm and by the end of the century had offices in New York, Singapore, Liverpool, and Copenhagen. These developments brought to Baku Russians affiliated with the provincial administration and attracted speculators, traders, and laborers. The population began to grow rapidly. In the early 1850s Baku had about 8,000 inhabitants, only slightly more than in the early part of the century. By the early 1860s the population had grown to nearly 13,000.[5]

The cultural and intellectual response of the Muslim intelligentsia to the Russian presence combined two opposite reactions—accommodation and resistance. By accommodation, we should understand not subservience or Russification (which occurred only on a small scale), but a shift away from the traditional Turco-Iranian Islamic *Weltanschauung* and way of life. Resistance means here not merely resistance to Russification and other Western influences, but also a positive assertion of the Muslim Turkic heritage. Thus on the one hand various signs of accommodation to the Russian presence began in the 1840s, including service in the tsarist bureaucracy, use of the Russian language, and acceptance of Western dress. Simultaneously this same bilingual intelligentsia produced histories of Azerbaijan and the Caucasus and plays written in the spoken Azerbaijani Turkish vernacular. The intelligentsia began to be aware of its ethnic identity, and its Turkic awareness soon replaced its traditional Iranian orientation.

THE OIL ECONOMY

The most striking feature of industrial-era Baku was the preeminence of the petroleum industry. More than the commercial growth or the transfer of the provincial capital to Baku, industrialization stimulated immigration, the physical expansion of the town, the growth of the local market, the concentration of capital, the sharpening of competition, and the creation of new industrial classes.

The oil rush that began in the 1870s exerted a more profound impact on Baku than any event since the acceptance of Shi'ism. The discovery of oil was not the decisive factor, since oil had been exported from the area for nearly a thousand years. It was two factors—the drilling of wells and land reform—that triggered Baku's oil rush. Until 1871 oil had been collected from pits dug to gather the substantial seepage of oil that was pushed to the surface over centuries by the pressure of subterranean natural gas. The first successful well was sunk in 1871 by the local concessionaire for the state monopoly, M. I. Mirzoev, a local Armenian. Wells soon proliferated, though hand extraction from pits continued into the twentieth century. Drilling produced spectacular gushers which often spewed oil and sand for days, making Baku world-famous. When a skeptical American visitor came to investigate the rumors, a local British oilman took him to see one of the renowned gushers which had spouted, seemingly, just for the occasion:

> They could see cascades of oil squirting from the damaged boarding of the derrick, itself already half-buried in sand, and they were deafened by the noise of the escaping oil projected with such terrific force against the massive iron blocks placed to check its upward flight. Rivers of oil and slimy sand ran in all directions, and hundreds of men in oil-soaked garments were engaged in shoveling away sand to make channels for leading the oil to enormous earthen reservoirs hastily constructed for its reception. The well was giving around 100,000 barrels of oil a day, mingled with at least 10,000 tons of sand and tens of millions of cubic feet of gas which saturated the air over a wide area.[6]

Such abundance not only led to jumps in oil output (from approximately 40 barrels (bbl) per day in 1872 to 12,000 bbl/day in 1897 and nearly 200,000 bbl/day in the peak production year, 1901),[7] but lured speculators from every corner of the Empire and abroad. Land parcels were small and multitudes of hastily built derricks appeared like forests so dense that one "could not swing a cat by the tail between them."

The second factor, land reform, was carried out the year after the first well was sunk. Prior to 1872 oil-bearing lands had belonged to the tsarist government and were leased out for a specified number of years to individual investors. Fees were paid to the local concessionaire, a state appointee. This state monopoly was abolished and replaced by the auction of land parcels. Investors' rights over their land were now secure, and oilmen invested more money and care in their operations. Under the state monopoly, all the concessionaires had been Armenian. The last concessionaire was M. I. Mirzoev. Shut out of the market by Kokorev and Gubonin, Baku's pioneer oil refiners, during the first segment of a four-week auction, Mirzoev subsequently succeeded in purchasing oil parcels by offering great sums that exceeded even those bid by Kokorev and Gubonin. "The state monopoly had only been replaced by a private duopoly" which dominated efforts by Russian and Armenian investors to mechanize and modernize the petroleum industry in its early years.[8]

The establishment of the Nobel Brothers' Petroleum Company also had a decisive impact on the development of the oil industry. In 1873 Robert Nobel, brother of the renowned Alfred Nobel, arrived in Baku to purchase lumber made from local walnut trees. He stayed and bought an oil refinery.[9] Within ten years the Nobel Company was the largest in the area; within thirty it was one of the major oil producers in the world. The Nobels invested in risky expansion on a scale totally unprecedented in Baku's oil industry. They imported the latest technology or created their own. They constructed massive projects in and around Baku, including the first pipeline from the oilfields to the refineries in the city, company towns, parks, villas, and the first modern oil tankers and railway cars used in the Empire. The Nobels subsequently became the Empire's largest manufacturer and marketer of diesel engines and produced and exported more oil than all other Baku firms combined. At its peak in 1883, their market share was 55 percent of all oil exported from the Empire.[10]

The petroleum industry spawned other industries, stimulated trade both directly and indirectly, and led to the development of transportation and communications networks. One of the first institutions to respond to the needs of the oil industry was the banking system of the Empire. In 1880 a branch of the State Bank was opened in Baku. In its first year of operation, this branch discounted 438,000 rubles' worth of bills. Five years later that figure had risen more than ten times to 4,913,000 rubles.[11] Other banking and financial institutions followed. In 1897 all Baku financial institutions issued a total of 5.6 million rubles in interest-bearing securities; the following two years, they issued 9.2 million and 11.4 million rubles respectively.[12]

By the turn of the century, these financial institutions were serving much more than a growing oil industry. Shipping—long an important concern—had been expanding during the last quarter of the nineteenth century. The number of ships on the Caspian had increased more than fourfold between 1887 and 1899, and their total tonnage had grown six times. Most of the fleet was aging. Half the ships were ten or more years old; a quarter were twenty-five years old or more.[13] This state of affairs led to a new spurt of shipbuilding in the twentieth century. In 1900, 40 percent of the ships of the Caspian fleet had been built inside the Russian Empire. By 1907 all the sailing ships and 40 percent of the steamers had been built inside the Empire, some in Baku's own shipyards.[14]

The machine-building industry grew directly out of the needs of the oil companies for equipment and parts. Oil companies themselves often set up machine-building operations. Machine production began in the

1880s, but did not grow into a large endeavor until the twentieth century. In the period 1901–1903, there were 184 mechanical enterprises in Baku with a total of 9,349 workers. By 1908–1910 Baku had 207 mechanical enterprises with 16,643 workers.[15]

Other industries that were not directly linked to oil also made contributions to the development of the city. Fishing and other food industries grew, as did trade in food items.[16] In general, the number of retail trade establishments, including restaurants, inns, hotels, stores, and other sellers of consumer goods, increased. In 1881 there were 1,334 retail trade establishments in Baku; in 1897, there were 1,620.[17] The first area textile mill was built by H. Z. A. Tagiev, Baku's wealthiest Muslim entrepreneur. It provided cheap cloth and over 1,500 jobs.

Lines of communication and transportation linked Baku to the outside world and its markets. Telegraph lines connected Baku to the rest of the Empire beginning with the first line to Tiflis in the 1860s. Within Baku a telephone system was created in the 1880s, laying the ground for a communications network as modern as those in contemporary Europe. Baku's oldest rail line was built in 1880 to connect the city with the oil districts Balakhano-Sabunchi and Surakhany. In 1884 the Transcaucasian Railway was completed, linking Baku to Batum on the Black Sea via Tiflis.

DEMOGRAPHIC CHANGE

Demographic change in the industrial era was striking. Baku's population grew from roughly 14,500 in the 1870s to nearly 112,000 in 1897—over 700 percent in about twenty-five years. Between 1897 and 1913 the population increased another 92 percent, making Baku one of the most rapidly growing cities in the Empire. Just outside the city villages were being transformed into industrial settlements. Industrialization drew workers, mostly male. By the eve of the war, men constituted 55 to 60 percent of the population in the city, 75 percent in the oil districts. Baku became a city of immigrants: 65 percent of the population was born outside Baku, 8 to 12 percent outside the Empire. Over 90 percent of the foreign population was from Iran. Data on their language use indicate they were Azerbaijani Turks, not ethnic Persians.[18]

The ethnoreligious composition of Baku shifted steadily in favor of Christian peoples in the early decades of industrialization. Between the 1860s and the census of 1897, the Iranian-speaking population (Tats and Talysh) declined and the number of Russians increased.[19] By 1897 over one-third of Baku's population was Russian. Thereafter, Russian immigration kept pace with the growth of the population as a whole. This was also true of the Armenian population, which remained at about 20 percent during the seventeen prewar years for which we have accurate census data. During this period the total number of Muslims shrank from over 40 percent to only one-third, mainly because of higher rates of immigration by Russians and Armenians. Native Azerbaijani Turks (called "Tatars" in pre-revolutionary Russia) increased slightly in absolute numbers, but only the flood of Azerbaijani Turks from Iran kept the proportion of Muslims from falling even further. (See Table 9.1.)

More important than their numbers is the way these groups fit into Baku's nascent industrial structure. The Russians tended to dominate the institutions of administration and surveillance. There were also many Russian skilled workers in the petroleum industry, especially in refinery work, in the machine industries, and in the crafts. Due to the immigration of thousands of peasants (25,000 of Baku's 39,000 peasants in 1897 were Russian) from southern Russia, they also formed the second largest group of unskilled laborers both in the oil industry and in the city's labor force in general. Armenians dominated large-scale trade. Most of the guild merchants of higher ranks (razriady) were Armenians. They also gave the greatest impetus to the early development of the petroleum industry, as noted above. Among the ranks of skilled workers as well as managerial and technical specialists, there were many Armenians. Finally, there was a small number of extremely wealthy Azerbai-

TABLE 9.1

Population Growth and Ethnic Composition in Baku, 1897–1913

	1897	1903	1913
Total population	111,904	155,876	214,672
Armenian	19,033	26,151	41,680
Azerbaijani Tk.	33,826	44,257	45,962
Iranian	8,982	11,132	25,096
Russian	38,975	65,955	76,288

SOURCE: *Pervaia vseobshchaia perepis' naseleniia rossiiskoi imperii, 1897 g. (St. Petersburg, 1897) (hereafter Perepis' 1897)*, v. 61, 50–53, 152–155; *Baku po perepisi 22 oktiabria 1903 g. (Baku, 1905) (Perepis' 1903)*, v. 1, pt. 2, tables between pp. 28–29; *Baku po perepisi 22 oktiabria 1913 g. (Baku, 1916) (Perepis' 1913)*, v. 3, pt. 1, 4–5.

NOTE: Categories in these three censuses are not comparable: the 1897 census was arranged by language and religion, the later censuses by nationality. This presented no problem for the Armenian and Russian populations since the different categories still encompassed the same people. For Muslims, the problem occurred because Turkic-speaking Iranians were classified in 1897 with local Turks (because they spoke the same language) and in the city censuses of 1903 and 1913 with ethnic Persians. To make all the columns comparable I subtracted 6,435 foreign citizens from the "Tatar-speaking" (i.e., Azerbaijani-speaking) category (use of the term "Tatar" indicates they were not Ottoman Turks) and added them to the "Iranian" total. I have used "Iranian" as a designation of citizenship instead of the ethnic term "Persian." Other data from these censuses show that the proportion of Turks among the Iranians was lowest in 1897, when the Turks constituted over 70 percent of the Iranian citizens in Baku.

jani Turkish merchant-industrialists, whose initial fortunes were made in either oil or trade but who then moved into other areas. Although not an important factor in the petroleum industry (the hundreds of Muslim oilmen identified in the 1913 census were almost exclusively owners of tiny, primitive operations), they dominated shipping and trade with Iran and were active in the silk and tobacco industries. The Muslims also formed the backbone of bazaar trade in Baku. Muslims accounted for most of the unskilled workers in Baku and the oil districts.

Table 9.2 gives a more detailed overview of the class structure of the three major communities of Baku in 1897. Aside from the exclusion of non-Russians from organs of administration, the table also indicates the low number of Azerbaijani Turks engaged in professions. This census also indicated that Muslims had the lowest rate of literacy of the three major groups—15 percent of the Azerbaijani Turkish males were literate, compared with over 50 percent of the Armenian and Russian males. It is also noteworthy that Russian women were more likely than either Armenian or Muslim women to be employed outside the home.

Table 9.3 indicates the composition of the male labor force for the three censuses, 1897, 1903, and 1913. Some of the main trends include the growth of the administrative–law enforcement category and the increased number of professionals. The law enforcement group, still overwhelmingly Russian, grew primarily because of a large increase in the number of police. We have noted the predominance of Russians in administration and law enforcement. Roughly 15 percent of all Russians in the labor force in 1913 fell into this category. The number of professionals also grew between 1897 and 1913. The greatest rates of increase were first among Russians (between 1897 and 1903) and then among Armenians (between 1903 and 1913). However, the number of Muslim professionals more than trebled between 1897 and 1913.

Tables 9.2 and 9.3, because they deal only with the city proper, do not give information on the workers in the oil districts. Unlike oil refining, which required a substantial proportion of skilled workers (which in Baku were mostly Russians), extraction of crude requires large numbers of unskilled workers. Most were Muslims, including a large component of Iranians; Russians were second. The extraction workers worked and lived in the oil districts. In 1903 there were 15,367 extraction workers in the oil districts, 54 percent of whom were classified as "Persians and Tatars," i.e., Azerbaijani Turks from Iran and the Caucasus. By 1913 the number of extraction workers had grown to 34,479, of whom 33 percent were Iranian citizens, 12 percent local Azerbaijani Turks, and 18 percent other Muslims, either from Kazan or Daghestan. Thus the Muslim component of oil workers constituted 63 percent, 51 percent without the local Azerbaijani Turks. Of the rest, 17 percent were Armenians, 15 percent Russians. These figures reflect the numbers of immigrants from Iran and other Muslim areas of the Russian

TABLE 9.2

Employment of 1897 Population of Baku, by Language Use

Job Category	Total M	Total F	Armenian M	Armenian F	Azer. Tk.ᵃ M	Azer. Tk.ᵃ F	Russian M	Russian F
Admin./Judic./Law Enforcement	3,002	11	313	0	324	0	1,345	10
Clergy: Orthodox	46	16	7	0	4	0	29	14
Other Christian	18	0	10	0	0	0	0	0
Non-Christian	151	0	0	0	134	0	0	0
Education/Medicine/Arts	627	326	97	25	73	14	293	203
Servants	10,661	3,145	1,991	100	4,143	136	2,460	2,448
Landowners	1,065	772	231	171	549	231	186	294
Agricult./Fishing/Mining	873	34	279	6	268	12	159	12
Handicrafts	4,768	11	773	1	426	0	2,960	11
Chemical prod.ᵇ	1,309	9	305	0	253	2	433	4
Production—food, tobacco, alcohol, clothing	2,943	715	1,214	71	656	64	531	464
Construction/Shipbuilding	3,661	1	679	0	1,364	0	1,369	1
Transport/Posts-Telegraphᶜ	7,236	62	413	2	3,540	7	2,430	51
All trade	6,021	235	1,924	20	2,742	45	568	137
Hygiene/Baths	457	496	124	26	241	55	23	384
Prostitution	0	213	0	2	0	22	0	135
Other	4,206	768	756	159	923	149	1,513	369
Total all occupations	47,386	6,828	9,167	585	15,807	738	14,394	4,553

SOURCE: *Perepis' 1897*, 105, 120–123.

NOTE: Data in this table do not include other groups in Baku, among which are 2,400 Germans, 2,000 Jews, 1,000 Tats, 900 Georgians, 800 Poles, 800 Ottoman Turks, 700 Daghestanis. The Tats and Daghestanis are native to the eastern Caucasus and Caucasus mountains.

ᵃBecause of classification by language (see note, Table 9.1), this column includes Iranian Turks as well as locals. Total number of former: 6,425.

ᵇIncludes oil refining, for which there was no separate category.

ᶜIncludes porters (*ambals*): 224 Armenian, 1,192 Az. Turkish, 274 Russian males, and 4 Russian females; city total: 1,810 males, 4 females.

TABLE 9.3

Male Occupation Patterns in Baku, 1897–1913

Category/Nationality[a]	1897	1903	1913
All income-earners	47,386	61,173	102,940
Armenian	9,167	10,948	18,389
Azerbaijani Turk[b]	15,807[c]	(23,658)[b]	15,807
Iranian[c]	2,571[c]	— [b]	17,018
Russian	14,394	25,614	37,645
Admin./Judic./Law Enf.	3,002	4,127[d]	7,609[e]
Armenian	313	(345)[f]	427
Azerbaijani Turk[b]	324[c]	(383)[b]	292
Iranian[c]	11[c]	— [b]	141
Russian	1,345	(2,361)[f]	5,588
Professionals[g]	627	2,210	4,072
Armenian	97	289	741
Azerbaijani Turk[b]	73[c]	165[b]	214
Iranian[c]	10[c]	— [b]	49
Russian	293	1,190	1,805
Crafts/Food-Clothing Mfg.	7,711	13,456	— [h]
Armenians	1,987	2,645	—
Azerbaijani Turk[b]	1,076[c]	(2,606)[b]	—
Iranian[c]	279[c]	— [b]	—
Russian	3,491	6,070	—
Oil/Chemical Prod.[i]	1,309	3,236	3,806
Armenian	305	518	997
Azerbaijani Turk[b]	253[c]	(1,045)[b]	333
Iranian[c]	186[c]	— [b]	439
Russian	433	1,355	1,381
Repair/Construction	3,661	4,417	— [h]
Armenian	679	1,028	—
Azerbaijani Turk[b]	1,364[c]	(1,502)[b]	—
Iranian[c]	65[c]	— [b]	—
Russian	1,369	1,692	—
Transport/Porters	7,236	9,463	11,380
Armenian	413	604	881
Azerbaijani Turk[b]	3,540[c]	—	1,157
Iranian[c]	206[c]	—	5,348
Russian	2,430	3,204	2,949
Trade—all types	6,021	14,945[j]	19,515[j]
Armenian	1,924	3,559	—
Azerbaijani Turk[b]	2,742[c]	(7,084)[b]	—
Iranian[c]	458[c]	— [b]	—
Russian	568	2,429	—

Empire working in Baku. They also indicate the degree to which local Turks, because of family networks, were able to avoid the dirty and dangerous work of the oilfields and find positions in the city. Although salaries in the oil industry were among the highest in the Empire, rates of injury and death were also high. Workers' living quarters were oil-covered, poorly ventilated, and overcrowded. Water was always a problem; roads were unpaved and unlit, providing excellent cover for frequent brigandage.[20]

Russians and Armenians complained loudest and struck most frequently, but Muslims often suffered much more. As unskilled workers they were confined to jobs with the lowest wages and highest accident rates. They were more often separated from village families to whom they intended to return. Russian and Armenian workers, by contrast, either brought wives and children (whom they could afford to support with their higher wages) or made a complete break with their villages. Thus differentials in wage structure and living conditions coincided with ethnoreligious divisions and aggravated traditional animosities.[21]

URBAN ENVIRONMENT

Baku's urban environment was a mix and synthesis of Eastern and Western elements.[22] The physical appearance of the town suggests the mixing of elements and their occasional synthesis. The old town, much of its stone wall intact, was now at the center of a European-style metropolis. Baku had begun to expand outward from its walled core even before industrialization. In the industrial period, especially in the 1890s and 1900s, dozens of new structures made of local cut stone were

---

SOURCE: *Perepis' 1897*, 120–123; *Perepis' 1903*, v. 1, pt. 2, table IV-b; *Perepis' 1913*, v. 3, pt. 2, 40–45 (table 6); M. A. Musaev, "Razvitie torgovli goroda Baku," dissertation (Baku, 1970).

[a]See Note for Table 9.1 re: categories of the various censuses.

[b]In the 1903 Census, data on employment gave a combined figure for "Tatars and Persians"; this is the figure in the Azerbaijani Turk line.

[c]Data regarding Iranian immigrants are not comparable to that in Table 9.1 (see Note in Table 9.1), nor are the 1897 data comparable to the 1913 data. The 1897 data are given by language usage, so that for the "Iranian" line in that column, figures concern only Persian speakers; similarly, Turkic-speaking Iranians are counted in the line for Azerbaijani Turks. The nature of these data did not permit the kind of correction made for Table 9.1.

[d]This figure includes 2,948 police, of whom 2,361 were Russian.

[e]This figure includes 5,149 "security forces."

[f]Data were incomplete; this figure is for police only.

[g]Professionals include those in education, science, the arts, medicine, and private law practice.

[h]There was no comparable category in the 1913 census.

[i]These data are for the city only, and exclude the oil districts, as noted in the text.

[j]These data are taken from M. A. Musaev, "Razvitie torgovli gor. Baku," pp. 91–93; no breakdown of these data are given for 1913.

erected to the north and west of the walls. Many new buildings comprising Baku's downtown and including the city council building, a girls' school, and a men's middle school (*uchilishche*) were built in European styles. The American consul in Batum remarked that Baku, with its European architecture, rapid expansion, paved and lighted streets, and rows of shops selling a large variety of goods, compared favorably with larger European cities.[23] Even much of the Inner City, within the walls, was rebuilt at this time. Some of Baku's new buildings were built in Mediterranean or local styles, such as the Ismailie building housing the Muslim Charitable Society. New mosques were also built.[24] Old buildings, some dating from pre-Islamic times, remained amid the new.

Russians were the most visible element of the population in the center of town. Arthur Beeby-Thompson, a British oil company manager living in Baku from 1898 to 1905, noted on his arrival both the European buildings and the low profile of the indigenous groups:

> Baku was in 1898 a city of some prominence and had a prosperous appearance. The main thoroughfares were wide and lined with houses and shops of artistic design, built of limestone quarried in the hills overlooking the city. Persians, Tatars [Azerbaijanis], Armenians were mostly in evidence in the country and in the [oil]fields, but in town the customary cosmopolitan population was to be found more or less segregated in separate quarters.[25]

Like most cities of the Muslim world, Baku was separated into quarters (*mahalla*). Although they were not divided by walls and gates as is sometimes the case, many quarters, especially those outside the central business district, were ethnoreligiously homogenous. The map shows a city plan from the 1913 city census. The Inner City on the bay (Quarter III) was called the Fortress by the Russians. This quarter and those west of an imaginary line drawn northward from the Inner City were predominantly Muslim. To the east in the center of town was the business district, which comprised several mixed quarters—probably the area Thompson referred to in his description. Further east were a few large quarters where oil refineries and other industries were concentrated. The population was predominantly Russian. North of the business district were the Armenian quarters, and in the extreme southwest were the administrative and military centers, populated overwhelmingly by Russians.

In all quarters except those with heavily Russian or Armenian populations, the majority of building owners were Azerbaijani Turks. In fact, 71 percent of all building owners in Baku in 1913 were Muslims. Armenian owners (12 percent) held property in the Armenian quarters and the western section of the central business district. Russian owners (7 percent) predominated in the southwestern administrative district and in one of the far-eastern industrial quarters. Private companies (7 percent) had holdings primarily in the industrial quarters. Data do not indicate the relative value of properties, however, and it is likely that much valuable property belonged to Armenians, Russians, and private companies. Nonetheless, the value of Muslim-owned property must have been considerable, for under the requirements for suffrage laid down by the urban reforms, Muslims formed over 80 percent of the electors for city council elections.[26]

Finally, the characteristics of the quarters themselves emphasized the "Eastern" nature of industrial-era Baku. Census data indicate that in Muslim quarters buildings opened onto inner courtyards, in keeping with traditional Islamic patterns based on the desire to keep private life separate from public. Horses, goats, and cows were kept, but not pigs, which are regarded by Muslims as unclean. In Armenian and Russian quarters, most buildings opened onto the street and pigs as well as other animals were kept.

Like the physical city, Baku's cultural and social life reflected not only Eastern and Western cultural elements, but, more significantly, the tension between them. The penetration of Western elements was so thorough that no group was left untouched. For the majority of Baku's Azerbaijani Turks, whose primary identity was as Shi'i Muslims, the tension between the two cultural forces was overt and external, involving choices between piety and impiety, between dictates of religion and tradition on the one hand and the demands of the marketplace and contemporary life on the other. For the educated, especially the intelligentsia, the tension was more often internal, personal, and a question of degree—how much reform, how much tradition? How much self-assertion, how much acquiescence? Tension was implicit in their mixed life style. Most of the secular intelligentsia had been educated in Russian or European universities and spoke perfect Russian; they were often engaged in Western professions. Would they stop throughout the day to perform the prayer? Muslim professional men in business suits married Muslim women, at least some of whom wore the veil. These families observed religious rites in marriage, circumcision, and burial. Would they spend a life's savings to make the *hajj* (pilgrimage) to Mecca?

Attitudes often revealed syntheses of cultural influences. Yet sometimes inner conflicts remained unresolved, and contradictory attitudes and actions coexisted. Educational reform, a program of vital importance for the whole community, reflected both syntheses and contradictions. At the First Conference of Muslim Teachers, convened in Baku in August 1906, discussion centered on the "nationalization of primary schools." Parents and teachers complained about the Russification of Azerbaijani Turkish ("Tatar") and about the lack of instruction in students' native language. They called for the use of Azerbaijani-language textbooks and improved training for teachers. The conference

appointed a committee to work out the details of the reform program. It
included the most educated and highly respected scholars of Azerbaijan,
men of varying political leanings. Häsän Bek Melikov-Zärdabi, a renowned scholar, pedagogue, and founder of *Ekinji* (Sower), the first
Azerbaijani-language newspaper (published 1875–77), cochaired this
committee with Näriman Närimanov, then head of the men's *gymnasium,* later a medical doctor, who was a member of the Baku Committee
of the Russian Social Democratic Workers' Party (RSDWP) and later
served in the Commissariat for the Nationalities under Lenin and
Stalin.

The committee report, published in January 1907, is noteworthy
mainly for its attempt to make use of the local language and preserve
Islamic culture while simultaneously preparing a new generation for
life in a Western, industrial society. The program called for parallel
instruction: Islamic law and custom (*Shari'a*) and the Azerbaijani language were to be taught in Azerbaijani Turkish while "practical" subjects, such as geography and accounting, were to be taught in Russian.
The Muslim children who graduated from these reformed schools
would be able to conduct business or pursue a higher education in either
language or culture. The objective seems to have been to keep as many
options open as possible.[27]

In keeping with the secular intelligentsia's oft-sounded call for
female emancipation, the educational reform committee recommended
improving educational facilities for girls. Commentaries in the press
supported this recommendation, and the city council later provided
funds for a girls' school. (The first Muslim Girls' School had been
established somewhat earlier by the millionaire philanthropist H. Z. A.
Tagiev.) Both press commentaries and speeches in the city council,
however, indicate that the basis for this campaign for women's emancipation had more to do with women's traditional role as culture-
bearers and child-rearers than with any belief in women's rights or
concern for their potential to develop intellectually. One Muslim city
council representative ended his rousing "down with the veil" speech
with an invocation to "make our women good citizens and good
mothers."[28]

One aspect of the committee's program is surprising—religious
education was recommended by a group of secularizing intellectuals.
The secular intelligentsia had consistently stood for increased secular-
ization in all walks of life. It was this group which had held up the
mullahs to unflagging ridicule at least since the middle of the preceding
century. The mullahs were portrayed as tradition-bound and ignorant.
Attacks against them and against the tendency of most Muslims to
follow them unthinkingly were no less virulent than subsequent Soviet
attacks. How was it that the secularizing intelligentsia placed the mullahs in so powerful a role in educational reform? A survey of Muslim

educational reform throughout the Empire in the early twentieth century shows that, despite the criticisms of their detractors, mullahs in
various areas of the Volga, Daghestan, and Zerbaijan often opened and
staffed reformed (as opposed to Koranic) schools. The committee members in Baku simply recognized that attitudes toward reform differed
from one mullah to another.[29]

The intelligentsia also attended to adult education. Baku's cultural
enlightenment societies offered night courses to combat illiteracy and
more generally to educate and train adults.[30] The success of these classes
and of the reforms of regular educational institutions was reflected in
increased literacy and the trebling of the number of Azerbaijani Turks in
professions. By 1913, 35 percent of the Azerbaijani Turkish males and 7
percent of the females could read and write as opposed to 15 and 1.7
percent, respectively, in 1897. The number of professionals in law,
medicine, and education increased during the same period from 73 to
214.[31]

In the realm of ideology and political thought, Azerbaijani Turks
responded to varied ideological currents of Eastern and Western origins.
The currents of the era included Islamic identity and Pan-Islamism,
embraced in Baku on a religious-cultural level rather than a political
level (in its extreme form the latter, like political Pan-Turkism, implied
unification under the Ottoman Sultan); ethnic Turkic identity and
cultural Pan-Turkism; liberalism, rationalism, and populism, together
with the principles they suggest such as constitutional rule and civil
liberties; and socialism of both Russian and Austrian Marxist types.

The Azerbaijani Turkish intelligentsia drew from all these trends.
The most far-reaching result was the development of a Muslim Turkic
identity devoid of the sectarian animosities that usually divided Shi'a
from Sunni. The creation of a Turkic consciousness was part of the
secular intelligentsia's attempt to distance itself and all of Russian
Azerbaijan from Iran and the increasingly powerful Iranian Shi'i clerical
hierarchy. The movement away from Iranian influence had begun with
the first generation under Russian rule. By the end of the nineteenth
century, under the influence of Pan-Turkism, many Azerbaijani Turks
combined criticism of Iran's religious hierarchy with criticism of the
Arabs, clearly marking the Azerbaijani's Islamic consciousness as Turkic. At the same time, their Turkic identity was Islamic—the Azerbaijani Turks referred only rarely to pre-Islamic Turkic legend or symbol
and exhibited no interest at all in non-Muslim Turks like the Yakut.
The Muslim-Turkic character of the Azerbaijanis' nascent identity was
shared by the Ottoman Turks who were experiencing their own ethnic
awakening at this time. The similarities between the renaissances of
these two closely related Turkic peoples provided a common ground
and sense of closeness between them.

In addition to the Muslim Turkic identity, "localism" was crucial to the development of the Azerbaijani Turkish national consciousness. "Localism" meant not merely the study of local history and language, which began soon after the Russian conquest, but pride in the local heritage. That pride manifested itself in demands for the use of Azerbaijani Turkish in the press and as a language of instruction in schools. It underlay, at least in part, the popularity of Mirza Fath Ali Akhundov (Akhundzade)'s plays satirizing local problems and written in the spoken vernacular.[32] Local pride fostered a sense of *noblesse oblige* in the wealthy and educated who established and supported charitable and cultural organizations. The Muslim Charitable Society aided the indigent in Baku and other areas of Azerbaijan. Two cultural enlightenment societies, Näshr Maarif and Nijat, not only established adult education classes but also set up acting troupes and reading rooms. Local pride had been fundamental to educational reform. The merging of local consciousness with the Muslim-Turkic identity defined the Azerbaijani Turks' national consciousness and contributed to the subsequent emergence of nationalism.[33]

National consciousness only gradually became the basis for political organization. The establishment of the Muslim Social Democratic Party, Hümmät, in fall 1904 marked the beginning of organized political life in Azerbaijan. Its character reflected disparate schools of thought rather than national consciousness. Hümmät existed as an autonomous organization of the Baku Committee of the RSDWP from late 1904 until its eclipse in 1908 and again after 1918. Although Social Democratic in name, in membership and program the Hümmät was not a purely Marxist organization. Some of its founders were members of the RSDWP, but the group's ranks swelled with intellectuals, members of the bourgeoisie, and possibly the religious establishment. Its program was reformist but not revolutionary; its leaflets were dated by the Muslim calendar. The group included many who would later join the nationalist Musavat Party. The Hümmät never denounced the localist trends, ethnic identity, or even Islam.[34] On the contrary, Hümmätists themselves shared the nascent Muslim-Turkic identity and concern for local issues. The cultural enlightenment society Nijat was founded and managed by Hümmätists. Hümmät leaders participated in Baku's educational reform program which supported religious education in the local language. For Baku's Muslim Social Democrats, there was no contradiction between adherence to Marxism and attempts to advance their community. Thus an avowed Marxist and Hümmät member concluded in an article entitled "What Is Happiness?" in a left-wing journal that the greatest joy was to give one's life for one's *vatan* (homeland).[35] By the same token, non-Marxists embraced ideals of economic opportunity and egalitarianism preached by Marxists. Baku's "bourgeois press" supported many of labor's demands and the utterly non-Marxist Muslim Union included labor items in its program.

The Muslim Union (*Ittifaq al-Muslimin*) was created at the First Muslim Congress, held secretly at Nizhnii Novgorod in August 1905, under the leadership of Crimean and Volga Tatars and Azerbaijani Turks. Unlike the Hümmät, the Muslim Union strove to represent and unite all Muslims of the Russian Empire regardless of class. Socialists were shunned. By the Second Muslim Congress in January 1906, the Muslim Union had already established an alliance with the Constitutional Democrats (Kadets). At the Second Congress, the Muslim Union declared itself a political party. Yusuf Akchuraoglu (Akchurin), a founding member of the Muslim Union, became a member of the Kadet Central Committee; so close was this tie that later critics referred to the Muslim Union as "Tatar Kadetism in a cloak and turban."[36] The Muslim Union advanced political demands on behalf of the Empire's Muslims. They proclaimed their loyalty to the tsar but called for the establishment of a constitutional monarchy and "rule of law." Their program stressed the need for equality for Muslims in political, civil, and religious rights and called for decentralized government and cultural autonomy (ideas borrowed from Austrian Marxists Karl Renner and Otto Bauer). They also supported a shorter workday and certain labor laws.[37] Although clearly inspired by Western ideas, the demands of the Muslim Union were aimed primarily at protecting the indigenous culture and securing for the Muslims of the Empire proportional representation and civil liberties.

By the time the Third Duma was convened, the Kadets had failed to exact any concessions from the monarchy for their own programs much less for their Muslim associates. The Muslim Union soon disappeared from the political scene. Although the Central Committee was nominally headquartered in Baku, home of Central Committee member and cofounder Ali Mardan Bey Topchibashev (Topchibashi), in fact no office was ever set up, and few other Azerbaijanis became involved in the Muslim Union. The Muslim Union's low profile on the Baku political scene and its quiet disappearance demonstrate the preoccupation of Baku's Muslims with local problems. Topchibashev, an attorney, newspaper publisher, and editor, was atypical. Elected to the First Duma, where he headed the Muslim faction, he signed the Vyborg Manifesto protesting the Duma's dissolution by the Tsar. He was thereafter active in Baku's politics only intermittently until the First World War. The many politicians in Baku who did not join the RDSWP after the suspension of the Hümmät's activities in 1908 hastened to join the Musavat (Equality) party when it was established around 1911–12. Initially a group with Pan-Islamic sentiments, the Musavat evolved under wartime pressures into Azerbaijan's first nationalist party.[38]

Baku's political organizations and ideas, products of diverse streams of thought, were characterized by inner tension. More crucial, inner tension was inherent in the Muslim-Turkic identity itself because that identity deviated from traditional Shi'ism and rejected historical ties to Iran in favor of a closer bond with Sunni Turks. Only in the Soviet period would Sunni-Shi'i divisiveness fade completely as Azerbaijani nationalism replaced, or more correctly, absorbed, Islam as the primary identity of the majority. Thus being an "Azerbaijani" came to be synonymous with being both a Muslim and a Turk. The pain of the earlier conflict of loyalties is eloquently expressed in an allegorical novel, *Ali and Nino*.[39] The devout Shi'i Sayyid Mustafa is horrified at the affinity of Baku's Shi'i for the Sunni Ottoman Turks and the willingness of the former to join the Ottoman Army in the World War. His conversation with Ali, the novel's protagonist, penetrated to the root of the ethnoreligious conflict for many Shi'i Turks. The Sayyid begins:

> For centuries the people of the Shiites have been mourning, blood has been flowing between us and the renegades [Sunni], who are worse than unbelievers. Shia here—Sunni there—there is no bridge between us. . . . Here in our Shiite town, men are longing for the Sunnites to come and destroy our faith. What does the Turk want?! Enver [Pasha] has advanced even to Urmia.* Iran will be cut in half. The True Faith is destroyed.

Ali questions him on the alternative: "Iran's sword is rusty. Whoever fights against the Turks is helping the Czar. Should we in Mohammad's name defend the Czar's cross against the Khalif's Half Moon? What shall we do Sayyid?" Ali then resumes his narration: "He looked at me and it seemed that all the despair of a dying millennium was in his eyes. Sayyid answered, 'What shall we do Ali Khan? I do not know.'"[40]

URBAN INSTITUTIONS

One of Baku's most influential institutions was the city council (*gorodskaia duma*) which came into being in 1878 under the terms set by the Municipal Statute of 1870.[41] The council offered Baku's Muslim elite its first opportunity to participate in local rule, though no more than half the council representatives could be non-Christians. The counterreform of 1892 tightened that restriction to no more than one-third. Of the electors who were eligible to vote in the first election (held in 1877), however, 85 percent were Muslims. Because suffrage was based on tax payment (based on property ownership or trade volume), the large number of Muslim electors indicates their relative economic strength. Even with the more stringent property qualifications imposed in 1892, over 80 percent of Baku's electors were Muslims.[42]

---

*Urmia refers to Lake Urmia in East Azerbaijan Province in Iran.

Although the provisions of 1892 remained the underlying law governing municipal administration until the end of the Empire, the one-third restriction against non-Christians was lifted in Baku province (and probably throughout the viceroyalty of the Caucasus) in December 1900.[43] Even the one-half restriction was circumvented in the elections of 1906, when slightly over half the elected representatives were Muslims. The council petitioned the viceroy (then the liberal Vorontsov-Dashkov) to permit the election results to stand. No new elections were ever held. In 1910, the duma petitioned the viceroy to rescind officially the one-half restriction (Statute 44). The viceroy first granted, then rejected the request. The Muslims seem to have ignored the latter action as they had ignored Statute 44 itself. The last prewar council, too, had a majority of Muslims.

This surprising series of interactions suggests there were limits to the state's (or the viceroy's) willingness to intervene in this issue. Perhaps the lax enforcement of the non-Christian restrictions in Baku was an attempt to conciliate the Muslim population. Since it coincided with various Russian moves against the Armenian community, such as the confiscation of Armenian Church lands, however, it was more likely part of the government's attempt to use traditional antagonisms between the Muslims and the Christian Armenians in its own anti-Armenian campaign. Possibly the authorities were reluctant to intervene because Baku was so volatile and because the city had such a large majority of Muslim electors. Vorontsov-Dashkov's own views were also a determining factor. His apparent liberalism was manifested in 1907–1908 when he sponsored a labor-management conference at a time of Empire-wide repression to the labor movement.

Despite early restrictions on their representation, Muslims were often accused of controlling the city council. Critics charged that council decisions were actually made in Tagiev's parlor. Some of the Christian representatives were regarded as "puppets" of Tagiev and other wealthy Muslims. These accusations reinforce the impression of Muslim power and fit in with the classic patron-client networks so common in Middle Eastern cities. In these networks, wealthy and prominent men had "clients" whom they aided financially or socially and represented unofficially to higher authorities. The clients repaid with loyalty and service, especially in times of the decline or disintegration of central authority when the patrons became political or military leaders. Tagiev seems to have been such a patron in Baku Muslim society, and his gifts to the poor and to local students placed many in his debt. Nonetheless, in actual council business, evenhandedness generally prevailed. When money was apportioned for some repairs to a mosque, money was also designated for repairs to an Orthodox or Armenian Gregorian church. Much council business dealt with common concerns, such as water supply problems, sanitation provisions aimed at combating the frequent cholera epidemics, and ceaseless attempts to end the city's budget deficit in the face of rising expenses for services. These issues generated little or no ethnoreligious conflict, except for the occasional complaint that this or that quarter was neglected. It was usually Muslims who made the complaint.

The atmosphere of the council meetings ranged from the formal to the comic, and boisterous debates were characteristic. The greatest difficulty for the chairman, after reaching a quorum, was often simply to keep order. One of many shouting matches was caused by a request of the Nobel Brothers Petroleum Company to build a tunnel under a public street linking two company buildings. The request had been sent to the city's executive board (*Uprava*). The mayor (*gorodskaia golova*), in the face of this unprecedented proposal, decided to permit construction, but to put a tax on the tunnel because of the economic benefits it would yield for the company. The company's manager, infuriated, wrote a letter to the mayor charging there was no basis for levying the tax and that its aim was purely to line the pockets of city officials. The manager further demanded that the matter be taken to the city council. When the mayor did so, he explained that the executive board had initially considered sending the letter back to the company manager because of its tone, but instead decided to bring the matter to the council.

One of the Muslim representatives, Mehti Bek Hajinskii, rose to agree with the mayor. He called the letter an insult to the city's administration and urged that it be returned and the request denied. Another representative suggested the council ought not to risk ruining good relations with the Nobels by such action. "You call these good relations?" Hajinskii fumed: "They give us a slap. If they later offer sweets, should we forgive everything?" Debate raged in the council chambers between these two points of view, with the Muslim representatives generally siding with Hajinskii. In the end, the vote was taken and the majority went with Hajinskii—the letter was rejected, along with the request to build the tunnel, and a letter was to be sent "to St. Petersburg" (possibly to the main Nobel office) explaining that the council's action was based on the "incorrect tone" of the company manager's letter.[44]

This incident and others like it support a general impression created by reading the Baku press of this period: despite the economic power of the Armenians and the administrative and judicial power of the Russians, the Muslims felt themselves to be in control of Baku. It was their city; the others were newcomers.

The Baku press, after many vicissitudes, emerged as a powerful urban institution. The Russo-Ottoman War of 1876–77 led to the closing of the first Azerbaijani-language newspaper, *Ekinji*, which was followed by a ban on publication in Azerbaijani Turkish. The Russian-language daily *Kaspii* (Caspian), financed by Tagiev and edited by Topchibashev, began publication in the following decade and filled the gap in Muslim news. Publication of Azerbaijani-language newspapers and journals was again permitted in 1905. Thereafter, Baku's press appears to have been remarkably untouched by censorship. At a time when the death of monarchs even by natural causes did not appear in Moscow or St. Petersburg newspapers, the Baku press reported on political assassinations and revolution in neighboring Iran and Turkey, pogroms in Russia, and strikes and riots in Baku. The major Russian-language dailies, *Kaspii* and *Baku*, were widely read; they printed useful information such as ferry boat schedules, advertisements for professional services and shops, local news, and reports of city council meetings. Papers were read aloud in the teahouses (*chaihanes*), so that illiteracy was no obstacle to being well informed. It is difficult to gauge the impact of the press on the majority of the population, but as a medium of debate for the intelligentsia it was a vigorous and unparalleled forum.

Commentaries and interpretive articles in the Baku press were written by and for the intelligentsia of all nationalities. Muslims criticized the veiling and seclusion of women and supported educational reform. Writers not only reported but commented on speeches of city councilmen or government spokesmen in Tiflis or St. Petersburg. They established a dialogue between the organs of local government and the press. Writers also engaged in lively and personal attacks on one another. Many articles were written on the national question in the Empire, and here proposals for a decentralized government along the lines advocated by the Austrian Marxists and adopted by the Muslim Union were put forth. *Kaspii* also had a section on "The Muslim World," which covered news from the opening of mosques in India or Egypt to discussions of the national question of the Ottoman Empire, with its obvious implications for Russia's national problem. Agaoglu Ahmet (Ahmet Agaev), one of the Baku's leading Turcophile political activists and commentators often wrote for *Kaspii* on the inherently democratic nature of Islam. In 1905 Agaoglu edited the Azerbaijani-language *Hayat* (Life), a "spinoff" from *Kaspii*, and with Baju's other leading Turkish, Hüseinzade Ali (Ali Guseinov), edited and contributed to a series of Azerbaijani-language newspapers and journals in the following years.[45]

COMMUNITY AND CONFLICT

Baku was a violent city. Simple brigandage was common. Serious conflict erupted in two forms—class conflict, as embodied in the labor movement, and ethnoreligious conflict. The former made Baku a major center of the Empire's revolutionary movement. The latter made it one of the bloodiest. Conflict between ethnoreligious communities took place at every social level and in many forms, from business competition to outright violence. It was often intertwined with class conflict. The bloody riots that broke out intermittently during the strikes of 1905 were the worst eruption of ethnoreligious violence. The transformation from class to ethnoreligious conflict raised the issue of primary loyalty. Sometimes Muslim, Armenian, and Russian workers struck together against (usually Christian) employers. At crucial historical moments, however, this class solidarity broke down and violence shifted to ethnoreligious lines. One of the most important and knotty issues one can raise about the prewar history of Baku is the question of overriding allegiance. Although space prevents a full treatment of this complex subject here, we can look at events and possible causes.

Initially Baku's strikes occurred mainly in tobacco factories rather than in the oilfields. Workers demanded increased wages and improved conditions.[46] The Social Democrats saw opportunity in the oil city and, in the late 1890s, began traveling to Baku. By 1900 the Russian Social Democratic Workers' Party had an organization in Baku—the Baku Committee.

Long hours, primitive living conditions, and dangerous working conditions constituted the basis of workers' discontent. The drop in oil production after the peak production year 1901 led to increased unemployment. Oil prices stayed high as demand for fuel grew in the industrializing Empire and abroad. Workers must have felt (or been told) that owners could afford to grant wage increases, and began to strike and demonstrate. After a series of individual strikes in the spring of 1903, Baku's first general strike took place in July. The catalyst seemed to be the failure of one oil company to provide a promised wage increase. Dock and tram workers, electric utility workers, and others soon joined the striking oil workers, paralyzing Baku. Although troops were brought in and some returned to work, the strike spread to other cities in the Caucasus and beyond. Only through widespread use of force for more than a week was the strike finally defeated.[47]

The spread of the strike might be attributed to simmering discontent, agitation by the Baku Committee, or the workers' perception that they had reasonable chances for success. Soviet sources credit the sharpening of contradictions between the working class and the capitalists. Arthur Beeby-Thompson, a British oilman in Baku, explained the first oil strikes more concretely:

Until 1903 there had been no serious labour troubles on the oilfields and remarkably few complaints, although wages and living conditions were deplorable. Discontent had been brewing amongst the more intelligent sections, but some surprise was occasioned when without warning the Armenians, who comprised a considerable proportion of the artisan [skilled labor] element, struck, and with little opposition secured all their demands. Such an immediate and unexpected success encouraged the organizers to make new demands. . . . [T]hese events led the Tatar workmen to believe that there must be some magic in the word *strike* for which there was no word in their language, and they were in consequence induced to join in and put forward extravagant demands. . . . So frivolous became the demands that the authorities were compelled to intervene with the aid of troops to check the wave of sabotage, incendiarism, intimidation, and other forms of violence that originated from the groundless charges made by agitators.[48]

Baku's second general strike was called in December 1904 by labor leaders Lev and Ilya Shendrikov, who had shortly before been expelled from the Baku Committee for "economism" by the Bolshevik faction. The Bolsheviks and the Mensheviks were at this time, and until 1907, part of the same Social Democratic organization in Baku, but had already come into conflict over the question of economic versus political demands. After the Bolsheviks rose to preeminence in the Baku Committee in fall 1904, they expelled the Shendrikovs and others. The Shendrikov brothers promptly began to organize workers around economic demands and quickly acquired a large following. They concentrated on organizing Russian workers in Baku; the Bolsheviks countered by attempting to organize Muslim workers in the oil districts. In December the Shendrikovs were strong enough to call for a general strike. The workers responded, and the ensuing month-long strike led to the first industrywide labor contract in the Russian Empire. Referred to as the "crude oil (*mazut*) constitution," it established the nine-hour workday, abolished systematic daily overtime, set the length of work shifts, established a salary schedule, and settled various other issues of contention between labor and management.[49] The provisions were poorly observed by the owners, however, and many subsequent strikes demanded observance of this "December Agreement." The Shendrikov brothers remained the single most powerful organizers in Baku throughout 1905. One member of the Baku Committee wrote: "From the end of 1904 until the beginning of 1906, the Shendrikovtsy actually led the Baku masses, and we, with all our political influence, had to fall in line (at least in the area of the economic struggle) along their front."[50]

The most volatile year in Baku was 1905. Plans were underway for a demonstration to protest the Bloody Sunday shooting of peaceful demonstrators in front of the Winter Palace in St. Petersburg. Tensions had soared and labor organizers had failed to channel them. Ethnoreligious riots broke out between the Muslim and Armenian communities. As a result of these riots, which bloodied Baku streets from 6 to 9 February 1905, martial law was declared. The secular leaders and clergy of both the Muslim and Armenian communities established a Peace Committee. Mullahs and priests were urged to calm their followers. Twelve wealthy members of each community pledged to accept full personal financial responsibility for any future damage done by members of their own ethnoreligious community, including indemnification to families of the deceased.[51] The Baku Committee swung into action. It denounced the riots as "fratricide," and blamed police provocateurs for trying to sidetrack workers from the labor movement. They argued, in leaflets and speeches, that workers must not lose sight of their real enemies— the autocracy and capitalists of all nationalities.

Strikes resurged in March with the Transcaucasian Railway strike, which spread to Baku from Elizavetpol (Ganje, now Kirovobad). May Day demonstrations were accompanied by more strikes. Oil owners sought to pacify workers by offering economic concessions. Simultaneously they urged the Minister of Finance to arrange a labor-management conference in St. Petersburg to work out differences among labor representatives, business, and the state. The Ministry announced plans for the conference and labor leaders in Baku set about arranging elections for representatives.[52] Yet the strikes went on because of the disunity of the labor movement. Only some were appeased by the promise of a conference.

By the summer, Baku was declared to be in a state of siege. Throughout the summer countless individual strikes broke out in the oilfields and the city among dock workers, typographers, porters (ambals), phaeton drivers, textile workers, and others. During June and July 1905, approximately three-quarters of the industrial enterprises of Baku, including oilfields, refineries, and factories, were on strike.[53] A general strike was planned for mid-August by the Baku Committee, which was boycotting the proposed labor-management conference. The Shendrikovs meanwhile were busy with preparations for the elections of workers' representatives to the conference.

The general strike began, as planned, on 16 August 1905. Also on this day Muslim-Armenian clashes began in the town of Shusha, to the west of Baku. Despite the efforts of the local press and the Peace Committee to calm the populace, strikers soon abandoned their class action and rechanneled their energies. Muslims and Armenians began killing each other. These riots lasted from 20 to 26 August and ended with widespread arson in the oil districts. Far worse than earlier isolated fires, those of August 1905 destroyed huge areas of the oilfields and many workers' homes. Hundreds were killed and thousands wounded in this conflict. The industry suffered a further decline in output and many workers lost their jobs. The industrialists, angered by inadequate police protection, demanded deployment of a special police force in the oilfields, interest-free loans to finance reconstruction, and the relocation of workers' settlements away from the oilfields.

After the fires of August Baku, exhausted and broken, settled down. As the promulgation of the October Manifesto split the political opposition throughout the Empire, the Minister of Finance's labor-management conference had a dampening effect on Baku's labor movement. Concessions included an end to overtime work without pay, equalization of salaries in some job categories, and the creation of mediation boards in factories. The major achievement was the recognition of factory committees that had first materialized in May 1905. The workers of Baku were quite happy with the concessions—so much so that when the Shendrikovs called for a strike in December, they received only a tepid response. The revolution had petered out in Baku, though individual strikes continued into 1906. However, as a result of the failed strike call and subsequent Social Democratic accusations that the Shendrikovs were in the pay of capitalists, the brothers soon lost power; Social Democratic predominance, despite Menshevik-Bolshevik clashes, was assured.[54]

In the summer of 1906, there were strikes in response to the arrest or injury of workers by police. Baku was sufficiently quiet that martial law was lifted in October 1906, after being in effect for nineteen months. Although repression deepened throughout the Empire in 1906 and 1907, the earlier liberalism prevailed in Baku. A representative of the viceroy suggested a meeting between oil company owners and labor representatives. This proposal was put forth in the spring of 1907. Given the conservatism of the government, such a proposal is surprising enough, but then both the government and the oil companies had to wait for almost a year while the Bolshevik-led Union of Oil Workers, the Menshevik-dominated Union of Mechanical Workers and the labor press debated what guarantees they would *require* before participating. In the end, a strongly-worded letter from Prime Minister P. A. Stolypin to Vorontsov-Dashkov deploring the liberal approach to "labor leaders and revolutionaries" put an end to the conference. Ensuing arrests and repression soon crushed the trade union movement in the Caucasus.[55]

Baku remained pacific until the summer of 1913. Even the Lena Goldfield incident of April 1912, in which the shooting of several unarmed strikers inflamed the labor movement elsewhere in the Empire, evoked little response in Baku. Because of police vigilance, socialist agitators had been exiled or forced underground, and trade unions had been strangled. Baku's enlarged police force seems also to have controlled ethnoreligious violence. The absence of further clashes after the costly fires of August 1905 until the disintegration of effective control in 1918 lends validity to the charge of provocation. The use of intercommunal conflict to distract workers from strikes, if this was official policy, had proven to be expensive.

Oil prices rose in 1913. Perhaps this or agitation by the skeleton Bolshevik underground made workers feel they stood to gain some concessions from owners. A few scattered strikes in the spring of 1913 blossomed into a revitalized labor movement in the heat of summer.

Exiled labor activists began to return to Baku. In July 1913 over seven
hundred workers struck at the Rothschild oilfields in Balakhany. By the
end of the month, 19,000 workers were on strike in eighty-eight firms.

In 1914 the number of strikes in Baku had reached the 1905 level.
Over 10,000 workers celebrated May Day 1914. A strike at the Mirzoev
oil company at the end of May 1914 led to nearly 20,000 workers going
on strike. The situation remained fluid. Whole firms returned to work,
with or without the promise of concessions from company owners;
others joined the strike. By June 30,000 were striking. The government
used troops to try to force the workers back to their jobs. Strikers
attacked non-striking workers. Police troops drove striking workers
from their company-owned homes. Owners were now less conciliatory.
Perhaps they were more aware of the left and its goals. Certainly they
were under government pressure, at least to the extent that they were
forbidden to discuss any "political" demands. But it is clear from their
own records that the decisive factor in their change of attitude was the
refusal of striking workers to settle with individual employers. This
demand for an industry-wide settlement bespoke a new-found solidarity. Material hardship began to take a serious toll on the workers and
their families; by the end of July only about 9,500 workers were still
refusing to return to work. Only the beginning of the war and mobilization, however, put an end to the crisis.[56]

WHY IN BAKU?

Certain characteristics of Baku's urban environment contributed
to, even caused, the outbreaks of the prewar period. Baku shared the
same problems of any industrializing town—overcrowding, masses of
uprooted immigrants from the countryside, inadequacy of city services,
the breakdown of the family and other traditional structures. Yet conditions specific to Baku exacerbated the conventional problems created by
rapid growth and industrialization.

The first of these conditions concerns the radically different, traditionally antagonistic cultures of the populace, both indigenous and
immigrant. Overt tension existed primarily between the two groups
native to this area, the Azerbaijani Turks and the Armenians, both of
whom had lived throughout Transcaucasus and northern Iran for many
centuries. Antagonism between these two groups sharpened in the close
physical proximity of the urban setting. More important was the rise of
Armenian nationalism, Pan-Islamism, and Pan-Turkism, all articulate
and dynamic movements of the late nineteenth century. The leaders of
the two camps (Pan-Islamism and Pan-Turkism complemented one
another for Russia's Muslims) formulated ideologies and advanced ter-
ritorial demands that denied or ignored those of the other. None of these

movements originated in Baku, and their broader conflicts had reper-
cussions far beyond the conflicts that took place there. But ideologists
and political activists of these movements worked in Baku, sowed seeds
of suspicion and hatred in the fertile ground of their respective communities.

However, it would be uninstructive and incorrect to dismiss the
problem solely as the work of fanatics. Armenians and Muslims had
always been proud of who they were; the new ideologies reinforced
identities and pride, but also pejorative stereotypes and distrust.
Perhaps inevitably the glorification of one culture leads to the denigra-
tion of others, if only by implication. Thus Muslims and Armenians felt
threatened not only by the demands of each other's extremists, but by
the very dynamism of each other's renaissances.

A second contributory factor is closely related to the first. Both the
Muslim and Armenian communities swelled with immigrants from
other areas of Transcaucasia and from abroad. Those Armenians from
the Ottoman Empire and Turks and Persians from Iran had come from
areas in which violence had already become a norm. Especially important for Baku were the Armenian-Turkish conflicts of Anatolia. Armenian immigrants to Baku were again facing a large Muslim Turkish
community, a condition militating toward retaliation in a new context
for injuries suffered in the old. Finally, the influx of huge numbers of
Russians from central and southern provinces of the Empire added new
competitors for jobs and increased the number of Christians, the new
majority of Baku. For many Muslims, it seemed the Islamic way of life
was under siege.

Commercial competition was another factor contributing to violence in the oil city. Armenian and Muslim merchants had long
competed in the Caspian area; the influx of wealth raised the stakes,
enlivened traditional competition, and accentuated deep-seated antagonism. In the oil industry, the situation was somewhat more complex.
In the upper echelons of the oil hierarchy, the ethnoreligious question
was not at issue. Those few Muslims who were among the very wealthiest of oil men did not behave as partisans in their business dealings
despite their influential role as cultural and social leaders of their
community. Thus oil company owners could present a united front
against the demands of workers. The workers themselves never
attained such consistent solidarity.

The major obstacle to enduring proletarian solidarity was the tension between Muslims and Christians. Muslim distrust of Christians
was the main obstacle to propaganda work by the Social Democrats of
Baku, who were primarily Russian, Armenian, and Georgian; it was for
this reason that the Baku Committee found the Muslim Social Democratic Hümmät indispensable. When Muslims did participate in
strikes—and we have ample evidence that they did[57]—they frequently

advanced such "religious" demands as prayer time without loss of pay, separate water carriers and bakers (items that passed through the hands of unbelievers were widely regarded as unclean), and the building of a mosque in the oil districts. The traditional, religious-based tensions were amplified by the coincidence of ethnoreligious lines with job categories. Muslims constituted the bulk of the poorly paid unskilled workers, while Christians generally filled the skilled, technical, white-collar, and managerial posts. Soviet and other Marxist writings stress the multinational character of Baku's proletariat and its class solidarity; ironically, because of its multinational composition, the labor movement carried within itself in true Marxist fashion the seeds of its own degeneration into ethnoreligious conflict.

Political factors also shaped Baku's conflicts. Transcaucasia was a colony of the Russian Empire and Baku a seat of Russian colonial administration. With the possible exception of Tiflis, the colonial status of the Caucasus was nowhere as clear as in Baku with its large and visible Russian population, Russian-dominated administrative, judicial, and police surveillance structures, and Russian interest in oil production and the transportation network that brought the oil to Russian markets. Furthermore, rule by Russian law had gradually displaced Islamic law in the decades since the conquest. Declarations of states of emergency and martial law brought Russian soldiers and Cossacks. Publication in the indigenous language had been banned for many years. Control engendered resentment, though the power of the Russian state discouraged open expression; it was channeled into subtler forms. The subtlety of its expression, however, does not mean resentment was negligible. Indeed, the Muslim community of Baku was fully part of the colonial world which delighted in Russia's defeat by an Asian power in the Russo-Japanese War (1904–1905) and took heart in revolutions in Iran (1905–11) and Turkey (1908).

Because of these various levels of discontentment Baku became fertile ground for Marxist agitation, itself another factor in Baku's conflict pattern. Baku's Social Democrats, the most successful of the radical groups, exploited actual discontent and injustice. They understood the nature of latent antagonism and attempted to channel it; they offered hope of a better life, one in which material need would be satisfied and in which ethnoreligious differences would be transcended. Finally, they offered a concrete program of action for achieving their utopian goals. Their program, specifically that of the Bolshevik faction, called for strikes, demonstrations, and the like, but even more important, for political education. The former without the latter would, for the Leninists, constitute a betrayal of the revolutionary goal.

These cultural, social, economic, and political factors provide a framework for analyzing two of the most volatile issues of Baku's history of this period—the degeneration of strikes into ethnoreligious riots in 1905 and the development of Azerbaijani Turkish nationalism. Contemporary investigators were never able to determine the immediate causes of the ethnoreligious riots of 1905. Any attempt to explain these outbreaks must take into account both underlying tensions and immediate provocations. Traditional religious and cultural antagonism, long-standing commercial rivalry which was intensified by Baku's growing commercial-industrial market, sharply differentiated employment stratification, and ideas and demands associated with nascent nationalism all helped kindle the conflict. Two outbreaks in 1905 came during periods of prolonged agitation on the labor front—the first in connection with Bloody Sunday, the second in preparation for the August general strike. Agitators aroused anger, but because of the strength of ethnoreligious feelings were unable to control its manifestations. Rumors then provided the catalyst needed to turn the tide of human energy. In one instance word spread that the Armenians were arming for an attack on the Muslim quarters; in another, that police would not interfere if the Muslims wanted to settle old scores with Armenians. As was the case in the pogroms against the Jews elsewhere in the Empire, there is clear evidence of instigation by agent provocateurs. In Baku the goal was to divert energy and attention from the labor movement. But the extent to which the same striking workers turned to intercommunal violence is unclear.

Some community leaders suggested that new Muslim immigrants from the countryside were largely responsible because of their rural conflicts with Armenians and because they were allegedly a more malleable element in the hands of provocateurs.[58] Though never mentioned in this connection, it is also possible that the bazaar merchants (*bazari*—the thousands of *meshchane* in the censuses), mirroring the religious conservatism and the volatile behavior of their Iranian counterparts, responded to urban tensions, rumors, or provocation with violence. The same might be said of the Armenian lower classes, including new migrants from the Caucasian countryside and the Ottoman Empire, where conflict with the Turks of Anatolia had already become violent. Furthermore, the activities of the radical Armenian nationalist Dashnaktsiutiun Party inflamed anti-Turk sentiments and gave them direction. Because the outbreaks of February and August 1905 began in the city proper rather than the oil districts, it seems likely that these lower urban classes, rather than the oil workers, played a key instigative role in the violence.

Conflict-ridden Baku was also the birthplace of Azerbaijani Turkish national consciousness, which first stirred among the community's intelligentsia. This group was better able than others to comprehend the roots and nature of conflict in Baku as well as parallel conflicts elsewhere in the Empire, the region, and the world. Although they were active on the cultural and political scenes, the intelligentsia's ultimate and most lasting response was in the realm of ideas. The Azerbaijani Turks' concern with their own local language, history, and education had come on the heels of the Russian conquest when they were faced with Russia's obvious military might and cultural flourishing. Later the great ideas of the nineteenth century also penetrated Baku—socialism and nationalism, Pan-Islamism and Pan-Turkism. These set the parameters within which Baku's Muslims sought answers to many ideological and political dilemmas.

Yet local concerns were decisive. Under the inescapable pressures of Baku's daily life—political discrimination from the Russian colonial rulers and economic competition from the powerful Armenian bourgeoisie—the Azerbaijani Turks' "localism" came to dominate Baku's political environment and to command the loyalty of the intelligentsia and the upper classes. Indeed, the beginning of true national consciousness came not with the Azerbaijani Turks' differentiation from the Christians with whom they had lived for centuries and in contrast to whom they had always recognized their own distinctness, but rather with the positive assertion of the uniqueness that distinguished them from other Muslim and Turkic peoples. For this reason, their involvement with local problems at the expense of commitment to Empire-wide Muslim movements must be recognized as a fundamental stage in their national formation.

The urban environment generally provides a high-tension context in which cultural, social, economic, political, and even psychological and emotional pressures are brought to bear with excruciating urgency. This was true for Baku in a particular way which might be described in terms of frontiers. In many senses Baku had always been a frontier town. For over ten centuries, it lay on the frontier between the Christian West and the Muslim East. Islamic civilization had shaped the society for over a millennium and gave Baku its underlying character. Industrial-era Baku was also a product of the Russian colonial system and the efforts of its multinational immigrant population: ethnic and colonial frontiers ran through Baku. The oil industry placed the city on the frontier of the Industrial Age, and Baku thus enjoyed the technological and cultural benefits of wealth and development. It also suffered the prejudice, violence, and bloodshed of an era of social, ideological, and political revolutions.

The Azerbaijani Turks asserted themselves not only as commercial competitors and political actors, but as modern heirs to their Turkic traditions and high Islamic culture. Their ideas and spheres of cultural and intellectual activity suggest not a rejection of their own heritage to adopt wholesale the cultural practices of powerful conquerors (a practice that characterized other colonial elites), but recognition and utilization of traditional strengths in new situations. They strove to fit into the contemporary world while sustaining their lifeline to the past.

NOTES

I wish to thank the International Research and Exchanges Board for support during 1980–81 when I was researching this paper in Baku. Thanks also go to the Russian Research Center of Harvard University for support and assistance during the writing of this paper, and to particular Fellows of the Center for their many helpful discussions, especially Olga Andriewsky and Teresa Rakowska-Harmstone.

1. The Turks of Azerbaijan are of the southwestern branch of the Oguz Turks, as are the Turks of Anatolia. Their languages are very similar and mutually intelligible. On the general history of the eastern Caucasus (now the Azerbaijan Soviet Socialist Republic), see the three-volume work by I. A. Guseinov et al., *Istoriia Azerbaidzhana* (Baku, 1960–63); also the following encyclopedias: *Azärbayjan Sovet Ensiklopediyasy (ASE)* under the entry *Baky*; all editions of the *Bol'shaia Sovetskaia entsiklopediia*, under entries Baku and Azerbaidzhan; either edition of *Encyclopedia Islam (EI)* under entries Baku or Sharwan. On the Shirvanshah dynasties, see V. Minorskii, trans., *A History of Sharvan and Darbend in the X–XI Centuries* (Cambridge, 1958), and *EI* under Sharwan (by V. V. Bartold). On the Russian conquest of the Caucasus, see J. Baddeley, *Russian Conquest of the Caucasus* (London, 1907), and Muriel Atkin's *Russia and Iran, 1780–1828* (Minneapolis, 1980).

2. The majority of Muslims by the nineteenth century were of the Shi'i sect, that is, those who believe the only legitimate leader of the community (Imam) is a descendant of the Prophet Muhammad through his cousin and son-in-law Ali and daughter Fatima. As for the other communities, we should note that virtually all of the Russians, Ukrainians, and Belorussians (who were often counted together because of the small number of the latter two groups) were Orthodox, with only a small number of Old Believers. The Armenians were all Gregorian, with only a tiny number of Catholics. The Armenian Gregorian Church had been an independent body from the time of the Armenians' conversion to Christianity in the fourth century.

3. Essad Bey, *Blood and Oil in the Orient* (New York, 1934), p. 1.

4. On the early years of Russian rule, see Atkin, *Russia and Iran*.

5. On population in this period, *ASE*, p. 551, gives an 1807 population of 3,000, an 1849 figure of 8,120; *EI²*, p. 967, in an article by A. Bennigsen, gives an early nineteenth-century figure of 5,000; and an 1859 figure of 13,000. A. Mil'man, *Politicheskii stroi Azerbaidzhana v XIX-nachale XX vekov* (Baku, 1966) states that the population in 1854–57 was 8,374, in 1874, 14,577. The population survey *Spiski naselennykh mest Rossiiskoi imperii* (Tiflis, 1870) gives the Baku population as 12,000 between the years 1859 and 1864.

6. A. Beeby-Thompson, *Oil Pioneer* (London, 1961), pp. 66–67.

7 These figures represent my conversion from poods as given in K. A. Pazhitnov, *Ocherki po istorii bakinskoi neftedobyvaiushchei promyshlennosti* (Moscow, 1940), p. 97, and, for the 1901 figure, M. A. Musaev, "Razvitie torgovli goroda Baku v period kapitalizma (1860–1917 gg)" (Ph. D. dissertation, Academy of Sciences of the Azerbaijan SSR Baku, 1970), p. 50: 1872—1,395 poods; 1897—421,727 poods; 1901—671,000,000 poods.

8. John McKay, "Entrepreneurship and the Emergence of the Russian Petroleum Industry, 1813–1883," in *Research on Economic History: A Research Annual*, ed. Paul Uselding (Greenwich, Conn., 1983), p. 54. McKay's is the clearest explanation of the changes in landholding. He also demonstrates that the Nobel capital was of Russian rather than foreign origin. For names of those who purchased parcels in the first auction (and the value and number of parcels purchased) see S. Gulishambarov, *Ocherki fabrik i zavodov bakinskoi gubernii* (Tiflis, 1870), p. 25.

9. On the Nobels, see McKay, "Entrepreneurship," and Robert Tolf, *The Russian Rockefellers: The Saga of the Nobel Family and the Russian Oil Industry* (Stanford, 1976).

10. McKay, "Entrepreneurship," p. 86.

11. A. A. Umaev, and A. M. Kasumov, "Rol' bankskogo i rostovshchiskogo kapitala v ekonomicheskom razvitii dorevoliutsionnogo Azerbaidzhana," in *Materialy po ekonomicheskoi istorii Azerbaidzhana* (Baku, 1970), p. 41. Hereafter, *Materialy*.

12. *Ezhegodnik Ministerstva finansov*, v. 25 (1899).

13. Guseinov, et al., 2:234; Dina Sadyg kizi Guseinova, "Razvitie morskogo transporta, formirovanie kadrov rabochikh-moriakov Azerbaidzhana i ikh revoliutsionnye vystupleniia (90-e gody xix v.–1907 g)" (Candidate dissertation, Baku, 1975), p. 17.

14. Figures from Guseinova, "Razvitie," p. 17, citing *Otchet nachal'niki bakinskogo porta za 1909 g.*

15. M. A. Ismailov, "Gornaia promyshlennost' i mekhanicheskoe proizvodstvo Azerbaidzhana v period kapitalizma," in *Materialy*, pp. 81–85.

16. On this topic, see Musaev's dissertation "Razvitie" and his subsequent monographs based thereon: *XX asrin ävvälärnda Baky shähärinin tijareti (1900–1917)* (Baku, 1975), and *XIX äsrin sonlarynda Baku shähärinin tijareti (1883–1900)* (Baku, 1972).

17. Musaev, "Razvitie," p. 32, 52.

18. Census data are drawn from *Pervaia vseobshchaia perepis' naseleniia rossiiskoi imperii, 1897 g.*, v. 61 (Bakinskaia guberniia) (St. Petersburg, 1905), hereafter *Perepis' 1897*; *Baku po perepisi 22 oktiabria 1903* (Baku, 1905), hereafter *Perepis' 1903*; and *Baku po perepisi 22 oktiabria 1913* (Baku, 1916), hereafter *Perepis' 1913*.

19. Iranian languages, which include Persian, Kurdish, Baluchi, Tajiki, and Tati, are Indo-European languages. Turkic languages are Altaic languages; they differ significantly from Indo-European languages. Azerbaijani Turkish, more than Anatolian Turkish, reflects considerable Persian influence in pronunciation, vocabulary, and, to a lesser degree, syntax.

20. An interesting description of life in the oil districts and socialist agitation there may be found in the memoirs of Eva Broido, a Menshevik agitator, *Memoirs of a Revolutionary*, trans. Vera Broido (London, 1967).

21. On accident and injury rates, see S. and L. Pershke, *Russkaia neftianaia promyshlennost', ee razvitie i sovremennoe polozhenie v statisticheskikh dannykh* (Tiflis, 1913) and on workers' families, A. D. Bok, "Usloviia byta rabochikh-neftianikov g.Baku," in *Usloviia byta rabochikh dorevoliutsionnoi Rossii* (Moscow, 1958).

22. For works on cities of the Muslim world, the reader could begin with Ibn Khaldun, *The Muqaddimah: An Introduction to History*, trans. Franz Rosenthal, ed. N. J. Dawood (New York, 1976), esp. Chapter 4; Albert Hourani and S. M. Stern, eds., *The Islamic City* (Oxford, 1970); and Ira Lapidus, *Muslim Cities in the Later Middle Ages* (Cambridge, Mass., 1967).

23. Report of U.S. Vice-Consul in Batum F. W. Caldwell, reported in *Oildom* (Bayonne, N.J., 1913), 3:131–32.

24. S. S. Fatullaev, *Gradostroitel'stvo Baku XIX–nachala XX vekov* (Leningrad, 1978) is an excellent survey of period construction.

25. Beeby-Thompson, *Oil Pioneer*, p. 55.

26. A. Mil'man, *Politicheskii stroi Azerbaidzhana v XIX–nachale XX vekov* (Baku, 1966), pp. 211–12.

27. *Baku*, 7 August and 12 September 1906; 13 January 1907; for more information on these conferences, see my forthcoming article "Dilemmas of Education Reform: The 1906 Muslim Teachers' Conference in Baku," in *Cahiers du Monde Russe et Sovietique* (1986).

28. *Kaspii*, 24 May 1908.

29. Mullahs are prayer leaders and teachers; ulama (sing. *alim*) are Muslim religious scholars, of which there were few if any in the Caucasus in this period. We cannot properly refer to a Muslim clergy, since in Islam there can be no clergy in the Christian sense—i.e., ministers who act as intermediaries between God and the believer such as in administering sacraments. For more on the religious establishment of Azerbaijan in the prewar period, see my "The Forgotten Factor: The Shi'i Mullahs of Pre-Revolutionary Baku," in the forthcoming *festschrift* in honor of Alexandre Bennigsen edited by Chantal Lemercier-Quelquejay and S. Enders Wimbush.

30. The major societies for adult education and other cultural activities were Näshr Maarif and the Hummat-affiliated Nijat. See note 33, below.

31. *Perepis' 1913*, v. 3, pt. 1, p. 11.

32. Mirza Fath Ali Akhundov (Akhundzade) (1812–1878), regarded as the father of Azerbaijani theater, was author of many satires of contemporary social mores. He was particularly critical of religious tradition and mullahs. One of his translators referred to him as the "Moliere of the Orient." He began his career as a translator in the tsarist administration in Tiflis and throughout his life advocated the learning and use of the Russian language. He was declared *kafir* (unbeliever) by the Shi'i ulama of Iran.

33. Most recent authors accept the notion that an ethnic group can be "other-identified," but a nation must be "self-identified." I am accepting that idea here. I am also in this context reserving the application of the term "nationalism" for that time when a nation advances a demand for independence. Among the most useful works on this subject are those of Walker Connor, especially his "A Nation Is a Nation, Is a State, Is an Ethnic Group, Is a . . . " in *Ethnic and Racial Studies*, I (October 1978):377–400. I am indebted to Prof. Teresa Rakowska-Harmstone for bringing this work to my attention, as well as for helpful discussions on this topic. On nationalism and the cultural-enlightenment movement in Baku, see my "The Azerbaijani Bourgeoisie and the Cultural-Enlightenment Movement in Baku: First Step towards Nationalism," in Ronald G. Suny, ed., *Transcaucasia: Nationalism and Social Change: Essays in the History of Armenia, Azerbaijan, and Georgia* (Ann Arbor, 1983).

34. On the Hümmät Party, see Tadeusz Swietochowski, "Himmat Party: Socialism and the National Question in Russian Azerbaijan, 1904–1920," in *Cahiers du Monde Russe et Sovietique*, 19, nos. 1–2 (1978):119–42.

35. Firuddin Köcherli, *Marksizm-Leninizm vä Azärbayjanda demokratik ijtimai fikir* (Baku, 1976), pp. 23–24, 52.

36. A. Arsharuni and Kh. Gabidullin, *Ocherki panislamizma i pantiurkizma v Rossii* (Moscow, 1931), on both the Muslim Congresses and the Muslim Union.

37. In English, see Alexandre Bennigsen and Chantal Lemercier-

Quelquejay, *Islam in the Soviet Union* (London, 1976), on the Muslim Union and various individual participants.

38. We will not deal with the Musavat Party here because most of its activity took place during the war, and until 1920 when the independent Azerbaijani republic was absorbed into Soviet Russia. For a history of the Party and the nationalist movement in Azerbaijan in this period, see the forthcoming monograph by Tadeusz Swietochowski.

39. Kurban Said (pseud.) *Ali and Nino*, trans. Jenia Graman (New York, 1972), was written in German and first published in 1937. It is reputed to be the work of an Azerbaijani Turk who fled Baku in 1920. Some believe he is also Essad Bey. See note 3.

40. *Ibid*, pp. 73–74.

41. Max Weber in *The City*, trans. and ed. Don Martindale and Gertrude Neuwirth (New York, 1958), argues the necessity of urban self-rule as precondition for the existence of a city; on the general provisions of these urban reforms, see the general introduction to this volume or Mil'man, *Politicheskii stroi*, which also gives data on the reforms' application in Azerbaijan. See also "Gorodskaia duma" in *Entsiklopedicheskii slovar* (St. Petersburg, 1890–1904).

42. See note 27. Mil'man, *Politicheskii stroi*, pp. 211–12.

43. Mil'man, p. 218.

44. *Kaspii*, June 6, 1980.

45. Agaoglu (1865–1939) and Hüseinzade (1864–1941) are included in Bennigsen and Lemercier-Quelquejay, *Islam*. The newspapers and journals to which they contributed included *Täzä Häyat* (new life), *Füyüzat* [abundance] (of which Hüseinzade was editor), and *Irshad* [guide], of which Agaoglu was editor).

46. Guseinov, et al., v 2, pp. 297–302, on the pre–1903 strikes.

47. Ibid., p. 494.

48. Beeby-Thompson, *Oil Pioneer*, pp. 72–73.

49. *Rabochee dvizhenie v Baku v period pervoi russkoi revoliutsii; dokumenty i materialy* (Baku, 1962), pp. 34–36.

50. Ronald G. Suny, *The Baku Commune, 1917–1918: Class and Nationality in the Russian Revolution* (Princeton, 1972), p. 35; for more detail on the Shrendrikovs see his "Labor and Liquidators: Revolutionaries and the 'Reaction' in Baku, May 1908–April 1912," *Slavic Review*, 34 (1975):319–40.

51. Numerous articles in *Baku*, 1905, especially July 21 and August 11 issues. The proposal that twelve members of each community be responsible for outbreaks is in September 11, 1905 issue.

52. Suny, *Baku Commune*, pp. 38–39.

53. Guseinov, et al., v. 2, p. 567.

54. Suny, *Baku Commune*, p. 39.

55. Ronald G. Suny, "A Journeyman for the Revolution: Stalin and the Labor Movement in Baku, June 1907–May 1908," *Soviet Studies*, no. 3 (1971):373–94.

56. On the strike movement during the war years, see Suny, *Baku Commune*, and various Russian-language sources cited in the bibliographic note at the end of this article; on the role of the Muslim workers in the prewar strike movement, see my "Muslim Workers and the Labor Movement in Pre-War Baku," paper presented at the First International Turkic Studies Conference, May 1983, Bloomington, Indiana.

57. See note 56 and my bibliographical note for sources on this topic.

58. This is reflected in numerous press commentaries of the time and is articulated by Meshadi Azizbekov (1876–1918), an engineer by profession and member of RSDWP, the Hümmät, later the Baku City Council, and, in 1918, the

Baku Commune. In his testimony before the Baku Adovcate's Special Commission on the causes of the riots, he argued that the disturbances could not have taken place without the acquiescence of the police. See Tsentral'nyi gosudarstrennyi istoricheskii arkhiv Azerbaidzhanskoi SSR (Baku), *fond* 486.

BIBLIOGRAPHICAL NOTE

The vast bulk of literature on Baku has, until recently, focused on the oil industry and the labor movement. As a result, the picture of Baku which these works produced suggested the city was nothing more than a European industrial enclave with an inconsequential history, lying in a faceless hinterland. Muslims seemed not to exist. Only within the last fifteen years, and primarily as a result of efforts by Azerbaijani Turkish scholars themselves, have we begun to see scholarly works that reflect Baku's diversity.

For a general history of Baku, the standard work, A. I. Guseinov et al., *Istoriia Azerbaidzhana*, 3 vols. (Baku, 1963), is the most logical starting point despite its lack of footnotes and need of revision. Also of interest are the *Encyclopedia of Islam* (both editions) under entries Baku and Sharwan; and the newly published *Azärbayjan Sovet Ensiklopediyasy* (Baku, 1976–) under the entry *Baky*. Invaluable for the industrial period are travelers' accounts: Charles Marvin, *Land of the Eternal Fire* (London, 1884), and Luigi Villari, *Fire and Sword in the Caucasus* (London, 1906), although one must keep in mind the Eurocentric views of these writers. On the city's construction, see Sh. S. Fatullaev, *Gradostroitel'stvo Baku XIX–nachala XX vekov* (Leningrad, 1978). The only source on administration is A. Mil'man, *Politicheskii stroi Azerbaidzhana XIX–nachale XX vekov* (Baku, 1966), but some of the data cited by Mil'man should be checked against *Entsiklopedicheskii slovar'* (St. Petersburg, 1890–1904), especially on regulations governing elections.

As noted, industrial development was the main focus of historians and contemporary observers. Many of the basic works can be found in the bibliography in each volume of Guseinov et al. More recent works include Suleiman S. Aliiarov, *Neftianye monopolii v Azerbaidzhane v period pervoi mirovoi voiny* (Baku, 1974), and John McKay's outstanding "Entrepreneurship and the Emergence of the Russian Petroleum Industry, 1813–1883," in *Research on Economic History: A Research Annual* (Greenwich, Conn., 1983). General information on Baku's industrial development can be found in various works by A. S. Sumbatzade (cited in Guseinov et al., v.2), especially his *Prisoedinenie Azerbaidzhana k Rossii i ego progressivnye posledstviia v oblasti ekonomiki i kultury* (Baku, 1955). M. A. Ismailov's *Promyshlennost' Baku v nachale XX veka* (Baku, 1976) is concise and based entirely on archival materials and other primary sources. Trade in general is treated in two monographs by M. A. Musaev, *XIX äsrin sonlarynda Baky shähärinin tijareti (1883–1900)* (Baku, 1972), and *XX äsrin ävvälärindä Baky shähärinin tijareti (1900–1917)* (Baku, 1974). Musaev uses archival materials and raises potentially controversial issues such as nationalities of merchants and their spheres of activity.

On the labor movement there are documents such as *Rabochee dvizhenie v Baku v gody pervoi russkoi revoliutsii; dokumenty i materialy* (Baku, 1962). Also useful are countless memoirs, published speeches and writings of participants in the labor movement, and reports by observers. Eva Broido's memoirs are cited in the Notes, and others are cited in Ronald G. Suny's *Baku Commune: Class and Nationality in the Russian Revolution* (Princeton, 1972). In addition, one should consult published speeches and writings of Nariman Narimanov, Meshadi Azizbekov, and S. M. Efendiev's *Iz istorii revoliutsionnogo dvizheniia azerbaidzhanskogo proletariata* (Baku, 1957). Space constraints prevent a listing of the extensive secondary literature on the labor movement in Baku.

The political, intellectual, and social aspects of Baku's history have been most neglected despite their richness and complexity. An excellent source for these topics is the Baku press which is discussed by Alexandre Bennigsen and Chantal Lemercier-Quelquejay in *La Presse et le Mouvement National chez les Musulmans de Russie avant 1920* (Paris, 1964). The press itself is crucial. Microfilm copies of *Mir Islama*, published 1911–13 in St. Petersburg, and *Kaspii* (partial) are available at the University of Chicago, while many Turkic-language Baku papers are in Columbia University's collection. Baku's first Turkic-language newspaper, *Ekinji*, has been published in monograph form in the current (Cyrillic) orthography (Baku, 1979). Secondary sources covering social, intellectual, and political history include Bennigsen and Lemercier-Quelquejay's *Islam in the Soviet Union* (London, 1967) and Bennigsen and S. Enders Wimbush, *Muslim National Communism in the Soviet Union* (Chicago, 1979). Also see various entries in the *Modern Encyclopedia of Russian and Soviet History* (e.g., Baku Commissars, Ali Guseinov, Hümmät, etc.) and relevant articles in R. G. Suny, ed., *Transcaucasia: Nationalism and Social Change* (Ann Arbor, 1983), as well as a forthcoming monograph by Tadeusz Swietochowski on the history of the Azerbaijani national movement. Other works on political life include *Istoriia kommunisticheskoi partii Azerbaidzhana* (Baku, 1959) and *Ocherki istorii kommunisticheskoi partii Azerbaidzhana* (Baku, 1963), V. Iu. Samedov *Rasprostranenie marksizma-leninizma v Azerbaidzhana* (Baku, 1966), and the satirical journals of the early twentieth century, *Molla Nasrettin* and *Zanbur*, both in the rare book collection of the University of Chicago. *Azerbaycan Yurt Bilgisi*, also available at University of Chicago, was an emigre journal published in the 1930s in Turkey. Among its contributors were such nationalist leaders as Mehmet Emin Rasulzade and Fath Ali Khankhoilu (Khankhoiskii).

The *Putevoditel'* to the Tsentral'nyi gosudarstvennyi istoricheskii arkhiv Azerbaidzhana (in Baku) can be found at the University of Illinois (Urbana), which also has scattered holdings of such useful prerevolutionary handbooks as *Kavkazskii kalendar*.

10.

Urban Revolution in the Late Russian Empire

DANIEL R. BROWER

Beneath the colorful diversity of city histories presented in this volume, there exists a commonality of subjects important to an understanding of the evolution of the Russian Empire from the mid-nineteenth to the early twentieth centuries. These cities, like the rest of the country, felt the impact of rapid industrial and commercial development and of internal population migration. Growing hostility among ethnic groups appeared in the border-lands, and class conflict erupted between workers and capitalists in the industrial cities. In municipal councils a new political leadership emerged which had to deal with a rapidly growing, turbulent urban population and at the same time to confront an authoritarian, often hostile autocratic regime. The urban perspective provides a clear focus on trends which fundamentally altered social and political relations in the decades before the fall of the Empire. These essays offer new insight into the problem that transcends all other issues of late tsarist history: namely, the origins of the great revolutionary upheaval of 1917. Thus they constitute an important contribution to the historical literature on the last years of the Russian Empire.

Of even greater interest than their topical coverage, in my opinion, is their exploration of a new area of Russian social history. From these individual "urban biographies," one can extract the outlines of Russian urban history, a subject as yet scarcely opened, in those decades of profound change. They suggest the existence of a pattern of urban development similar in some ways to that of Western Europe yet in others unique. In turn, this synthesis of urban change fits into the still larger story of the transformation of Russian society in the late tsarist period. The goal of this concluding chapter is to seek out that underlying pattern of urbanization and to assess its significance in the context of Russian social and political history. It represents a challenging task.

It is so in part as a result of the conceptual confusion regarding the historical significance of urbanization. One concept proposed in recent years to interpret global social change of particular relevance to urban development is modernization. It enjoyed a period of considerable vogue in the 1960s, when the creation of new states in formerly colonial lands and an optimistic faith in progress through national self-determination led American social scientists to look for a single dominant global trend. The modernization theories, though diverse in detail, tended in the words of one critic, Dean Tipps, "to evaluate the progress of nations . . . by their proximity to the institutions and values of Western, and particularly Anglo-American societies.[1] Countries such as Russia that experienced violent revolutions deviated from the proper path of political and social development. Revolution revealed political backwardness. In the opinion of the political scientist Samuel Huntington, its occurrence was an indication of the failure of modernization brought about when "the processes of . . . political development have lagged behind the processes of social and economic change."[2] The term "modernization" created an ahistorical standard of judgment. Research into the development of "modernizing" countries, past and present, examined such important phenomena as urbanization from the perspective of the Western historical experience. In modern Russian history this tendency gained strength by drawing on the venerable practice of Westernized Russian intellectuals of making invidious comparisons between contemporary conditions in their country and the West.

William Blackwell, the author of the conclusion to a previous volume of essays devoted to Russian urban history, used this concept to survey ten centuries in the history of cities in Russia. Modernization provided him with criteria of historical change by which to periodize Russian urban development, which he suggested moved from its "premodern" to its "modernizing" phase around the year 1860. Later in his essay, he refined his usage of the term by differentiating between constructive "dynamic modernization," in which he included "expanding cities" and "sophisticated urban culture," and destructive "breakdown," by which he designated "poverty, slums, social disorientation, and increasing political instability."[3] Following thus in the judgmental tradition of the theorists of modernization, he could both periodize Russian urban history and distinguish between good and bad aspects of social change by referring to a "modern" condition. Blackwell's working definition, derived from the writing of the historian Cyril Black,

associated modernization with a formative process involving "the impact on societies of the scientific and technological revolution."[4]

Such vague critieria are easily broadened, as Tipps has observed, to
"encompass within a single concept virtually every 'progressive' social
change since the seventeenth century."[5] The Black definition, similar in
this respect to other modernization theories, makes the actions of state
institutions and personnel an important measure by which to judge the
"success" of modernization, a perspective adopted by Frederick Skinner
in this volume. The focus shifts from issues of socioeconomic causation
to political decisions, evaluated by those "modern" attributes of development judged appropriate or necessary for Russia at a particular
period in its recent history.

As an organizing concept for the study of Russian urban history, the
theory of modernization suffers from serious deficiencies. In the first
place, it does not clearly identify characteristics which distinguish
important historical periods. "Modern" and "premodern" are labels,
not meaningful points of reference for precise social, economic, or
political changes pertinent to such topics as urbanization. "Premodern"
is roughly synonymous with the equally vague term "tradition." "Modern" conveys the implicit meaning of progressive change, defined by
whatever social and political criteria the historian wishes to apply.
Presented as a polar dichotomy, the two expressions create an artificial
historical "turning point" masking a highly complex and varied process
of social and political change. They are, in the words of L. E. Shiner, "an
ideal type gone astray."[6]

In the second place, the modernization model diverts attention
from the major issues of historical context and causes. Its global and
comparative perspectives, easily confused with the Western model of
development, look toward results, not origins, and in doing so lose real
conceptual clarity. It appears in this light "an illusion . . . represented as
a scientific concept."[7] Emphasis on the role of political policies and
leadership in achieving—or failing to achieve—certain results such as
balanced urbanization cannot replace study of the conditions in which
Russia's urban areas grew to become a new and vital sector of the
country's economy and society.

The debate over modernization has had the merit of posing the
important issue of explicit measures of change applicable to social
processes such as urbanization. The elaboration of appropriate indica-
tors of urban development in particular societies poses serious problems, however. In the great diversity of individual cities in mid–
nineteenth century Russia, how can one discern any common social and
economic traits? The introductory essay points to underlying political
and economic similarities. I would suggest that the economic factors
were most influential in determining the level of urbanization in those
prereform years. Every chapter in this collection provides indices of lack

of development, such as slow econonic growth, social immobility, and little population expansion, to characterize the level of urban life in mid-century Russia.

Kiev, despite its venerable past and substantial population, remained at the end of the eighteenth century "three separate settlements" that had the appearance of villages. From this perspective it resembled the spatial divisions of Moscow, separated into a vast outlying territory "beyond the Ring" consisting of "settlement-villages" bound at a distance to the "market-town" in the center. Though obviously not villages in any literal sense of the word, these urban areas had evolved in close contact with the rural population and agricultural activities of the surrounding areas. The borderland towns, with a long history of commercial activity, closely resembled unchanging medieval trade centers. Mid-nineteenth century Riga's Old Town retained, in Henriksson's opinion, the look of a medieval German stronghold cut off from its suburbs by high stone walls and a fetid moat. No one term clearly characterizes urban relations in these mid-century towns, yet all experienced little or no change in economic condition and social structure. From the perspective of the lower classes, they were in this sense "village-like."[8]

This term, of dubious precision to define the mid-century level of development, acquires greater significance by contrast with urban life a half-century later. The changes in Moscow appear so significant that Bradley concludes the city now resembled in some respects a "metropolis." Though he is careful not to imply a complete transformation of the city, his use of the term suggests the type of urban society toward which Moscow was evolving, especially by comparison with the "village" relations of mid-century. The characteristics to which he refers, such as great occupational diversity, an increasing flow of migrants from the surrounding region, active economic exchange with large areas of the country, and intense cultural life, emerged as well in the other major cities in the same years.

In their particular configuration these traits were unique to the Russian Empire, yet their overall impact was to create "economic, social and cultural linkages" not unlike those appearing about the same time or slightly earlier in certain large urban areas in Western Europe and the United States.[9] John Dyos, until his recent death England's leading urban historian, observed that the "metropolitanisation" of London involved both the concentration of England's social and economic forces within the city and the "growing share of the national life" assumed by London.[10] The patterns that he and others have uncovered in nineteenth-century Europe suggest criteria by which to interpret the direction of change in Russia. The terms "village" and "metropolis" (if divorced from their old sociological associations with "community" and "society") provide measures by which to evaluate the extent of social and economic development in Russia's major cities. However oversimplified, they do identify socioeconomic stages providing points of reference to levels of urban development within the historical context of the Empire. What forces pulled these urban areas out of their mid-century somnolence? How did the new urban environment influence the attitudes and behavior of the city dwellers? These questions, the real point of departure of urban history, are the central topics addressed in this essay.

Urbanization in late tsarist Russia had a direct impact on the fate of the state itself, for it led to serious social and political conflict in the early twentieth century. In fact, one might conceive of the urban transformation of Russia in two phases: (1) the period dominated by city building—"urbanization" in its traditional sense of explosive demographic growth and economic expansion, to the end of the nineteenth ceutury; (2) the period of urban activism when groups, divided along ethnic, class, and political lines, at times fought and at times cooperated among themselves in revolutionary combat with the autocracy. This periodization is schematic, for "urbanization" remained a constant force throughout the later years of social and political activism, whose origins in turn were clearly discernible by the 1880s. It does focus attention on the transforming forces at work both in the reorganization of Russian society and, ultimately, in the process leading to the overthrow of the tsarist regime. Not backwardness but development provides the thematic focus of this concluding essay. The rich histories of the individual cities provide the bulk of the evidence for this tentative synthesis of Russian urban history.

ECONOMIC GROWTH

The rapid growth of the major cities of the Empire in the last decades of the nineteenth century was closely associated with economic development. The form taken by the new commercial and manufacturing forces varied appreciably from one region to another. Riga assumed a major role as transshipment point for agricultural produce from Russia's heartland to Western Europe, and industrial enterprises appeared there to meet the demand for machinery, chemicals, and textiles. In the southeast, Baku serviced the needs for machinery and commercial supplies of the vast oil fields nearby. Kiev expanded its role as processor as well as shipping point for the crops of the central Ukraine. Reflecting the diversity of economic activities of the Empire, its cities assumed a multitude of tasks.

Important similarities nonetheless bound the cities to a common pattern of economic growth. All depended on the expanding transportation system for the movement of goods they produced or handled.

Traders and manufacturers, especially in cities confronting serious competition like Odessa, continued to complain of problems of shipment. However, they no longer were forced to rely solely on natural waterways or a few state roads, whose inadequacies earlier in the century had provoked pathetic appeals to the Russian state for aid. In the mid-nineteenth century, a new river-canal system had opened between the Volga basin and the Baltic suitable for heavy barge traffic. In the third quarter of the century a railroad network gradually spread out to link every major region of the country. Hamm makes clear the extent to which a city such as Kiev, enjoying by the 1870s a river link through the southern Ukraine and rail connections with Black Sea ports and with northern Russia, prospered through these transportation facilities.

The importance of commercial activities is apparent in every major city. Through both local and long-distance trade these urban centers became important marketing points, opening opportunities for commercial venture and employment for large numbers of laborers and employees. Cities such as Moscow and Kiev, located in the middle of productive manufacturing and agricultural regions, expanded their trade activities to bring enormous areas into their commercial "hinterland." Kiev became the center for the sugar beet trade and acquired its industrial character through the processing of beets and other produce.

Though we lack accurate figures on urban commerce, the evidence suggests that the single most important economic factor behind the growth of these cities was commercial expansion. Government fiscal data from 1889 indicate that in the entire country the working capital invested in trade was five times greater than that in manufacturing.[11] Conditions varied among the major urban centers. Riga and St. Petersburg appear to have maintained a balance between industry and commerce; Bater's figures on employment, though no indication of the relative profitability of the two sectors, reveal that in 1914 almost as many Petersburg residents found work in commerce as in industry. Even this degree of industrial activity was the exception, not the rule. Moscow, despite its textile production, distinguished itself to contemporary observers and to statisticians by the importance of its trading activities—the "real commercial capital of Russia," in the words of the British consular official in 1898. The yearly fairs were becoming an outmoded enterprise; even the great fair of Nizhnii Novgorod appeared by then an extension of Moscow's trading network.

Urban commercial activities developed in a variety of directions. International and national markets expanded; wholesale commercial exchange became a year-round affair; intracity trade became increasingly active. With increased marketing came more intense competition among trading cities. The lower costs offered by competing Black Sea ports such as Nikolaev may well have been more important to the decline of Odessa than the inadequacy of municipal and Imperial investments, suggested by Skinner to be the principal cause. Overall, the intensification and expansion of economic activities owed much to the dynamic force of growing commerce. This trend, which had made itself felt in all these cities by the end of the century, continued during the years of economic boom after 1905.

Opportunities for work multiplied many times as a result of commercial and industrial expansion. International commerce and even large commercial transactions were the affair of a small number of companies and traders, who in a city such as Odessa were often of foreign origin or were employed by Western companies. While significant, the number of their employees and laborers remained relatively small within the urban work force. The employment figures for Moscow, indicative of trends elsewhere, revealed that the proportion of white-collar workers was growing, especially in the last years before World War I. Many of these people were educated professionals, including some who found work in local and state agencies, expanding rapidly in those years.

Serving these groups with food, clothing, etc., were a multitude of small-scale traders and artisans. In Warsaw the census of 1897 revealed that one-tenth of the entire population consisted of artisans—62,000—twice the number of factory workers, and more than five times the number of artisans counted in the city in the 1860s. Handicraft remained the principal form of production in Kiev, which, Hamm observes, remained largely a city of artisans throughout these decades of exceptional growth. Even where industrial growth was most spectacular, as in St. Petersburg, the artisanal workers remained almost as large a group as factory workers; in Moscow at the turn of the century the former were half again as numerous as the latter.[12] All these cities proved their economic vigor through the expansion of many occupations. None had a predominantly industrial character.

Thus the outstanding characteristic of the Russian urban economy of the late tsarist years appears to be its combination of capitalist operations in commerce and industry and many petty enterprises in trade and artisanry. Moscow's commercial and industrial boom carried along with it an expansion of small-scale production and distribution. Bradley designates this development a "dual economy"; on the one hand, an increasing concentration in manufacturing and other economic enterprises with fewer (and increasingly corporate) owners and more wage and salaried employees; and on the other "the institutions of barter, haggle, and street vending and peasant entrepreneurs." The capitalist expansion fits well our image of the "metropolis," but Bradley makes clear that this trend in Moscow was accompanied by and was in fact ideally suited to sustain small-scale, informal economic organizations. There the semiskilled, individualistic, and petty operations of "village economy" had adapted to the needs of expanded urban markets.

The other major cities reveal similar traits. In Tiflis as elsewhere, commercial affairs were concentrated in the hands of a few large enterprises. Suny argues that "individualistic small tradesmen" were giving way in some manufacturing sectors to wage labor in the employ of capitalist employers. Yet he notes as well that in early twentieth-century Tiflis "the dominant position in local industry was held by small-scale handwork," a trait typical of the other cities. Thus there appear to be solid grounds for questioning the validity of the old picture of the "steady transformation of the traditional artisanal economy into a capitalist industrial one." More persuasive than this theory of uni-linear economic change is the view of a dual urban economy, incorporating the substantial evidence of parallel growth of small-scale handicraft and commerce alongside large-scale enterprise.

The reasons for the pervasiveness and tenacity of this artisan-trader economy, while not clear, are certainly linked with the pattern of urban migration. The consequences, equally difficult to discern, have a direct bearing on the manner in which the city populations reacted to the new urban setting. The urban types of "village" and "metropolis" reveal themselves in economic terms most clearly as forms of economic association dependent on each other in that period of urbanization.

URBAN SOCIETY

These economic trends responded to and stimulated the massive influx of population into the Empire's large cities. The urban population figures compiled by the census takers are comparable in scope and scale of growth only to those in North American cities of the last century. The absolute increase for the urban centers studied in these essays represented on an average 400 to 500 percent from mid-century to the eve of World War I. The growth of Moscow and St. Petersburg, while lower in percentage terms since both started with much larger populations, constituted a tremendous expansion—over one million in each case. At the other extreme, Baku and Tiflis, which expanded their populations more than ten times, were both very small at mid-century. This sudden growth opened vast opportunities for economic development based on cheap manpower, but also placed overwhelming demands on the urban facilities, especially housing and sanitation.

Where did these additional townspeople come from? In almost all cases they were migrants, largely from the countryside but also from other towns. The census entry for place of birth provides the only uniform indicator of place of origin, though it may hide as much significant information as it reveals. The data assembled by the authors suggest a "typical" pattern of urban migration. In every case, by the turn of the century over half of the population was born outside the city of residence; in the capitals, almost three-fourths of the inhabitants were by this measure migrants (as was the case in the early 1880s). The census of 1897 revealed that as many as half of the migrants had come from another province to seek a new life in the big city.

The demographic profile of these new townspeople in the various cities is sufficiently similar to allow us to draw a portrait of the typical migrant. During the years of greatest urban influx at the turn of the century, this migrant appears to have been a young, single, male peasant, who had left his family behind to find work as an unskilled or semiskilled laborer. Only the Warsaw migrant (predominantly Polish) tended more often to arrive with his family (or to marry soon after arrival someone from the same place of origin); only in Odessa did the "urban" estate of the petty bourgeoisie (*meshchanstvo*) constitute the largest group of new arrivals (most of whom originated in the Yiddish villages of the Pale of Settlement). In each of these cities the reason for its peculiarity lay in the special ethnic composition of the migrants. Overall, urban growth occurred largely as a result of the influx of laborers, to whom the metropolis appeared as a workplace.

It is an obvious—if presumptuous—deduction that they were drawn to the city primarily by the lure of employment. Certainly the evidence from the essays points to a wide variety of opportunities for the enterprising and adventuresome. Even when many actually were trapped in the grinding poverty of the city's slums, as Corrsin argues with regard to Warsaw, "in the vibrant commercial and industrial life of the city" they had a chance. In other words, they came with the hope of improvement, heeding the call of the city summed up in the Latvian saying that "all roads lead to Riga."

This picture of urban migration resembles the experience of other European countries in the nineteenth century. However, as both Bradley and Bater discovered, the mobility of migrants in Moscow and St. Petersburg was vastly greater than the increase in population revealed. At the end of the last century, approximately 20 percent of the inhabitants present in the city at a given time had either just arrived or would leave before the end of the year. This tremendous turnover, accumulating over the last two decades of the century, brought into Moscow two to three million immigrants, leaving behind a net increase of 400,000. One might envisage these urban centers as great revolving doors through which passed a significant proportion of the population of large regions of Russia.

Did the other cities resemble the capitals in this respect? Data available leave the answer in doubt, but one might suppose that, at least in the Russian lands, the urban centers experienced a similar level of migrant mobility. Temporary migration (in Russian, *otkhodnichestvo*, from *otkhodnik*, "he who leaves [temporarily]") had been a characteristic of the population, urban as well as rural, for centuries; as cities grew (and as the total population of the country expanded), so did the scale of this temporary migration. Contemporaries estimated that in the 1890s over six million Russians moved from their place of residence yearly to seek work. Like magnets, the large towns drew in migrants from near and far, yet many more found only temporary abode there than made permanent residence. This transience was partly due to the disappointments encountered by the migrants in actual conditions of the city. The long tradition of temporary migration, however, suggests that among the Russian population many continued to view the city and its opportunities as a transitory attraction.

The ethnic diversity of the urban migration profoundly affected the social and cultural life of the new urban centers. It played a particularly important role in the "borderland" cities from west to south to east. Because in Riga "until the very end of the nineteenth century the overwhelming majority of newcomers were Latvian" the proportion of townspeople there of Latvian nationality rose from one-fifth in mid-century to two-fifths by 1900. In Odessa (and to a lesser extent in Kiev), the migration of Jews from their villages in the Pale of Settlement to the big city swelled the size of the Jewish community, Yiddish in culture and still strongly tied to religious traditions, to a point where Jews constituted a major part of the urban population. As a result of the influx of Georgian villagers, Tiflis became for the first time a city with more Georgians than Armenians. Baku, a city created from a market town by the oil boom, took on the characteristics of a multinational center where Russians, though the largest national group, constituted only one-third of the population alongside Azerbaijani Turks and Armenians. Several of the Russian Empire's largest cities remained predominantly non-Russian (Warsaw, Riga, Tiflis), or grew through migration in such a manner as to leave Russians a plurality (Baku), or at best a bare majority (Odessa, Kiev). The "heterogeneous ethnicity" of cities such as Odessa created serious political problems for the state and a growing danger of communal conflict for the various ethnic communities. To the economic complexity of cities with a "dual economy" was added a highly transient population, split frequently into diverse ethnic communities.

The boundaries separating these groups were for some townspeople easily crossed. The lure of social mobility induced the ambitious to adopt another language and hence a new national loyalty. The process of assimilation at times entailed the adoption of a new religion as well. In Riga, Henriksson emphasizes, for generations "upwardly mobile Latvians had Germanized as a matter of course," since "to be Latvian was to be lower class." In Kiev, large numbers of Ukrainians apparently adopted the Russian language, desirable for entry into the city's economy and—as in the case of the Latvians in Riga—for social advancement. Even a small proportion of the Jewish population of cities such as

Warsaw, Kiev, and Odessa abandoned the Yiddish culture to adopt the language and style of life of the emancipated Poles or Russians.

Often, though, the adoption of the language and dress of the foreigners left cultural identity intact. Corrsin finds that the Polonized Jews of Warsaw "remained consciously, ethnically Jewish." In Baku, Westernized Muslims "had been educated in Russian or European universities and spoke perfect Russian; they were often engaged in Western professions." Yet privately they maintained an Islamic way of life. Even when these cities provided the setting for cultural assimilation and integration, the mixing of peoples remained limited and superficial.

The dominant trend in these cities at the turn of the century appears to have been a strengthening of ethnic community ties, not a weakening. Even where both status and economic opportunity had for centuries dictated assimilation into the dominant group, as in Riga, the transformation of the urban environment included a dramatic modification in the pattern of social mobility. The former preeminence of Germans in Riga had declined by the late nineteenth century. The increased proportion of Latvians in the "national composition" of the city provided strong evidence, not only of geographical migration patterns, but of lessening Germanization. There, as elsewhere, urban growth stimulated an increased awareness of ethnicity based on what Suny suggests are bonds of "social communication." What forces created these bonds? The issue is both complex and crucial to our understanding of nineteenth-century history. Among the important factors mentioned by the authors are growing economic opportunities and competition, the need for stronger social ties within a larger and far more diverse community than the village, and a heightened sense of cultural identity stimulated by newspapers and other forms of mass urban culture yet still shaped by strong religious loyalties.

The evidence for these developments rests largely on indications of growing hostility among ethnic groups. The persecution of the Jewish inhabitants of cities such as Warsaw, Odessa, and Kiev was too widespread to be attributable simply to tsarist manipulation. Russians, Ukranians, and Poles provided the cohorts for riotous mobs, tolerated but not organized by the local authorities. Anti-Semitism in those regions was not new; the eruption of such antagonism within major urban centers did, however, mark a new stage in the urban transformation there, and coincides roughly with the end of the first major period in urban growth at the turn of the twentieth century. These attacks provided the catalyst for the strengthening of bonds within the Jewish communities in these cities. A similar pattern of rising communal solidarity and worsening relations among ethnic groups occurred in the Caucasian cities, where Muslim confronted Armenian in Baku and Georgian confronted Armenian in Tiflis. These conflicts too became prominent in the first years of this century. Only shared enmity toward the Russian autocracy, it seemed, could temporarily make these groups forget their antagonism.

A new social structure emerged from these conditions of urbanization. It was the product in part of more general trends within the Empire. The landed nobility, in decline in almost all the regions of the country, lost its traditional social eminence in the cities. In Tiflis as in Moscow, mansions long the possession of noble families passed into the hands of wealthy entrepreneurs. Polish nobles, "thrown from the saddle" by the state's repression of the 1863 uprising, came to Warsaw "to try to rebuild their fortunes." There as in other urban areas an untold number would fail, finding modest clerical positions or even falling in with the drunkards and drifters (to provide models for literary types such as the Baron in Gorky's play *The Lower Depths*). For others these cities provided a quiet refuge where, after selling their estates, they lived on income from stocks and bonds (one-half of St. Petersburg's 140,000 nobles in 1910 classified themselves *rentiers*[13]). Still others found opportunities to create new careers, some as powerful bureaucrats, others as outstanding writers (and a few, as Suny suggests, as revolutionary socialist intellectuals). Their varied experiences provide us with a partial measure of the potential influence of the urban environment to reshape the lives of their inhabitants.

Profound social changes within these cities resulted from conditions peculiar to urban Russia. Rapid economic growth and increasingly high rates of population mobility produced major adjustments in the structure of these urban societies. All the authors describe lower and upper classes identified by the officially recognized estates, yet they also make clear that often the groups so labeled bore only a remote resemblance—or no resemblance at all—to the original designation. Skinner's list of trades practiced by Odessa's petty bourgeoisie (*meshchanstvo*) reveals clearly that this estate grouping in fact "ranged across the broad middle spectrum of the social order, bridging wealth and poverty, connecting 'bourgeois to underworld.'"

How then ought one to describe the social relations and structure of urban societies which combined elements of both old and new ways of life? The criteria by which social historians classify social diversification and stratification are ambiguous and still subject to debate.[14] For the purposes of this essay, the pragmatic approach appears the most suitable—even if too vague for the purist. Evidence from the individual city histories provides categories of analysis specific to the Russian historical context. The image proposed by Bradley of a "dual economy" in Moscow suggests a conceptual approach to social analysis of Russia's urban development. Instead of viewing these urban centers as either "capitalist" or "precapitalist," we ought to conceive of a process of social transformation in which occupational groups possessing new skills and productive property emerged in communities where older crafts and property-holders were adapting as well to new conditions. The substantial differences of interests and outlook existed between these "two societies," just as within each group important divisions emerged along lines of wealth and occupation. Both "societies" offered new opportunities to the ambitious and left the unfortunate or disadvantaged to a condition of social hardship. The urban environment emerging in late tsarist Russia appears to have been one of increasing social diversity and complexity, of expanded opportunities and growing inequalities. Our task is to seek to draw out the major lines of these social trends as they appear from the individual portraits of Russia's major cities.

The crude social indices of employer or employee, propertied or propertyless, provide only a vague indication of the urban hierarchy. Within the older economy of "haggle and barter" existed a myriad of petty entrepreneurs whose numbers grew as the city economy expanded. The bazaar tradesmen of Tiflis, Suny reminds us, remained a "powerful social group" down to the twentieth century. Many of these small-scale "businessmen" in Moscow, as Bradley indicates, were "first- or second-generation peasant immigrants." While one must not assume all peasants were recent arrivals, the indication of large peasant ownership suggests that migrants could aspire realistically to a place among the cities' propertied. The well-known dominant position of Iaroslavl' peasants in Moscow's booming tavern trade is but one example of a time-honored path to social and economic advancement for one group of peasant migrants. Similarly, many of the Jewish migrants to Warsaw sought out a place among the artisans.

As indicated above, it appears likely that the adaptation of artisanry to the new economic conditions led to increased size of shops, with larger numbers of workers and correspondingly fewer opportunities for ownership available to these workers and new migrants. Bradley points out as well that the possibility of upward mobility declined for most women, increasingly relegated to the numerous lowly positions in domestic service. Small-scale trade or artisanry implied a modest place in urban society; yet it represented a type of employment sought after by many and enjoyed by the largest group of property owners in these major towns. The enormous numbers of these "petty bourgeois" townspeople carrying on small-scale trade or a petty handicraft business created an urban society dominated by people of small means (referred to scornfully by political activists as the *obyvateli*, literally "residents" but figuratively the "silent majority"). Hamm points out that in prewar Kiev only 9,000 property owners paid any real estate tax; one half of the traders and artisans of Khar'kov, a city similar to Moscow in type of economic activity, held property of so little value they were excluded from the property-tax rolls.[15] The stereotypical Odessites out for a "quick profit" repelled the city prefect looking for patriotism and "civic consciousness," but they had the qualities needed to survive or get ahead in that booming center of commerce and contraband. They, not the great merchants or industrialists, constitute the typical "bourgeois" of these major urban areas.

The most dramatic changes in urban society were the consequence of the new economic trends. The expansion of the sector of "large-scale enterprises" created conditions of significant structural mobility. Wherever one looked at the turn of the century, a few families with great wealth earned through commerce, finance, or industry had emerged at the pinnacle of urban society.[16] Within the new commercial and industrial enterprises themselves, new occupations at the "white-collar" level such as clerks and salespeople multiplied to such a point that in Moscow, as Bradley points out, in the period between 1882 and 1912 "the most rapidly growing labor category was professionals and salaried employees." The construction of the country's railroad network, in cities like Kiev, meant employment for thousands of white-collar employees and skilled workers, a consideration important enough to the city council to donate municipal land for the construction of the Southwestern Railroad's Railway Colony. The spread of factory production brought opportunities for large numbers of factory labor, another area where migrants predominated. For the able and industrious, factory work offered the chance of becoming a skilled and "citified" worker. Young Semen Kanatchikov, brought from his village at age sixteen by his father, seized on these opportunities and temptations after he entered Moscow's metalworking industry in the 1890s.[17] His case was closer to the exception than the rule, however. The numbers of unskilled workers remained large, even growing in textiles and metalworking as mechanization spread.

Even more lowly was the position of the great mass of transportation workers in the ports and around the railroad freight centers, from whom were demanded only physical strength and endurance. They, like other day laborers, presented the cases of most obvious misery, enduring the worst living conditions, constituting probably the most "transient" of the urban population. They appeared to municipal and tsarist authorities, such as Tsaritsyn's provincial governor, "generally undisciplined and extremely inclined to drunkenness and disorder."[18] Among the disorders for which they were blamed were anti-Semitic pogroms. The assertion is plausible but conjectural; we lack real evidence that in cities like Odessa the mass of "20,000 homeless dockworkers" had any major part in the terrible pogroms there. The social distance separating capitalist from dockworker was enormous and the potential for social conflict correspondingly great.

Among the new groups in urban society the increasingly numerous professionals and white-collar workers in public service were particularly important. In each account of the development of the major cities of the Empire one finds reference to highly educated Russians whose special skills earned them positions with municipalities, zemstvos, the state—and for a few an independent career. The 400 members of Odessa's branch of the Imperial Russian Technical Society were included in their numbers, as were the artists and writers who brought fame to Warsaw—and a prestigious career for themselves.

In these cities were located the training centers for those aspiring to join their ranks: the institutions of higher education. The numbers of young people in these schools remained small in proportion to the total urban population (though Hamm notes that in Kiev in 1913 there were as many advanced students as factory workers). Still, their standing among townspeople remained high. Though some tended to exaggerate their importance to society and to their country's future, they did enjoy a privileged position that provided access to a secure, influential place in urban society. Concurrently, these schools became the seed bed for revolutionary opposition to the tsarist regime. One need only recall the case of an obscure theological seminary in Tiflis to appreciate the new directions taken by educational life in these urban centers.

While the social transformation brought about by the rapid growth of these cities created conditions for massive assimilation of new townspeople into both the "petty bourgeois" and "bourgeois" groups of urban society, it also created conditions of serious social conflict. Opportunities were numerous for those with modest ambitions. We have no reason to doubt that most townspeople aspired to no more. Yet by the end of the century more and more signs pointed to emerging hostility and outright violence dividing various urban groups. The interests and outlook of workers and employers were becoming increasingly antagonistic, a process which historians have for long taken for granted but only now are beginning to study in detail.[19]

As important was the emergence by the turn of the century within certain cities of large and dynamic ethnic communities divided among themselves along both national and class lines. In the cities around the borderlands, ethnic and class divisions tended to reinforce one another in a manner closely resembling what one sociologist studying American society has clumsily labeled "ethclass."[20] In Riga, Latvian workers confronted German factory owners. In Tiflis, Georgian laborers identified Armenian capitalists as their class and national enemies; around Baku, social and ethnic boundaries separated Muslim oil workers and traders from wealthy Armenian well-owners and merchants. Finally, in cities such as Odessa the dominance of Jews among the wealthy merchants acted as a catalyst for the anti-Semitic hostility of Russian and Ukrainian workers and tradesmen. In every case the opposing classes included sizable minorities from the other nationality. The merchants of Tiflis included Georgians as well as Armenians; Jews were numerous among the poor workers of Odessa alongside their Orthodox neighbors. The social conflicts resulted as much from deep cultural and psychological strains, creating ethnic stereotypes, as from confrontation over labor conditions and inequalities of wealth. The antagonism among ethnic and class groups emerged from the same conditions that created opportunities for social betterment. Russian urban development produced both social integration and conflict.

MUNICIPALITIES AND URBAN IMPROVEMENTS

Within these rapidly growing urban areas municipal governments and imperial administrators sought to deal with a host of complex and unsettling problems. The priorities of these political leaders at times diverged so widely they became adversaries. The weight of Imperial power and decrees gave governors and city prefects the final word in disputes, but daily involvement in the affairs of the major cities gave municipal leaders considerable latitude to pursue their own objectives. As a careful reading of the essays in this volume makes clear, there existed no simple institutional dichotomy of autocracy versus municipalities, nor did the pattern of municipal policies respect a simple ideological division between liberalism and conservatism. Though several authors emphasize the serious shortcomings of civic measures dealing with the acute problems posed by urbanization, one can argue that the urban improvements undertaken by the municipalities represented major achievements in the social and political conditions of those years. Yet these civic works benefited the urban population unevenly.

Both the institutional framework of the municipalities and urban leadership changed over the last half of the nineteenth century, though to a much lesser degree than the urban economy and society. After a few years of regional experimentation in the 1860s, the municipal reform of 1870 established uniformity of municipal institutions throughout the Empire. Still, autocratic controls did not determine the actual conditions of self-government, a fact of political life previously made apparent in those cities which had received self-rule under the Statute of 1785.

Catherine II's dream that a Russian "third estate" would emerge in her self-governing cities had proved illusory. Municipal rule had decayed in the first half of the century to such an extent that it became merely an extension of Imperial administration. While authoritarian-minded provincial governors found the situation satisfactory (and later would harken back with nostalgia to these "good old days"), neither Alexander II's advisers nor civic-minded urban leaders judged the 1785 Municipal Statute suitable to contemporary needs. Both groups agreed that municipal self-government had to be revived. The state tried first to bring the nobility and bureaucracy into urban leadership, adapting in the 1860s to Moscow, Odessa, and Tiflis the Petersburg 1846 Statute granting separate representation to these and to the urban estates. For reasons which are still not clear, it quickly abandoned the formula for municipal government through estates in favor of a system of broad representation based on property holding and commercial activity.

For all its defects, the Municipal Statute of 1870 did widen suffrage and grant the municipalities considerable autonomy in local rule. It lasted only twenty-two years. It was replaced under Alexander III by a new statute which, while retaining the property basis for representation, excluded all small and medium property owners and substantially increased the powers of the provincial administration over the municipal policies. This "counterreform" ended the paltry "democratization" of municipal representation permitted in the 1870 Statute. In every major Imperial city (excluding Warsaw, deprived of municipal rule), however, it neither curtailed policies for civic improvements nor substantially altered the social composition of municipal leadership.

The reasons for this continuity lay in the attitudes of the municipal electorate under the old statute and in the concerns of the small political elite that ran these cities. Voters, save in Riga, represented on an average thirty percent or less of the electorate. Those who did vote deferred to their social betters by sending to the councils delegates largely from the merchant and honorary citizen estates. Nobles played a leading role for only a few years after the 1870 Statute took effect, disappearing from the councils and the administrative boards of cities such as Moscow and Tiflis by the end of the 1870s. City leadership proved remarkably stable, for a handful of activists retained power over many years. Though we know little of their actions, they appear to have built political "machines." The "German elite" of Riga had its counterparts in Mayor Eisman's supporters in Kiev and in the Pitoev-Izmailov-Matinov "party" in Tiflis. In every case the 1892 reform appears to have left the existing political factions in place, since their influence depended not on democratic rule but on control over a small electorate and over a few essential levers of power. The sources of support for these groups and the political direction they gave to their municipalities differed widely; they embodied only in a loose sense "class rule" of the wealthy townspeople.

The divisions among municipal leaders generally produced two political tendencies. On the one hand were those one might designate the "conservatives," that is, defenders of propertied townspeople whose major concern consisted in keeping the budget at its minimum level while fulfilling state-imposed obligations. To this group belonged the Tiflis "merchants of the old school," an expression that aptly describes their political views, if not their precise occupations. On the other side were the reformers or "liberals," whose goals included major capital investments in municipal services and active development of public services such as health care and education. The characterization of "conservative" and "liberal" has a strictly fiscal meaning, for the most acute issue confronting mayors and city councils was the insufficiency of municipal revenues. Conservatives considered any increase in property-tax rates or any municipal borrowing anathema; the liberals, such as Moscow's "civic-minded businessmen, professionals, and philanthropists," viewed taxes and indebtedness the sole means to indispensable civic improvements.

The emergence of the liberals in the major cities dated from the 1880s; Moscow's dynamic mayor Nikolai Alekseev, a young civic activist wealthy through his family's textile enterprises yet himself uninterested in a business career, typified the new type of municipal leaders. More often, the leadership of this liberal group came from the growing body of educated professionals in the cities, the "modernizers" whom Skinner identifies in Odessa. Their role expanded as their numbers grew and as the business communities themselves looked increasingly to them for new policies. The trends in composition of municipal leadership, concluded a Soviet historian studying Moscow in the last decades of the nineteenth century, "were based less on the new municipal law of 1892 than on the economic and political development of the country."[21] Gradually these elective municipal institutions came to articulate new concerns of ethnic communities in their cities and at times to express *sotto voce* partisan views on the political future of the Empire as a whole. These new issues emerged largely after the turn of the century, however. Until then, the little world of urban problems and personal interest determined the policies of the municipal leadership.

The debates between conservatives and liberals at times generated great bitterness, yet both sides accepted certain urban conditions and recognized certain limits. In the first place, the overriding reality present in the minds of all municipal leaders was that extraordinary "tempo of change" transforming the society and economy of their cities. Conservatives viewed rapid urbanization and its attendant problems in the same light as epidemic disease, namely an affair "in the hands of God." Liberals sought at least partial solutions to acute social problems such as unclean water, uncollected filth, impassable streets, and miserable housing for the poor. Gradually resistance to civic improvements dwindled in the face of overwhelming pressures, both from within the urban population and from the tsarist administration. Differences increasingly centered on priorities, not on the need for social investments *per se.* In the second place, the tsarist government made greater demands of municipalities for funds and services to meet its own needs for urban governance. The expansion of urban police forces, particularly after 1880, came at the government's insistence and at

municipal expense. Third, fiscal constraints remained a constant restriction on action. Even the municipalities' ability to raise funds
through borrowing had limits. These countervailing pressures of growing needs and tax limits set the bounds for municipal action, whose
effects ought to be judged from this dual perspective.

The social and cultural background of the municipal leaders also
strongly influenced the policies of urban reform. They were men of
some education, usually considerably above average even for the trading
classes. Still, their interests and concerns centered on the economic life
of their city and on its settled population. All shared the view of the
Moscow city council that municipal welfare ought to go the city's poor,
not to vagrants and beggars from elsewhere. Similarly, civic improvements appeared solely as practical questions posed by local needs, not as
questions of ethical principle. The areas they judged in particular need
of capital investment were those of commercial business and administration, not only because many were in commerce (or were supported by
business interests) but also because they valued most highly productive
activities by people like themselves. In this manner "class" interests
definitely shaped their view of urban change, and guided their selection
of appropriate policies. Nonetheless, they confronted a considerable
range of choices regarding the direction of municipal involvement in
the transformation of their cities. Within those narrow limits there
emerged a gradual pattern of reform that had a measurable impact on
Russia's great cities.

Municipal policies affected the urban population through three
major areas of expenditure: health, welfare, and education. Of these, the
first required the greatest expenditure and (perhaps debatably) had the
greatest influence on the quality of urban life. Urban migration created a
condition of acute overcrowding in housing; Moscow's density rate in
1912 of 8.5 persons per housing unit fell probably close to the average of
the other major cities of the empire. These urban areas (save the "Western" cities of Warsaw and Riga) had possessed in mid-century no public
facilities to handle the basic needs of the population for water and
removal of waste. Sudden population growth within a few decades
confronted the municipalities with a major public health hazard, threatening the welfare of even the well-to-do. Whether elected or (in Warsaw's case) appointed by the tsarist administration, their first major
public projects not surprisingly were directed toward removal of sewage
and toward construction of water mains to provide reasonably clean
water to the urban population. Many of these facilities were completed
by the late 1880s, though as several authors make clear the arduous
struggle to improve them continued down to the war.

Results proved uneven. Central areas of the city received the best
service; outlying areas largely peopled by migrants and laborers (constantly expanding as new cheap housing was built) such as Warsaw's

Praga or Kiev's Shuliavka benefited hardly at all. Overall, the joint impact of these projects combined with the more limited expansion of public medical care appears to have curtailed drastically the impact of deadly disease.

Our only measure, an imperfect one, is the mortality rate, reflecting "preventive" health measures such as improvements in food consumption as well as the salutary effects of public health projects, particularly new sewage and water systems. The statistics from all cities reveal a significant decline in rates, higher than thirty per thousand before 1880 (Moscow's 1870 figure, cited by Bradley, proved exceptionally low) down to the mid- or low twenties by the turn of the century.[22] In Odessa, the fall coincided with the completion of these projects. Certain infectious diseases such as typhus and cholera ceased to be a constant threat to the entire urban population, though St. Petersburg had the sorry distinction of actually increasing its typhus rate between 1880 and 1914. The insalubrious conditions of the "desperate" city outskirts bore the major responsibility for the persistence of these diseases. The major typhus epidemic of 1892 did not threaten any major Imperial city, however, while ill-equipped port cities such as Astrakhan and new industrial settlements like Iuzovka suffered severely. To this limited extent one can conclude that the public authorities did succeed in bettering urban living conditions. In spite of municipal partisan conflicts and shortsighted public concern of the city leaders, in spite too of population boom and shortage of funds, municipalities eased in some respects the social crisis confronting Russia's major cities.

Did these improvements have a significant impact on urban life in general in those last decades of the Empire? A fair answer ought to take into account both the conditions in the cities in mid-century and the demands placed on urban leaders by economic development and population growth. A considerable body of opinion, reflected by some authors in this collection, would conclude that failures in most areas of municipal activities outweigh such limited improvements as those just described. These critical judgments appear most forcefully when comparisons are made with Western European conditions. The contrast was great, a point emphasized by Russian intellectuals convinced of the backwardness of their country and of the incompetence of the political regime, including the municipal oligarchy. Their evaluation of the political crisis of their country associated traditional autocratic rule with the continued existence of the "dark" masses, whose presence they discerned in both town and countryside. Though many educated Russians participated in efforts, notable especially in Moscow, "to spread learning and culture to the general public," writers on urban affairs repeatedly stressed the continued inferiority of their cities to those of the West. Their high expectations led them to conclude that urban conditions were worsening, a situation they blamed on reactionary public officials.

One might object, however, that their focus on conditions in cities such as Berlin created an unfair standard. A crude measure more revealing in the Russian context is the increase in municipal expenditures. It reveals striking growth among all the major cities. Moscow's budget expanded 700 percent between 1870 and 1914, far outstripping population growth, while Riga (in this respect too the "exemplary city") raised its budget 900 percent in the same period. In one decade between 1895 and 1905 Odessa doubled its budgetary outlays. Income could not cover the totality of these expenditures, forcing municipalities to borrow heavily (a policy once judged intolerable to conservative councilors). In that specific context debt represented an unavoidable consequence of a policy of major investment in public services. Municipal leaders struggled to keep up with mushrooming urban needs, leaving behind a mixed record in the important areas of public health, welfare, and education. One might well conclude with Bater that the tempo of change outstripped the ability of civic officials to respond adequately. On the other hand, if one compares conditions prevalent in mid-century with those of sixty years later, improvements in public life appear everywhere. The "metropolis" was absorbing the "village." Even Baku, at the crossroads of the Middle East and Europe, with a population which had grown more rapidly than any other major city of the Empire, impressed the American consul visiting shortly before World War I with its public amenities. In these terms the Imperial municipalities had made an appreciable impact on the urban transformation of their cities.

Yet there remain troubling facts to challenge this somewhat roseate view. The conservative groups in the city councils continued in the face of acute need to obstruct improvements so as to curtail municipal expense. Hamm traces the protracted battle in Kiev over the extension and upgrading of the city's water and sewage systems. "Desperate outskirts" suffered repeated cholera epidemics; yet influential municipal councilors preferred to protect the interests of the city's property owners (including increasingly large numbers of landlords) by choosing "cheap water to pure water." Similar conditions existed in St. Petersburg and Odessa, where districts deprived of satisfactory water experienced morality rates fifty percent higher than the central districts.

These shortcomings reflected not only the acute public health problems posed by rapid urban growth but also the narrow perception of urban interests of a sizable group among the propertied electorate. By comparison with the other Imperial cities, Warsaw enjoyed a favored regime of urban public services under direct tsarist administration unobstructed by electoral parties. The search for new sources of revenue inspired a movement for "municipalization" of public services—that is,

operation of services by the municipality instead of private concessionaires—and did, as it were incidentally, bring in certain cities better
conditions in public transport or meat slaughtering. Local and class
interests impeded even those improvements within the means of the
cities.

The combination of rapid growth on city outskirts and municipal
attention primarily to the needs of the city center created a form of
urban spatial segregation making visible the inequalities of public services. The "transportation revolution" brought by electric streetcars
had scarcely touched the great cities of Russia. Kiev had been in the
1890s the first city in the Empire to electrify its public transportation,
using streetcars to help townspeople travel over its hills. The Petersburg
council finally resolved its dispute over the electrification of transport
after 1905. The central city remained the most desirable living place, its
land most valuable, its rents highest. Elimination of the infamous
Khitrov market section of central Moscow, a major project of the Moscow municipality in the early 1900s, was the result as much of rising
land values as of revulsion at the squalid living conditions there.
"Streetcar suburbs" belonged to the Western world;[23] around Russia's
major cities the poor people lived in districts whose very names conveyed to contemporaries a sense of isolation. Tiflis had its Nakhalovka,
Kiev its Shuliavka, St. Petersburg its Vyborg district, and so on for every
other urban area.

The isolation of these areas was due largely to the amenities denied
them but granted central districts. Housing conditions were bad,
though conditions equally deplorable existed in the central city as well.
The absence of public services marked these areas particularly. Street
paving and lighting were sparse or nonexistent; water was available in
wells or ponds, sewage dumped outdoors in streams or lowlying areas.
The districts frequently contained large factories, established by law
away from mid-city and on cheaper "suburban" land. In Moscow 90
percent of the factory workers congregated there. Scholars frequently
referred to these neighborhoods as "working-class districts," yet Bater
makes clear that in Petersburg residential segregation did not reflect
social segregation. In these outlying districts lived migrants and poor
townspeople, petty tradesmen and peddlers, artisans and factory workers. They were found in other areas as well, including the center. The
transience of the population assured wide distribution of the lower
classes. Though Baku's case may be atypical, it suggests that the ethnic
communities in the borderland cities tended to congregate more closely
than did particular classes. If this were the case, it gave even greater
explosive power to the mixture of ethnic and social grievance noted
earlier. The hardships to which the residents of these "desperate" districts gave voice reflected the relative deprivation of these areas by

contrast with city centers as well as the economic exploitation which the laborers there experienced.

The result of these conditions was the appearance of what might be called a "dual city." The central areas benefited from private and public investments in buildings and services to become a new urban environment. They provided those amenities associated with the metropolitan centers of the West, as the American consul to Baku had noted with surprise. They offered a great contrast both to their earlier condition of "stagnant" towns and to the squalor of their outlying areas. They were built partly in the oldest sections of the cities, which benefited from major capital improvements. The newness of the poor districts enhanced their isolation, for it reinforced the inclination of municipal councils to ignore their needs. The "other Riga" ringing the "sparkling center" appeared to municipal officials in the 1880s to suffer from "horrifying" conditions, which they concluded were inescapable. The neglect did not go unnoticed. Hamm provides the reader with the most eloquent cry of protest at civic discrimination against the outlying areas. It came in 1907 from one Shuliavka resident, damning Kiev's leaders for his district's cholera epidemic: "Do the authorities even know where Shuliavka is?"

Similarly, the urban police maintained public order in the outlying districts in a manner substantially different than in the central areas. It employed there a special set of operating laws and punishments, and set much higher limits on tolerable public violence. Until the early years of this century, the mass fist-fight battles organized in Russian urban areas for Sunday entertainment of workingmen could occur without obstacle in these districts; a mid-town battle in Moscow in the 1880s brought immediate police attention.[24] The disdain with which their inhabitants were treated by police was reciprocated. Kanatchikov found among Petersburg workers in the district where he lived a conviction that "to beat or to kill a policeman was a victory."[25] The arbitrary rule characteristic of so many aspects of tsarist administration appears particularly pervasive in these "marginal" areas of urban society.

On the other hand, one should not exaggerate the isolation of the outlying areas of the Russian cities. In the first place, these areas depended in many ways on the urban core for employment. The boundaries of the "dual city" do not coincide with that "dual economy" of large enterprise and small-scale trade and handicraft outlined by Bradley. The factories of the industrial districts belonged to the capitalist urban economy; many of the unskilled laborers living in the outskirts found work in the central regions. Economically the two urban areas were linked together through those years of rapid growth.

A second force at work to unite populations of the central and outer areas of the major cities was the spread of mass literate culture. The evidence gathered in these essays and other studies of late-century urban society in the Empire points to a remarkable diffusion of the printed word among townspeople, especially in the major cities. The indices include the increase in literacy among urban dwellers and the rapid growth in the circulation of inexpensive newspapers, the "penny press." A large Russian city such as Moscow in those years was, in the words of one historian of Russian popular culture, "an environment filled with printed words."[26] Hamm points out that Kiev had in mid-century only one newspaper (in fact a government bulletin), while by the turn of the century the number had grown to nine. Rotary presses in all major cities turned out tens of thousands of papers at cheap prices every day. The total daily sales of Warsaw's Polish papers mounted to 123,000, one for every six residents and nine times their circulation forty years earlier. In this manner the cities of the Empire became the centers for the diffusion of popular as well as elite learning among their populations.

The figures on newspaper circulation are indicative of an explosion of popular culture through books, brochures, pamphlets, and papers. A similar process occurred through the dissemination of learning by a wide variety of officially tolerated public readings and literacy schools, as well as through informal contacts (such as those facilitated by the ubiquitous tavern). The tsarist authorities attempted to place strict controls on the information disseminated in these urban areas. The publication in the 1880s by Moscow's first successful penny paper, *Moskovskii listok*, of the serialized popular novel *Razboinik Churkin* (The Bandit Churkin) earned its editor a summons and warning by the governor-general, upset at the glorification of a Robin Hood–type hero; the bandit met a sudden death shortly thereafter. The public readings first authorized in 1872 in St. Petersburg by the city prefect had the quaint purpose of "the struggle against drunkenness, the elimination of coarse manners and the improvement of the moral and intellectual level of the people."[27] The dissemination of information was not so easily guided and controlled, however. Altstadt-Mirhadi finds the press of Baku particularly influential in the early years of this century, since it was "remarkably untouched by censorship" and could become "a vigorous and unparalleled forum of debate for the intelligentsia." The Tiflis press provided by the 1890s the principal voice of the major political tendencies, including Marxist, of that city's intellectuals. Censorship struck here and there, yet the power of the printed word (illegal as well as legal) overcame official repression.

Knowledge served many masters, though. Hamm points out that in Kiev access to the new learning by the literate urban population "promoted hatred, bigotry, and class conflict." The conservative press of cities such as Odessa and Kiev cultivated the deepest fears and prejudices of its readers in order to stir up support for the autocracy and hostility toward political opponents. This press bore great responsibility for the anti-Semitic hatred that erupted in those cities; certainly the effects of their lurid stories strengthened racial stereotypes and jingo patriotism. The sorry fate to which Kuprin subjects his character Sasha, violinist in Odessa's Gambrinus tavern who refused in 1905 to play the national anthem "in honor of our beloved monarch," owed nothing directly to the conservative press. Indirectly, it epitomized the end which vocal conservative writers and editors vowed for all "enemies of Orthodox Russia." To this extent reading strengthened political reaction.

On the other hand, the new mass culture within the cities did offer activities and aspirations to be shared by the inhabitants of the outlying districts as well as by those of the center. The penny press reached them, and Sunday outings offered a chance to glimpse the life of the "other city." Municipal elementary schools gradually penetrated these areas. Literacy societies and "people's clubs" (*Narodnye doma*) provided cultural activities and contacts between educated and lower-class townspeople, at least until the tsarist authorities shut them down. The cultural effects of the "dual city" present complex problems whose dimensions and nature are still poorly understood. The "citified worker," a model temporarily for the young peasant migrant Kanatchikov, represented a real form of adaptation to "big-city life" for the inhabitant of the poor districts.

How widely and profoundly did these institutions and aspirations penetrate among the population? A few scattered clues suggest that they reached far enough to arouse interest even in dangerous questions of oppression and exploitation. The spread of literacy and other manifestations of urban culture played a direct role in forming bonds around new political ideals and new political movements. The printed word, Hamm suggests, was also capable of "breaking down class and national barriers," promoting tolerance and interest in reform, and stimulating thought about "equity, justice, and authority."

There existed in these large cities of the Empire powerful forces acting by the early years of this century to create shared cultural aspirations and forms of social solidarity as well as new divisions among the townspeople. The image proposed here of the dual city highlights primarily the substantial political and cultural isolation from "civic society" in which poor urban districts existed. They evolved in a manner distinct from the central areas, to a certain degree "marginal" societies dependent on and exploited by the center. Out of these conditions of municipal activism, social and ethnic antagonism, and social disorder evolved political movements which defied the old order, sometimes by violent means.

URBAN REVOLUTION

Organized opposition to the tsarist regime represented the most notable development in Russia's urban history after 1900. It manifested itself principally in three political movements familiar to any student of the nineteenth-century revolutions in Europe. Liberalism, socialism, and nationalism had all acquired by the late nineteenth century a corpus of theoretical writings and had developed organizational ties and patterns of action, violent and nonviolent, suitable to their goals. They provided the models for similar movements in the Russian Empire, whose major cities were the centers for political study and action. Only Baku, at the "crossroads of East and West," saw yet another form of opposition emerge in the Pan-Islamic movement defending the cultural-religious identity of the city's Muslims.

The cities were at the center of the revolutionary conflict of the early twentieth century. They became both the crucible in which these movements took on real life and the spark igniting opposition in other parts of the country. The process by which the Western oppositional models were adapted to conditions in the Empire involved complex cultural and social forces dating to the pre-emancipation period. Its ramifications extend far beyond the limits of Russian urban history and pose conceptual problems considerably different from those addressed in this concluding chapter. The focus of attention here, as in most of the essays in this collection, is directed to the influence of the urban environment itself on the emergence and evolution of mass movements powerful enough to shake the foundations of the autocracy.

The urban transformation of the late nineteenth century profoundly altered the potential for collective action there. Mob violence in cities had a long history. Moscow's "plague riot" of 1775 had deeply concerned Empress Catherine II, confronted with rebelliousness among the population of Russia's first capital. The cholera epidemics of the first half of the nineteenth century had similarly mobilized angry and violent mobs. Factory populations rioted here and there during that century when serious grievances went unheeded. While increased garrison and police forces curtailed the risk of violence in the major cities, events occasionally overwhelmed the authorities. A new tax on the Tiflis population united Armenian and Georgian guild members and workers in a riot in 1865 which, as Suny describes it, bore a strong resemblance to the action of those "urban mobs" which throughout Europe had sought redress from wrongs by direct, violent action.[28] Though directed against the authorities, this kind of action was not revolutionary; its participants assumed correction of abuses would come from the tsarist institutions whose administrators they were attacking. Violence remained an integral part of collective action into the new century, present alongside and at times within those revolutionary movements seeking to modify profoundly or to overthrow the tsarist regime.

The revolutionary potential of urbanization did not escape the notice of authorities, even before the revolution of 1905. The disorders of the last years of Alexander II's reign had led to a major increase and arming of the urban police forces, including for the first time mounted police in cities judged particularly dangerous. The municipal counterreform of 1892 received the support of certain provincial governors eager to reestablish their authority and repress "democratic" elements among the urban electorate. This rhetoric, perhaps formulated at the time largely to please the tsar, did not lead to concrete action until after 1905. Prefect Tolmachev's manipulation of Odessa municipal elections to strengthen the loyal Nationalist Party represented an extreme example of Imperial efforts to eliminate subversive liberalism. Russification policies led to similar authoritarian efforts at domination in the borderlands; attacks on Riga's German culture and repression of Armenian leadership in the Caucasian cities represented separate aspects of a campaign to end nationalist movements in these areas where Russians were a minority in the cities. That the Caucasus viceroy would violate the terms of the 1892 statute on limitation of non-Christian representation in order to keep a Muslim majority on the Baku city council is one good indication of autocratic difficulties in controlling its major municipalities.

In fact the municipal "oligarchy" itself became at times a center of mild resistance to the autocracy. One should not glorify all such cases as liberal opposition. The conflicts that sporadically broke out between the Moscow municipality and the Moscow governor-general in the 1870s owed much to the sense of dignity and privilege which the nobles then in positions of leadership brought with them to office.[29] In Riga the corporate solidarity of the German political elite led them temporarily to defy tsarist policies of Russification—only to abandon the campaign when its futility became apparent.

Yet there is evidence that municipal self-government encouraged some urban leaders in "vain dreams" of liberal reform. The "liberalism" of municipal spending for public works resembled the "small deeds" of zemstvo activists, some of whom also came to support the ideals of representative government for the good of all the people. The Empire's cities, multi-class and often ethnically mixed, embodied in microcosm the diversity of the country as a whole: their good governance provided municipal activists the experience on which to build the conviction that their liberal faith and leadership was best for the country. Suny points to the support of Tiflis's "first generation" of Georgian intellectuals for public service in municipal government to "most effectively influence the people." This movement, difficult to trace, apparently remained alive there and elsewhere in the Empire's municipalities. In

1905 the municipal councilors of Tiflis, along with those of Moscow and many other cities, joined the liberal campaign against Nicholas II's regime to obtain political reforms.

It is particularly noteworthy that, incorporated in the program of strikers and demonstrators that year, the liberal demands for constitutional government and individual liberties appeared frequently. The revolutionary turmoil of 1905 did reveal a striking degree of urban solidarity, at least in the first months. A historian of Moscow's revolution concluded that "the entire urban community, from top to bottom, was moved to action" that year.[30] To the extent that political unity formed around liberal ideals, it owed its existence partly to the leadership of municipal activists, partly also to the intellectual web spun by the new press and to the muffled calls for political liberty sounded in writings and discussions within these cities.

Much easier to document is the rise of the socialist labor movement. The essays in this collection examine the emergence of worker protest and its links with socialism from the perspective of urban development. This approach proves particularly valuable in bringing out two important characteristics of this protest movement. In the first place, the leading role played by the better-paid, skilled urban workers appears especially important in organizing and initiating strike action. In the second place, strikes which swept across large areas of the Empire, especially in 1905, owed their remarkable scope and synchronization in part to the fact that most were urban based; it was in the cities that the coordination of socialist activists proved particularly effective.

The wave of strikes in southern Russia in 1903 marked the first large-scale labor protest the country had known; before that time individual cities such as Tiflis or Riga or St. Petersburg had experienced serious outbursts, but never concurrently. The most likely reason for this important new development in the labor movement is the presence of socialist agitators, sometimes intellectuals and at other times former workers, capable of appealing to and mobilizing workers. The Odessa prefect sought some measure of excuse for his powerlessness during the three days of general strike in 1903 by stressing, as Skinner notes, "the degree to which the railway and factory workers had been politicized by socialist propaganda."

In all the cities there existed organized groups of socialist intellectuals and workers, a subject much studied in recent years by scholars interested in the origins of the socialist movement. From the Hümmät socialists of Baku to the Social Democrats and Bundists of Riga, the socialist movement had formed urban networks to reach the workers. Their success remained uneven; internal divisions weakened their effectiveness. They could at times, as in 1903, provide the impetus for coordinated strike action. At other times splinter groups like the Shendrikov brothers and their followers in Baku found the key to unleashing major strikes beyond the power of the regular Social Democratic committees. One might include in this "sub-elite" Father Gapon and his followers in the St. Petersburg Assembly of Factory Workers. For these beleaguered but zealous militants, the city environment provided the best conditions for their work of social and political mobilization.

The group that furnished the cohorts for this action came from the skilled factory and artisanal workers of the cities. The urban strike movements of the early years of this century acquired the greatest power when they joined in large numbers. The term "skilled" implies that autonomy and craft solidarity often associated with artisans, with whom skilled factory workers at that period had much in common. In the 1905 Baku strikes, an English observer noted, the initiative came from the Armenian "artisan (skilled labor) element," whose successful action incited the "Tatar workmen" of the oilfields to join in and—if the account is accurate—to launch "a wave of sabotage, incendiarism, intimidation and other forms of violence." Such violence, a constant undercurrent in many protest actions, usually brought immediate police repression and was vigorously resisted by both socialist activists and worker militants in those years.

These organizers and activists were largely skilled workers. The unskilled, temporary workers of Kiev's sugar industry, though very poorly paid, were among the least militant in that city. When the July 1903 and January 1905 strike waves reached that city, Hamm indicates that they were supported by the city's railroad employees and metalworkers. A recent study of the worker movement in Moscow and St. Petersburg lays particular emphasis on role of the skilled workers there. Having "acquired a social identity as urban 'workers' and a sense of their relative status and self-worth," they developed a "craft consciousness and factory patriotism" which made them "exceptionally active in every form of labor association" that year.[31] They included the blue-collar workers (especially printers) of the inner city as well as the skilled factory workers of those "outer cities" around both capitals. They thus stood out not only because of their economic skills but also by the sociocultural attributes acquired through their urban experience. The city in this case represented more than a setting for the socialist movement; it proved to be an active force unifying the groups most influential in its development.

The third major revolutionary force strongly influenced by urbanization was nationalism. Its roots lay in the social and cultural evolution of the urban communities in the previous half-century. Like liberalism and socialism, it symbolized and reflected the transformation of the country's urban society. The intellectual ferment among townspeople, noted by several of the authors, played a powerful role of its own; Henriksson concludes that Riga over the last half of the nineteenth century became "the crucible for Latvian literary culture." A prime agent there for the crystallization of a Latvian national movement was the Latvian Association, more concerned with social, cultural, and political resistance to German domination than with economic issues. Tiflis played a role similar to Riga in the rise of Georgian nationalism. In Baku social contacts with Armenians and Russians and direct exposure to Western culture obliged Turkish intellectuals, as Altstadt-Mirhadi suggests, to adopt Western ways and institutions in order to resist the West, creating a unique "Muslim-Turkic consciousness." Their voice reached out through urban cultural channels to the literate population of the city. So too did Warsaw's Polish and Jewish writers reach their audience, readers of a press which Corrsin finds "integrative within each ethnic group."

The institutions of municipal self-government that had been intended to unify and strengthen urban life became by the early twentieth century the arena for nationalist political expression. The conflict in Riga between Germans and Latvians turned the local elections into contests of "symbolic value" for the latter and brought out an unusually high percentage of voters from among the tiny electorate of wealthy property owners. Georgians sought to supplant Armenians at the head of the Tiflis city council, even going to the lengths of allying with the Russian party. In Odessa and Kiev the Nationalist party found a strong backing among voters (and among tsarist administrators) by championing Russian national unity.

As elsewhere in Europe, nationalist movements in those cities expressed a deep hostility toward other nationalities. This potential for conflict reached its peak in places where social and ethnic divisions coincided (at least sufficiently to create cultural stereotypes). The power of the Georgian Marxist movement in Tiflis sprang from the deep hostility toward the "Armenian merchants," on whose shoulders Georgians could lay the blame for cultural and economic oppression. Similarly, in Riga the Latvian factory workers found Germans in the positions of managers and owners (as well as in control of the city council) frequently enough to color their socialist convictions with an anti-German hue. The creation in that city in 1906 of the German National Union marked the first appearance of a German Nationalist organization there, offering a new form of political action to Germans confronted for the first time with an organized and powerful Latvian nationalist movement.

Under these circumstances only opposition to the autocracy provided the grounds for united political action among the nationalist groups. The tsarist regime proved in its blundering way as capable of provoking unity among nationalities as it was of bringing together the liberal and socialist opposition—at least for short periods of time. The revolutionary movement of the first half of 1905 (like that in the early months of 1917) rested on just such alliances. The subject of much historical literature, a few examples of this united action will suffice here, drawn from the 1905 upheaval in three major cities of the empire. The dramatic collapse of tsarist authority in Tiflis resulted from the "unity among the various social groups and nationalities," including "workers and city council deputies, Georgian intellectuals and Armenian businessmen." In Moscow, the strikes and violence in September forged the "liberal-radical, professional-proletarian alliance that succeeded in October in bringing the autocracy to a standstill.[32] Both tsarist and municipal institutions in Riga vanished that fall, replaced by "a federated Latvian-Russian-Jewish socialist committeee [which] functioned as an *ad hoc* city government, enacting laws, regulating prices and rents and using its militia as a police force." While they lasted, these alliances held the power to undermine the autocracy. Events in these cities pointed the way to the revolutionary democracy of 1917.

Still, the dominant trend of urban political movements through the early years of the twentieth century appears to have been weakness and division. Only the most resolutely optimistic revolutionaries could ignore the disturbing signs of social and ethnic conflicts dividing the opposition to the autocratic regime, or could claim leadership of the population at large. Worker soviets were often confined to the "desperate" districts, the darker side to the "dual city." Kiev's soviet emerged in the midst of the Shuliavka area, stepchild of the Kiev municipality. Its geographical isolation typified the real gap that continued to separate liberal and socialist, intellectual and worker in those urban societies.

This gap manifested itself clearly by the fall of 1905 in the disputes that broke out among previous allies against the autocracy in cities such as Tiflis. The result there was the collapse of "the broad oppositional front" formed that spring. In certain cities the competition among political movements acquired the colors of different national groups. When the Polish National Democrats warned in 1906 that "Warsaw is in danger!," they conjured up a devil in liberal-Jewish garb to defeat their electoral rivals. The terrible wave of anti-Semitic riots that swept the Ukrainian cities in the fall of 1905 was not the result solely of the action of a few "Black Hundreds" gangs or of a tsarist conspiracy, as liberals and intellectuals charged. It expressed as well the profound antagonism of Christian for Jew which penetrated deeply those urban societies. In Baku the efforts of press and clergy could not halt the bloody riots of August 1905 between Muslim and Christian that ended all strike activity and reduced a large area of the oil fields and worker settlements to ashes and rubble. No amount of political and intellectual activity could paper over the deep divisions that separated townspeople into separate and often hostile groups. This situation reemerged in 1917 to weaken the efforts of the tsar's heirs in the Provisional Government to bring together a unified state based on the free choice of the population.

The political turmoil of early twentieth-century Russia did not arise in conditions of urban "backwardness." If this term has any meaning at all in the context of urban history in the last half-century of tsarist rule, it has to designate the level of urban development in the middle of the nineteenth century. The characteristics of urban life differed greatly between Baku and Warsaw, Moscow and Riga, yet overall their social and economic activities still functioned then at a level of small towns or villages. Their transformation in the following decades was so sweeping and profound that it might well be described an urban revolution. The expansion of commercial and industrial affairs brought them into close market relations with other Russian urban areas, with the large rural hinterland, and with economies of the Western world.

These cities appeared as places of opportunity to the crowds of migrants who swelled their labor force, arriving in numbers so great and moving about so quickly they created an urban population in constant turnover. Out of this dynamic economic activity there emerged new classes of urban dwellers and a revitalized network of small-scale trading and artisanal enterprises. Inequalities of wealth and power emerged in new forms to separate this "one-story" urban society from its capitalist counterpart, and to divide the latter between employee-worker and manager-owner in a manner familiar to Western Europeans. At the same time a mass literate culture in the last decades of tsarist rule provided an increasingly large proportion of the population with access to the printed word and to all the images and ideals of a new life it could convey. These cities offered new opportunities and risks to old and new inhabitants. The threat of sudden death or illness from epidemics of communicable disease still hung over the poorer sections, yet by comparison with mid-nineteenth century health conditions they assured greater physical security to more people than ever before. These cities, once quiet towns dominated by administrative activities, manifested by the early twentieth century many of the linkages and relations characteristic of a metropolis.

Their development made them centers of social and political conflict. They became increasingly divided internally by economic, social, and ethnic differences. It is perhaps historical hindsight which incites us to search for signs of division within this urban society. The vitality of these cities demonstrated the ability to their inhabitants to adapt to new conditions and to seize new opportunities requiring greater social interaction and cooperation. Yet much evidence points to conditions of increasing diversity in social and ethnic classes, to the growth of hostility among urban groups producing new forms of unrest and conflict. Municipalities attempted to cope with overwhelming problems of urbanization and in doing so deepened the disparities in living conditions between their prosperous central districts and new outlying settlements. Ethnic groups competed among each other and forged stronger bonds of identity and solidarity than had ever existed among nationalities within the Empire. Factories and artisanal shops provided openings for workers to acquire the skills of a "master," yet these favored wage earners appear to have been the first to use the term "worker" to identify themselves with the masses of exploited laborers in the cities. Their initiative played a key role in the successful strike waves of the first years of this century, a movement so powerful it challenged the autocracy itself.

These cities provided their inhabitants with unheard-of opportunities to free themselves from old bonds and habits of subservience—and in so doing created conditions of social and cultural ferment and political assertiveness. Townspeople could think of themselves as members of a nation, of a class, or free citizens of a state that ought to be of their own making. The opportunities, though fraught with risk, opened up new worlds to them. New social bonds were formed and new enemies discovered. Isaac Bashevis Singer, recalling his departure by train from wartime Warsaw after seven harsh years of learning and discovery, is an eloquent witness to the dangers and challenges thrown up by this new urban life to a youth such as he: "Like a king or a great wizard, I rode through the world, no longer fearing every soldier, policeman, Gentile boy, or bum."

NOTES

1. Dean Tipps, "Modernization Theory and the Comparative Study of Societies: A Critical Perspective," *Comparative Studies in Society and History*, XV (March, 1973):206.

2. Samuel Huntington, *Political Order in Changing Societies* (New Haven, 1968), pp. 265, 274; his views are criticized by Alexander Groth, "The Institutional Myth: Huntington's Order Revisited," *The Review of Politics*, 41 (April 1979):203–34.

3. William Blackwell, "Modernization and Urbanization in Russia: A Comparative View," in Michael Hamm, ed., *The City in Russian History* (Lexington, Ky., 1976), pp. 294, 306.

4. Ibid., p. 293.

5. Tipps, p. 218.

6. L. E. Shiner, "Tradition/Modernity: An Ideal Type Gone Astray," *Comparative Studies in Society and History*, XVII (April 1975):245–52; the empirical case against this dichotomy is made in Tipps, pp. 212–15.

7. Tipps, p. 222.

8. For a study of the level of urban development in mid-century in European Russia, see my article, "Urbanization and Autocracy: Russian Urban Development in the First Half of the Nineteenth Century," *Russian Review*, 42 (October 1983):377–402.

9. A brief discussion of the rise of metropolitan centers in the U.S. is found in Allen Wakstein, *The Urbanization of America: An Historical Anthology* (New York, 1970), pp. 341–42.

10. John Dyos, "Greater and Greater London," in D. Cannadine, ed., *Exploring the Urban Past: Essays in Urban History by H. J. Dyos* (Cambridge, 1982), p. 39.

11. Pavel G. Ryndziunskii, *Utverzhdenie kapitalizma v Rossii* (Moscow, 1978), table 41, p. 236.

12. For a careful analysis of the labor force of the two capital cities, see Victoria Bonnell, *Roots of Rebellion: Workers' Politics and Organizations in St. Petersburg and Moscow, 1900–1914* (Berkeley, Calif., 1983), esp. table 1, p. 23.

13. V. Laverychev, *Krupnaia burzhuaziia v poreformennoi Rossii* (Moscow, 1974), p. 69.

14. A recent brief survey of the issues and literature on these issues is found in Kathleen Conzen, "Quantification and the New Urban History," *Journal of Interdisciplinary History*, XIII (Spring 1983), esp. pp. 669–75.

15. D. Brower, "Urban Russia on the Eve of World War One: A Social Profile," *Journal of Social History*, 13 (Spring 1980):428.

16. For an exhaustive (though somewhat flawed) discussion of the rise of a Russian capitalist class, see Alfred Rieber, *Merchants and Entrepreneurs in Imperial Russia* (Chapel Hill, N.C., 1982).

17. Semen Kanatchikov, *Iz istorii moego bytiia* (Moscow, 1930); the first chapters of his autobiography provide a vivid picture of the experience of one young urban migrant.

18. Cited in D. Brower, "Labor Violence in Russia in the Late Nineteenth Century," *Slavic Review*, 41 (Sept. 1982):418.

19. Reginald Zelnik provides, through the study of the autobiographies of two workers, one of them Kanatchikov, a fascinating interpretation of the development of worker revolutionaries, in "Russian Bebels: An Introduction to the Memoirs of the Russian Workers Semen Kanatchikov and Matvei Fisher," *Russian Review*, 35 (July, 1976):249–89, and 35 (October, 1976):417–47.

20. Cited in John McClymer, "The Study of Community and the 'New' Social History," *Journal of Urban History*, 7 (November 1980):114.

21. L.F. Pisar'kova, *Moskovskoe gorodskoe obshchestvennoe upravlenie s serediny 1880-kh godov do pervoi russkoi revoliutsii: Avtoreferat dissertatsii* (Moscow, 1980), p. 14.

22. One could write an entire essay on the reliability and correct interpretation of Russian mortality statistics in the late nineteenth century. The influx of migrants makes the analysis of urban data particularly difficult. Only when the proportion of migrants remained constant—as in Moscow between 1882 and 1902—can one extract an approximate mortality trend line. The Moscow figures, about the most reliable for any Russian city, indicate a decline from an average of thirty-four per 1000 in the early 1880s (1880–84) to twenty-six in the early 1900s. See Thomas McGivney, "The Lower Classes in the City of Moscow," (Ph.D. dissertation, New York University, 1978), table 40, p. 191.

23. For a study of the impact of urban public transportation in Europe, see John McKay, *Tramways and Trolleys: The Rise of Urban Mass Transportation in Europe* (Princeton, 1976).

24. D. Brower, "Labor Violence in Russia," pp. 425–26.

25. Kanatchikov, p. 153.

26. Jeffrey Brooks, "Readers and Reading at the End of the Tsarist Era," in William Todd, ed., *Literature and Society in Imperial Russia, 1800–1914* (Stanford, 1978), p. 142.

27. Cited in L. M. Ivanov, "Ideologicheskoe vozdeistvie burzhuazii i tsarizma na proletariat," in *Rossiiskii proletariat: Oblik, bor'ba, gegemoniia* (Moscow, 1970), p. 323.

28. Eric Hobsbawm, *Primitive Rebels* (New York, 1965), pp. 110–11.

29. A careful study of the conflicts then and in the 1880s between tsarist administrators and municipal leaders is found in V. A. Nardova, *Gorodskoe samoupravlenie v Rossii v 6okh—nachale 9okh godov XIX veka* (Leningrad, 1984), ch. 4.

30. Laura Engelstein, *Moscow 1905: Working-Class Organization and Political Conflict* (Stanford, 1982), p. 13; Terence Emmons's careful examination of the results of the elections in 1906 to the First Duma provides convincing evidence of the strength of the liberal movement among voters in Russia's large cities (*The Formation of Political Parties and the First National Elections in Russia* [Stanford, 1983], p. 277; table 11, pp. 278–79).

31. Bonnell, *Roots of Rebellion*, p. 190.

32. Engelstein, p. 96.

BIBLIOGRAPHY OF ENGLISH-LANGUAGE WORKS ON THE IMPERIAL RUSSIAN CITY AND RELATED TOPICS, 1860–1917

The bibliographical notes at the end of the essays are intended for the specialist. This list, intended for the general reader, is limited to English-language sources. For additional sources on the urban worker, the reader may consult Victoria Bonnell, *Roots of Rebellion*, pp. 511–43.

Anderson, Barbara. *Internal Migration during Modernization in Late Nineteenth Century Russia.* Princeton: Princeton University Press, 1980.

Bater, James H. "The Journey to Work in St. Petersburg, 1860–1914." *The Journal of Transport History*, vol. 3, no. 2 (1974):214–33.

———. *St. Petersburg: Industrialization and Change.* Montreal: McGill University Press, 1976.

———. "Transience, Residential Persistence, and Mobility in Moscow and St. Petersburg, 1900–1914." *Slavic Review*, vol. 39, no. 2 (1980):239–54.

Blackwell, William L. "Modernization and Urbanization in Russia: A Comparative View." In Hamm, ed., *The City in Russian History,* pp. 291–330.

Bonnell, Victoria E. "Radical Politics and Organized Labor in Pre-Revolutionary Moscow, 1905–1914." *Journal of Social History*, vol. 12, no. 2 (1979):282–300.

———. *Roots of Rebellion. Workers' Politics and Organizations in St. Petersburg and Moscow, 1900–1914.* Berkeley: University of California Press, 1983.

———. "Trade Unions, Parties, and the State in Tsarist Russia: A Study of Labor Politics in St. Petersburg and Moscow." *Politics and Society*, vol. 9, no. 3 (1980):299–322.

———. "Urban Working Class Life in Early Twentieth-Century Russia: Some Problems and Patterns," *Russian History*, vol. 8, no. 3 (1981):360–78.

———, ed. *The Russian Worker: Life and Labor under the Tsarist Regime.* Berkeley: University of California Press, 1983.

Bradley, Joseph. "The Moscow Workhouse and Urban Welfare Reform." *The Russian Review*, vol. 41, no. 4 (1982):427–44.

———. *Muzhik and Muscovite: Urbanization in Late Imperial Russia.* Berkeley: University of California Press, 1984.

Brooks, Jeffrey. "Readers and Reading at the End of the Tsarist Era." In *Literature and Society in Imperial Russia, 1800–1914,* ed. William Mills Todd. Stanford: Stanford University Press, 1978.

Brower, Daniel. *Estate, Class, and Community: Urbanization and Revolution in Late Tsarist Russia.* University of Pittsburgh, Carl Beck Paper No. 302, 1983.

———. "Labor Violence in the Late Nineteenth Century." *Slavic Review*, vol. 41, no. 3 (1982):417–53.

———. "Urban Russia on the Eve of World War One: A Social Profile," *Journal of Social History* 13 (1980):424–36.

———. "Urbanization and Autocracy: Russian Urban Development in the First Half of the Nineteenth Century." *The Russian Review*, vol. 42 (1983):377–402.

Corrsin, Stephen. "The Changing Composition of the City of Riga, 1867–1913."
    Journal of Baltic Studies, vol. 13, no. 1 (1982):19–39.
———. "Urbanization and the Baltic Peoples: Riga and Tallinn before the First
    World War." *East European Quarterly*, vol. 12 (1978):69–84.
Dudgeon, Ruth A. "The Forgotten Minority: Women Students in Imperial
    Russia, 1872–1977." *Russian History*, vol. 9, no. 1 (1982):1–26.
Engelstein, Laura. *Moscow, 1905: Working-Class Organization and Political
    Conflict.* Stanford: Stanford University Press, 1982.
Fedor, Thomas. *Patterns of Urban Growth in the Russian Empire during the
    Nineteenth Century.* Chicago: University of Chicago Department of
    Geography, 1975.
Fox, D. J. "Odessa." *Scottish Geographical Magazine*, vol. 79, no. 1 (1963):5–22.
Frieden, Nancy. *Russian Physicians in an Era of Reform and Revolution.* Prince-
    ton: Princeton University Press, 1982.
Gleason, William E. "The All-Russian Union of Towns and the Politics of Urban
    Reform in Tsarist Russia." *The Russian Review*, vol. 35, no. 3 (1976):295–
    302.
Glickman, Rose. *Russian Factory Women, Workplace and Society 1880–1914.*
    Berkeley: University of California Press, 1984
Gliksman, Jerzy G. "The Russian Urban Worker: From Serf to Proletarian." In
    The Transformation of Russian Society, ed. Cyril Black. Cambridge, Mass.:
    Harvard University Press, 1960, pp. 311–23.
Gohstand, Robert. "The Shaping of Moscow by Nineteenth-Century Trade." In
    Hamm, ed., *The City in Russian History*, pp. 160–81.
Guroff, Gregory and Carstenson, Fred V. *Entrepreneurship in Imperial Russia
    and the Soviet Union.* Princeton: Princeton University Press, 1983.
Guroff, Gregory and Starr, S. Frederick. "A Note on Urban Literacy in Russia,
    1890–1914." *Jahrbücher für Geschichte Osteuropas*, vol. 19 (1971):520–31.
Haimson, Leopold. "The Problem of Social Stability in Urban Russia, 1905–
    1917." *Slavic Review*, part 1, vol. 23, no. 4 (1964):619–42; part 2, vol. 24, no.
    1 (1965):1–22.
Hamm, Michael F. "The Breakdown of Urban Modernization: A Prelude to the
    Revolutions of 1917." In Hamm, ed., *The City in Russian History*, pp.
    182–200.
———. "Khar'kov's Progressive Duma, 1910–1914: A Study in Russian Munici-
    pal Reform." *Slavic Review*, vol. 40, no. 1 (1981):17–36.
———. "The Modern Russian City: An Historiographical Analysis." *Journal of
    Urban History*, vol. 4, no. 1 (1977):39–76.
———. "Riga's 1913 City Election: A Study in Baltic Urban Politics." The
    Russian Review, vol. 34, no. 4 (1980):442–61.
———, ed. *The City in Russian History.* Lexington: University Press of Ken-
    tucky, 1976.
Hanchett, Walter. "Tsarist Statutory Regulation of Municipal Government in
    the Nineteenth Century." In Hamm, ed., *The City in Russian History*, pp.
    91–114.
Harcave, Sidney. *First Blood: The Russian Revolution of 1905.* New York,
    Macmillan, 1964.
Harris, Chauncy. *Cities of the Soviet Union.* Chicago: Rand McNally, 1970.
Hasegawa, Tsuyoshi. *The February Revolution: Petrograd, 1917.* Seattle: Uni-
    versity of Washington Press, 1981.
Henriksson, Anders. "Minorities and the Industrialization of Imperial Russia:
    The Case of the Baltic German Urban Elite." *Canadian Slavonic Papers*, vol.
    24 (1982):115–27.

————. *The Tsar's Loyal Germans. The Riga German Community: Social Change and the Nationality Question, 1855–1905.* Boulder: East European Monographs, 1983.

Herlihy, Patricia. "Death in Odessa: A Study of Population Movements in a Nineteenth-Century City." *Journal of Urban History,* vol. 4, no. 4 (1978):417–42.

————. "The Ethnic Composition of the City of Odessa in the Nineteenth Century." *Harvard Ukrainian Studies,* vol. 1, no. 1 (1977):53–78.

————. "Odessa: Staple Trade and Urbanization in New Russia." *Jahrbücher für Geschichte Osteuropas,* vol. 11, no. 2 (1973):184–95.

————. "Ukrainian Cities in the Nineteenth Century." In Ivan L. Rudnytsky, ed., *Rethinking Ukrainian History.* Edmonton: Canadian Institute of Ukrainian Studies, 1981, pp. 135–55.

Hooson, David J. M. "The Growth of Cities in Pre-Soviet Russia." In *Urbanization and Its Problems: Essays in Honour of E. W. Gilbert,* ed. R. P. Beckinsale and J. M. Houston. Oxford: Basil Blackwell, 1970, pp. 254–76.

Iukneva, N. V. "Ethnic Aspects of Study of the Population of Prerevolutionary St. Petersburg." *Soviet Sociology,* vol. 18, no. 4 (1979–80):23–37.

Johnson, Robert Eugene. "Family Relations and the Rural-Urban Nexus: Patterns in the Hinterland of Moscow, 1880–1900." In Ransel, ed., *The Family in Imperial Russia,* pp. 263–79.

————. *Peasant and Proletarian: The Working Class of Moscow in the Late Nineteenth Century.* New Brunswick: Rutgers University Press, 1979.

————. "Peasant Migration and the Russian Working Class: Moscow at the End of the Nineteenth Century." *Slavic Review,* vol. 35, no. 4 (December 1976):652–64.

Keep, John. *The Russian Revolution: A Study in Mass Mobilization.* New York: Norton, 1976.

Khatissian, Alexander, "The Memoirs of a Mayor." *The Armenian Review,* part I, vol. 2, no. 3 (1949):40–47; Part II, vol. 2, no. 4 (1949):104–15; Part III, vol. 3, no. 1 (1950):87–106; Part IV, vol. 3, no. 4 (1950):106–12.

Koenker, Diane. *Moscow Workers and the 1917 Revolution.* Princeton: Princeton University Press, 1981.

————. "Urban Families, Working-Class Youth Groups, and the 1917 Revolution in Moscow." In Ransel, ed., *The Family in Imperial Russia,* pp. 280–304.

Lewis, Robert A. and Rowland, Richard. "Urbanization in Russia and the USSR, 1897–1979." In Hamm. ed., *The City in Russian History,* pp. 205–21.

Lindenmyer, Adele. "A Russian Experiment in Voluntarism: The Municipal Guardianships of the Poor, 1894–1914." *Jahrbücher für Geschichte Osteuropas,* vol. 30, no. 3 (1982):429–51.

McKay, John P. *Pioneers for Profit: Foreign Entrepreneurship and Russian Industrialization, 1885–1913.* Chicago: University of Chicago Press, 1970.

McKinsey, Pamela Sears. "From City Workers to Peasantry: The Beginning of the Russian Movement 'To the People.'" *Slavic Review,* vol. 38, no. 4 (1979):629–49.

Manning, Roberta Thompson. *The Crisis of the Old Order in Russia: Gentry and Government.* Princeton: Princeton University Press, 1982.

Owen, Thomas C. *Capitalism and Politics in Russia: A Social History of the Moscow Merchants, 1855–1905.* New York: Cambridge University Press, 1981.

Phillips, G. W. "Urban Proletarian Politics in Tsarist Russia: Petersburg and Moscow, 1912–1914." *Comparative Urban Research,* vol. 3 (1976):11–20.

Pipes, Richard. *Social Democracy and the St. Petersburg Labor Movement, 1855–1897.* Cambridge: Harvard University Press, 1963.

Puryear, Vernon J. "Odessa: Its Rise and International Importance, 1815–50." *Pacific Historical Review,* vol. 3 (1934):192–215.

Rabinowitch, Alexander. *The Bolsheviks Come to Power: The Revolution of 1917 in Petrograd.* New York: Norton, 1976.

——. *Prelude to Revolution: The Petrograd Bolsheviks and the July 1917 Uprising.* Bloomington: Indiana University Press, 1968.

Ransel, David L., ed., *The Family in Imperial Russia.* Urbana: University of Illinois Press, 1978.

Reichman, Henry. "The Rostov General Strike of 1902. *Russian History,* vol. 9, pt. 1 (1982):67–85.

Rieber, Alfred. *Merchants and Entrepreneurs in Imperial Russia.* Chapel Hill: University of North Carolina Press, 1982.

Rimlinger, Gaston V. "Autocracy and the Factory Order in Early Russian Industrialization." *Journal of Economic History,* vol. 20, no. 1 (1960):67–92.

——. "The Management of Labor Protest in Tsarist Russia." *International Review of Social History,* vol. 3, part 2 (1960):226–48.

Roosa, Ruth Amende. "Russian Industrialists and 'State Socialism,' 1906–1917." *Soviet Studies,* vol. 23, no. 3 (1972):395–417.

——. "Workers' Insurance Legislation and the Role of the Industrialists in the Period of the Third State Duma." *The Russian Review,* vol. 34, no. 4 (1975):410–52.

Rosenberg, William G. "Workers and Workers' Control in the Russian Revolution." *History Workshop,* no. 5 (1978):89–97.

Rowland, Richard. "Urban In-Migration in Late Nineteenth-Century Russia." In Hamm, ed., *The City in Russian History,* pp. 115–24.

Ruckman, Jo Ann. *The Moscow Business Elite: A Social and Cultural Portrait of Two Generations, 1840–1905.* De Kalb: Northern Illinois University Press, 1984.

Ruud, Charles A. *Fighting Words: Imperial Censorship and the Russian Press, 1804–1906.* Toronto: University of Toronto Press, 1982.

——. "The Printing Press as an Agent of Political Change in Early Twentieth-Century Russia." *The Russian Review,* vol. 40, no. 4 (1981):378–95.

Sablinksy, Walter. *The Road to Bloody Sunday: Father Gapon and the St. Petersburg Massacre of 1905.* Princeton: Princeton University Press, 1976.

Skinner, Frederick W. "Trends in Planning Practices: The Building of Odessa, 1794–1917." In Hamm, ed., *The City in Russian History,* pp. 129–59.

Smith, S. A. *Red Petrograd: Revolution in the Factories 1917–1918.* Cambridge: Cambridge University Press, 1983.

Starr, S. Frederick. "The Revival and Schism of Urban Planning in Twentieth-Century Russia." In Hamm, ed., *The City in Russian History,* pp. 222–42.

Suny, Ronald Gregor. "Labor and Liquidators: Revolutionaries and the 'Reaction' in Baku, May 1908–April 1912." *Slavic Review,* vol. 34, no. 2 (1975):319–40.

——. "'The Peasants Have Always Fed Us': The Georgian Nobility and the Peasant Emancipation, 1856–1871." *The Russian Review,* vol. 38 (1979):27–51.

——. "Populism, Nationalism, and Marxism: The Origins of Revolutionary Parties among the Armenians of the Caucasus." *The Armenian Review,* vol. 32 (1979):134–51.

——. "Russian Rule and Caucasian Society, 1801–1856: The Georgian Nobility and the Armenian Bourgeoisie." *Nationalities Papers,* vol. 7 (1979):53–78.

Surh, Gerald D. "Petersburg's First Mass Labor Organization: The Assembly of Russian Workers and Father Gapon." *The Russian Review*, part 1, vol. 40, no. 3 (1981):241–262; part 2, vol. 40, no. 4 (1981):412–41.

Swain, G. R. "Bolsheviks and the Metal Workers on the Eve of the First World War." *Journal of Contemporary History*, vol. 16, no. 2 (1981):273–91.

Thiede, Roger. "Industry and Urbanization in New Russia from 1860 to 1910." In Hamm, ed., *The City in Russian History*, pp. 125–38.

Thurston, Robert W. "Police and People in Moscow, 1906–1914." *The Russian Review*, vol. 39, no. 3 (1980):320–38.

Walkin, Jacob. "The Attitude of the Tsarist Government Toward the Labor Problem." *American Slavic and East European Review*, vol. 13, no. 2 (1954):163–184.

Weissman, Neil B. *Reform in Tsarist Russia: The State Bureaucracy and Local Government, 1900–1914.* New Brunswick: Rutgers University Press, 1981.

CONTRIBUTORS

Michael F. Hamm, Associate Professor of History at Centre College, is editor and coauthor of *The City in Russian History* (1976), and author of articles on Russian politics during the First World War and on prerevolutionary urban life in Riga and Khar'kov. He is currently writing a history of Kiev and Khar'kov in the nineteenth and twentieth centuries.

Audrey Altstadt-Mirhadi is Lecturer in History at the University of Wisconsin-Madison. She has published articles on Azerbaijani history and is working on studies of the prerevolutionary Azerbaijani and Central Asian intelligentsia and on the role of the Caucasian Muslim Social Democrats in the Iranian Constitutional Revolution of 1905–1911.

James H. Bater, Professor of Geography, is Dean of the Faculty of Environmental Studies at the University of Waterloo. He is the author of *St. Petersburg: Industrialization and Change* (1976), *The Soviet City: Ideal and Reality* (1980), and articles on Russian and North American urban and economic geography. He is working on a book to be entitled *The Russian City: Image and Reality.*

Joseph Bradley is Assistant Professor of History at the University of Tulsa. He has written *Muzhik and Muscovite: Urbanization in Late Imperial Russia* (1985) and several articles on Moscow and on the Russian working class. He is preparing works on Moscow after the Revolutions of 1917 and on the Colt Mission and American-Russian technological transfer.

Daniel R. Brower, Professor of History at the University of California, Davis, has published *Training the Nihilists: Education and Radicalism in Tsarist Russia* (1976), *The New Jacobins: The French Communist Party and the Popular Front* (1968), and articles on Russian social and urban history. He is working on a general study of the consequences of urbanization in Russia.

Stephen D. Corrsin is a Cataloguer in Slavic and Germanic languages at the Princeton University Library. His articles include surveys of prerevolutionary Riga and Tallinn and of Polish sources for the study of migration to America. He is at work on a book entitled *Warsaw before the First World War: Poles and Jews in a Conquered City.*

Anders Henriksson is Assistant Professor of History at Shepherd College. He has published articles on Baltic history and on the humorous side of history teaching as well as *The Tsar's Loyal Germans. The Riga German Community: Social Change and the Nationality Question, 1855–1905* (1983).

Frederick W. Skinner is Associate Professor of History at the University of Montana. The author of "Trends in Planning Practices: The Building of Odessa, 1794–1917," which appeared in *The City in Russian History* (1976), and of several entries for reference works on modern Russian history, he is currently working on a book-length study of Odessa.

Ronald Grigor Suny is Alex Manoogian Professor of Modern Armenian History at the University of Michigan. His publications include *The Baku Commune, 1917–18: Class and Nationality in the Russian Revolution* (1972), *Armenia in the Twentieth Century* (1983), and articles on the history of the Caucasus. He is editor of *Transcaucasia: Nationalism and Social Change* (1983).

INDEX